The Essential Philo

PHILO JUDAEUS

The Essential Philo

EDITED BY NAHUM N. GLATZER

SCHOCKEN BOOKS • NEW YORK

CONTENTS

PREFACE

The ideas closest to the heart of Western man emerged not in the great empires of antiquity but in the politically insignificant realms of Greece and Judaea. The mature issues of each—philosophic thought and biblical faith—met in Egyptian Alexandria in the person of Philo Judaeus (ca. 25 B.C.—ca. 45 A.D.). The synthesis, or, better, symbiosis, of Greek philosophy and Mosaic religion, as it presented itself to Philo's mind, was of significance neither to Greek philosophers nor to teachers of Judaism. However, Philo's work was of decisive importance to the early theologians of Christianity: to the second-century Clement of Alexandria and to his pupil, Origen, to the Latin Father Ambrose, and, later, to the thinkers of Islam.

They, too, faced the task of correlating, combining, harmonizing the truth of revelation with Greek wisdom; Philo pointed the way. Indeed, as Harry A. Wolfson has demonstrated in his monumental work *Philo: Foundations of Religious Philosophy in Judaism, Christianity, and Islam,* the philosophy of Philo was "in its main features the most dominant force in the history of philosophy down to the seventeenth century"—when it was overthrown by Spinoza.

In their time, Philo's work and other literary products of Hellenistic Judaism—e.g., the Fourth Book of Maccabees, the second part of the Wisdom of Solomon, the Letter of Aristeas—expressed the concerns of small, though significant, groups of diaspora Judaism. These groups lived, intellectually, in two cultures, symbolically represented by Moses and Plato, respectively. Central elements in both merge and unite in Philo. By means of allegorical interpretation—a method borrowed from the Stoa—Scripture is made to yield Greek philosophical concepts insofar as they are

acceptable to the Jew in Philo. By the same token, Scripture (in
its Greek translation, the Septuagint) is read with utmost care
and concern, with sections unacceptable to the Hellenist in Philo
bypassed in silence. He knows Homer and Euripides; he adores
the "great" Plato; Parmenides, Empedocles, Zeno, Cleanthes are
in his eyes "divine men," members of "a sacred society."

He accepted Plato's doctrine of ideas and theory of creation.
The Stoics taught him certain psychological and ethical theories,
tenets of world-pervading divine reason and of divine *logoi* acting
in the universe. However, Philo rejects the Stoa's materialistic
metaphysics—determinism and fatalism—and transforms the
logos concept, giving it a great variety of meaning. He knew the
Pythagoreans' numbers symbolism and adapted it to his purposes.
His God, whose essence is inaccessible to human reason, is more
than Plato's "Idea of the Good"; "He is the absolute, transcend-
ent Being, Which, at the same time, fills the world" and Who
relates to man like a father to his children. Although Philo uses
Platonic and Stoic terminology in speaking of the aspects of the
deity, his basic views are biblical and Jewish. The human soul can
experience an "extasy of love" of God. Philo's belief in providence militates against the Epicureans. The "four virtues" which
the Platonic and Stoic schools expounded appear in Philo, not
without having been augmented by the virtues of piety and humanity. A person undergoes the normal course of studies, com-
prising literature, rhetoric, mathematics, music, and logic (the
"Encyclia"), symbolically represented by Hagar, the handmaiden,
in preparation for "philosophy" in the Philonic sense, a contemplation represented by Sarah.

What ultimately emerges is not a new, systematic philosophy
or doctrinal scheme but a vision of a religious personality. In his
treatises "On Abraham," "On the Migration of Abraham," and
"On the Life of Moses" (included in the present volume), Philo
presents men who have transcended the material aspects of existence and have ascended the ladder of mystic perfection, until the
one, Abraham, has become "the unwritten law and justice of
God" (p. 138), and the other, Moses, "transformed . . . into a
most sun-like mind . . . wholly possessed by inspiration" (p.
269). "God accounts a wise man [Moses] as entitled to equal

honour with the world itself, having both created the universe and raised the perfect man from the things earthly up to himself by the same Word" ("On the Sacrifices of Abel and Cain," III). Having reached this high station, Moses is implored to show others the way: "O Sacred Guide, even if we close the eye of our soul and take no care to understand such mysteries . . . , be you our prompter . . . and introduce those who are duly initiated to the hidden light of the sacred Scriptures . . . which is invisible to those who are uninitiated" ("On Dreams," XXVI).

In an allegorical interpretation of the "cities of refuge" (Numbers xxxv. 9–28), three of which were situated west of the river Jordan and three across the river, Philo pictures the gradual progression in the life of faith. Man is to escape the ordinary pursuit of life and take refuge in the negative commandments of the law—the nearest city; from there he proceeds to the positive commandments—the next city; and then to the third that represents divine forgiveness and mercy. If he is prepared to cross the river, he will find three cities symbolizing God's cosmic law, His creative energy, and finally the manifestation of God's being: the *logos* ("On Fugitives").

Philo maintains that "the divine and secret ordinances" are to be imparted only to "those initiated persons who are worthy of the knowledge of the most holy mysteries. And those who are thus worthy are they who, with all modesty, practice genuine piety. The Sacred Revelation is not for those who are afflicted with the uncurable disease of pride of language" ("On the Cherubim," XII). The "initiates," Erwin R. Goodenough tells us (*An Introduction to Philo Judaeus,* Oxford, 1962, p. 46), are "those Jews who had learned to look beyond the letter of the Torah, and, through the lenses of allegory, to discern as the true objective of Jewish revelation a great new immaterial world of mystic accomplishment."

In a rare reference to his own life, Philo, at once thinker and, as a member of a prominent family, man of affairs, speaks of the time when, "devoting myself to philosophy and to contemplation of the world . . . , when I lived among the divine themes and verities. I appeared to be raised on high and borne aloft by a certain inspiration of the soul, and to dwell in the regions of the

sun and the moon and the whole heaven and universe. At that
time, looking down from above and straining the eye of the mind
as from a watch-tower, I surveyed the multitudinous world-wide
spectacles of earthly things, and looked upon myself as happy at
having escaped from all the calamities of mortal life. . . . Implanted in my soul from early youth, I have a desire for instruction. . . . I survey all the things around me, being eager to imbibe
something of a life pure and unmixed with evils. . . . I open the
eyes of my soul . . . and I am irradiated with the light of wisdom"
("On the Special Laws," beginning of Book III).

Philo's absorption by the spiritual aspect in individual life is
paralleled by his deep admiration for the Essenes who cultivate a
saintly life on a community level (see "On the Virtuous Being
also Free" in this volume), and for the Therapeutae, a Jewish
sect in Egypt, dedicated to contemplation (see "On a Contemplative Life" in this volume).

However, this emphasis on spiritualization of faith, on mystical experience and contemplative life, and on the harmony between Moses and Plato, Torah and philosophy, is but one—however fundamental—side of Philo's thought. Another aspect of his
many-sided, if not complex, personality is his demand that the
literal meaning of the Law be observed, even if allegory discovers
an underlying spiritual significance that raises the human mind
above the practical, earthy "Thou shalt" or "Thou shalt not." Or
his affirmation that Israel is not only a symbol of "man who sees
God" (as he interpreted the name), not only a community "consecrated to priesthood" on behalf of mankind (p. 213 in this volume), but a veritable people, a nation with its own peculiar historic fate.

Compared with other nations, Philo says, the Jewish people
are in the position of an orphan. If misfortunes fall upon any of
the nations, they, "owing to international intercourse," have help-
ers who come to their aid. Whereas the Jewish nation has none to
take its part, "because it lives under exceptional laws . . . imposing on them austere standards of virtue." Such austerity is dis-
liked by the majority of men, who favor pleasures. Yet, "as
Moses tells us," the orphan-like position of His people is always
an object of pity and compassion to the Ruler of the Universe

Whose portion it is: They have been set apart from within the human race "as a kind of first fruits to the Maker and Father" ("On the Special Laws," IV).

The political situation of the Alexandrian Jews was indeed precarious and forced Philo to descend from the lofty heights of his philosophy and to take a stand on the practical issues of the day. He wrote *Against Flaccus,* the prefect of Egypt who was responsible for a wholesale persecution of Jews in Alexandria. In 39–40 Philo headed a delegation to emperor Gaius Caligula on behalf of the Jewish community, an event he described in *The Embassy to Gaius.*

Philo's writings—most of which, in the form of biblical commentaries, were preserved by the Church for their theological implications—fall into two main categories: writings addressed to interested gentiles and writings of concern to a group of enlightened, educated Jews.

The first group comprises treatises "On the Creation of the World," "On Abraham" (essays on Isaac and Jacob are lost), "On the Life of Moses," "On the Decalogue" (not included in this selection), "On the Special Laws" (of which the section "On the Ten Festivals" is here included), "On Virtues" (not included), "On a Contemplative Life," and various fragments.

The second group, an allegorical commentary to Genesis i–xx, comprises today eighteen treatises, while at least nine are lost. Our selection includes the first book of the allegorical interpretation of Genesis ii–iii ("On the Allegories of the Sacred Laws"), which deals with the second account of Creation, "On the Cherubim," and "On the Migration of Abraham." In addition, Philo addressed the rank and file of Alexandrian Jews in "On Rewards and Punishments," the first part of which ("On Rewards") is here included. Also included is the section on the sect of the Essenes from the treatise "On the Virtuous Being also Free."

It is hoped that the volume presents the essential aspects of Philo's work—as an introduction to Hellenistic Judaism, information on the background of early Christian thought, and as a chapter in the intellectual history of antiquity—for Philo prepares the way for Neoplatonism, as shown by H. Guyot, F. Heinemann, and A. Altmann. The translation from the Greek by C. D. Yonge has been used (*The Works of Philo Judaeus*, 4 vols., London, 1854), corrected in a number of places. The notes are designed to provide basic explanations, to point to Philo's sources, and to supplement the references given in the body of the book. The occasional use of the annotations in the German translation by Leopold Cohn and I. Heinemann (*Die Werke Philo's von Alexandria*, Breslau, 1909 *et seq.*) and in the English Philo rendition by F. H. Colson and G. H. Whitaker (in The Loeb Classical Library, Cambridge, Mass., and London, 1929 *et seq.*) is gratefully acknowledged.

N. N. Glatzer

Brandeis University
April 1970

The Essential Philo

A TREATISE

THE CREATION OF THE WORLD,

AS GIVEN BY MOSES.

I. Of other lawgivers, some have set forth what they considered to be just and reasonable, in a naked and unadorned manner, while others, investing their ideas with an abundance of amplification, have sought to bewilder the people, by burying the truth under a heap of fabulous inventions. But Moses, rejecting both of these methods, the one as inconsiderate, careless, and unphilosophical, and the other as mendacious and full of trickery, made the beginning of his laws entirely beautiful, and in all respects admirable, neither at once declaring what ought to be done or the contrary, nor (since it was necessary to mould beforehand the dispositions of those who were to use his laws) inventing fables himself or adopting those which had been invented by others.

And his exordium, as I have already said, is most admirable; embracing the creation of the world, under the idea that the law corresponds to the world and the world to the law, and that a man who is obedient to the law, being, by so doing, a citizen of the world, arranges his actions with reference to the intention of nature, in harmony with which the whole universal world is regulated. Accordingly no one, whether poet or historian, could ever give expression in an adequate manner to the beauty of his ideas respecting the creation of the world; for they surpass all the power of language, and amaze our hearing, being too great and venerable to be adapted to the senses of any created being. That, however, is not a reason for our yielding to indolence on the subject, but rather from our affection for the Deity we ought to endeavour to exert ourselves even beyond our powers in describing them: not as having much, or indeed anything to say of our own, but instead of much, just a little, such as it may be probable that human intellect may attain to, when wholly occupied with a love of and desire for wisdom.

For as the smallest seal receives imitations of things of colossal magnitude when engraved upon it, so perchance in some instances the exceeding beauty of the description of the creation of the world as recorded in the Law, overshadowing with its brilliancy the souls of those who happen to meet with it, will be delivered to a more concise record after these facts have been first premised which it would be improper to pass over in silence.

II. For some men, admiring the world itself rather than the Creator of the world, have represented it as existing without any maker, and eternal; and as impiously as falsely have represented God as existing in a state of complete inactivity, while it would have been right on the other hand to marvel at the might of God as the creator and father of all, and to admire the world in a degree not exceeding the bounds of moderation.

But Moses, who had early reached the very summits of philosophy, and who had learnt from the oracles of God the most numerous and important of the principles of nature, was well aware that it is indispensable that in all existing things there must be an active cause, and a passive subject; and that the active cause is the intellect of the universe, thoroughly unadulterated and thoroughly unmixed, superior to virtue and superior to science, superior even to abstract good or abstract beauty; while the passive subject is something inanimate and incapable of motion by any intrinsic power of its own, but having been set in motion, and fashioned, and endowed with life by the intellect, became transformed into that most perfect work, this world. And those who describe it as being uncreated, do, without being aware of it, cut off the most useful and necessary of all the qualities which tend to produce piety, namely, providence: for reason proves that the father and creator has a care for that which has been created; for a father is anxious for the life of his children, and a workman aims at the duration of his works, and employs every device imaginable to ward off everything that is pernicious or injurious, and is desirous by every means in his power to provide everything which is useful or profitable for them. But with regard to that which has not been created, there is no feeling of interest as if it were his own in the breast of him who has not created it.

It is then a pernicious doctrine, and one for which no one should contend, to establish a system in this world, such as anarchy is in a city, so that it should have no superintendant, or regulator, or judge, by whom everything must be managed and governed.

But the great Moses, thinking that a thing which has not been uncreated is as alien as possible from that which is visible before our eyes (for everything which is the subject of our senses exists in birth and in changes, and is not always in the same condition), has attributed eternity to that which is invisible and discerned only by our intellect as a kinsman and a brother, while of that which is the object of our external senses he had predicated generation as an appropriate description. Since, then, this world is visible and the object of our external senses, it follows of necessity that it must have been created; on which account it was not without a wise purpose that he recorded its creation, giving a very venerable account of God.

III. And he says that the world was made in six days, not because the Creator stood in need of a length of time (for it is natural that God should do everything at once, not merely by uttering a command, but by even thinking of it); but because the things created required arrangement; and number is akin to arrangement; and, of all numbers, six is, by the laws of nature, the most productive: for of all the numbers, from the unit upwards, it is the first perfect one, being made equal to its parts, and being made complete by them; the number three being half of it, and the number two a third of it, and the unit a sixth of it, and, so to say, it is formed so as to be both male and female, and is made up of the power of both natures; for in existing things the odd number is the male, and the even number is the female; accordingly, of odd numbers the first is the number three, and of even numbers the first is two, and the two numbers multiplied together make six. It was fitting therefore, that the world, being the most perfect

of created things, should be made according to the perfect
number, namely, six : and, as it was to have in it the causes
of both, which arise from combination, that it should be formed
according to a mixed number, the first combination of odd and
even numbers, since it was to embrace the character both of
the male who sows the seed, and of the female who receives it.
And he allotted each of the six days to one of the portions of
the whole, taking out the first day, which he does not even call
the first day, that it may not be numbered with the others, but
entitling it one, he names it rightly, perceiving in it, and
ascribing to it the nature and appellation of the limit.

IV. We must mention as much as we can of the matters
contained in his account, since to enumerate them all is impossible ; for he embraces that beautiful world which is perceptible only by the intellect, as the account of the first day will
show : for God, as apprehending beforehand, as a God must
do, that there could not exist a good imitation without a good
model, and that of the things perceptible to the external
senses nothing could be faultless which was not fashioned with
reference to some archetypal idea conceived by the intellect,
when he had determined to create this visible world, previously
formed that one which is perceptible only by the intellect, in
order that so using an incorporeal model formed as far as possible on the image of God, he might then make this corporeal
world, a younger likeness of the elder creation, which should
embrace as many different genera perceptible to the external
senses, as the other world contains of those which are visible
only to the intellect.

But that world which consists of ideas, it were impious in
any degree to attempt to describe or even to imagine : but
how it was created, we shall know if we take for our guide a
certain image of the things which exist among us.

When any city is founded through the exceeding ambition
of some king or leader who lays claim to absolute authority,
and is at the same time a man of brilliant imagination, eager
to display his good fortune, then it happens at times that some
man coming up who, from his education, is skilful in archi-
tecture, and he, seeing the advantageous character and beauty
of the situation, first of all sketches out in his own mind
nearly all the parts of the city which is about to be completed—the temples, the gymnasia, the prytanea, the markets,

the docks, the streets, the arrangement of the
uations of the dwelling houses, and of the public
ldings. Then, having received in his own mind,
tablet, the form of each building, he carries in
image of a city, perceptible as yet only by the
images of which he stirs up in memory which is
and, still further, engraving them in his mind
workman, keeping his eyes fixed on his model, he
aise the city of stones and wood, making the corporeal substances to resemble each of the incorporeal ideas.
Now we must form a somewhat similar opinion of God, who,
having determined to found a mighty state, first of all conceived its form in his mind, according to which form he made
a world perceptible only by the intellect, and then completed
one visible to the external senses, using the first one as a
model.

V. As therefore the city, when previously shadowed out in
the mind of the man of architectural skill had no external
place, but was stamped solely in the mind of the workman, so
in the same manner neither can the world which existed in
ideas have had any other local position except the divine
reason which made them; for what other place could there be
for his powers which should be able to receive and contain, I
do not say all, but even any single one of them whatever, in
its simple form? And the power and faculty which could be
capable of creating the world, has for its origin that good which
is founded on truth; for if any one were desirous to investigate the cause on account of which this universe was created, I
think that he would come to no erroneous conclusion if he
were to say as one of the ancients did say: " That the Father
and Creator was good; on which account he did not grudge the
substance a share of his own excellent nature, since it had nothing
good of itself, but was able to become everything." For the
substance was of itself destitute of arrangement, of quality, of
animation, of distinctive character, and full of all disorder and
confusion; and it received a change and transformation to
what is opposite to this condition, and most excellent, being
invested with order, quality, animation, resemblance, identity,
arrangement, harmony, and everything which belongs to the
more excellent idea.

VI. And God, not being urged on by any prompter (for

ld there have been to prompt him?) but guided
le will, decided that it was fitting to benefit with
d abundant favours a nature which, without the
as unable of itself to partake of any good thing;
ts it, not according to the greatness of his own
hey are illimitable and eternal, but according to
the power of that which is benefited to receive his graces.
For the capacity of that which is created to receive benefits
does not correspond to the natural power of God to confer
them; since his powers are infinitely greater, and the thing
created being not sufficiently powerful to receive all their
greatness would have sunk under it, if he had not measured
his bounty, allotting to each, in due proportion, that which was
poured upon it. And if any one were to desire to use more
undisguised terms, he would not call the world, which is perceptible only to the intellect, any thing else but the reason of
God, already occupied in the creation of the world; for neither
is a city, while only perceptible to the intellect, anything else
but the reason of the architect, who is already designing to
build one perceptible to the external senses, on the model of
that which is so only to the intellect—this is the doctrine of
Moses, not mine. Accordingly he, when recording the creation of man, in words which follow, asserts expressly, that
he was made in the image of God—and if the image be a part
of the image, then manifestly so is the entire form, namely,
the whole of this world perceptible by the external senses,
which is a greater imitation of the divine image than the
human form is. It is manifest also, that the archetypal seal,
which we call that world which is perceptible only to the intellect, must itself be the archetypal model, the idea of ideas,
the Reason of God.

VII. Moses says also; "In the beginning God created the
heaven and the earth:" taking the beginning to be, not as
some men think, that which is according to time; for before
the world time had no existence, but was created either
simultaneously with it, or after it; for since time is the interval of the motion of the heavens, there could not have been
any such thing as motion before there was anything which
could be moved; but it follows of necessity that it received
existence subsequently or simultaneously. It therefore follows
also of necessity, that time was created either at the same

assert that it is older than the world is absolutely inconsistent with philosophy. But if the beginning spoken of by Moses is not to be looked upon as spoken of according to time, then it may be natural to suppose that it is the beginning according to number that is indicated; so that, " In the beginning he created," is equivalent to " first of all he created the heaven;" for it is natural in reality that that should have been the first object created, being both the best of all created things, and being also made of the purest substance, because it was destined to be the most holy abode of the visible Gods who are perceptible by the external senses; for if the Creator had made everything at the same moment, still those things which were created in beauty would no less have had a regular arrangement, for there is no such thing as beauty in disorder. But order is a due consequence and connection of things precedent and subsequent, if not in the completion of a work, at all events in the intention of the maker; for it is owing to order that they become accurately defined and stationary, and free from confusion.

In the first place therefore, from the model of the world, perceptible only by intellect, the Creator made an incorporeal heaven, and an invisible earth, and the form of air and of empty space: the former of which he called darkness, because the air is black by nature; and the other he called the abyss, for empty space is very deep and yawning with immense width. Then he created the incorporeal substance of water and of air, and above all he spread light, being the seventh thing made; and this again was incorporeal, and a model of the sun, perceptible only to intellect, and of all the light-giving stars, which are destined to stand together in heaven.

VIII. And air and light he considered worthy of the pre-eminence. For the one he called the breath of God, because it is air, which is the most life-giving of things, and of life the causer is God; and the other he called light, because it is surpassingly beautiful: for that which is perceptible only by intellect is as far more brilliant and splendid than that which is seen, as I conceive, the sun is than darkness, or day than night, or the intellect than any other of the outward senses by which men judge (inasmuch as it is the guide of the entire soul), or the eyes than any other part of the body. And the

invisible divine reason, perceptible only by intellect, he calls
the image of God. And the image of this image is that light,
perceptible only by the intellect, which is the image of the
divine reason, which has explained its generation. And it is
a star above the heavens, the source of those stars which are
perceptible by the external senses, and if any one were to call
it universal light he would not be very wrong; since it is from
that the sun and the moon, and all the other planets and fixed
stars derive their due light, in proportion as each has power
given to it; that unmingled and pure light being obscured
when it begins to change, according to the change from that
which is perceptible only by the intellect, to that which is
perceptible by the external senses; for none of those things
which are perceptible to the external senses is pure.

IX. Moses is right also when he says, that " darkness was
over the face of the abyss." For the air is in a manner
spread above the empty space, since having mounted up it
entirely fills all that open, and desolate, and empty place,
which reaches down to us from the regions below the moon.
And after the shining forth of that light, perceptible only to
the intellect, which existed before the sun, then its adversary
darkness yielded, as God put a wall between them and separated them, well knowing their opposite characters, and the
enmity existing between their natures. In order, therefore,
that they might not war against one another from being continually brought in contact, so that war would prevail instead
of peace, God, turning want of order into order, did not only
separate light and darkness, but did also place boundaries in
the middle of the space between the two, by which he separated the extremities of each. For if they had approximated
they must have produced confusion, preparing for the contest,
for the supremacy, with great and unextinguishable rivalry, if
boundaries established between them had not separated them
and prevented them from clashing together, and these boundaries are evening and morning; the one of which heralds in
the good tidings that the sun is about to rise, gently dissipating the darkness: and evening comes on as the sun sets,
receiving gently the collective approach of darkness. And
these, I mean morning and evening, must be placed in the
class of incorporeal things, perceptible only by the intellect;
for there is absolutely nothing in them which is perceptible by

the external senses, but they are entirely ideas, and measures, and forms, and seals, incorporeal as far as regards the generation of other bodies. But when light came, and darkness retreated and yielded to it, and boundaries were set in the space between the two, namely, evening and morning, then of necessity the measure of time was immediately perfected, which also the Creator called " day," and He called it not " the first day," but " one day ;" and it is spoken of thus, on account of the single nature of the world perceptible only by the intellect, which has a single nature.

X. The incorporeal world then was already completed, having its seat in the Divine Reason ; and the world, perceptible by the external senses, was made on the model of it ; and the first portion of it, being also the most excellent of all made by the Creator, was the heaven, which he truly called the firmament, as being corporeal ; for the body is by nature firm, inasmuch as it is divisible into three parts ; and what other idea of solidity and of body can there be, except that it is something which may be measured in every direction? therefore he, very naturally contrasting that which was perceptible to the external senses, and corporeal with that which was perceptible only by the intellect and incorporeal, called this the firmament. Immediately afterwards he, with great propriety and entire correctness, called it the heaven, either because it was already the boundary* of everything, or because it was the first of all visible things which was created; and after its second rising he called the time day, referring the entire space and measure of a day to the heaven, on account of its dignity and honour among the things perceptible to the external senses.

XI. And after this, as the whole body of water in existence was spread over all the earth, and had penetrated through all its parts, as if it were a sponge which had imbibed moisture, so that the earth was only swampy land and deep mud, both the elements of earth and water being mixed up and combined together, like one confused mass into one undistinguishable and shapeless nature, God ordained that all the water which was salt, and destined to be a cause of barrenness to seeds and trees, should be gathered together, flowing forth out of all

* Philo means that οὐρανος was derived either from ὅρος, a boundary, or from ὁράω, to see, ὁρατὸς, visible.

the holes of the entire earth; and he commanded dry land to appear, that liquid which had any sweetness in it being left in it to secure its durability. For this sweet liquid, in due proportions, is as a sort of glue for the different substances, preventing the earth from being utterly dried up, and so becoming unproductive and barren, and causing it, like a mother, to furnish not only one kind of nourishment, namely meat, but both sorts at once, so as to supply its offspring with both meat and drink; wherefore he filled it with veins, resembling breasts, which, being provided with openings, were destined to pour forth springs and rivers. And in the same way he extended the invisible irrigations of dew pervading every portion of arable and deep-soiled land, to contribute to the most liberal and plenteous supply of fruits. Having arranged these things, he gave them names, calling the dry, " land," and the water which was separated from it he called " sea."

XII. After this he began to adorn the land, for he bade it bring forth grass, and bear corn, producing every kind of herb, and plains clothed with verdure, and everything which was calculated to be fodder for cattle, or food for men. Moreover he commanded every kind of tree to spring up, omitting no kind, either of those which are wild or of those which are called cultivated. And simultaneously with their first production he loaded them all with fruit, in a manner different from that which exists at present; for now the different fruits are produced in turn, at different seasons, and not all together at one time; for who is there who does not know that first of all comes the sowing and the planting; and, in the second place, the growth of what has been sown and planted, in some cases the plants extending their roots downwards like foundations, and in others raising themselves upwards to a height and displaying long stalks? After that come the buds, and the putting forth of leaves, and then after everything else comes the production of fruit. And again, the fruit when first produced is not perfect, but it contains in itself all kinds of change, with reference both to its quantity in regard of magnitude, and to its qualities in its multiform appearance: for the fruit is produced at first like indivisible grains, which are hardly visible from their diminutive size, and which one might correctly enough pronounce to be the first things per-

ceptible by the external senses; and afterwards by little and
little, from the nourishment conveyed in channels, which
waters the tree, and from the wholesome effect of the breezes,
which blow air at the same time cold and gentle, the fruit is
gradually vivified, and nursed up, and increased, advancing
onward to its perfect size; and with its change of magnitude
it changes also its qualities, as if it were diversified with
varying colours by pictorial science.

XIII. But in the first creation of the universe, as I have
said already, God produced the whole race of trees out of the
earth in full perfection, having their fruit not incomplete but
in a state of entire ripeness, to be ready for the immediate and
undelayed use and enjoyment of the animals which were about
immediately to be born. Accordingly he commanded the
earth to produce these things. And the earth, as though it
had for a long time been pregnant and travailing, produced
every sort of seed, and every sort of tree, and also of fruit, in
unspeakable abundance; and not only were these produced
fruits to be food for living animals, but enough also to serve as
a preparation for the continuous production of similar fruits
hereafter; covering substances consisting of seed, in which are
the principles of all plants undistinguishable and invisible,
but destined hereafter to become manifest and visible in the
periodical maturity of the fruit. For God thought fit to
endue nature with a long duration, making the races that he
was creating immortal, and giving them a participation in
eternity. On which account he led on and hastened the
beginning towards the end, and caused the end to turn backwards to the beginning: for from plants comes fruit, as the end
might come from the beginning; and from the fruit comes the
seed, which again contains the plant within itself, so that a
fresh beginning may come from the end.

XIV. And on the fourth day, after he had embellished the
earth, he diversified and adorned the heaven: not giving the
precedence to the inferior nature by arranging the heaven
subsequently to the earth, or thinking that which was the
more excellent and the more divine worthy only of the second
place, but acting thus for the more manifest demonstration of
the power of his dominion. For he foreknew with respect
to men who were not yet born, what sort of beings they would
be as to their opinions, forming conjectures on what was

likely and probable, of which the greater part would be reasonable, though falling short of the character of unadulterated
truth ; and trusting rather to visible phenomena than to God,
and admiring sophistry rather than wisdom.   And again he
knew that surveying the periods of the sun and moon, to
which are owing the summers and winters, and the alternations
of spring and autumn, they would conceive the revolutions of
the stars in heaven to be the causes of all the things which
every year should be produced and generated on the earth,
accordingly that no one might venture either through shameless impudence or inordinate ignorance to attribute to any
created thing the primary causes of things, he said : "Let
them run over in their minds the first creation of the universe,
when, before the sun or the moon existed, the earth brought
forth all kinds of plants and all kinds of fruits : and seeing
this in their minds let them hope that it will again also bring
forth such, according to the appointment of the Father, when
it shall seem good to him, without his having need of the aid
of any of the sons of men beneath the heavens, to whom he
has given powers, though not absolute ones." For as a charioteer holding the reins, or a helmsman with his hand upon the
rudder, he guides everything as he pleases, in accordance with
law and justice, needing no one else as his assistant ; for all
things are possible to God.

XV. This is the cause why the earth bore fruit and herbs
before God proceeded to adorn the heaven.   And next the
heaven was embellished in the perfect number four, and if
any one were to pronounce this number the origin and source
of the all-perfect decade he would not err.   For what the
decade is in actuality, that the number four, as it seeems, is in
potentiality, at all events if the numerals from the unit to four*
are placed together in order, they will make ten, which is the
limit of the number of immensity, around which the numbers
wheel and turn as around a goal.

Moreover the number four also comprehends the principles
of the harmonious concords in music, that in fours, and in

* By addition, that is 1
                       2
                       3
                       4
                       ──
                       10

fifths, and the diapason, and besides this the double diapason
from which sounds the most perfect system of harmony is produced. For the ratio of the sounds in fourths is as four to
three ; and in fifths as three to two ; and in the diapason that ratio
is doubled : and in the double diapason it is increased fourfold,
all which ratios the number four comprehends.   At all
events the first, or the epistritus, is the ratio of four to three ;
the second, or the hemiolius, is that of three to two : the twofold ratio is that of two to one, or four to two : and the fourfold ratio is that of four to one.

XVI. There is also another power of the number four which
is a most wonderful one to speak of and to contemplate. For
it was this number that first displayed the nature of the solid
cube, the numbers before four being assigned only to incorporeal things. For it is according to the unit that that thing
is reckoned which is spoken of in geometry as a point : and a
line is spoken of according to the number two, because it is
arranged by nature from a point ; and a line is length without
breadth. But when breadth is added to it, it becomes a
superficies, which is arranged according to the number three.
And a superficies, when compared with the nature of a solid
cube, wants one thing, namely depth, and when this one thing
is added to the three, it becomes four. On which account it
has happened that this number is a thing of great importance,
inasmuch as from an incorporeal substance perceptible only
by intellect, it has led us on to a comprehension of a body
divisible in a threefold manner, and which by its own nature
is first perceived by the external senses. And he who does
not comprehend what is here said may learn to understand it
from a game which is very common. Those who play with
nuts are accustomed when they have placed three nuts on the
floor, to place one more on the top of them producing a figure
like a pyramid. Accordingly the triangle stands on the floor,
arranged up to the number three, and the nut which is placed
upon it makes up four in number, and in figure it produces a
pyramid, being now a solid body.

And in addition to this there is this point also of which we
should not be ignorant, the number four is the first number
which is a square, being equal on all sides, the measure of
justice and equality. And that it is the only number the
nature of which is such that it is produced by the same numbers

whether in combination, or in power. In combination when
two and two are added together; and again in power when we
speak of twice two;* and in this it displays an exceedingly
beautiful kind of harmony, which is not the lot of any other
number.

If we examine the number six which is composed of two
threes, if these two numbers are multiplied it is not the number
six that is produced, but a different one, the number nine.
And the number four has many other powers also, which we
must subsequently show more accurately in a separate essay
appropriated to it. At present it is sufficient to add this that
it was the foundation of the creation of the whole heaven and
the whole world. For the four elements, out of which this
universe was made, flowed from the number four as from a
fountain. And in addition to the four elements the seasons of
the year are also four, which are the causes of the generation
of animals and plants, the year being divided into the quadruple
division of winter, and spring, and summer, and autumn.

XVII. The aforesaid number therefore being accounted
worthy of such pre eminence in nature, the Creator of necessity
adorned the heaven by the number four, namely by that most
beautiful and most godlike ornament the light-giving stars. And
knowing that of all existing things light is the most excellent,
he made it the instrument of the best of all the senses, sight.
For what the mind is in the soul, that the eye is in the body.
For each of them sees, the one beholding those existing things
which are perceptible only to the intellect, and the other those
which are perceptible to the external senses.

But the mind is in need of knowledge in order to distinguish
incorporeal things, and the eyes have need of light in order to
be able to perceive bodies, and light is also the cause of many
other good things to men, and particularly of the greatest,
namely philosophy. For the sight being sent upwards by light
and beholding the nature of the stars and their harmonious
movement, and the well-ordered revolutions of the fixed stars,
and of the planets, some always revolving in the same manner
and coming to the same places, and others having double
periods in an anomalous and somewhat contrary manner, beholding also, the harmonious dances of all these bodies arranged
according to the laws of perfect music, causes an ineffable

* Thus $2+2=4$, or $2 \times 2=4$.

joy and delight to the soul. And the soul, feasting on a continuous series of spectacles, for one succeeds another, has an insatiable love for beholding such. Then, as is usually the case, it examines with increased curiosity what is the substance of these things which are visible; and whether they have an existence without having been created, or whether they received their origin by creation, and what is the character of their movement, and what the causes are by which everything is regulated. And it is from inquiries into these things that philosophy has arisen, than which no more perfect good has entered into human life.

XVIII. But the Creator having a regard to that idea of light perceptible only by the intellect, which has been spoken of in the mention made of the incorporeal world, created those stars which are perceptible by the external senses, those divine and superlatively beautiful images, which on many accounts he placed in the purest temple of corporeal substance, namely in heaven. One of the reasons for his so doing was that they might give light; another was that they might be signs; another had reference to their dividing the times of the seasons of the year, and above all dividing days and nights, months and years, which are the measures of time; and which have given rise to the nature of number. And how great is the use and how great the advantage derivable from each of the aforesaid things, is plain from their effect. But with a view to a more accurate comprehension of them, it may perhaps not be out of place to trace out the truth in a regular discussion.

Now the whole of time being divided into two portions day and night, the sovereignty of the day the Father has assigned to the Sun, as a mighty monarch: and that of the night he has given to the moon and to the multitude of the other stars. And the greatness of the power and sovereignty of the sun has its most conspicuous proof in what has been already said: for he, being one and single has been allotted for his own share and by himself one half portion of all time, namely day; and all the other lights in conjunction with the moon have the other portion, which is called night. And when the sun rises all the appearances of such numbers of stars are not only obscured but absolutely disappear from the effusion of his beams; and when he sets then they all assembled together, begin to display their own peculiar brilliancy and their separate qualities,

XIX. And they have been created, as Moses tells us, not only that they might send light upon the earth, but also that they might display signs of future events. For either by their risings, or their settings, or their eclipses, or again by their appearances and occultations, or by the other variations observable in their motions, men oftentimes conjecture what is about to happen, the productiveness or unproductiveness of the crops, the birth or loss of their cattle, fine weather or cloudy weather, calms and violent storms of wind, floods in the rivers or droughts, a tranquil state of the sea and heavy waves, unusual changes in the seasons of the year when either the summer is cold like winter, or the winter warm, or when the spring assumes the temperature of autumn or the autumn that of spring. And before now some men have conjecturally predicted disturbances and commotions of the earth from the revolutions of the heavenly bodies, and innumerable other events which have turned out most exactly true : so that it is a most veracious saying that " the stars were created to act as signs, and moreover to mark the seasons." And by the word seasons the divisions of the year are here intended. And why may not this be reasonably affirmed ? For what other idea of opportunity can there be except that it is the time for success ? And the seasons bring everything to perfection and set everything right ; giving perfection to the sowing and planting of fruits, and to the birth and growth of animals.

They were also created to serve as measures of time ; for it is by the appointed periodical revolutions of the sun and moon and other stars, that days and months and years are determined. And moreover it is owing to them that the most useful of all things, the nature of number exists, time having displayed it ; for from one day comes the limit, and from two the number two, and from three, three, and from the notion of a month is derived the number thirty, and from a year that number which is equal to the days of the twelve months, and from infinite time comes the notion of infinite number.

To such great and indispensable advantages do the natures of the heavenly bodies and the motions of the stars tend. And to how many other things might I also affirm that they contribute which are as yet unknown to us ? for all things are

not known to the will of man ; but of the things which contribute towards the durability of the universe, those which are
established by laws and ordinances which God has appointed
to be unalterable for ever, are accomplished in every instance
and in every country.

XX. Then when earth and heaven had been adorned with
their befitting ornaments, one with a triad, and the other, as has
been already said, with a quaternion, God proceeded to create the
races of mortal creatures, making the beginning with the
aquatic animals on the fifth day, thinking that there was no
one thing so akin to another as the number five was to animals ; for animate things differ from inanimate in nothing
more than in sensation, and sensation is divided according to
a five-fold division, into sight, hearing, taste, smell, and
touch. Accordingly, the Creator allotted to each of the senses
its appropriate matter, and also its peculiar faculty of judgment, by which it should decide on what came before it. So
sight judges of colours, and hearing of sounds, and taste of
juices, and smell of vapours, and touch of softness and hardness, and of heat and cold, and of smoothness and roughness ;
therefore He commanded all the races of fish and sea-monsters
to stand together in their places, animals differing both in
their sizes and in their qualities ; for they vary in different
seas, though in some cases they are the same, and every
animal was not formed to live every where. And was not this
reasonable ? For some of them delight in marshy places,
and in water which is very deep ; and some in sewers and
harbours, being neither able to crawl up upon the land, nor to
swim off far from the land. Some, again, dwell in the middle
and in the deep sea, and avoid all the projecting promontories
and islands and rocks : some also exult in fine weather and
in calms, and some in storms and heavy surf. For being
exercised by continual buffetings, and being in the habit of
withstanding the current by force, they are very vigorous and
become stout.

After that he created the races of birds as akin to the races
of aquatic animals (for they are each of them swimmers),
leaving no species of creatures which traverse the air un-
finished.

XXI. So now when the air and the water had received
their appropriate races of animals as an allotment that was

their due, God again summoned the earth for the creation of that share which still remained : and after the production of plants, the terrestrial animals still remained. And God said, " Let the earth bring forth cattle and beasts, and creeping things of each kind." And the earth did as it was commanded, and immediately sent forth animals differing in their formation and in their strength, and in the injurious or beneficial powers that were implanted in them.

And after all He made man. But how he made him I will mention presently, after I have first explained that he adopted the most beautiful connection and train of consequences according to the system of the creation of animals which he had sketched out to himself; for of souls the most sluggish and the most weakly formed has been allotted to the race of fishes ; and the most exquisitely endowed soul, that which is in all respects most excellent, has been given to the race of mankind, and one something between the two to the races of terrestrial animals and those which traverse the air ; for the soul of such creatures is endowed with more acute sensations than the soul of fishes, but is more dull than that of mankind. And it was on this account that of all living creatures God created fishes first, inasmuch as they partake of corporeal substance in a greater degree than they partake of soul, being in a manner animals and not animals, moving soulless things, having a sort of semblance of soul diffused through them for no object beyond that of keeping their bodies alive (just as they say that salt preserves meat), in order that they may not easily be destroyed. And after the fishes, he created winged and terrestrial animals : for these are endowed with a higher degree of sensation, and from their formation show that the properties of their animating principle are of a higher order. But after all the rest, then, as has been said before, he created man, to whom he gave that admirable endowment of mind—the soul, if I may so call it, of the soul, as being like the pupil to the eye ; for those who most accurately investigate the natures of things affirm, that it is the pupil which is the eye of the eye.

XXII. So at last all things were created and existing together. But when they all were collected in one place, then some sort of order was necessarily laid down for them for the sake of the production of them from one another which was

hereafter to take place. Now in things which exist in part,
the principle of order is this, to begin with that which is most
inferior in its nature, and to end with that which is the most
excellent of all; and what that is we will explain. It has been
arranged that seed should be the principle of the generation of
animals. It is plainly seen that this is a thing of no importance, being like foam; but when it has descended into the
womb and remained there, then immediately it receives
motion and is changed into nature; and nature is more excellent than seed, as also motion is better than quiet in created
things; and nature, like a workman, or, to speak more correctly, like a faultless art, endows the moist substance with
life, and fashions it, distributing it among the limbs and parts
of the body, allotting that portion which can produce breath,
and nourishment, and sensation to the powers of the soul: for
as to the reasoning powers, we may pass over them for the
present, on account of those who say, that the mind enters
into the body from without, being something divine and
eternal.

Nature therefore began from an insignificant seed, and
ended in the most honourable of things, namely, in the formation of animals and men. And the very same thing took
place in the creation of every thing: for when the Creator
determined to make animals the first created in his arrangement were in some degree inferior, such as the fishes, and the
last were the best, namely, man. And the others the terrestrial and winged creatures were between these extremes,
being better than the first created, and inferior to the last.

XXIII. So then after all the other things, as has been
said before, Moses says that man was made in the image and
likeness of God. And he says well; for nothing that is born on
the earth is more resembling God than man. And let no one
think that he is able to judge of this likeness from the characters of the body: for neither is God a being with the form of a
man, nor is the human body like the form of God; but the
resemblance is spoken of with reference to the most important
part of the soul, namely, the mind: for the mind which
exists in each individual has been created after the likeness
of that one mind which is in the universe as its primitive
model, being in some sort the God of that body which carries
it about and bears its image within it. In the same rank

that the great Governor occupies in the universal world, that same as it seems does the mind of man occupy in man; for it is invisible, though it sees everything itself; and it has an essence which is undiscernible, though it can discern the essences of all other things, and making for itself by art and science all sorts of roads leading in divers directions, and all plain; it traverses land and sea, investigating everything which is contained in either element. And again, being raised up on wings, and so surveying and contemplating the air, and all the commotions to which it is subject, it is borne upwards to the higher firmament, and to the revolutions of the heavenly bodies. And also being itself involved in the revolutions of the planets and fixed stars according to the perfect laws of music, and being led on by love, which is the guide of wisdom, it proceeds onwards till, having surmounted all essence intelligible by the external senses, it comes to aspire to such as is perceptible only by the intellect: and perceiving in that, the original models and ideas of those things intelligible by the external senses which it saw here full of surpassing beauty, it becomes seized with a sort of sober intoxication like the zealots engaged in the Corybantian festivals, and yields to enthusiasm, becoming filled with another desire, and a more excellent longing, by which it is conducted onwards to the very summit of such things as are perceptible only to the intellect, till it appears to be reaching the great King himself. And while it is eagerly longing to behold him pure and unmingled, rays of divine light are poured forth upon it like a torrent, so as to bewilder the eyes of its intelligence by their splendour.

But as it is not every image that resembles its archetypal model, since many are unlike, Moses has shown this by adding to the words " after his image," the expression, " in his likeness," to prove that it means an accurate impression, having a clear and evident resemblance in form.

XXIV. And he would not err who should raise the question why Moses attributed the creation of man alone not to one creator, as he did that of other animals, but to several. For he introduces the Father of the universe using this language: " Let *us* make man after our image, and in our likeness." Had he then, shall I say, need of any one whatever to help him, He to whom all things are subject? Or, when he was making the heaven and the earth and the sea, was he in need of no one to co-operate with him; and yet was he unable himself by his own power to make man an animal so short-lived and so exposed to the assaults of fate without the assistance of others? It is plain that the real cause of his so acting is known to God alone, but one which to a reasonable conjecture appears probable and credible, I think I should not conceal; and it is this.

Of existing things, there are some which partake neither of virtue nor of vice; as for instance, plants and irrational animals; the one, because they are destitute of soul, and are regulated by a nature void of sense; and the other, because they are not endowed with mind or reason. But mind and reason may be looked upon as the abode of virtue and vice; as it is in them that they seem to dwell. Some things again partake of virtue alone, being without any participation in any kind of vice; as for instance, the stars, for they are said to be animals, and animals endowed with intelligence; or I might rather say, the mind of each of them is wholly and entirely virtuous, and unsusceptible of every kind of evil. Some things again are of a mixed nature, like man, who is capable of opposite qualities, of wisdom and folly, of temperance and dissoluteness, of courage and cowardice, of justice and injustice, in short of good and evil, of what is honourable and what is disgraceful, of virtue and vice. Now it was a very appropriate task for God the Father of all to create by himself alone, those things which were wholly good, on account of their kindred with himself. And it was not inconsistent with his dignity to create those which were indifferent since they too are devoid of evil, which is hateful to him. To create the beings of a mixed nature, was partly consistent and partly inconsistent with his dignity; consistent by reason of the more excellent idea which is mingled in them; inconsistent because of the opposite and worse one.

It is on this account that Moses says, at the creation of man alone that God said, "Let *us* make man," which expression shows an assumption of other beings to himself as assistants, in order that God, the governor of all things, might have all the blameless intentions and actions of man, when he does right attributed to him; and that his other assistants might bear the imputation of his contrary actions. For it was fitting that the Father should in the eyes of his children be free from all imputation of evil ; and vice and energy in accordance with vice are evil.   And very beautifully after he had called the whole race " man," did he distinguish between the sexes, saying, that " they were created male and female ;" although all the individuals of the race had not yet assumed their distinctive form ; since the extreme species are contained in the genus, and are beheld, as in a mirror, by those who are able to discern acutely.

XXV. And some one may inquire the cause why it was that man was the last work in the creation of the world. For the Creator and Father created him after every thing else as the sacred scriptures inform us.   Accordingly, they who have gone most deeply into the laws, and who to the best of their power have investigated everything that is contained in them with all diligence, say that God, when he had given to man to partake of kindred with himself, grudged him neither reason, which is the most excellent of all gifts, nor anything else that is good ; but before his creation, provided for him every thing in the world, as for the animal most resembling himself, and dearest to him, being desirous that when he was born, he should be in want of nothing requisite for living, and for living well ; the first of which objects is provided for by the abundance of supplies which are furnished to him for his enjoyment, and the other by his power of contemplation of the heavenly bodies, by which the mind is smitten so as to conceive a love and desire for knowledge on those subjects ; owing to which desire, philosophy has sprung up, by which, man, though mortal, is made immortal.   As then, those who make a feast do not invite their guests to the entertainment before they have provided everything for festivity, and as those who celebrate gymnastic or dramatic contests, before they assemble the spectators, provide themselves with an abundance of competitors and spectacles, and sweet sounds, with which to fill the theatres and the stadia ; so in the same manner did the Ruler of all, as a man proposing games, or giving a banquet and being about to invite others to feast and to behold the spectacle, first provide everything for every kind of entertainment, in order that when man came into the world he might at once find a feast ready for him, and a most holy theatre ; the one abounding with everything which the earth, or the rivers, or the sea, or air, brings forth for use and enjoyment, and the other being full of every description of light, which has either its essence or its qualities admirable, and its motions and revolutions worthy of notice, being arranged in perfect order, both as to the proportions of its numbers, and the harmony of its periods. And a man would not be far wrong who should say that in all these things there might be discovered that archetypal and real model music, the images of which the subsequent generations of mankind engraved in their own souls, and in this way handed down the art which is the most necessary and the most advantageous to human life.

XXVI. This is the first reason on account of which it seems that man was created after all other animals. And there is another not altogether unreasonable, which I must mention. At the moment of his first birth, man found all the requisites for life ready prepared for him that he might teach them to those who should come afterwards. Nature all but crying out with a distinct voice, that men, imitating the Author of their being, should pass their lives without labour and without trouble, living in the most ungrudging abundance and plenty. And this would be the case if there were neither irrational pleasures to obtain mastery over the soul raising up a wall of gluttony and lasciviousness, nor desires of glory, or power, or riches, to assume dominion over life, nor pains to contract and warp the intellect, nor that evil councillor—fear, to restrain the natural inclinations towards virtuous actions, nor folly and cowardice, and injustice, and the incalculable multitude of other evils to attack them. But now that all the evils which I have now been mentioning are vigorous, and that men abandon themselves without restraint to their passions, and to those unbridled and guilty inclinations, which it is impious even to mention, justice encounters them as a suitable chastiser of wicked habits; and therefore, as a punishment for wrong doers, the necessaries of life have been made difficult of acquisition. For men ploughing up the plains with difficulty, and bringing streams from rivers, and fountains by channels, and sowing and planting, and submitting indefatigably day and night to the labour of cultivating the ground, provide themselves every year with what is necessary, even that at times being attended with pain; and not very sufficient in quantity, from being injured by many causes. For either a fall of incessant rain has carried away the crops, or the weight of hail which has fallen upon them has crushed them altogether, or snow has chilled them, or the violence of the winds has torn them up by the roots; for water and air cause many alterations, tending to destroy the productiveness of the crops. But if the immoderate violence of the passions were appeased by temperance, and the inclination to do wrong and depraved ambition were corrected by justice, and in short if the vices and unhallowed actions done in accordance with them, were corrected by the virtues, and the energies in accordance with them, the war of the soul being terminated, which is in good truth the most grievous and heavy of all wars, and peace being established, and founding amid all our faculties, a due regard for law, with all tranquillity and mildness, then there would be hope that God, as being a friend to virtue, and a friend to honour, and above all a friend to man, would bestow upon the race of man, all kinds of spontaneous blessings from his ready store. For it is evident that it is easier to supply most abundantly the requisite supplies without having recourse to agricultural means, from treasures which already exist, than to bring forth what as yet has no existence.

XXVII. I have now mentioned the second reason. There is also a third, which is as follows:—God, intending to adapt the beginning and the end of all created things together, as being all necessary and dear to one another, made heaven the beginning, and man the end: the one being the most perfect of incorruptible things, among those things which are perceptible by the external senses; and the other, the best of all earth-born and perishable productions—a short-lived heaven if one were to speak the truth, bearing within himself many starlike natures, by means of certain arts and sciences, and illustrious speculations, according to every kind of virtue. For since the corruptible and the incorruptible, are by nature opposite, he has allotted the best thing of each species to the beginning and to the end. Heaven, as I before said, to the beginning, and man to the end.

XXVIII. And besides all this, another is also mentioned among the necessary causes. It was necessary that man should be the last of all created beings; in order that being so, and appearing suddenly, he might strike terror into the other animals. For it was fitting that they, as soon as they first saw him should admire and worship him, as their natural ruler and master; on which account, they all, as soon as they saw him, became tame before him; even those, who by nature were most savage, becoming at once most manageable at the first sight of him; displaying their unbridled ferocity to one another, and being tame to man alone. For which reason the Father who made him to be a being dominant over them by nature not merely in fact, but also by express verbal appointment, established him as the king of all the animals, beneath the moon, whether terrestrial or aquatic, or such as traverse the air. For every mortal thing which lives in the three elements, land, water or air, did he put in subjection to him, excepting only the beings that are in heaven, as creatures who have a more divine portion. And what is apparent to our eyes is the most evident proof of this. For at times, innumerable herds of beasts are led about by one man, not armed, nor wearing iron, nor any defensive weapon, but clad only in a skin for a garment, and carrying a staff, for the purpose of making signs, and to lean upon also in his journeys if he become weary. And so the shepherd, and the goatherd, and the cowherd, lead numerous flocks of sheep, and goats, and herds of oxen; men neither vigorous, nor active in their bodies, so as to strike those who behold them with admiration because of their fine appearance; and all the might and power of such numerous and well-armed beasts (for they have means of self-defence given them by nature), yet dread them as slaves do their master, and do all that is commanded them. Bulls are yoked to the plough to till the ground, and cutting deep furrows all day, sometimes even for a long space of time together, while some farmer is managing them. And rams being weighed down with heavy fleeces of wool, in the spring season, at the command of the shepherd, stand quietly, and lying down, without resistance, permit their wool to be shorn off, being accustomed naturally, like cities, to yield a yearly tribute to their sovereign. And moreover, that most spirited of animals, the horse, is easily guided after he has been bridled; in order that he may not become frisky, and shake off the rein; and he hollows his back in an admirable manner to receive his rider and to afford him a good seat, and then bearing him aloft, he gallops at a rapid pace, being eager to arrive at and carry him to the place to which he is urging him. And the rider without any toil, but in the most perfect quiet, makes a rapid journey, by using the body and feet of another animal.

XXIX. And any one who was inclined to dwell upon this subject might bring forward a great many other instances, to prove that there is no animal in the enjoyment of perfect liberty, and exempt from the dominion of man; but what has been already said is sufficient by way of example. We ought, however, not to be ignorant of this also, that it is no proof because man was the last created animal that he is the lowest in rank, and charioteers and pilots are witnesses of this; for the charioteers sit behind their beasts of burden, and are placed at their backs, and yet when they have the reins in their hands, they guide them wherever they choose, and at one time they urge them on to a swift pace, and at another time they hold them back, if they are going on at a speed greater than is desirable. And pilots again, sitting in the hindmost part of the ship, that is the stern are, as one may say, the most important of all the people in the ship, inasmuch as they have the safety of the ship and of all those who are in it, in their hands. And so the Creator has made man to be as it were a charioteer and pilot over all other animals, in order that he may hold the reins and direct the course of every thing upon earth, having the superintendence of all animals and plants, as a sort of viceroy of the principal and mighty King.

XXX. But after the whole world had been completed according to the perfect nature of the number six, the Father hallowed the day following, the seventh, praising it, and calling it holy. For that day is the festival, not of one city or one country, but of all the earth; a day which alone it is right to call the day of festival for all people, and the birthday of the world. And I know not if any one would be able to celebrate the nature of the number seven in adequate terms, since it is superior to every form of expression. But it does not follow that because it is more admirable than anything that can be said of it, that on that account one ought to keep silence; but rather we ought to try, even if one cannot say everything which is proper, or even that which is most proper, at all events to utter such things as may be attainable by our capacities.

XLIV. So Moses, summing up his account of the creation of the world, says in a brief style, " This is the book of the creation of the heaven and of the earth, when it took place, in the day on which God made the heaven and the earth, and every green herb before it appeared upon the earth, and all the grass of the field before it sprang up." Does he not here manifestly set before us incorporeal ideas perceptible only by the intellect, which have been appointed to be as seals of the perfected works, perceptible by the outward senses. For before the earth was green, he says that this same thing, verdure, existed in the nature of things, and before the grass sprang up in the field, there was grass though it was not visible. And we must understand in the case of every thing else which is decided on by the external senses, there were elder forms and motions previously existing, according to which the things which were created were fashioned and measured out. For although Moses did not describe everything collectively, but only a part of what existed, as he was desirous of brevity, beyond all men that ever wrote, still the few things which he has mentioned are examples of the nature of all, for nature perfects none of those which are perceptible to the outward senses without an incorporeal model.

XLV. Then, preserving the natural order of things, and having a regard to the connection between what comes afterwards and what has gone before, he says next, "And a fountain went up from the earth and watered the whole face of the earth." For other philosophers affirm that all water is one of the four elements of which the world was composed. But Moses, who was accustomed to contemplate and comprehend matters with a more acute and far-sighted vision, considers thus : the vast sea is an element, being a fourth part of the entire universe, which the men after him denominated the ocean, while they look upon the smaller seas which we sail over in the light of harbours. And he drew a distinction between the sweet and drinkable water and that of the sea, attributing the former to the earth, and considering it a portion of the earth, rather than of the ocean, on account of the reason which I have already mentioned, that is to say, that the earth may be held together by the sweet qualities of the water as by a chain ; the water acting in the manner of glue. For if the earth were left entirely dry, so that no moisture arose and penetrated through its holes rising to the surface in various directions, it would split. But now it is held together, and remains lasting, partly by the force of the wind which unites it, and partly because the moisture does not allow it to become dry, and so to be broken up into larger and smaller fragments.

This is one reason ; and we must also mention another,

which is aimed at the truth like an arrow at a mark. It is not
the nature of anything upon the earth to exist without a moist
essence. And this is indicated by the throwing of seed, which
is either moist, as the seed of animals, or else does not shoot up
without moisture, such as the seeds of plants ; from which it is
evident that it follows that the aforesaid moist essence must be
a portion of the earth which produces everything, just as the
flux of the catamenia is a part of women. For by men who are
learned in natural philosophy, this also is said to be the corporeal essence of children. Nor is what we are about to say
inconsistent with what has been said ; for nature has bestowed
upon every mother, as a most indispensable part of her conformation, breasts gushing forth like fountains, having in this
manner provided abundant food for the child that is to be
born. And the earth also, as it seems, is a mother, from
which consideration it occurred to the early ages to call her
Demetra, combining the names of mother (μήτηρ), and earth
(γῆ or δη). For it is not the earth which imitates the woman, as
Plato has said, but the woman who has imitated the earth which
the race of poets has been accustomed with truth to call the
mother of all things, and the fruit-bearer, and the giver of all
things, since she is at the same time the cause of the generation
and durability of all things, to the animals and plants. Rightly,
therefore, did nature bestow on the earth as the eldest and most
fertile of mothers, streams of rivers, and fountains like
breasts, in order that the plants might be watered, and that all
living things might have abundant supplies of drink.

XLVI. After this, Moses says that "God made man,
having taken clay from the earth, and he breathed into his
face the breath of life." And by this expression he shows
most clearly that there is a vast difference between man as
generated now, and the first man who was made according to
the image of God. For man as formed now is perceptible to
the external senses, partaking of qualities, consisting of body
and soul, man or woman, by nature mortal. But man, made
according to the image of God, was an idea, or a genus, or a
seal, perceptible only by the intellect, incorporeal, neither male
nor female, imperishable by nature. But he asserts that the
formation of the individual man, perceptible by the external
senses is a composition of earthy substance, and divine spirit.
For that the body was created by the Creator taking a lump of

clay, and fashioning the human form out of it ; but that the soul proceeds from no created thing at all, but from the Father and Ruler of all things.   For when he uses the expression, " he breathed into," &c., he means nothing else than the divine spirit proceeding from that happy and blessed nature, sent to take up its habitation here on earth, for the advantage of our race, in order that, even if man is mortal according to that portion of him which is visible, he may at all events be immortal according to that portion which is invisible ; and for this reason, one may properly say that man is on the boundaries of a better and an immortal nature, partaking of each as far as it is ne-cessary for him ; and that he was born at the same time, both mortal and the immortal.   Mortal as to his body, but immortal as to his intellect.

XLVII. But the original man, he who was created out of the clay, the primeval founder of all our race, appears to me to have been most excellent in both particulars, in both soul and body, and to have been very far superior to all the men of subsequent ages from his pre-eminent excellence in both parts. For he in truth was really good and perfect.   And one may form a conjecture of the perfection of his bodily beauty from three considerations, the first of which is this : when the earth was now but lately formed by its separation from that abundant quantity of water which was called the sea, it hap-pened that the materials out of which the things just created were formed were unmixed, uncorrupted, and pure ; and the things made from this material were naturally free from all imperfection.   The second consideration is that it is not likely that God made this figure in the present form of a man, work-ing with the most sublime care, after he had taken the clay from any chance portion of earth, but that he selected carefully the most excellent clay of all the earth, of the pure material choosing the finest and most carefully sifted portion, such as was especially fit for the formation of the work which he had in hand.   For it was an abode or sacred temple for a reason-able soul which was being made, the image of which he was about to carry in his heart, being the most God-like looking of images.   The third consideration is one which admits of no comparison with those which have been already mentioned, namely, this : the Creator was good both in other respects, and also in knowledge, so that every one of the parts of the

body had separately the numbers which were suited to it, and
was also accurately completed in the admirable adaptation to
the share in the universe of which it was to partake. And
after he had endowed it with fair proportions, he clothed it
with beauty of flesh, and embellished it with an exquisite complexion, wishing, as far as was possible, that man should
appear the most beautiful of beings.

XLVIII. And that he is superior to all these animals in
regard of his soul, is plain. For God does not seem to have
availed himself of any other animal existing in creation as his
model in the formation of man; but to have been guided, as I
have said before, by his own reason alone. On which account,
Moses affirms that this man was an image and imitation of
God, being breathed into in his face in which is the place of
the sensations, by which the Creator endowed the body with a
soul. Then, having placed the mind in the dominant part as
king, he gave him as a body of satellites, the different powers
calculated to perceive colours and sounds, and flavours and
odours, and other things of similar kinds, which man could
never have distinguished by his own resources without the sensations. And it follows of necessity that an imitation of a
perfectly beautiful model must itself be perfectly beautiful, for
the word of God surpasses even that beauty which exists in the
nature which is perceptible only by the external senses, not
being embellished by any adventitious beauty, but being itself,
if one must speak the truth, its most exquisite embellishment.

XLIX. The first man, therefore, appears to me to have
been such both in his body and in his soul, being very far superior to all those who live in the present day, and to all those who
have gone before us. For our generation has been from men:
but he was created by God. And in the same proportion as
the one Author of being is superior to the other, so too is the
being that is produced. For as that which is in its prime is
superior to that the beauty of which is gone by, whether it be
an animal, or a plant, or fruit, or anything else whatever of the
productions of nature; so also the first man who was ever
formed appears to have been the height of perfection of our
entire race, and subsequent generations appear never to have
reached an equal state of perfection, but to have at all times
been inferior both in their appearance and in their power, and
to have been constantly degenerating, which same thing I have

also seen to be the case in the instance of the sculptors' and painters' art. For the imitations always fall short of the original models. And those works which are painted or fashioned from models must be much more inferior, as being still further removed from the original. And the stone which is called the magnet is subject to a similar deterioration. For any iron ring which touches it is held by it as firmly as possible, but another which only touches that ring is held less firmly. And the third ring hangs from the second, and the fourth from the third, and the fifth from the fourth, and so on one from another in a long chain, being all held together by one attractive power, but still they are not all supported in the same degree. For those which are suspended at a distance from the original attraction, are held more loosely, because the attractive power is weakened, and is no longer able to bind them in an equal degree.

And the race of mankind appears to be subject to an influence of the same kind, since in men the faculties and distinctive qualities of both body and soul are less vivid and strongly marked in each succeeding generation. And we shall be only saying what is the plain truth, if we call the original founder of our race not only the first man, but also the first citizen of the world. For the world was his house and his city, while he had as yet no structure made by hands and wrought out of the materials of wood and stone. And in this world he lived as in his own country, in all safety, removed from any fear, inasmuch as he had been thought worthy of the dominion over all earthly things; and had everything that was mortal crouching before him, and taught to obey him as their master, or else constrained to do so by superior force, and living himself surrounded by all the joys which peace can bestow without a struggle and without reproach.

L. But since every city in which laws are properly established, has a regular constitution, it became necessary for this citizen of the world to adopt the same constitution as that which prevailed in the universal world. And this constitution is the right reason of nature, which in more appropriate language is denominated law, being a divine arrangement in accordance with which everything suitable and appropriate is assigned to every individual. But of this city and constitution there must have been some citizens before man, who might be justly called citizens of a mighty city, having received the

greatest imaginable circumference to dwell in ; and having
been enrolled in the largest and most perfect commonwealth.
And who could these have been but rational divine natures,
some of them incorporeal and perceptible only by intellect, and
others not destitute of bodily substance, such in fact as the
stars ? And he who associated with and lived among them was
naturally living in a state of unmixed happiness. And being
akin and nearly related to the ruler of all, inasmuch as a great
deal of the divine spirit had flowed into him, he was eager both
to say and to do everything which might please his father and
his king, following him step by step in the paths which the
virtues prepare and make plain, as those in which those souls
alone are permitted to proceed who consider the attaining a
likeness to God who made them as the proper end of their
existence.

LI. We have now then set forth the beauty of the first
created man in both respects, in body and soul, if in a way
much inferior to the reality, still to the extent of our power,
and the best of our ability. And it cannot be but that his
descendants, who all partake of his original character, must
preserve some traces of their relationship to their father,
though they may be but faint. And what is this relationship ?
Every man in regard of his intellect is connected with divine
reason, being an impression of, or a fragment or a ray of
that blessed nature ; but in regard of the structure of his body
he is connected with the universal world. For he is composed
of the same materials as the world, that is of earth, and water,
and air and fire, each of the elements having contributed its
appropriate part towards the completion of most sufficient materials, which the Creator was to take in order to fashion this
visible image. And, moreover, man dwells among all the
things that have been just enumerated, as most appropriate
places having the closest connection with himself, changing
his abode, and going at different times to different places. So
that one may say with the most perfect propriety that man is
every kind of animal, terrestrial, aquatic, flying, and celestial.
For inasmuch as he dwells and walks upon the earth he is a
terrestrial animal ; but inasmuch as he often dives and swims,
and sails, he is an aquatic creature. And merchants and cap-
tains of ships and purple dyers, and all those who let down
their nets for oysters and fish, are a very clear proof of what is

here said. Again, inasmuch as his body is raised at times above the earth and uses high paths, he may with justice be pronounced a creature who traverses the air; and, moreover, he is a celestial animal, by reason of that most important of the senses, sight; being by it brought near the sun and moon, and each of the stars, whether planets or fixed stars.

LII. And with great beauty Moses has attributed the giving of names to the different animals to the first created man, for it is a work of wisdom and indicative of royal authority, and man was full of intuitive wisdom and self-taught, having been created by the grace of God, and, moreover, was a king. And it is proper for a ruler to give names to each of his subjects. And, as was very natural, the power of domination was excessive in that first-created man, whom God formed with great care and thought worthy of the second rank in the creation, making him his own viceroy and the ruler of all other creatures. Since even those who have been born so many generations afterwards, when the race is becoming weakened by reason of the long intervals of time that have elapsed since the beginning of the world, do still exert the same power over the irrational beasts, preserving as it were a spark of the dominion and power which has been handed down to them by succession from their first ancestor.

Accordingly, Moses says, that " God brought all the animals to man, wishing to see what names he would give to each." Not because he was in doubt, for nothing is unknown to God, but because he knew that he had formed in mortal man a rational nature capable of moving of its own accord, in order that he might be free from all participation in vice. But he was now trying him as a master might try his pupil, stirring up the disposition which he had implanted in him; and moreover exciting him to a contemplation of his own works, that he might extemporise them names which should not be inappropriate nor unbecoming, but which should well and clearly display the peculiar qualities of the different subjects. For as the rational nature was as yet uncorrupted in the soul, and as no weakness, or disease, or affliction had as yet come upon it, man having most pure and perfect perceptions of bodies and of things, devised names for them with great felicity and correctness of judgment, forming very admirable opinions as to the qualities which they displayed, so that their natures were at once perceived and correctly described by him. And he was so excellent in all good things that he speedily arrived at the very perfection of human happiness.

LIII. But since nothing in creation lasts for ever, but all mortal things are liable to inevitable changes and alterations, it was unavoidable that the first man should also undergo some disaster. And the beginning of his life being liable to reproach, was his wife. For, as long as he was single, he resembled, as to his creation, both the world and God; and he represented in his soul the characteristics of the nature of each, I do not mean all of them, but such as a mortal constitution was capable of admitting. But when woman also was created, man perceiving a closely connected figure and a kindred formation to his own, rejoiced at the sight, and approached her and embraced her. And she, in like manner, beholding a creature greatly resembling herself, rejoiced also, and addressed him in reply with due modesty. And love being engendered, and, as it were, uniting two separate portions of one animal into one body, adapted them to each other, implanting in each of them a desire of connection with the other with a view to the generation of a being similar to themselves. And this desire caused likewise pleasure to their bodies, which is the beginning of iniquities and transgressions, and it is owing to this that men have exchanged their previously immortal and happy existence for one which is mortal and full of misfortune.

LIV. But while man was still living a solitary life, and before woman was created, the history relates that a paradise was planted by God in no respect resembling the parks which are seen among men now. For parks of our day are only lifeless woods, full of all kinds of trees, some evergreen with a view to the undisturbed delectation of the sight; others budding and germinating in the spring season, and producing fruit, some eatable by men, and sufficient, not only for the necessary support of nature as food, but also for the superfluous enjoyment of luxurious life; and some not eatable by men, but of necessity bestowed upon the beasts. But in the paradise, made by God, all the plants were endowed in the souls and reason, producing for their fruit the different virtues, and, moreover, imperishable wisdom and prudence, by which honourable and dishonourable things are distinguished from one another, and also a life free from disease, and exempt from corruption, and all other qualities corresponding to these already mentioned. And these statements appear to me to be dictated by a philosophy which is symbolical rather than strictly accurate. For no trees of life or of knowledge have ever at any previous time appeared upon the earth, nor is it likely that any will appear hereafter. But I rather conceive that Moses was speaking in an allegorical spirit, intending by his paradise to intimate the dominant character of the soul, which is full of innumerable opinions as this figurative paradise was of trees. And by the tree of life he was shadowing out the greatest of the virtues—namely, piety towards the gods, by means of which the soul is made immortal; and by the tree which had the knowledge of good and evil, he was intimating that wisdom and moderation, by means of which things, contrary in their nature to one another, are distinguished.

LV. Therefore, having laid down these to be boundaries as it were in the soul, God then, like a judge, began to consider to which side men would be most inclined by nature. And when he saw that the disposition of man had a tendency to wickedness, and was but little inclined to holiness or piety, by which qualities an immortal life is secured, he drove them forth as was very natural, and banished him from paradise; giving no hope of any subsequent restoration to his soul which had sinned in such a desperate and irremediable manner. Since even the opportunity of deceit was blameable in no slight degree, which I must not pass over in this place.

It is said that the old poisonous and earthborn reptile, the serpent, uttered the voice of a man. And he on one occasion coming to the wife of the first created man, reproached her with her slowness and her excessive prudence, because she delayed and hesitated to gather the fruit which was completely beautiful to look at, and exceedingly sweet to enjoy, and was, moreover, most useful as being a means by which men might be able to distinguish between good and evil. And she, without any inquiry, prompted by an unstable and rash mind, acquiesced in his advice, and ate of the fruit, and gave a portion of it to her husband. And this conduct suddenly changed both of them from innocence and simplicity of character to all kinds of wickedness; at which the Father of all was indignant. For their actions deserved his anger, inasmuch as they, passing by the tree of eternal life, the tree which might have endowed them with perfection of virtue, and by means of which they might have enjoyed a long and happy life, preferred a brief and mortal (I will not call it life, but) time full of unhappiness ; and, accordingly, he appointed them such punishment as was befitting.

LVI. And these things are not mere fabulous inventions, in which the race of poets and sophists delights, but are rather types shadowing forth some allegorical truth, according to some mystical explanation. And any one who follows a reasonable train of conjecture, will say with great propriety, that the aforesaid serpent is the symbol of pleasure, because in the first place he is destitute of feet, and crawls on his belly with his face downwards. In the second place, because he uses lumps of clay for food. Thirdly, because he bears poison in his teeth, by which it is his nature to kill those who are bitten by him. And the man devoted to pleasure is free from none of the aforementioned evils ; for it is with difficulty that he can raise his head, being weighed down and dragged down, since intemperance trips him up and keeps him down. And he feeds, not on heavenly food, which wisdom offers to contemplative men by means of discourses and opinions ; but on that which is put forth by the earth in the varying seasons of the year, from which arise drunkenness and voracity, and licentiousness, breaking through and inflaming the appetites of the belly, and enslaving them in subjection to gluttony, by which they strengthen the impetuous passions, the seat of which is beneath the belly ; and make them break forth. And they lick up the result of the labours of cooks and tavern-keepers ; and at times some of them in ecstasy with the flavour of the delicious food, moves about his head and reaches forward, being desirous to participate in the sight. And when he sees an expensively furnished table, he throws himself bodily upon the delicacies which are abundantly prepared, and devotes himself to them, wishing to be filled with them all together, and so to depart, having no other end in view than that he should allow nothing of such a sumptuous preparation to be wasted. Owing to which conduct, he too, carries about poison in his teeth, no less than the serpent does ; for his teeth are the ministers and servants of his insatiability, cutting up and smoothing everything which has a reference to eating, and committing them, in the first place to the tongue, which decides upon, and distinguishes between the various flavours, and, subsequently, to the larynx. But immoderate indulgence in eating is naturally a poisonous and deadly habit, inasmuch as what is so devoured is not capable of digestion, in consequence of the quantity of additional food which is heaped in on the top of it, and arrives before what was previously eaten is converted into juice.

And the serpent is said to have uttered a human voice, because pleasure employs innumerable champions and defenders who take care to advocate its interests, and who dare to assert that the power over everything, both small and great, does of right belong to it without any exception whatever.

LVII. Now, the first approaches of the male to the female have a pleasure in them which brings on other pleasures also, and it is through this pleasure that the formation and generation of children is carried on. And what is generated by it appears to be attached to nothing rather than to it, since they rejoice in pleasure, and are impatient at pain, which is its contrary. On which account even the infant when first brought forth cries, being as it seems in pain at the cold. For coming forth on a sudden into the air from a very warm, and indeed, hot region—namely, the womb, in which it has been abiding a considerable time, the air being a cold place and one to which it is wholly unaccustomed, it is alarmed, and pours forth tears as the most evident proof of its grief and of its impatience at pain. For every animal, it is said, hastens to pleasure as to the cud which is most indispensable and necessary to its very existence ; and, above all other animals, this is the case with man. For other animals pursue pleasure only in taste and in the acts of generation ; but man aims at it by means of his other senses also, devoting himself to whatever sights or sounds can impart pleasure to his eyes or ears. And many other things are said in the way of praise of this inclination, especially that it is one most peculiar and kindred to all animals.

LVIII. But what has been already said is sufficient to show what the reasons were on account of which the serpent appears to have uttered a human voice. And it is on this account that Moses appears to me in the particular laws also which he issued in the respect to animals, deciding what were proper to be eaten, and what were not, to have given especial praise to the animal called the serpent fighter. This is a reptile with jointed legs above its feet, by which it is able to leap and to raise itself on high, in the same manner as the tribe of locusts. For the serpent fighter appears to me to be no other than temperance expressed under a symbolical figure, waging an interminable and unrelenting warfare against intemperance and pleasure. For temperance especially embraces economy and frugality, and pares down the necessities to a small number, preferring a life of austerity and dignity. But intemperance is devoted to extravagance and superfluity, which are the causes of luxury and effeminacy to both soul and body, and to which it is owing that in the opinion of wise men life is but a faulty thing, and more miserable than death.

LIX. But its juggleries and deceits pleasure does not venture to bring directly to the man, but first offers them to the woman, and by her means to the man; acting in a very natural and sagacious manner. For in human beings the mind occupies the rank of the man, and the sensations that of the woman. And pleasure joins itself to and associates itself with the sensations first of all, and then by their means cajoles also the mind, which is the dominant part. For, after each of the senses have been subjected to the charms of pleasure, and has learnt to delight in what is offered to it, the sight being fascinated by varieties of colours and shapes, the hearing by harmonious sounds, the taste by the sweetness of flowers, and the smell by the delicious fragrance of the odours which are brought before it, these all having received these offerings, like handmaids, bring them to the mind as their master, leading with them persuasion as an advocate, to warn it against rejecting any of them whatever. And the mind being immediately caught by the bait, becomes a subject instead of a ruler, and a slave instead of a master, and an exile instead of a citizen, and a mortal instead of an immortal. For we must altogether not be ignorant that pleasure, being like a courtesan or mistress, is eager to meet with a lover, and seeks for panders in order by their means to catch a lover. And the sensations are her panders, and conciliate love to her, and she employing them as baits, easily brings the mind into subjection to her. And the sensations conveying within the mind the things which have been seen externally, explain and display the forms of each of them, setting their seal upon a similar affection. For the mind is like wax, and receives the impressions of appearances through the sensations, by means of which it makes itself master of the body, which of itself it would not be able to do, as I have already said.

LX. And those who have previously become the slaves of pleasure immediately receive the wages of this miserable and incurable passion. For the woman having received vehement pains, partly in her travail, and partly such as are a rapid succession of agonies during the other portions of her life, and especially with reference to the bringing forth and bringing up of her children, to their diseases and their health, to their good or evil fortune, to an extent that utterly deprives her of her freedom and subjects her to the dominion of the man who is her companion, finds it unavoidable to obey all his commands. And the man in his turn endures toils and labours, and continual sweats, in order to the providing of himself with necessaries, and he also bears the deprivation of all those spontaneous good things which the earth was originally taught to produce without requiring the skill of the farmer, and he is subjected to a state in which he lives in incessant labour, for the purpose of seeking for food and means of subsistence, in order to avoid perishing by hunger.

For I think that as the sun and the moon do continually give light, ever since they were originally commanded to do so at the time of the original creation of the universe, and as they constantly obey the divine injunction, for the sake of no other reason but because evil and disobedience are banished to a distance far from the boundaries of heaven : so in the same way would the fertile and productive regions of the earth yield an immense abundance in the various seasons of the year, without any skill or co-operation on the part of the husbandman. But at present the ever-flowing fountains of the graces of God have been checked, from the time when wickedness began to increase faster than the virtues, in order that they might not be supplying men who were unworthy to be benefited by them. Therefore, the race of mankind, if it had met with strict and befitting justice, must have been utterly destroyed, because of its ingratitude to God its benefactor and its Saviour. But God, being merciful by nature, took pity upon them, and moderated their punishment. And he permitted the race to continue to exist, but he no longer gave them food as he had done before from ready prepared stores, lest if they were under the dominion of his evils, satiety and idleness, they should become unruly and insolent.

LXI. Such is the life of those who originally were men of innocence and simplicity, and also of those who have come to prefer vice to virtue, from whom one ought to keep aloof. And in his beforementioned account of the creation of the world, Moses teaches us also many other things, and especially five most beautiful lessons which are superior to all others. In the first place, for the sake of convicting the atheists, he teaches us that the Deity has a real being and existence. Now, of the atheists, some have only doubted of the existence of God, stating it to be an uncertain thing ; but others, who are more audacious, have taken courage, and asserted positively that there is no such thing ; but this is affirmed only by men who have darkened the truth with fabulous inventions.

In the second place he teaches us that God is one ; having reference here to the assertors of the polytheistic doctrine ; men who do not blush to transfer that worst of evil constitutions, ochlocracy, from earth to heaven.

Thirdly, he teaches, as has been already related, that the world was created ; by this lesson refuting those who think that it is uncreated and eternal, and who thus attribute no glory to God.

In the fourth place we learn that the world also which was thus created is one, since also the Creator is one, and he, making his creation to resemble himself in its singleness, employed all existing essence in the creation of the universe. For it would not have been complete if it had not been made and composed of all parts which were likewise whole and complete. For there are some persons who believe that there are many worlds, and some who even fancy that they are boundless in extent, being themselves inexperienced and ignorant of the truth of those things of which it is desirable to have a correct knowledge.

The fifth lesson that Moses teaches us is, that God exerts his providence for the benefit of the world. For it follows of necessity that the Creator must always care for that which he has created, just as parents do also care for their children. And he who has learnt this not more by hearing it than by his own understanding, and has impressed on his own soul these marvellous facts which are the subject of so much contention—namely, that God has a being and existence, and that he who so exists is really one, and that he has created the world, and that he has created it one as has been stated, having made it like to himself in singleness ; and that he exercises a continual care for that which he has created will live a happy and blessed life, stamped with the doctrines of piety and holiness.

THE FIRST BOOK

OF THE TREATISE ON

THE ALLEGORIES OF THE SACRED LAWS,

AFTER THE WORK OF THE SIX DAYS OF CREATION.

I. " And the heaven and the earth and all their world was completed."* Having previously related the creation of the mind and of sense, Moses now proceeds to describe the perfection which was brought about by them both. And he says that neither the indivisible mind nor the particular sensations received perfection, but only ideas, one the idea of the mind, the other of sensation. And, speaking symbolically, he calls the mind heaven, since the natures which can only be comprehended by the intellect are in heaven. And sensation he calls earth, because it is sensation which has obtained a corporeal and somewhat earthy constitution. The ornaments of the mind are all the incorporeal things, which are perceptible only by the intellect. Those of sensation are the corporeal things, and everything in short which is perceptible by the external senses.

II. " And on the sixth day God finished his work which he had made." It would be a sign of great simplicity to think that the world was created in six days, or indeed at all in time; because all time is only the space of days and nights, and these things the motion of the sun as he passes over the earth and under the earth does necessarily make. But the sun is a portion of heaven, so that one must confess that time

* Genesis ii. 1.

is a thing posterior to the world.   Therefore it would be correctly said that the world was not created in time, but that time had its existence in consequence of the world.   For it is the motion of the heaven that has displayed the nature of time.

When, therefore, Moses says, " God completed his works on the sixth day," we must understand that he is speaking not of a number of days, but that he takes six as a perfect number. Since it is the first number which is equal in its parts, in the half, and the third and sixth parts, and since it is produced by the multiplication of two unequal factors, two and three.   And the numbers two and three exceed the incorporeality which exists in the unit; because the number two is an image of matter being divided into two parts and dissected like matter. And the number three is an image of a solid body, because a solid can be divided according to a threefold division.   Not but what it is also akin to the motions of organic animals.   For an organic body is naturally capable of motion in six directions, forward, backwards, upwards, downwards, to the right, and to the left.   And at all events he desires to show that the races of mortal, and also of all the immortal beings, exist according to their appropriate numbers ; measuring mortal beings, as I have said, by the number six, and the blessed and immortal beings by the number seven.   First, therefore, having desisted from the creation of mortal creatures on the seventh day, he began the formation of other and more divine beings.

III. For God never ceases from making something or other ; but, as it is the property of fire to burn, and of snow to chill, so also it is the property of God to be creating.   And much more so, in proportion as he himself is to all other beings the author of their working.   Therefore the expression, " he caused to rest," is very appropriately employed here, not " he rested." For he makes things to rest which appear to be producing others, but which in reality do not effect anything ; but he himself never ceases from creating.   On which account Moses says, " He caused to rest the things which he had begun." For all the things that are made by our arts when completed stand still and remain ; but all those which are accomplished by the knowledge of God are moved at subsequent times.   For their ends are the beginnings of other things ; as, for instance, the end of day is the beginning of night.   And in the same

way we must look upon months and years when they come to
an end as the beginning of those which are just about to follow
them. And so the generation of other things which are destroyed, and the destruction of others which are generated is
completed, so that that is true which is said that—

> And nought that is created wholly dies;
> But one thing parted and combined with others
> Produces a fresh form.

IV. But nature delights in the number seven. For there
are seven planets, going in continual opposition to the daily
course of the heaven which always proceeds in the same direction. And likewise the constellation of the Bear is made up
of seven stars, which constellation is the cause of communication and unity among men, and not merely of traffic. Again,
the periodical changes of the moon, take place according to the
number seven, that star having the greatest sympathy with the
things on earth. And the changes which the moon works in
the air, it perfects chiefly in accordance with its own configura-
tions on each seventh day. At all events, all mortal things,
as I have said before, drawing their more divine nature from
the heaven, are moved in a manner which tends to their preservation in accordance with this number seven. For who is
there who does not know that those infants who are born at
the end of the seventh month are likely to live, but those who
have taken a longer time, so as to have abided eight months in
the womb, are for the most part abortive births? And they
say that man is a reasoning being in his first seven years, by
which time he is a competent interpreter of ordinary nouns and
verbs, making himself master of the faculty of speaking. And
in his second period of seven years, he arrives at the perfection
of his nature; and this perfection is the power of generating
a being like himself; for at about the age of fourteen we are
able to beget a creature resembling ourselves. Again, the
third period of seven years is the termination of his growth;
for up to the age of one and twenty years man keeps on increasing in size, and this time is called by many maturity.

Again, the irrational portion of the soul is divisible into
seven portions; the five senses, and the organ of speech, and
the power of generation. Again, the motions of the body are
seven; the six organic motions, and the rotatory motion.

Also the entrails are seven—the stomach, the heart, the spleen, the liver, the lungs, and the two kidneys.

In like manner the limbs of the body amount to an equal number—the head, the neck, the chest, the two hands, the belly, the two feet. Also the most important part of the animal, the face, is divisible according to a sevenfold division—the two eyes, and the two ears, and as many nostrils, and in the seventh place, the mouth.

Again, the secretions are seven — tears, mucus from the nose, saliva, the generative fluid, the two excremental discharges, and the sweat that proceeds from every part of the body.

Moreover, in diseases the seventh day is the most critical period—and in women the catamenial purifications extend to the seventh day.

V. And the power of this number has extended also to the most useful of the arts—namely, to grammar. At all events, in grammar, the most excellent of the elements, and those which have the most powers, are the seven vowels. And likewise in music, the lyre with seven strings is nearly the best of all instruments; because the euharmonic principle which is the most dignified of all the principles of melody, is especially perceived in connection with it.

Again, it happens that the tones of the voice are seven—the acute, the grave, the contracted, the aspirate, the lene, the long and the short sound. The number seven is also the first number which is compounded of the perfect number, that is to say of six, and of the unit. And in some sense the numbers which are below ten are either generated by, or do themselves generate those numbers which are below ten, and the number ten itself. But the number seven neither generates any of the numbers below ten, nor is it generated by any of them. On which account the Pythagoreans compare this number to the Goddess always a virgin who was born without a mother,* because it was not generated by any other, and will not generate any other.

VI. " Accordingly, on the seventh day, God caused to rest from all his works which he had made."† Now, the meaning of this sentence is something of this kind. God ceases from forming the races of mortal creatures when he begins to create

* *i. e.* Minerva   † Genesis ii. 2,.

the divine races, which are akin to the nature of the number seven. And the reference which is here contained to their moral character is of the following nature. When that reason which is holy in accordance with the number seven has entered into the soul the number six is then arrested, and all the mortal things which this number appears to make.

VII. " And God blessed the seventh day, and hallowed it." God blesses the manners which are formed in accordance with the seventh and divine light, as being truly light, and immediately declares them holy. For that which is blessed, and that which is holy, are closely connected with one another. On this account he says, concerning him who has vowed a great vow, that " If a sudden change comes over him, and pollutes his mind, he shall no longer be holy."*

But the previous days were not taken into the calculation, as was natural. For those manners which are not holy are not counted, so that which is blessed is alone holy. Correctly therefore, did Moses say that " God blessed the seventh day and hallowed it," because on it he "caused to rest from all his works which he had begun to make." And this is the reason why he who lives and conducts himself in accordance with the seventh and perfect light is blessed and holy, since it is in accordance with his nature, that the creation of mortal beings was terminated. For the case is thus : when the light of virtue, which is brilliant and really divine, rises up, then the generation of the contrary nature is checked. And we have shown that God never desists from creating something, but that when he appears to do so he is only beginning the creation of something else ; as being not only, the Creator, but also the Father of everything which exists.

VIII. "This is the book of the generation of heaven and earth, when they were created."† This is perfect reason, which is put in motion in accordance with the number seven, being the beginning of the creation of that mind which was arranged according to the ideas, and also of the sensation arranged according to the ideas, and perceptible only by the intellect, if one can speak in such a manner. And Moses calls the word of God a book, in which it is come to pass that the formations of other things are written down and engraved. But, lest you should imagine that the Deity does anything ac-

* Numbers vi. 9.   † Genesis ii. 4.

cording to definite periods of time, while you should rather think that everything done by him is inscrutable in its nature, uncertain, unknown to, and incomprehensible by the race of mortal men.   Moses adds the words, " when they were created," not defining the time when by any exact limitation, for what has been made by the Author of all things has no limitation.   And in this way the idea is excluded, that the universe was created in six days.

IX.   " On which day God created the heaven and the earth, and every green herb of the field, before it appeared upon the earth, and all the grass of the field before it sprang up.   For God did not rain upon the earth, and man did not exist to cultivate the earth."   This day Moses has previously called a book, since at least he describes the generation of both heaven and earth in each place.   For by his most conspicuous and brillant word, by one command, God makes both things : the idea of mind, which, speaking symbolically, he calls heaven, and the idea of sensation, which by a sign he named earth.   And he likens the idea of mind, and the idea of sensation to two fields ; for the mind brings forth fruit, which consists in having intellectual perception ; and sensation brings forth other fruits which consist in perceiving by the agency of the external senses.   And what he says has the following meaning ;—as there was a previously existing idea of the particular mind, and also of the indivisible minds to serve as an archetype and model for either ; and also a pre-existent idea of particular sensation, being, so to say, a sort of seal which gave impressions of forms, so before particular things perceptible only by the intellect had any existence, there was a pre-existent abstract idea of what was perceptible only by intellect, by participation in which the other things also received their names ; and before particular objects perceptible by the external senses, existed, there was also a generic something perceptible by the external senses, in accordance with a participation in which, the other things perceptible by the external senses were created.

By " the green herb of the field," Moses means that portion of the mind which is perceptible only by intellect.   For as in the field green things spring up and flourish, so also that which is perceptible only by the intellect is the fruit of the mind.   Therefore, before the particular something perceptible only by intellect existed, God created the general something perceptible only by intellect, which also he correctly denominated the universe. For since the particular something perceptible only by intellect is incomplete, that is not the universe ; but that which is generic is the universe, as being complete.

X. " And all the grass of the field," he proceeds, " before it sprang up." That is to say, before the particular things perceptible by the external senses sprang up, there existed the generic something perceptible by the external senses through the fore-knowledge of the Creator, which he again called " the universe." And very naturally he likened the things perceptible by the external senses to grass. For as grass is the food of irrational animals, so also that which is perceptible by the external senses is assigned to the irrational portion of the soul. For why, when he has previously mentioned " the green herb of the field," does he add also " and all the grass," as if grass were not green at all ? But the truth is, that by the green herb of the field, he means that which is perceptible by the intellect only, the budding forth of the mind. But grass means that which is perceptible by the external senses, that being likewise the produce of the irrational part of the soul.

" For God did not rain upon the earth, and man did not exist to cultivate the earth," speaking in the strictest accordance with natural philosophy. For if God did not shed the perceptions of things subject to them, like rain upon the senses, in that case the mind too would not labour nor employ itself about sensation. For he himself would be unable to effect anything by himself, unless he were to pour forth, like rain or dew, colours upon the sight, and sounds upon the hearing, and flavour on the tastes, and on all the other senses, the things proper to produce the requisite effects. But when God begins to rain sensation on the things perceptible by the external senses, then also the mind is perceived to act like the cultivator of fertile soil. But the idea of sensation, which he, speaking figuratively, has called the earth, is in no need of nourishment. But the nourishment of the senses, are the particular objects perceptible by the external senses ; and these objects are bodies. But an idea is a thing different from bodies.

Before, therefore, there existed any individual compound substances, God did not rain upon that idea of sensation to which he gave the name of the earth.   And that means that he did not furnish it with any nourishment ; for, indeed, it had altogether no need of any object perceptible by the external senses

But when Moses says, " And man did not exist to cultivate the earth," that means that the idea of intellect did not labour upon the idea of the sensations.   For my intellect and yours work up the sensations by means of things perceptible by the the external senses : but the idea of mind as must be the case while there is no individual body connected with it does not work upon the idea of sensation.   For if it did so work, it would of course work by means of objects, perceptible by the external senses.   But there is no such object in ideas.

XI. " But a fountain went up upon the earth, and watered all the face of the earth."   He here calls the mind the fountain of the earth, and the sensations he calls the face of the earth, because there is the most suitable place in the whole body for them, with reference to their appropriate energies, a place that nature which foreknows everything, has assigned to them.   And the mind waters the sensations like a fountain, sending appropriate streams over each.

See now how all the powers of a living animal depend upon one another like a chain.   For as the mind, and sensations, and the object perceptible by the external sense are three different things, the middle term is sensation ; and the mind, and the object perceptible by the external sense, are the two extremes.   But the mind is unable to work ; that is to say, to energize according to sensation, unless God rains upon and irrigates the object perceptible by the external senses, nor is there any advantage from the object perceptible to the external sense when watered, unless the mind, like a fountain, extending itself as far as the sensation, puts it in motion when it is quiet, and leads it on to a comprehension of the subject. So that the mind, and the object perceptible by the external senses, are always endeavouring to reciprocate with one another, the one the being subject to the sensations as a kind of material would be, and the mind stirring up the sensations towards the external object, as a workman would do, in order to create an appetite.   For a living animal is superior to that which is not a living animal in two points, imagination and appetite.   Accordingly, imagination consists in the approach of the external object striking the mind by means of the sensations.   And appetite is the brother of imagination, according

to the intensive power of the mind, which the mind keeps on
the stretch, by means of the sensation, and so touches the subject matter, and comes over to it, being eager to arrive at and
comprehend it.

XII. " And God created man, taking a lump of clay from
the earth, and breathed into his face the breath of life : and
man became a living soul." The races of men are twofold ;
for one is the heavenly man, and the other the earthly man.
Now the heavenly man, as being born in the image of God,
has no participation in any corruptible or earth-like essence.
But the earthly man is made of loose material, which he calls
a lump of clay. On which account he says, not that the
heavenly man was made, but that he was fashioned according
to the image of God ; but the earthly man he calls a thing
made, and not begotten by the maker. And we must consider
that the man who was formed of earth, means the mind which
is to be infused into the body, but which has not yet been so
infused. And this mind would be really earthly and corruptible, if it were not that God had breathed into it the spirit of
genuine life ; for then it " exists," and is no longer made
into a soul ; and its soul is not inactive, and incapable of
proper formation, but a really intellectual and living one.
" For man," says Moses, " became a living soul."

XIII. But some one may ask, why God thought an earth-
born mind, which was wholly devoted to the body, worthy of
divine inspiration, and yet did not treat the one made after
his own idea and image in the same manner. In the second
place he may ask, what is the meaning of the expression
" breathed into." And thirdly, why he breathed into his face :
fourthly also, why, since he knew the name of the Spirit when
he says, " And the Spirit of God moved upon the face of the
waters,"* he now speaks of breath, and not of the Spirit.
Now in reply to the first question we must say this one thing ;
God being very munificent gives his good things to all men,
even to those who are not perfect ; inviting them to a participation and rivalry in virtue, and at the same time displaying
his abundant riches, and showing that it is sufficient for those
also who will not be greatly benefited by it ; and he also
shows this in the most evident manner possible in other cases;
for when he rains on the sea, and when he raises up fountains

* Genesis i. 2.

in desert places, and waters shallow and rough and unproductive land, making the rivers to overflow with floods, what else is he doing but displaying the great abundance of his riches and of his goodness? This is the cause why he has created no soul in such a condition as to be wholly barren of good, even if the employment of that good be beyond the reach of some people. We must also give a second reason, which is this: Moses wished to represent all the actions of the Deity as just—therefore a man who had not had a real life breathed into him, but who was ignorant of virtue, when he was chastised for the sins which he had committed would say that he was punished unjustly, in that it was only through ignorance of what was good that he had erred respecting it; and that he was to blame who had not breathed any proper wisdom into him; and perhaps he will even say, that he has absolutely committed no offence whatever; since some people affirm that actions done involuntarily and in ignorance have not the nature of offences.

Now the expression "breathed into" is equivalent to "inspired," or "gave life to" things inanimate: for let us take care that we are never filled with such absurdity as to think that God employs the organs of the mouth or nostrils for the purpose of breathing into anything; for God is not only devoid of peculiar qualities, but he is likewise not of the form of man, and the use of these words shows some more secret mystery of nature; for there must be three things, that which breathes in, that which receives what is breathed in, and that which is breathed in. Now that which breathes in is God, that which receives what is breathed in is the mind, and that which is breathed in is the spirit. What then is collected from these three things? A union of the three takes place, through God extending the power, which proceeds from himself through the spirit, which is the middle term, as far as the subject. Why does he do this, except that we may thus derive a proper notion of him? Since how could the soul have perceived God if he had not inspired it, and touched it according to his power? For human intellect would not have dared to mount up to such a height as to lay claim to the nature of God, if God himself had not drawn it up to himself, as far as it was possible for the mind of man to be drawn up, and if he had not formed it according to those powers which can be comprehended.

And God breathed into man's face both physically and morally. Physically, when he placed the senses in the face: and this portion of the body above all others is vivified and inspired; and morally, in this manner, as the face is the dominant portion of the body, so also is the mind the dominant portion of the soul. It is into this alone that God breathes; but the other parts, the sensations, the power of speech, and the power of generation, he does not think worthy of his breath, for they are inferior in power. By what then were these subordinate parts inspired? beyond all question by the mind; for of the qualities which the mind has received from God, it gives a share to the irrational portion of the soul, so that the mind is vivified by God, and the irrational part of the soul by the mind; for the mind is as it were a god to the irrational part of the soul, for which reason Moses did not hesitate to call it "the god of Pharaoh."*

For of all created things some are created by God, and through him: some not indeed by God, but yet through him: and the rest have their existence both by him and through him.

At all events Moses as he proceeds says, that God planted a paradise, and among the best things as made both by God and through God, is the mind. But the irrational part of the soul was made indeed by God but not through God, but through the reasoning power which bears rule and sovereignty in the soul; and Moses has used the word "breath," not "spirit," as there is a difference between the two words; for spirit is conceived of according to strength, and intensity, and power; but breath is a gentle and moderate kind of breeze and exhalation; therefore the mind, which was created in accordance with the image and idea of God, may be justly said to partake in his spirit, for its reasoning has strength: but that which is derived from matter is only a partaker in a thin and very light air, being as it were a sort of exhalation, such as arises from spices; for they, although they be preserved intact, and are not exposed to fire or fumigation, do nevertheless emit a certain fragrance.

* Exodus vii. 1.

XIV. "And God planted a paradise in Eden, in the east: and there he placed the man whom he had formed:" * for he called that divine and heavenly wisdom by many names; and he made it manifest that it had many appellations; for he called it the beginning, and the image, and the sight of God. And now he exhibits the wisdom which is conversant about the things of the earth (as being an imitation of this archetypal wisdom), in the plantation of this Paradise. For let not such impiety ever occupy our thoughts as for us to suppose that God cultivates the land and plants paradises, since if we were to do so, we should be presently raising the question of why he does so : for it could not be that he might provide himself with pleasant places of recreation and pastime, or with amusement. Let not such fabulous nonsense ever enter our minds; for even the whole world would not be a worthy place or habitation for God, since he is a place to himself, and he himself is full of himself, and he himself is sufficient for himself, filling up and surrounding everything else which is deficient in any respect, or deserted, or empty; but he himself is surrounded by nothing else, as being himself one and the universe.

God therefore sows and implants terrestrial virtue in the human race, being an imitation and representation of the heavenly virtue. For, pitying our race, and seeing that it is exposed to abundant and innumerable evils, he firmly planted terrestrial virtue as an assistant against and warder-off of the diseases of the soul; being, as I have said before, an imitation of the heavenly and archetypal wisdom which he calls by various names.

Now virtue is called a paradise metaphorically, and the appropriate place for the paradise is Eden; and this means luxury : and the most appropriate field for virtue is peace, and ease, and joy; in which real luxury especially consists. Moreover, the plantation of this paradise is represented in the east; for right reason never sets, and is never extinguished, but it is its nature to be always rising. And as I imagine, the rising sun fills the darkness of the air with light, so also does virtue when it has arisen in the soul, irradiate its mist and dissipate the dense darkness. " And there," says Moses, " he placed the man whom he had formed :" for God being good, and having formed our race for virtue, as his work which

* Genesis ii. 8.

was most akin to himself, places the mind in virtue, evidently in order that it, like a good husband, may cultivate and attend to nothing else except virtue.

XV. And some one may ask here, why, since it is a pious action to imitate the works of God, it is forbidden to me to plant a grove near the altar, and yet God plants a paradise? For Moses says, " You shall not plant a grove for yourself; you shall not make for yourself any tree which is near the altar of the Lord your God."* What then are we to say? That it is right for God to plant and to build up the virtues in the soul. But the selfish and atheistical mind, thinking itself equal with God while it appears to be doing something, is found in reality to be rather suffering. And though God sows and plants good things in the soul, the mind which says, "I plant," is acting impiously. You shall not plant therefore where God is planting : but if, O mind, you fix plants in the soul, take care to plant only such trees as bear fruit, and not a grove ; for in a grove there are trees of a character to bear cultivation, and also wild trees. But to plant vice, which is unproductive in the soul, along with cultivated and fertile virtue, is the act of a double-natured and confused leprosy. If, however, you bring into the same place things which ought not to be mingled together, you must separate and disjoin them from the pure and incorrupt nature which is accustomed to make blameless offerings to God ; and this is his altar ; for it is inconsistent with this to say that there is any such thing as a work of the soul, when all things are referred to God, and to mingle barren things with those which are productive ; for this would be faulty : but they are blameless things which are offered to God. If therefore you transgress any one of these laws, O soul! you will be injuring yourself, not God. On this account God says, " You shall not plant for yourself :" for no one works for God, and especially what is evil does not. And again, Moses adds: "You shall not make for yourself." And in another place he says, "You shall not make gods of silver with me, and you shall not make gods of gold for yourselves." For he who conceives either that God has any distinctive quality, or that he is not one, or that he is not uncreated and imperishable, or that he is not unchange-able, injures himself and not God. " For you shall not make

* Deuteronomy xvi. 21.

them for yourselves," is what he says. For we must conceive that God is free from distinctive qualities, and imperishable, and unchangeable; and he who does not conceive thus of him is filling his own soul with false and atheistical opinions. Do you not see that—even though God were to conduct us to virtue, and though when we had been thus conducted we were to plant no tree which was barren, but only such as produce fruit, he would still command us to purify its impurity, that is to say, the appearing to plant. For he here orders us to cut away vain opinions; and vain opinions are a thing impure by nature.

XVI. "And the man whom he had formed," Moses says, "God placed in the Paradise,"* for the present only. Who, then, is he in reference to whom he subsequently says that "The Lord God took the man whom he had formed, and placed him in the Paradise to cultivate it and to guard it."† Must not this man who was created according to the image and idea of God have been a different man from the other, so that two men must have been introduced into the Paradise together, the one a fictitious man, and the other modelled after the image of God? Therefore, the man modelled after the idea of God, is perceived not only amid the planting of the virtues, but, besides this, he is their cultivator and guardian; that is to say, he is mindful of the things which he has heard and practised. But the man who is factitious, neither cultivates the virtues, nor guards them, but is only introduced into opinions by the abundant liberality of God, being on the point of immediately becoming an exile from virtue. Therefore, he calls that man whom he only places in Paradise, factitious; but him whom he appoints to be its cultivator and guardian he calls not factitious, but "the man whom he had made." And him he takes, but the other he casts out. And him whom he takes he thinks worthy of three things, of which goodness of nature especially consists: namely, expertness, perseverance, and memory. Now, expertness is his position in Paradise; memory is the guarding and preservation of holy opinions; perseverance is the effecting of what is good, the performance of virtuous actions. But the factitious mind neither remembers what is good, nor does it, but is only expert, and nothing more; on which account, after it has been

* Gen. ii. 8.　　　　　† Gen. ii. 15.

placed in Paradise, in a short time afterwards it runs away, and is cast out.

XVII. "And God caused to rise out of the earth every tree which is pleasant to the sight and good for food, and the tree of life he raised in the middle of the Paradise, and also the tree of the knowledge of good and evil." He here gives a sketch of the trees of virtue which he plants in the soul. And these are the particular virtues, and the energies in accordance with them, and the good and successful actions, and the things which by the philosophers are called fitting; these are the plants of the Paradise. Nevertheless, he describes the characteristics of these same trees, showing that that which is desirable to be beheld is likewise most excellent to be enjoyed. For of the arts some are theoretical and not practical, such as geometry and astronomy. Some, again, are practical and not theoretical, such as the art of the architect, of the smith, and all those which are called mechanical arts. But virtue is both theoretical and practical; for it takes in theory, since the road which leads to it is philosophy in three of its parts—the reasoning, and the moral, and the physical part. It also includes action; for virtue is art conversant about the whole of life; and in life all actions are exhibited. Still, although it takes in both theory and practice, nevertheless it is most excellent in each particular. For the theory of virtue is thoroughly excellent, and its practice and observation is a worthy object to contend for. On which account Moses says that the tree was pleasant to the sight, which is a symbol of theoretical excellence; and likewise good for food, which is a token of useful and practical good.

XVIII. But the tree of life is that most general virtue which some people call goodness; from which the particular virtues are derived, and of which they are composed. And it is on this account that it is placed in the centre of the Paradise; having the most comprehensive place of all, in order that, like a king, it may be guarded by the trees on each side of it. But some say that it is the heart that is meant by the tree of life; since that is the cause of life, and since that has its position in the middle of the body, as being, according to them, the dominant part of the body. But these men ought to be made aware that they are expounding a doctrine which has more reference to medical than to natural science. But we, as has been said before, affirm that by the tree of life is meant the most general virtue. And of this tree Moses expressly says, that it is placed in the middle of the paradise ; but as to the other tree, that namely of the knowledge of good and evil, he has not specified whether it is within or outside of the Paradise ; but after he has used the following expression, " and the tree of the knowledge of good and evil," he says no more, not mentioning where it is placed, in order that any one who is uninitiated in the principles of natural philosophy, may not be made to marvel at his knowledge.

What then must we say? That this tree is both in the Paradise and also out of it. As to its essence, indeed, in it ; but as to its power, out of it. How so ? The dominant portion of us is capable of receiving everything, and resembles wax, which is capable of receiving every impression, whether good or bad. In reference to which fact, that supplanter Jacob makes a confession where he says, " all these things were made for me."* For the unspeakable formations and impressions of all the things in the universe, are all borne forward into, and comprehended by the soul, which is only one. When, therefore that receives the impression of perfect virtue, it has become the tree of life ; but when it has received the impression of vice, it has then become the tree of the knowledge of good and evil, and vice and all evil have been banished from the divine company. Therefore the dominant power which has received it is in the Paradise according to its essence ; for there is in it that characteristic of virtue, which is akin to the Paradise. But again, according to its power it is not in it, because the form of virtue is inconsistent with the divine operations ; and what I here say, any one may understand in this manner. At this moment, the dominant part is in my body, according to its essence, but according to its power it is in Italy, or Sicily, when it applies its consideration to those countries, and in heaven when it is contemplating the heaven. On which principle it often happens that some persons who are in profane places, according to their essence, are in the most sacred places, thinking of those things which relate to virtue. And again, others who are in the temples of the gods, are profane in their minds, from the fact of their minds receiving a change for the worse, and evil impressions ; so that vice is neither in

* Genesis xlii. 36.

the Paradise, nor not in it.   For it is possible that it may be
in it according to its essence, but it is not possible that it
should be according to its power.

XIX. " And a river goes forth out of Eden to water the
Paradise. From thence it is separated into four heads: the
name of the one is Pheison.   That is the one which encircles
the whole land of Evilat.   There is the country where there
is gold, and the gold of that land is good.   There also are the carbuncle and the sapphire stone.   And the name of the second
river is Gihon ; this is that which encircles the whole land of
Ethiopia.   And the third river is the Tigris.   This is the river
which flows in front of the Assyrians.   And the fourth river is
the Euphrates."*   In these words Moses intends to sketch
out the particular virtues.   And they also are four in number,
prudence, temperance, courage, and justice.   Now the greatest
river from which the four branches flow off, is generic virtue,
which we have already called goodness ; and the four branches
are the same number of virtues.   Generic virtue, therefore,
derives its beginning from Eden, which is the wisdom of God ;
which rejoices and exults, and triumphs, being delighted at
and honoured on account of nothing else, except its Father,
God.   And the four particular virtues, are branches from the
generic virtue, which like a river waters all the good actions of
each, with an abundant stream of benefits.

Let us examine the expressions of the writer : " A river,"
says he, " goes forth out of Eden, to water the Paradise."
This river is generic goodness ; and this issues forth out of
the Eden of the wisdom of God, and that is the word of God.
For it is according to the word of God, that generic virtue was
created.   And generic virtue waters the Paradise : that is to
say, it waters the particular virtues.   But it does not derive its
beginnings from any principle of locality, but from a principle
of pre-eminence.   For each of the virtues is really and truly a
ruler and a queen.   And the expression, " is separated," is
equivalent to " is marked off by fixed boundaries ;" since wisdom appoints them settled limits with reference to what is to
be done.   Courage with respect to what is to be endured ;
temperance with reference to what is to be chosen ; and justice
in respect of what is to be distributed.

XX. " The name of one river is Pheison.   This is that
* Genesis ii. 13.

river which encircles all the land of Evilat ; there is the country where there is gold.   And the gold of that land is good ; there also are the carbuncle and the sapphire stone." One of the four virtues is prudence, which Moses here calls Pheison : because the soul abstains * from, and guards against, acts of iniquity.   And it meanders in a circle, and flows all round the land of Evilat ; that is to say, it preserves a mild, and gentle, and favourable constitution.   And as of all fusible essences, the most excellent and the most illustrious is gold, so also the virtue of the soul which enjoys the highest reputation, is prudence.   And when he uses the expression, " that is the country where there is gold," he is not speaking geographically, that is, where gold exists, but that is the country in which that valuable possession exists, brilliant as gold, tried in the fire, and valuable, namely, prudence.   And this is confessed to be the most valuable possession of God.

But with reference to the geographical position of virtue, there are two personages, each invested with distinctive qualities.   One, the being who has prudence, the other, the being who exerts it ; and these he likens to the carbuncle and the emerald.

XXI.   " And the name of the second river is Gihon.   This is that which encircles all the land of Ethiopia." Under the symbol of this river courage is intended.   For the name of Gihon being interpreted means chest, or an animal which attacks with its horns ; each of which interpretations is emblematical of courage.   For courage has its abode about the chest, where also is the seat of the heart, and where man is prepared to defend himself.   For courage is the knowledge of what is to be withstood, and of what is not to be withstood, and of what is indifferent.   And it encircles and surrounds Ethiopia, making demonstrations of war against it ; and the name of Ethiopia, being interpreted, means humiliation.   And cowardice is a humiliating thing ; but courage is adverse to humiliation and to cowardice.

" And the third river is the Tigris ; this is that which flows in front of Assyria."   The third virtue is temperance, which resolutely opposes that kind of pleasure which appears to be the directress of human infirmity.   For the translation of the name Assyrians in the Greek tongue is εὐθύνοντες, (directors).

* Φεισών, from φείδομαι, to spare, or abstain from.

And he has likened desire to a tiger, which is the most untameable of beasts ; it being desire about which temperance is
conversant.

XXII. It is worth while therefore to raise the question why
courage has been spoken of as the second virtue, and temperance as the third, and prudence as the first ; and why Moses
has not also explained the course of action of the other virtues.
Now we must understand that our soul is divided into three
parts, and that it has one portion which is conversant about
reason ; another which is subject to passion ; and another
which is that in which the desires are conceived. And we
find that the proper place and abode of the reasoning part of
the soul, is the head ; of the passionate part, the chest ; and of
the part in which the desires are conceived, the stomach.
And we find that appropriate virtues are adapted to each of
these parts. To the rational part, prudence ; in it is the office
of reason, to have a knowledge of what one might, and of what
one ought not to do, And the virtue of the passionate part of
the soul is courage : and of the appetitive part, temperance.
For it is through temperance that we remedy and cure the
appetites. For as the head is the principle and uppermost
part of the animal, and the chest the next highest, and the
liver the third, in point both of importance and of position ; so
in the soul again, the first is the rational part, the second
the passionate part, and the third the appetitive part. In the
same way again of the virtues ; the first is that which is conversant about the first portion of the soul, which is the reasoning portion, and which at the same time has its abode in the
head of the body ; in short it is prudence. And the second
of the virtues is courage, because it is conversant about the
second portion of the soul, namely, about passion, and has its
abode in the second portion of the body, namely, in the chest.
And the third virtue is temperance, which is placed in the
stomach which is the third portion of the body, and it
is conversant about the appetitive part, which has been
allotted the third part of the soul, as being its subject
matter.

XXIII. " And the fourth river," continues Moses, " is the
river Euphrates." And this name Euphrates means fertility ;
and symbolically taken, it is the fourth virtue, namely, justice,
which is most truly a productive virtue, and one which gladdens

the intellect. When therefore does this happen? When the the three parts of the soul are all in harmony with one another; and harmony among them is in reality the predominance of the most important; as for instance, when the two inferior parts, the passionate and the appetitive part, are disposed to yield to the superior part, then justice exists. For it is just that the better portion should rule at all times, and in all places, and that the inferior part should be ruled. Now the rational part is the better part, and the appetitive and the passionate parts are the inferior ones. But when, on the contrary, passion and appetite get riotous and disobey the reins, and by the violence of their impetuosity throw off and disregard the charioteer, that is to say reason, and when each of these passions get hold of the reins themselves, then there is injustice. For it is inevitable, that through any ignorance or vice of the charioteer, the chariot must be borne down over precipices, and must fall into the abyss; just as it must be saved when the charioteer is endowed with skill and virtue.

XXIV. Again, let us look at the subject in this way also. Pheison, being interpreted, is the change of the mouth; and Evilat means bringing forth, and by these two names prudence is signified. For people in general think a man prudent who is an inventor of sophistical expressions, and clever at explaining that which he has conceived in the mind. But Moses considered such an one a man fond of words, but by no means a prudent man. For in the changing of the mouth, that is to say of the power of speaking and explaining one's ideas, prudence is seen. And prudence is not a certain degree of acuteness in speech, but ability which is beheld in deeds and in serious actions. And prudence surrounds Evilat, which is in travail, as it were with a wall, in order to besiege it and destroy it. And "bringing forth," is an especially appropriate name for folly, because the foolish mind, being always desirous of what is unattainable, is at all times in travail. When it is desirous of money it is in labour, also when it thirsts for glory, or when it is covetous of pleasure, or of any thing else. But, though always in labour, it never brings forth. For the soul of the worthless man is not calculated by nature to bring any thing to perfection which is likely to live. But every thing which it appears to bring forth is found to be abortive and immature. " Eating up the half of its flesh, and being like a death of the soul."* On which account that holy word Aaron entreats the pious Moses, who was beloved by God, to heal the leprosy of Miriam, in order that her soul might not be occupied in the labour of bringing forth evil things. And in consequence he says: "Let her not become like unto death, as an abortion proceeding out of the womb of her mother, and let her not devour the half of her own flesh."†

XXV. "That," says Moses, "is the country, where there is gold." He does not say that that is the only place where there is gold, but simply that is the country where there is gold. For prudence which he likened to gold, being of a nature free from deceit, and pure, and tried in the fire, and thoroughly tested, and honourable, exists there in the wisdom of God. And being there, it is not a possession of wisdom, but something belonging to the God who is its creator and owner, whose work and possession this wisdom likewise is. "And the gold of that land is good." Is there, then, any other gold which is not good? Beyond all doubt; for the nature of prudence is twofold, there being one prudence general, and another particular. Therefore, the prudence that is in me, being particular prudence, is not good; for when I perish that also will perish together with me; but general or universal prudence, the abode of which is the wisdom of God and the house of God, is good; for it is imperishable itself, and dwells in an imperishable habitation.

XXVI. "There also is the carbuncle and the emerald." The two beings endowed with distinctive qualities, the prudent man and the man who acts prudently, differ from one another; one of them existing according to prudence, and the other acting wisely according to the rules of wisdom. For it is on account of these two beings thus endowed with distinctive qualities God implanted prudence and virtue in the earth-born man. For what would have been the use of it, if there had been no reasoning powers in existence to receive it, and to give impressions of its form? So that virtue is very properly conjoined with prudence, and the prudent man is rightly joined with him who displays prudence in his actions; the two being like two precious stones. And may not they be Judah and Issachar? For the man who puts in practice the prudence of God confesses himself to be bound to feel gratitude, and to

* Numbers xii. 12.   † Numbers xii. 13.

feel it towards him who has given him what is good without grudging; and he also does honourable and virtuous actions. Accordingly Judah is the symbol of a man who makes this confession " in respect of whom Leah ceased from child-bearing."* But Issachar is the symbol of the man who does good actions, " For he put forth † his shoulder to labour and became a man tilling the earth." With respect to whom Moses says, hire is in his soul after he has been sown and planted, so that his labour is not imperfect, but is rather crowned and honoured with a reward by God.

And that he is making mention of these things, he shows when speaking on other subjects; when describing the garment, which reached to the feet he says, " And thou shalt weave in it sets of stones in four rows. The row of stones shall be the sardine stone, the topaz, and the emerald are the first row." Reuben, Simeon, and Levi are here meant. " And the second row," he says, " are the carbuncle and the sapphire."‡ And the sapphire is the same as the green stone. And in the carbuncle was inscribed the name of Judah, for he was the fourth son: and in the sapphire the name of Issachar. Why then as he had called the sapphire the green stone, did he not also speak of the red stone? Because Judah, as the type of a disposition inclined to confession, is a being immaterial and incorporeal. For the very name of confession (ἐξομολογήσεως) shows that it is a thing external to (ἐκτὸς) himself. For when the mind is beside itself, and bears itself upwards to God, as the laughter of Isaac did, then it makes a confession to him who alone has a real being. But as long as it considers itself as the cause of something, it is a long way from yielding to God, and confessing to him. For this very act of confessing ought to be considered as being the work not of the soul, but of God who teaches it this feeling of gratitude. Accordingly Judah, who practises confession, is an immaterial being.

But Issachar who came forth out of labour is in need of corporeal matter; since if it were otherwise how could a studious man read without his eyes? And how could any one hear words exhorting him to any cause, if he were not endowed with hearing? And how could he obtain meat and drink without a belly, and without a wonder working art exercised

---

* Genesis xxix. 35.   † Genesis xlix. 15.   ‡ Exodus xxviii. 17.

towards it? And it is on this account that he was likened to a precious stone.

Moreover the colours of the two are different. For the colour of a coal when on fire is akin to that of the man who is inclined to confession: for he is inflamed by gratitude to God, and he is intoxicated with a certain sober intoxication: but the colour of the green stone is more appropriate to the man who is still labouring: for those who are devoted to constant labour are pale on account of the wearing nature of toil, and also by reason of their fear that perhaps they may not attain to such an end of their wish as is desired in their prayers.

XXVII. And it is worth while to raise the question why the two rivers the Pheison and the Gihon encircle certain countries, the one surrounding Evilat, and the other Ethiopia, while neither of the other rivers is represented as encompasing any country. The Tigris is indeed said to flow in front of the land of the Assyrians, but the Euphrates is not mentioned in connection with any country whatever. And yet in real truth the Euphrates does both encircle some countries, and has several also in front of it. But the truth is that the sacred writer is here speaking not of the river, but of the correction of manners. It is necessary therefore to say that prudence and courage are able to raise a wall and a circle of fortification against the opposite evils, folly, and cowardice; and to take them captives: for both of them are powerless and easy to be taken. For the foolish man is easily to be defeated by the prudent one; and the coward falls before the valiant man. But temperance is unable to surround appetite and pleasure; for they are formidable adversaries and hard to be subdued. Do you not see that even the most temperate men are compelled by the necessities of their mortal body to seek meat and drink; and it is in those things that the pleasures of the belly have their existence. We must be content therefore to oppose and contend with the genus appetite. And it is on this account that the river Tigris is represented as flowing in front of the Assyrians, that is to say temperance is in front of or arrayed against pleasure.

But justice, according to which the river Euphrates is represented, neither besieges any one, nor draws lines of circumvallation round any one, nor opposes any one;—why so? Because justice is conversant about the distribution of things according to merit, and does not take the part either of accuser or of defendant, but acts as a judge. As therefore a judge does not desire beforehand to defeat any one, nor to oppose and make war upon any one; but delivers his own opinion and judges, deciding for the right, so also justice, not being the adversary of any one, distributes its due to every thing.

XXVIII. "And the Lord God took the man whom he had made and placed him in the Paradise, to cultivate and to guard it." The man whom God made differs from the factitious man, as I have said before. For the factitious mind is somewhat earthly; but the created mind is purer and more immaterial, having no participation in any perishable matter, but having received a purer and more simple constitution. Accordingly God takes this pure mind, not permitting it to proceed out of itself, and after he has taken it, he places it among the virtues which are firmly rooted and budding well, that it may cultivate and guard them. For many men who were originally prac- tisers of virtue, when they come to the end fall off; but he to whom God gives lasting knowledge is also endowed by him with both qualities, namely with the disposition to cultivate the virtues, and the resolution never to desert them, but always to minister to and guard every one of them. So Moses here uses the expression "cultivate" as equivalent to "act," and the word "guard" instead of "remember."

XXIX. "And the Lord God commanded Adam, saying, Of every tree that is in the Paradise thou mayest freely eat; but of the tree of the knowledge of good and evil ye shall not eat; but in the day on which ye eat of it ye shall die the death."

A question may arise here to what kind of Adam he gave this command and who, this Adam was. For Moses has not made any mention of him before; but now is the first time that he has named him.

Are we then to think that he is desirous to supply you with the name of the factitious man? "And he calls him," continues Moses, "Earth." For this is the interpretation of the name of Adam. Accordingly, when you hear the name Adam, you must think that he is an earthly and perishable being; for he is made according to an image, being not earthly but heavenly. But we must inquire how it was that after he had given names to all the other animals, he did not give one also to himself.

What then are we to say about this? The mind which is in each of us is able to comprehend all other things, but has not the capability of understanding itself. For as the eye sees all other things, but cannot see itself, so also the mind perceives the nature of other things but cannot understand itself. For if it does, let it tell us what it is, or what kind of thing it is, whether it is a spirit, or blood, or fire, or air, or any other substance: or even only so much whether it is a substance at all, or something incorporeal. Are not those men then simple who speculate on the essence of God? For how can they who are ignorant of the nature of the essence of their own soul, have any accurate knowledge of the soul of the universe? For the soul of the universe is according to our definition,—God.

XXX. It is therefore very natural that Adam, that is to say the mind, when he was giving names to and displaying his comprehension of the other animals, did not give a name to himself, because he was ignorant of himself and of his own nature. A command indeed is given to man, but not to the man created according to the image and idea of God; for that being is possessed of virtue without any need of exhortation, by his own instinctive nature, but this other would not have wisdom if it had not been taught to him: and these three things are different, command, prohibition, and recommendation. For prohibition is conversant about errors, and is directed to bad men, but command is conversant about things rightly done; recommendation again is addressed to men of intermediate character, neither bad nor good. For such a one does not sin so that any one has any need to direct prohibition to him, nor does he do right in every case in accordance with the injunction of right reason. But he is in need of recommendation, which teaches him to abstain from what is evil, and exhorts him to aim at what is good. Therefore there is no need of addressing either command, or prohibition, or recommendation to the man who is perfect, and made according to the image of God; For the perfect man requires none of these things; but there is a necessity of addressing both command and prohibition to the wicked man, and recommendation and instruction to the ignorant man. Just as the perfect grammarian or perfect musician has need of no instruction in the matters which belong to his art, but the man whose theories on such subjects are imperfect stands in need of certain rules, as it were, which contain in themselves commands and prohibitions, and he who is only learning the art requires instruction.

Very naturally, therefore, does God at present address commands and recommendations to the earthly mind, which is neither bad nor good, but of an intermediate character. And recommendation is employed in the two names, in that of the Lord and of God. For the Lord God commanded that if man obeyed his recommendations, he should be thought worthy of receiving benefits from God; but if he rejected his warnings, he should then be cast out to destruction by the Lord, as his Master and one who had authority over him. On which account, when he is driven out of Paradise, Moses repeats the same names; for he says, " And the Lord God sent him forth out of the Paradise of happiness, to till the ground from which he had been taken."* That, since the Lord had laid his commands on him as his Master, and God as his Benefactor, he might now, in both these characters, chastise him for having disobeyed them; for thus, by the same power by which he had exhorted him does he also banish him, now that he is disobedient.

XXXI. And the recommendations that he addresses to him are as follows: " Of every tree that is in the Paradise thou mayest freely eat."† He exhorts the soul of man to derive advantage not from one tree alone nor from one single virtue, but from all the virtues; for eating is a symbol of the nourishment of the soul, and the soul is nourished by the reception of good things, and by the doing of praiseworthy actions. And Moses not only says, " thou mayest eat," but he adds " freely," also; that is to say, having ground and prepared your food, not like an ordinary individual, but like a wrestler, you shall thus acquire strength and vigour. For the trainers recommend the wrestlers not to cut up their food by biting large pieces off, but to masticate it slowly, in order that it may contribute to their strength; for I and an athlete are fed in different manners. For I feed merely for the purpose of living, but the wrestler feeds for the purpose of acquiring flesh and deriving strength from it; on which account one of his rules of training and exercise is to masticate his food. This is the meaning of the expression, " Thou mayest freely eat."

Again let us endeavour to give a still more accurate expla-

* Genesis iii. 23.   † Genesis ii. 16.

nation of it. To honour one's parents is a nourishing and cherishing thing. But the good and the wicked honour them in different manners. For the one does it out of habit, as men eat who do not eat freely, but who merely eat. When, then, do they also eat freely? When having investigated and developed the causes of things they form a voluntary judgment that this is good, and the causes of their eating freely, that is to say, of their honouring their parents in a proper spirit, is— they became our parents; they nourished us; they instructed us; they have been the causes of all good things to us. Again, to honour the living God is spoken of symbolically as to eat. But to eat "freely," is when it is done with a proper explanation of the whole matter, and a correct assignment of the causes of it.

XXXII. "But of the tree of the knowledge of good and evil ye shall not eat." Therefore this tree is not in the Paradise. For God encourages them to eat of every tree that is in the Paradise. But when he forbids them to eat of this tree, it is plain that it is not in the Paradise; and this is in accordance with natural philosophy. For it is there in its essence, as I have said before, and it is not there in its power. For as in wax there are potentially many seals, but in actual fact only one which has been carved on it, so also in the soul, which resembles wax, all impressions whatever are contained potentially; but in really one single characteristic which is stamped upon it has possession of it; until it is effaced by some other which makes a deeper and more conspicuous impression.

Again, this, also, may be made the subject of a question. When God recommends men to eat of every tree in the Paradise, he is addressing his exhortation to one individual: but when he forbids him to eat of the tree of the knowledge of good and evil he is speaking to him as to many. For in the one case he says, "Thou mayest freely eat of all;" but in the second instance, "Ye shall not eat;" and "In the day in which ye shall eat," not "thou shalt eat;" and "Ye shall die," not "Thou shalt die." We must, therefore, say this,—that the first good is rare, imparted to but few; but the evil is comprehensive. On this account it is a hard matter to find one single man wise and faithful, but the number of bad men is beyond all computation. Very appropriately, therefore, God does not address his exhortation to nourish one's self amid the virtues, to one individual, but he encourages many to abstain from extravagant wickedness; for innumerable men are addicted to it.

In the second place, for the due comprehension and adoption of virtue man requires one thing alone, namely reason. But the body not only does not co-operate in it at all, but rather impedes the progress of the reason towards it. For it may be almost called the peculiar task of wisdom to alienate itself from the body and from the corporeal appetites. But for the enjoyment of evil it is not only necessary for a man to have mind in some degree, but also senses, and reason, and a body. For the bad man has need of all these things for the completion of his own wickedness. Since how will he be able to divulge the sacred mysteries unless he has the organ of voice? And how will he be able to indulge in pleasures if he be deprived of the belly and the organs of sensation? Very properly, therefore, does Moses address reason alone on the subject of the acquisition of virtue, for reason is, as I have said before, the only thing of which there is need for the establishment of virtue. But for indulgence in vice a man requires many things—soul, and reason, and the external senses of the body; for it is through all these organs that vice is exhibited.

XXXIII. Accordingly God says, "In the day in which ye eat of it ye shall die the death." And yet, though they have eaten of it, they not only do not die, but they even beget children, and are the causes of life to other beings besides themselves. What, then, are we to say? Surely that death is of two kinds; the one being the death of the man, the other the peculiar death of the soul—now the death of the man is the separation of his soul from his body, but the death of the soul is the destruction of virtue and the admission of vice; and consequently God calls that not merely "to die," but "to die the death;" showing that he is speaking not of common death, but of that peculiar and especial death which is the death of the soul, buried in its passions and in all kinds of evil. And we may almost say that one kind of death is opposed to the other kind. For the one is the separation of what was previously existing in combination, namely, of body and soul. But this other death, on the contrary, is a combination of them both, the inferior one, the body, having the predominance, and the superior one, the soul, being made subject to it

When, therefore, God says, "to die the death," you must remark that he is speaking of that death which is inflicted as punishment, and not of that which exists by the original ordinance of nature. The natural death is that one by which the soul is separated from the body. But the one which is inflicted as a punishment, is when the soul dies according to the life of virtue, and lives only according to the life of vice.

Well, therefore, did Heraclitus say this, following the doctrine of Moses; for he says, "We are living according to the death of those men; and we have died according to their life." As if he had said, Now, when we are alive, we are so though our soul is dead and buried in our body, as if in a tomb. But if it were to die, then our soul would live according to its proper life, being released from the evil and dead body to which it is bound.

that there he may endure unmitigated and everlasting misery.

Since we see Agar, by whom we understand the middle kind of instruction which is confined to the encyclical system, twice going forth from Sarah, who is the symbol of predominant virtue, and once returning back by the same road, inasmuch as after she had fled the first time, without being banished by her mistress, she returned to see her master's house, having been met by an angel, as the holy scriptures read*: but the second time, she is utterly cast out, and is never to be brought back again.†

II. And we must speak of the causes of her first flight, and then again of her second perpetual banishment.

Before the names of the two were changed, that is to say, before they had been altered for the better as to the characteristics of their souls, and had been endowed with better dispositions, but while the name of the man was still Abram, or the sublime father, who delighted in the lofty philosophy which investigates the events which take place in the air, and the sublime nature of the beings which exist in heaven, which mathematical science claims for itself as the most excellent part of natural philosophy, and the name of the woman was still Sarai; the symbol of my authority, for she is called my authority, and she had not yet changed her nature so as to become generic virtue, and all genus is imperishable, but was as yet classed among things particular and things in species; that is to say, such as the prudence which is in me, the temperance which is in me, the courage, the justice, and so on in the same manner; and these particular virtues are perishable, because the place which receives them, that is to say I, am also perishable. Then Agar, who is the middle kind of encyclical instruction, even if she should endeavour to escape from the austere and stern life of the lovers of virtue, will again return to it, since it is not, as yet, able to receive the generic and imperishable excellencies of virtue, but can only touch the particular virtues, and such as are spoken of in species, in which it is sufficient to attain to mediocrity instead of extreme perfection.

But when Abram, instead of an inquirer into natural philosophy, became a wise man and a lover of God, having his name changed to Abraham, which being interpreted means

* Genesis xvi. 9. † Genesis xxi. 14.

the great father of sounds; for language when uttered sounds, and the father of language is the mind, which has attained to what is virtuous. And when Sarai instead of being my authority, had her name also changed to Sarah, the meaning of which is princess, and this change is equivalent to becoming generic and imperishable virtue, instead of virtue special and perishable: then will arise the genus of happiness, that is to say, Isaac; and he, when all the feminine affections * have ceased, and when the passion of joy and cheerfulness are dead, will eagerly pursue, not childish amusements, but divine objects; then too those elementary branches of instruction which bear the name of Agar, will be cast out, and their sophistical child will also be cast out, who is named Ishmael.

III. And they shall undergo eternal banishment, God himself confirming their expulsion, when he bids the wise man obey the word spoken by Sarah, and she urges him expressly to cast out the serving woman and her son; and it is good to be guided by virtue, and especially so when it teaches such lessons as this, that the most perfect natures are very greatly different from the mediocre habits, and that wisdom is a wholly different thing from sophistry; for the one labours to devise what is persuasive for the establishment of a false opinion, which is pernicious to the soul, but wisdom, with long meditation on the truth by the knowledge of right reason, brings real advantage to the intellect. Why then do we wonder if God once for all banished Adam, that is to say, the mind out of the district of the virtues, after he had once contracted folly, that incurable disease, and if he never permitted him again to return, when he also drives out and banishes from wisdom and from the wise man every sophist, and the mother of sophists, the teaching that is of elementary instruction, while he calls the names of wisdom and of the wise man Abraham, and Sarah.

IV. Then also, "The flaming sword and the cherubim have an abode allotted to them exactly in front of paradise." The expression, "in front," is used partly to convey the idea of a resisting enemy, and partly as suitable to the notion of judgment, as a person whose cause is being decided appears in front of his judge: partly also in a friendly sense, in order

---

* The Greek text here is corrupt and unintelligible. I have followed the Latin translation of Mangey.

that they may be perceived, and may be considered in closer connection by reason of the more accurate view of them that is thus obtained, just as archetypal pictures and statues are placed in front of painters and statuaries.

Now the first example of an enemy placed directly in front of one is derived from what is said in the case of Cain, that " he went out from the face of God, and dwelt in the land of Nod, in the front of Eden."* Now Nod being interpreted means commotion, and Eden means delight. The one therefore is a symbol of wickedness agitating the soul, and the other of virtue which creates for the soul a state of tranquillity and happiness, not meaning by happiness that effeminate luxury which is derived from the indulgence of the irrational passion of pleasure, but a joy free from toil and free from hardship, which is enjoyed with great tranquillity. And it follows of necessity that when the mind goes forth from any imagination of God, by which it would be good and expedient for it to be supported, then immediately, after the fashion of a ship, which is tossed in the sea, when the winds oppose it with great violence, it is tossed about in every direction, having disturbance as it were for its country and its home, a thing which is the most contrary of all things to steadiness of soul, which is engendered by joy, which is a term synonymous with Eden.

V. Now of the kind of opposition of place which is connected with standing in front of a judge for judgment, we have an example in the case of the woman who has been suspected of having committed adultery. For, says Moses, " the priest shall cause the woman to stand in front of her lord, and she shall uncover her head."† Let us now examine what he intends to show by this direction.

It often happens that what ought to be done is not done, in the manner in which it ought to be done, and sometimes too that which is not proper is nevertheless done in a proper manner. For instance, when the return of a deposit is not made in an honest spirit, but is intended either to work the injury of him who receives it back again, or by way of a snare to bear out a denial in the case of another deposit of greater value, in that case a proper action is done in an improper manner. On the other hand, for a physician not to tell the exact truth to a sick patient, when he has decided on purging

* Genesis iv. 16.　　　　　　　　† Numbers v. 18.

him, or performing some operation with the knife or with the cautery for the benefit of the patient, lest if the sick man were to be moved too strongly by the anticipation of the suffering, he might refuse to submit to the cure, or through weakness of mind might despair of its succeeding; or in the case of a wise man giving false information to the enemy to secure the safety of his country, fearing lest through his speaking the truth the affairs of the adversaries should succeed, in this case an action which is not intrinsically right is done in a proper manner.

In reference to which distinction Moses says, "to pursue what is just justly,"* as if it were possible also to pursue it unjustly, if at any time the judge who gives sentence does not decide in an honest spirit. Since therefore what is said or done is openly notorious to all men, but since the intention, the consequence of which what is said is said, and what is done is done, is not notorious, but it is uncertain whether it be a sound and healthy motive, or an unhealthy design, stained with numerous pollutions; and since no created being is capable of discerning the secret intention of an invisible mind, but God alone; in reference to this Moses says that "all secret things are known to the Lord God, but only such as are manifest are known to the creature." And therefore it is enjoined to the priest and prophet, that is to say to reason, "to place the soul in front of God, with the head uncovered,"† that is to say, the soul must be laid bare as to its principal design, and the sentiments which it nourished must be revealed, in order that being brought before the judgment seat of the most accurate vision of the incorruptible God, it may be thoroughly examined as to all its concealed disguises, like a base coin, or, on the other hand, if it be found to be free from all participation in any kind of wickedness, it may wash away all the calumnies that have been uttered against its bringing him for a testimony to its purity, who is alone able to behold the soul naked.

VI. This, then, is the meaning of coming in front of one's judge, when brought up for judgment. But the case of coming in front of any one which has a bearing upon connection or familiarity, may be illustrated by the example of the all-wise Abraham. "For," says Moses, "he was still standing in front of God."‡ And a proof of his familiarity is contained in the expression that "he came near to God, and spoke." For it

* Deuteronomy xvi. 20.   † Numbers v. 18.   ‡ Genesis xviii. 22.

is fitting for one who has no connection with another to stand at a distance, and to be separated from him, but he who is connected with him should stand near to him. And to stand, and to have an unchangeable mind comes very near to the power of God, since the Divinity is unchangeable, but that which is created is intrinsically and essentially changeable. Therefore, if any one, restraining the changeableness natural to all created things by his love of knowledge, has been able to put such violence on any thing as to cause it to stand firm, let him be sure that he has come near to the happiness of the Deity.

But God very appropriately assigns to the cherubim and to the flaming sword a city or abode in front of Paradise, not as to enemies about to oppose and to fight him, but rather as to near connections and friends, in order that in consequence of a continued sight and contemplation of one another, the two powers might conceive an affection for one another, the all-bounteous God inspiring them with a winged and heavenly love.

VII. But we must now consider what the figurative allusions are which are enigmatically expressed in the mention of the cherubim and of the flaming sword which turned every way. May we not say that Moses here introduces under a figure an intimation of the revolutions of the whole heaven? For the spheres in heaven received a motion in opposite directions to one another, the one sphere receiving a fixed motion towards the right hand, but the sphere of the other side receiving a wandering motion towards the left. But that outermost circle of what are called the fixed stars is one sphere, which also proceeds in a fixed periodical revolution from east to west. But the interior circle of the seven planets, whose course is at the same time compulsory and voluntary, has two motions, which are to a certain degree contrary to one another. And one of these motions is involuntary, like that of the planets. For they appear every day proceeding onwards from the east to the west. But their peculiar and voluntary motion is from west to east, according to which last motion we find that the periods of the seven planets have received their exact measure of time, moving on in an equal course, as the Sun, and Lucifer, and what is called Stilbon. For these three planets are of equal speed; but some of the others are unequal in point of time, but preserve a certain sort of relative proportion to one another and to the other three which have been mentioned.

Accordingly, by one of the cherubim is understood the extreme outermost circumference of the entire heaven, in which the fixed stars celebrate their truly divine dance, which always proceeds on similar principles and is always the same, without ever leaving the order which the Father, who created them, appointed for them in the world.

But the other of the cherubim is the inner sphere which is contained within that previously mentioned, which God originally divided in two parts, and created seven orbits, bearing a certain definite proportion to one another, and he adapted each of the planets to one of these; and then, having placed each of these stars in its proper orbit, like a driver in a chariot, he did not entrust the reins to any one of them, fearing that some inharmonious sort of management might be the result, but he made them all to depend upon himself, thinking that, by that arrangement, the character of their motion would be rendered most harmonious. For every thing which exists in combination with God is deserving of praise; but every thing which exists without him is faulty.

VIII. This, then, is one of the systems, acccording to which what is said of the cherubim may be understood allegorically. But we must suppose that the sword, consisting of flame and always turning in every direction, intimates their motion and the everlasting agitation of the entire heaven. And may we not say, according to another way of understanding this allegory, that the two cherubim are meant as symbols of each of the hemispheres? For they say that they stand face to face, inclining towards the mercy-seat; since the two hemispheres are also exactly opposite to one another, and incline towards the earth which is the centre of the whole universe, by which, also, they are kept apart from one another.

But the only one of all the parts of the world that stands firmly was most appropriately named Vesta* by the ancients, in order that there might be an excellently arranged revolution of the two hemispheres around some object firmly fixed in the middle. And the flaming sword is a symbol of the sun; for as he is a collection of an immense body of flame, he is

* In Greek Ἑστίη, as standing (ἑστῶσα.)

the swiftest of all existing things, to such a degree that in one
day he revolves round the whole world.

IX. I have also, on one occasion, heard a more ingenious
train of reasoning from my own soul, which was accustomed
frequently to be seized with a certain divine inspiration, even
concerning matters which it could not explain even to itself;
which now, if I am able to remember it accurately, I will
relate.   It told me that in the one living and true God there
were two supreme and primary powers—goodness and authority;
and that by his goodness he had created every thing, and by
his authority he governed all that he had created; and that
the third thing which was between the two, and had the effect
of bringing them together was reason, for that it was owing to
reason that God was both a ruler and good.

Now, of this ruling authority and of this goodness, being two
distinct powers, the cherubim were the symbols, but of reason
the flaming sword was the symbol.   For reason is a thing
capable of rapid motion and impetuous, and especially the
reason of the Creator of all things is so, inasmuch as it was
before everything and passed by everything, and was conceived
before everything, and appears in everything.   And do thou,
O my mind, receive the impression of each of these cherubims
unadulterated, that thus becoming thoroughly instructed about
the ruling authority of the Creator of all things and about his
goodness, thou mayest receive a happy inheritance; for immediately thou shalt understand the conjunction and combination
of these imperishable powers, and learn in what respects God
is good, his majesty arising from his sovereign power being
all the time conspicuous; and in what he is powerful, his
goodness, being equally the object of attention, that in this
way thou mayest attain to the virtues which are engendered
by these conceptions, namely, a love and a reverential awe of
God, neither being uplifted to arrogance by any prosperity
which may befall thee, having regard always to the greatness
of the sovereignty of thy King; nor abjectly giving up hope of
better things in the hour of unexpected misfortune, having
regard, then, to the mercifulness of thy great and bounteous
God.   And let the flaming sword teach thee that these things
might be followed by a prompt and fiery reason combined with
action, which never ceases being in motion with rapidity and

energy to the selection of good objects, and the avoidance of all such as are evil.

X. Do you not see that even the wise Abraham, when he began to measure everything with a reference to God, and to leave nothing to the creature, took an imitation of the flaming sword, namely, "fire and a sword,"* being eager to slay and to burn that mortal creature which was born of him, that so being raised on high it might soar up to God, the intellect being thus disentangled from the body.

Moses also represents Balaam, who is the symbol of a vain people, stripped of his arms, as a runaway and deserter, well knowing the war which it becomes the soul to carry on for the sake of knowledge ; for he says to his ass, who is here a symbol of the irrational designs of life which every foolish man entertains, that "If I had had a sword, I should ere now have slain thee."† And great thanks are due to the Maker of all things, because he, knowing the struggles and resistance of folly, did not give to it the power of language, which would have been like giving a sword to a madman, in order that it might have no power to work great and iniquitous destruction among all whom it should meet with. But the reproaches which Balaam utters are in some degree expressed by all those who are not purified, but are always talking foolishly, devoting themselves to the life of a merchant, or of a farmer, or to some other business, the object of which is to provide the things necessary for life. As long, indeed, as everything goes on prosperously with respect to each individual, he mounts his animal joyfully and rides on cheerfully, and holding the reins firmly he will by no means consent to let them go. And if any one advises him to dismount and to set bounds to his appetites, because of his inability to know what will befall him hereafter, he reproaches him with jealousy and envy, saying that he does not address him in this way out of good will. But when any unexpected misfortune overtakes him, he then looks upon those who have given him warning as good prophets and men able, above all others, to foresee the future, and lays the blame of his distress on what is absolutely the cause of no evil whatever, on agriculture, on commerce, or on any other pursuit which he may have thought fit to select for the purpose of making money.

* Genesis xxii. 6.   † Numbers xxii. 29.

XI. But these pursuits, although they are destitute of the
organs of speech, will, nevertheless, through the medium of
actions, utter a language clearer than any speech which proceeds from the tongue, and will say, "O you sycophant and
false accuser, are not we the pursuits which you mounted upon
holding your head high, as you might have mounted upon a
beast of burden? And have we, by any insolence or obstinacy
of ours, caused you any suffering? Behold reason armed and
standing in opposition to God, by whom all good and all bad
fortune is brought to its accomplishment. Do you not see it?
Why, then, do you reproach us now, when you formerly had no
fault to find with us, while your affairs were proceeding prosperously? For we are the same as we were before, having
changed nothing of our nature, not the slightest jot. But you
are now applying tests which have no soundness in them, and
in consequence are unreasonably violent against us; for if you
had understood from the beginning that it is not the pursuits
which you follow that are the causes of your participation in
good or in evil, but rather the divine reason, which is the
helmsman and governor of the universe, then you would more
easily have borne the events which have befallen you, ceasing to bring false accusations against us, and to attribute
to us effects which we are unable to produce.

" If therefore this reason now again, putting an end to that
strife, and dispersing the sad and desponding ideas which arise
from it, should promise you tranquillity of life, you will then
again, with cheerfulness and joy, give us your right hand
though we shall be like what we are now. But we are
neither puffed up by your friendly favour, nor do we think it
of great importance if you are angry with us; for we know
that we are not the causes of either good or evil fortune, not
even if you believe that we are, unless indeed you attribute to
the sea the cause of sailors making favourable voyages, or of
the shipwrecks which at times befall them, and not rather to
the variations of the winds, which blow at one time gently,
and at another with the most violent impetuosity; for as all
water is by its own nature tranquil, accordingly, when a
favourable gale blows upon the stern of a ship, every rope is
bent, and the ship is in full sail, conveying the mariners to the
harbour; but when on a sudden the wind changes to the opposite direction, and blows against the head of the vessel, it

then raises a heavy swell and great disturbance in the water, and upsets the ship; and the sea, which was in no respect the cause of what has happened is blamed for it, though it notoriously is either calm or stormy according to the gentleness or violence of the winds."

By all these considerations I think it has been abundantly shown, that nature has made reason the most powerful coadjutor of man, and has made him, who is able to make a proper use of it, happy and truly rational; but him who has not this faculty, she has rendered irrational and unhappy.

A TREATISE

ON THE

LIFE OF THE WISE MAN MADE PERFECT BY INSTRUCTION

OR, ON

THE UNWRITTEN LAW, THAT IS TO SAY, ON ABRAHAM.

I. THE sacred laws having been written in five books, the first is called and inscribed Genesis, deriving its title from the creation (γένεσις) of the world, which it contains at the beginning; although there are ten thousand other matters also introduced which refer to peace and to war, or to fertility and barrenness, or to hunger and plenty, or to the terrible destructions which have taken place on earth by the agency of fire and water; or, on the contrary, to the birth and rapid propagation of animals and plants in accordance with the admirable arrangement of the atmosphere, and the seasons of the year, and of men, some of whom lived in accordance with virtue, while others were associated with wickedness.

But since of these things some are portions of the world, and some are accidents, and since the world is the most perfect and complete of all things, he has nominally assigned the whole book to that subject.

We have then examined with all the accuracy that was in our power, in what manner the creation of the world was arranged in our previous treatises; but since it is necessary, to be consistent with the regular order in which the sacred history proceeds to go on, now to investigate the laws, we will for the present postpone the particular laws which are copies as it were; and first of all examine the more general laws which are, as it were, the models of the others. Now these are those men who have lived irreproachably and admirably, whose virtues are durably and permanently recorded, as on pillars in the sacred scriptures, not merely with the object of praising the men themselves, but also for the sake of exhorting those who read their history, and of leading them on to emulate their conduct; for these men have been living and rational laws; and the lawgiver has magnified them for two reasons; first, because he was desirous to show that the injunctions which are thus given are not inconsistent with nature; and, secondly, that he might prove that it is not very difficult or laborious for those who wish to live according to the laws established in these books, since the earliest men easily and spontaneously obeyed the unwritten principle of legislation before any one of the particular laws were written down at all.

So that a man may very properly say, that the written laws are nothing more than a memorial of the life of the ancients, tracing back in an antiquarian spirit, the actions and reasonings which they adopted; for these first men, without ever having been followers or pupils of any one, and without ever having been taught by preceptors what they ought to do or say, but having embraced a line of conduct consistent with nature from attending to their own natural impulses, and from being prompted by an innate virtue, and looking upon nature herself to be, what in fact she is, the most ancient and duly established of laws, did in reality spend their whole lives in

making laws, never of deliberate purpose doing anything
open to reproach, and for their accidental errors propitiating
God, and appeasing him by prayers and supplications, so as to
procure for themselves the enjoyment of an entire life of virtue
and prosperity, both in respect of their deliberate actions, and
those which proceeded from no voluntary purpose.

II. Since then the beginning of all participation in good
things is hope, and since the soul devoted to virtue pioneers
and opens this path as a plain and easy one, being anxious to
attain to that which is really honourable, the sacred historian
has named the first lover of hope, Enos, giving him the common name of the whole race as an especial favour.   For the
Chaldæans call man Enos; as if he were the only real man,
who lived in expectation of good things, and who is established
in good hopes; from which it is evident that they do not look
upon the man devoid of hope as a man at all, but rather as an
animal resembling a man, inasmuch as he is deprived of that
most peculiar possession of the human soul, namely hope.
For which reason, being desirous to deliver an admirable
panegyric on the hopeful man, the sacred historian tells us,
first, that "he hoped in the father and creator of the
universe," * and adds in a subsequent passage, "This is the
book of the generation of men," † and of their fathers, and
grand-fathers who had existed previously; but he conceived
that they were the ancestors of the mixed race, that is to say,
of that purer and thoroughly sifted race which is the really
rational one; for, as the poet Homer, though the number of
poets is beyond all calculation, is called "the poet" by way of
distinction, and as the black [ink] with which we write is
called "the black," though in point of fact everything which
is not white is black; and as that archon at Athens is
especially called "the archon," who is the archon eponymus
and the chief of the nine archons, from whom the chronology
is dated; so in the same manner the sacred historian calls
him who indulges in hope, "a man," by way of pre-eminence,
passing over in silence the rest of the multitude of human
beings, as not being worthy to receive the same appellation.

And he has very properly called his first volume, the Book
of the Generation of the Real Man, speaking with perfect correctness; because the man who is full of good hope is worthy

* Genesis iv. 26.   † Genesis v. 1.

of being described and remembered, not with such a memory as is given by a record in papers, which are hereafter to be destroyed by bookworms, but by that which exists in immortal nature, where the virtuous actions are regularly recorded.

If then any one were to reckon the generations, from the first man, who was made out of the earth, he will find him who, by the Chaldæans is called Enos, and in the Greek language ἄνθρωπος (the man), to be the fourth in succession, and in numbers the number four is honoured among other philosophers, who have studied and admired the incorporeal essences, appreciable only by the intellect, and especially by the all-wise Moses, who magnifies the number four, and says that it is " holy and praiseworthy ;"* and the reasons for which this character has been given to it are mentioned in a former treatise. And the man who is full of good hope is likewise holy and praiseworthy ; as, on the contrary, he who has no hope is accursed and blameable, being always associated with fear, which is an evil counsellor in any emergency ; for they say, that there is no one thing so hostile to another, as hope is to fear and fear to hope, and perhaps this may be correctly said, for both fear and hope are an expectation, but the one is an expectation of good things, and the other, on the contrary, of evil things ; and the natures of good and evil are irreconcileable, and such as can never come together.

III. What has now been said about hope is sufficient ; and nature has placed her at the gates to be a sort of doorkeeper to the royal virtues within, which no one may approach who has not previously paid homage to hope. Therefore the lawgivers, and the laws in every state on earth, labour with great diligence to fill the souls of free men with good hopes ; but he who, without any recommendation and without being enjoined to be so, is nevertheless hopeful, has acquired this virtue by an unwritten, self-taught law, which nature has implanted in him.

That which is placed in the next rank after hope is repentance for errors committed, and improvement ; in reference to which principle Moses mentions next in order to Enos, the man who changed from a worse system of life to a better, who is called among the Hebrews Enoch, but as the Greeks would say, " gracious," of whom the following statement is made, " that Enoch pleased God, and was not found, because God transported him."† For transportation shows a change and

* Leviticus xix. 24.   † Genesis v. 24.

alteration : and such a change is for the better, because it takes place through the providence of God ; for every thing that is with God is in every case honourable and advantageous, since that which is destitute of any divine superintendence is useless and unprofitable.

And the expression, "he was not found," is very appropriately employed of him whose place was changed, either from the fact of his ancient blameable life being wiped out and effaced, and being no longer found, just as if it had never existed at all, or else because he whose place has been changed, and who is enrolled in a better class, is naturally difficult to be discovered. For wickedness is a very multiform and extensive thing, on which account it is known to many persons; but virtue is rare, so that it is not comprehended even by a few. And besides, the bad man runs about through the marketplace, and theatres, and courts of justice, and council halls, and assemblies, and every meeting and collection of men whatever, like one who lives with and for curiosity, letting loose his tongue in immoderate, and interminable, and indiscriminate conversation, confusing and disturbing every thing, mixing up what is true with what is false, what is unspeakable with what is public, private with public things, things profane with things sacred, what is ridiculous with what is excellent, from never having been instructed in what is the most excellent thing in season, namely silence. And pricking up his ears, because of the abundance of his leisure, and his superfluous curiosity, and love of interference, he is eager to make himself acquainted with the business of other people, whether good or bad, so as at once to envy those who are prosperous, and to rejoice over those who are not so ; for the bad man is by nature envious and a hater of all that is good, and a lover of all that is evil.

IV. But the good man, on the contrary, is a lover of that mode of life which is not troubled by business, and withdraws, and loves solitude, desiring to escape the notice of the many, not out of misanthropy, for he is a lover of mankind, if any one in the world is so, but because he eschews wickedness, which the chief multitude eagerly embraces, rejoicing at what it ought to mourn over, and grieving at what it is becoming rather to rejoice. On which account the good man shuts himself up, and remains for the most part at home, scarcely going over his threshold, or if he does go out, for the sake of avoiding the crowds who come to visit him, he generally goes out of the city, and makes his abode in some country place, living more pleasantly with such companions as are the most virtuous of all mankind, whose bodies, indeed, time has dissolved, but whose virtues the records which are left of them keep alive, in poems and in prose, histories by which the soul is naturally improved and led on to perfection.

It is on this account that the sacred historian has said that the man whose place was changed was not found, inasmuch as he is difficult to find and hard to seek out. Therefore, such a man emigrates from ignorance to instruction, and from folly to wisdom, and from cowardice to courage, and from impiety to piety ; and, again, from devotion to pleasure to temperance, and from vain-gloriousness to simplicity, qualities superior to all riches, and more valuable as a possession than any royal or imperial power. For if one may speak the plain truth, that wealth which is not blind, but which is clear-sighted, is the abundance of virtues, which we must at once conclude to be the genuine and legitimate predominance of good in comparison of all other bastard and falsely named powers, and to be the just and lawful superior of them all. But we must not be ignorant that repentance occupies the second place only, next after perfection, just as the change from sickness to convalescence is inferior to perfect uninterrupted health. Therefore, that which is continuous and perfect in virtues is very near divine power, but that condition which is improvement advancing in process of time is the peculiar blessing of a well-disposed soul, which does not continue in its childish pursuits, but by more vigorous thoughts and inclinations, such as really become a man, seeks a tranquil steadiness of soul, and which attains to it by its conception of what is good.

V. For which reason the sacred historian very naturally classes the lover of God and the lover of virtue next in order to him who repents ; and this man is in the language of the Hebrews called Noah, but in that of the Greeks, " rest," or " the just man," both being appellations very well suited to the wise man. That of " the just man " most evidently so, for nothing is better than justice, which is the chief among virtues, and which receives the highest honours like the most beautiful member of a company ; and the appellation " rest " is likewise appropriate, since the opposite quality to rest is unnatural agitation, the cause of confusions, and tumults, and seditions, and wars, which the wicked pursue; while those who pay due honour to excellence cultivate a tranquil, and quiet, and stable, and peaceful life.

And in strict consistency with himself, the lawgiver also calls the seventh day " rest, " which the Hebrews call " the sabbath; " not as some persons fancy, because after six days the multitude was restrained from its habitual employments, but because in real truth, the number seven is both in the world and in ourselves free from seditions and from wars, and is of all the numbers that which is the most averse to contention, and the greatest lover of peace. And a proof of what I have here asserted may be found in the powers which exist in us; for six of those powers, namely the five outward senses and uttered speech, stir up continued and ceaseless war, both by sea and land, some of them doing so from a desire for the objects of the outward senses, which if they cannot obtain they are grieved, and the last by divulging with unbridled mouth numbers of things which ought to be buried in silence. But the seventh power is that which proceeds from the dominant mind, which is more glorious than the other six powers, and which has by pre-eminent vigour obtained the mastery over them all, and when that retires, choosing solitude, and its own society, and living by itself, as one that has no need of any other, and that is all-sufficient for itself, being then emancipated from the cares and troubles that are found in the human race, embraces a calm and tranquil life.

VI. And the lawgiver magnifies the lover of virtue in such a way, that even when he is giving his genealogy, he does not trace him as he usually does other persons, by giving a catalogue of his grandfathers and great grandfathers, and ancestors who are numbered as men and women, but he gives a list of certain virtues; and almost asserts in express words that there is no other house, or kindred, or country whatever to a wise man, except the virtues and the actions in accordance with virtues.

"For these," says he, "are the generations of Noah; Noah was a just man, perfect in his generation, and one who pleased God."* But we must not be ignorant that when he says man

* Genesis vi. 9.

here, he does not mean merely to use the common expression for a rational mortal animal, but that he means to indicate in an eminent degree him who verifies the name, having driven away all the untameable and furious passions and brutal wickednesses of the soul; and as a proof of this, after the word man he adds as an epithet, "the just," saying, "a just man," as if no unjust person were a man at all, but to speak more properly a beast in the likeness of a man, and as if he alone were a man who is an admirer of justice; he also says that he was "perfect," intimating by this expression that he was possessed not of one virtue only but of all, and that being so possessed of them, he constantly exhibited every one of them according to his power and opportunities; and finally crowning him like a wrestler who has gained a glorious victory, he honours him moreover with a most noble proclamation, saying that "he pleased God," (and what can there be in nature that is more excellent than this panegyric?) which is the most visible proof of excellence; for if they who displease God are miserable, those who please him are by all means happy.

VII. It is not then without great correctness that after he has praised the man as being possessed of such great virtues he adds, "that he was perfect in his generation." Showing that he was not perfect absolutely, but that he was good in comparison with the others who lived at that time; for in a little time he will also speak of other wise men who were possessed of unconquerable and incomparable virtue, not merely if contrasted with the wicked, nor because they were better than the other men of their age, and as such were considered worthy of acceptance and pre-eminence, but because having received a well disposed nature, they preserved it without any error or change for the worse; not fleeing from evil habits, but never having once fallen into them, and being by deliberate purpose practisers of all virtuous actions and speeches, by which system they have adorned their life.

Those then are the most admirable of all men who have adopted free and noble inclinations, not in imitation of or by way of contrast to others, but from an inclination to genuine virtue and justice for its own sake; he also is to be admired who is superior to his own generation and his own age, and who is overcome by none of those things which the multitude follows; and he will be classed in the second rank, and nature

will give to such men the best of her prizes; and the second
prize is of itself a great thing; for what is not a great and
most desirable object which God offers to, and bestows upon
men? And the greatest proof of this is to be found in the
exceeding graces which this man attained to; for as that time
bore an abundant crop of injustice and impiety, and so every
country, and nation, and city, and house, and every separate
individual was full of wicked practices, all men of free will and
of deliberate purpose, as if in an arena, living with one another
for the first rank in iniquity, and strove with all possible zeal
and rivalry, every one seeking to surpass his neighbour in the
magnitude of his wickedness, and failing in nothing which
might render life blameable and accursed.

VIII. At whom God, being naturally indignant, and being
angry that that which appeared to be the most excellent of
animals, and which had been thought worthy of being reckoned
akin to himself by reason of his participation in reason, when
he ought to have practised virtue, devoted himself rather to
wickedness, and to every species of vice, appointed a fitting
punishment for them, and determined to destroy the whole
race at that time existing by a deluge; and not only those who
dwelt in the champaign country and in the lower districts,
but those also who lived in the most lofty mountains, for the
great deep,* being raised to a height which it had never
reached before, burst through its mouths with its whole collective impetuosity into the seas existing among us, and they
overflowed and inundated all the islands and continents; and
incessant floods of everlasting fountains, and of native rivers
and torrents combined together, mingled with one another,
and rising to a vast height, so as to surmount everything.
Nor indeed was the air tranquil, for a deep and unbroken
cloud overspread the whole heaven, and there were fearful
storms of wind, and roarings of thunder, and flashes of lightning, and rapid hurlings of thunderbolts, ceaseless storms of
rain being poured forth, so that one might have thought that
all the parts of the universe were hastening to dissolve themselves into the one element of the nature of water, until,
while the water from above kept pouring down, and that below
kept bursting up, the streams were raised to a height above

---

* Genesis vii. 11.

everything, so that they not only overwhelmed and hid from sight all the plains and all the level ground, but even the tops of the highest mountains, for every part of the earth was under water, so that it was wholly buried and carried away, and the world was mutilated of huge portions, and appeared in all its wholeness and integrity, fearful as it is to say or even to imagine such a thing, to be utterly crippled and destroyed.

And likewise the air, with the exception of that small portion which is about the moon, was wholly obscured, being overcast by the violence and impetuosity of the water which overran all the region belonging to it with irresistible might. Then were speedily destroyed all the crops and all the trees, for an unlimited quantity of water is as destructive to them as a scarcity, and innumerable flocks of animals, both tame and wild, perished at the same time; for it was natural when the most excellent race of all, that of man, had been destroyed, that none of the inferior races should be left, since they were only created to be slaves to his necessities, and to be in a manner subject to his authoritative commands as their master.

When such numbers then of such mighty evils had burst forth which that time poured out—for all the portions of the world, except the heaven itself, were moved in an unnatural manner—as if they were stricken with a terrible and deadly disease.

And one house alone, that of the aforesaid just and God-loving man who had received the two highest of all gifts, was preserved; one gift being, as I have said already, the not being destroyed with all the rest of mankind, the other that of becoming himself, at a subsequent period, the founder of a new generation of mankind; for God thought him worthy to be both the end of our race and the beginning of it, the end of those men who lived before the deluge, and the beginning of those who lived after the deluge.

IX. Such was he who was the most virtuous of all the men of his age, and such were the rewards which were allotted to him which the holy scriptures enumerate; and the arrangement and classification of the aforesaid three, whether you call them men or dispositions of the soul, is very symmetrical, for the perfect man is entire from the beginning; but he who has his place changed is but half entire, having appropriated the earlier period of his life to wickedness, and the subsequent time to virtue to which he afterwards came over, and with which at that subsequent time he lived. But he who hopes, as his very name shows, has still a defect, for though he is always wishing for what is good, he is not as yet able to attain to it, but he is like those who are on a voyage, who while they are eager to reach the harbour, are still kept at sea without being able to anchor in port.

X. I have now then explained the character of the first triad of those who desire virtue. There is also another more important company of which we must now proceed to speak, for the former resembles those branches of instruction which are allotted to the age of childhood, but this resembles rather the gymnastic exercises of athletic men, who are really preparing themselves for the sacred contests, who, despising all care of getting their body into proper condition, labour to bring about a healthy state of the soul, being desirous of that victory which is to be gained over the adverse passions.

The particulars then on which each individual differs from the other, though all are hastening to one and the same end, we will hereafter examine more minutely; but it is necessary not to pass over in silence what it seems desirable to premise concerning the whole three taken together.

It happens then that they are all three of one household and of one family, for the last of the three is the son of the middle one, and the grandson of the first; and they are all lovers of God, and beloved by God, loving the only God, and being loved in return by him who has chosen, as the holy scriptures tell us, by reason of the excess of their virtues in which they lived, to give them also a share of the same appellation as himself; for having added his own peculiar name to their names he has united them together, appropriating to himself an appellation composed of the three names: "For," says God, "this is my everlasting name: I am the God of Abraham, and the God of Isaac, and the God of Jacob,"* using there the relative term instead of the absolute one; and this is very natural, for God stands in no need of a name. But though he does not stand in any such need, nevertheless he bestows his own title on the human race that they may

* Exodus iii. 15.

have a refuge to which to betake themselves in supplications and prayers, and so may not be destitute of a good hope.

XI. This then is what appears to be said of these holy men; and it is indicative of a nature more remote from our knowledge than, and much superior to, that which exists in the objects of outward sense; for the sacred word appears thoroughly to investigate and to describe the different dispositions of the soul, being all of them good, the one aiming at what is good by means of instruction, the second by nature, the last by practice; for the first, who is named Abraham, is a symbol of that virtue which is derived from instruction; the intermediate Isaac is an emblem of natural virtue; the third, Jacob, of that virtue which is devoted to and derived from practice. But we must not be ignorant that each of these men was endowed with all these powers, but that each derived his name from that one which predominated in him and mastered the others; for neither is it possible for instruction to be made perfect without natural endowments and practice, nor is nature able to arrive at the goal without instruction and practice, nor is practice unless it be founded on natural gifts and sound instruction.

Very appropriately, therefore, has he represented, as united by relationship, these three, which in name indeed are men, but in reality, as I have said before, virtues, nature, instruction, and practice, which men also call by another name, and entitle them the three graces (χάριτες), either from the fact of God having bestowed (κεχαρίσθαι) on our race those three powers, in order to produce the perfection of life, or because they themselves have bestowed themselves on the rational soul as the most glorious of gifts, so that the eternal name, as set forth in the scriptures, may not be used in conjunction with three men, but rather with the aforesaid powers; for the nature of mankind is mortal, but that of the virtues is immortal; and it is more reasonable that the name of the everlasting God should be conjoined with what is immortal than with what is mortal, since what is immortal is akin to what is imperishable, but death is hostile to it.

XII. We must, however, not remain in ignorance that the sacred historian has represented the first man, him who was formed out of the earth as the father of all those who existed before the deluge; and him who, with his whole family, was

the only person left out of so universal a destruction, because of
his justice and his other excellencies and virtues, as the founder
of the new race of men which was to flourish hereafter.   And
that venerable, and estimable, and glorious triad is comprehended by the sacred scriptures under one class, and called,
" A royal priesthood, and a holy nation."*   And its name
shows its power ; for the nation is further called, in the language of the Hebrews, Israel, which name being interpreted
means, " seeing God."

But of sight, that which is exercised by means of the eyes
is the most excellent of all the outward senses, since by that
alone all the most beautiful of existing things are comprehended, the sun and the moon, and the whole heaven, and the
whole world ; but the sight of the soul which is exercised,
through the medium of its dominant part excels all the other
powers of the soul, as much as the powers of the soul excel all
other powers ; and this is prudence, which is the sight of the
mind.   But he to whose lot it falls, not only by means of his
knowledge, to comprehend all the other things which exist in
nature, but also to behold the Father and Creator of the
universe, has advanced to the very summit of happiness.   For
there is nothing above God ; and if any one, directing towards
him the eye of the soul, has reached up to him, let him then
pray for ability to remain and to stand firm before him ; for
the roads which lead upwards to him are laborious and slow,
but the descent down the declivity, being rather like a rapid
dragging down than a gradual descent, is swift and easy.   And
there are many things urged downwards, in which there is no
use whatever, when God having made the soul to depend on
his own powers, drags it up towards himself with a more
vigorous attraction.

XIII. Let thus much, then, be said generally about the
three persons, since it was absolutely necessary ; but we must
now proceed in regular order, to speak of those qualities in
which each separate individual surpasses the others, beginning
with him who is first mentioned.   Now he, being an admirer
of piety, the highest and greatest of all virtues, laboured
earnestly to follow God, and to be obedient to the injunctions
delivered by him, looking not only on those things as his commands which were signified to him by words and facts, but

* Exodus xix. 6.

those also which were indicated by more express signs through the medium of nature, and which the truest of the outward senses comprehends before the uncertain and untrustworthy hearing can do so; for if any one observes the arrangement which exists in nature, and the constitution according to which the world goes on, which is more excellent than any kind of reasoning, he learns, even though no one speaks to him, to study a course of life consistent with law and peace, looking to the example of good men. But the most manifest demonstrations of peace are those which the scriptures contain; and we must mention the first which also occurs the first in the order in which they are set down.

XIV. He being impressed by an oracle by which he was commanded to leave his country, and his kindred, and his father's house, and to emigrate like a man returning from a foreign land to his own country, and not like one who was about to set out from his own land to settle in a foreign district, hastened eagerly on, thinking to do with promptness what he was commanded to do was equivalent to perfecting the matter. And yet who else was it likely would be so undeviating and unchangeable as not to be won over by and as not to yield to the charms of one's relations and one's country? The love for which has in a manner—

"Grown with the growth and strengthened with the strength,"

of every individual, and even more, or at all events not less than the limbs united to the body have done.

And we have witnesses of this in the lawgivers who have enacted the second punishment next to death, namely, banishment, against those who are convicted of the most atrocious crimes: a punishment which indeed is not second to any, as it appears to me, if truth be the judge, but which is, in fact, much more grievous than death, since death is the end of all misfortunes, but banishment is not the end but the beginning of new calamities, inflicting instead of our death unaccompanied by pain ten thousand deaths with acute sensation.

Some men also, being engaged in traffic, do out of desire for gain sail over the sea, or being employed in some embassy, or being led by a desire to see the sights of foreign countries, or by a love for instruction, having various motives which attract them outwards and prevent their remaining where they are,

some being led by a love of gain, others by the idea of being
able to benefit their native city at its time of need in the most
necessary and important particulars, others seeking to arrive
at the knowledge of matters of which before they were ignorant,
a knowledge which brings, at the same time, both delight and
advantage to the soul.   For men who have never travelled are
to those who have, as blind men are to those who see clearly,
are nevertheless anxious to behold their father's threshold and
to salute it, and to embrace their acquaintances, and to enjoy
the most delightful and wished-for sight of their relations and
friends ; and very often, seeing the affairs, for the sake of
which they left their country, protracted, they have abandoned
them, being influenced by that most powerful feeling of longing
for a union with their kindred.

But this man with a very few companions, or perhaps I
might say by himself, as soon as he was commanded to do so,
left his home, and set out on an expedition to a foreign country
in his soul even before he started with his body, his regard for
mortal things being overpowered by his love for heavenly things.
Therefore giving no consideration to anything whatever, neither
to the men of his tribe, nor to those of his borough, nor to his
fellow disciples, nor to his companions, nor to those of his blood
as sprung from the same father or the same mother, nor to his
country, nor to his ancient habits, nor to the customs in which
he had been brought up, nor to his mode of life and his mates,
every one of which things has a seductive and almost irresistible attraction and power, he departed as speedily as possible,
yielding to a free and unrestrained impulse, and first of all
he quitted the land of the Chaldæans, a prosperous district,
and one which was greatly flourishing at that period, and went
into the land of Charran, and from that, after no very distant
interval, he departed to another place, which we will speak of
hereafter, when we have first discussed the country of Charran.

XV. The aforesaid emigrations, if one is to be guided by
the literal expressions of the scripture, were performed by a
wise man ; but if we look to the laws of allegory, by a soul
devoted to virtue and busied in the search after the true God.
For the Chaldæans were, above all nations, addicted to the
study of astronomy, and attributed all events to the motions
of the stars, by which they fancied that all the things in the
world were regulated, and accordingly they magnified the

visible essence by the powers which numbers and the analogies of numbers contain, taking no account of the invisible essence appreciable only by the intellect. But while they were busied in investigating the arrangement existing in them with reference to the periodical revolutions of the sun, and moon, and the other planets, and fixed stars, and the changes of the seasons of the year, and the sympathy of the heavenly bodies with the things of earth, they were led to imagine that the world itself was God, in their impious philosophy comparing the creature to the Creator.

The man who had been bred up in this doctrine, and who for a long time had studied the philosophy of the Chaldæans, as if suddenly awakening from a deep slumber and opening the eye of the soul, and beginning to perceive a pure ray of light instead of profound darkness, followed the light, and saw what he had never seen before, a certain governor and director of the world standing above it, and guiding his own work in a salutary manner, and exerting his care and power in behalf of all those parts of it which are worthy of divine superintendence.

In order, therefore, that he may the more firmly establish the sight which has thus been presented to him in his mind, the sacred word says to him, My good friend, great things are often made known by slight outlines, at which he who looks increases his imagination to an unlimited extent; therefore, having dismissed those who bend all their attention to the heavenly bodies, and discarding the Chaldæan science, rise up and depart for a short time from the greatest of cities, this world, to one which is smaller; for so you will be the better able to comprehend the nature of the Ruler of the universe.

It is for this reason that Abraham is said to have made his first migration from the country of the Chaldæans into the land of Charran.

XVI. But Charran, in the Greek language, means "holes," which is a figurative emblem of the regions of our outward senses; by means of which, as by holes, each of those senses is able to look out so as to comprehend the objects which belong to it. But, some one may say, what is the use of these holes, unless the invisible mind, like the exhibition of a puppet show, does from within prompt its own powers, which at one time losing and allowing to roam, and at another time holding back and restraining by force? He gives sometimes an harmonious motion, and sometimes perfect quiet to his puppets. And having this example at home, you will easily comprehend that being, the understanding of whom you are so anxious to arrive at ; unless, indeed, you fancy that the world is situated in you as the dominant part of you, which the whole common powers of the body obey, and which each of the outward senses follows ; but that the world, the most beautiful, and greatest, and most perfect of works, of which everything else is but a part, is destitute of any king to hold it together, and to regulate it, and govern it in accordance with justice.

And if it be invisible, wonder not at that, for neither can the mind which is in thee be perceived by the sight. Any one who considers this, deriving his proofs not from a distance but close at hand, both from himself and from the circumstances around him, will clearly see that the world is not the first God, but that it is the work of the first God and Father of all things, who, being himself invisible, displays every thing, showing the nature of all things both small and great. For he has not chosen to be beheld by the eyes of the body, perhaps because it was not consistent with holiness for what is mortal to touch what is everlasting, or perhaps because of the weakness of our sight ; for it would never have been able to stand the rays which are poured forth from the living God, since it cannot even look straight at the rays of the sun.

XVII. And the most visible proof of this migration in which the mind quitted astronomy and the doctrines of the Chaldæans, is this. For it is said in the scriptures that the very moment that the wise man quitted his abode, " God appeared unto Abraham,"* to whom, therefore, it is plain that he was not visible before, when he was adhering to the studies of the Chaldæans, and attending to the motions of the stars, not properly comprehending any nature whatever, which was well arranged and appreciable by the intellect only, apart from the world and the essence perceptible by the outward senses. But after he changed his abode and went into another country he learnt of necessity that the world was subject, and not independent ; not an absolute ruler, but governed by the great cause of all things who had created it, whom the mind then for the first time looked up and saw ; for previously a great mist was shed over it by the objects of the

* Genesis xii. 7.

external senses, which she, having dissipated by fervent and vivid doctrines, was scarcely able, as if in clear fine weather, to perceive him who had previously been concealed and invisible.

But he, by reason of his love for mankind, did not reject the soul which came to him, but went forward to meet it, and showed to it his own nature as far as it was possible that he who was looking at it could see it. For which reason it is said, not that the wise man saw God but that God appeared to the wise man; for it was impossible for any one to comprehend by his own unassisted power the true living God, unless he himself displayed and revealed himself to him.

XVIII. And there is evidence in support of what has here been said to be derived from the change and alteration of his name: for he was anciently called Abram, but afterwards he was named Abraham: the alteration of sound being only that which proceeds from one single letter, alpha, being doubled, but the alteration revealing in effect an important fact and doctrine; for the name Abram being interpreted means "sublime father;" but Abraham signifies, "the elect father of sound." The first name being expressive of the man who is called an astronomer, and one addicted to the contemplation of the sublime bodies in the sky, and who was versed in the doctrines of the Chaldæans, and who took care of them as a father might take care of his children. But the last name intimating the really wise man; for the latter name, by the word sound, intimates the uttered speech; and by the word father, the dominant mind. For the speech which is conceived within is naturally the father of that which is uttered, inasmuch as it is older than the latter, and as it also suggests what is to be said. And by the addition of the word elect his goodness is intimated.

For the evil disposition is a random and confused one, but that which is elect is good, having been selected from all others by reason of its excellence. Therefore, to him who is addicted to the contemplation of the sublime bodies of the sky there appears to be nothing whatever greater than the world; and therefore he refers the causes of all things that exist to the world. But the wise man, beholding with more accurate eyes that more perfect being that rules and governs all things, and is appreciable only by the intellect, to whom all things are subservient as to a master, and by whom every thing is

directed, very often reproaches himself for his former way of
life, and if he had lived the existence of a blind man, leaning
upon objects perceptible by the outward senses, on things by
their very nature worthless and unstable.

The second migration is again undertaken by the virtuous
man under the influence of a sacred oracle, but this is no
longer one from one city to another, but it is to a desolate
country, in which he wandered about for a long time without
being discontented at his wandering and at his unsettled condition, which necessarily arose from it.   And yet, what other man
would not have been grieved, not only at departing from his own
country but also at being driven away from every city into an
inaccessible and impassable district? And what other man would
not have turned back and returned to his former home, paying
but little attention to his former hopes, but desiring to escape
from his present perplexity, thinking it folly for the sake of
uncertain advantages to undergo admitted evils?   But this
man alone appears to have behaved in the contrary manner,
thinking that life which was remote from the fellowship of
many companions the most pleasant of all.

And this is naturally the case; for those who seek and
desire to find God, love that solitude which is dear to him,
labouring for this as their dearest and primary object, to
become like his blessed and happy nature.   Therefore, having
now given both explanations, the literal one as concerning the
man, and the allegorical one relating to the soul, we have
shown that both the man and the mind are deserving of love;
inasmuch as the one is obedient to the sacred oracles, and
because of their influence submits to be torn away from things
with which it is hard to part; and the mind deserves to be
loved because it has not submitted to be for ever deceived and
to abide permanently with the essences perceptible by the outward senses, thinking the visible world the greatest and first
of gods, but soaring upwards with its reason it has beheld
another nature better than that which is visible, that, namely,
which is appreciable only by the intellect; and also that being
who is at the same time the Creator and ruler of both.

XIX. These, then, are the first principles of the man who
loves God, and they are followed by actions which do not
deserve to be lightly esteemed.   But the greatness of them is
not evident to every one, but only to those who have tasted of

virtue, and who are wont to look with ridicule upon the objects which are admired by the multitude, by reason of the greatness of the good things of the soul. Therefore, God, having approved of his conduct which I have mentioned, presently rewarded the virtuous man with a great gift, inasmuch as he preserved sound and free from all pollution his marriage, which was in danger of being plotted against by a powerful and incontinent man.

And the cause of this man's design upon it arose from this beginning; there having been a barrenness and scarcity of crops for a long time, owing to a long and immoderate period of rain which prevailed at one time, and to a great drought and heat which ensued afterwards. The cities of Syria being oppressed by a long continuance of famine, became destitute of inhabitants, all of them being dispersed in different directions for the purpose of seeking food and providing themselves with necessaries. Therefore, Abraham, hearing that there was unlimited abundance and plenty in Egypt, since the river there irrigated the fields with its inundations at the proper season, and since the winds by their salutary temperature brought up and nourished rich and heavy crops of corn, rose up with all his household to quit Syria and to go thither. And he had a wife of a most excellent disposition, who was also the most beautiful of all the women of her time. The Egyptian magistrates, seeing her and admiring her exquisite form, for nothing ever escapes the notice of men in authority, gave information to the king. And the king, sending for the woman and beholding her extraordinary beauty, gave but little heed to the dictates of modesty or to the laws which had been established with respect to the honour due to strangers, but yielding to his incontinent desires, conceived the intention in name, indeed, to marry her in lawful wedlock, but, in fact to seduce and defile her. But she, being destitute of all succour, as being in a foreign land, before an incontinent and cruel-minded ruler (for her husband had no power to protect her, fearing the danger which impended over him from princes mightier than he), at last, with him, took refuge in the only alliance remaining to her, the protection of God.

And the merciful and gracious God, who takes compassion on the stranger, and who fights on behalf of those who are unjustly oppressed, inflicted in a moment painful sufferings and

terrible chastisements on the king, filling his body and soul
with all kinds of miseries difficult to be escaped or remedied,
so that all his inclinations tending to pleasure were cut short,
and, on the contrary, he was occupied with nothing but
cares, seeking an alleviation from his endless and intolerable
torments by which he was harassed and tortured day and
night ; and his whole household also received their share of
his punishment, because none of them had felt any indignation at his lawless conduct, but had all consented to it, and
had all but co-operated actively in his iniquity.

In this manner the chastity of the woman was preserved,
and God condescended to display the excellence and piety
of her husband, giving him the noblest reward, namely, his
marriage free from all injury, and even from all insult, so as
no longer to be in danger of being violated; a marriage
which however was not intended to produce any limited
number of sons and daughters, but an entire nation—the
most God-loving of all nations— and one which appears to
me to have received the offices of priesthood and prophecy
on behalf of the whole human race.

XX. I have heard men versed in natural philosophy in-
terpreting this passage in an allegorical manner with no
inconsiderable ingenuity and propriety ; and their idea is,
that the man here is a symbolical expression for the virtuous
mind, conjecturing from the interpretation of his name that
what is intended to be indicated is the virtuous disposition
existing in the soul; and that by his wife is meant virtue,
for the name of his wife is, in the Chaldæan language,
Sarah, but in Greek " princess," because there is nothing
more royal or more worthy of pre-eminence than virtue.
And the marriage in which pleasure unites people comprehends the connection of the bodies, but that which is
brought about by wisdom is the union of reasonings which
desire purification, and of the perfect virtues; and the two
kinds of marriage here described are extremely opposite to
one another; for in the marriage of the bodies it is the
male partner which sows the seed and the female which
receives it, but in the union which takes place with regard
to the soul it is quite the contrary, and it is virtue which
appears to be there in the place of the woman, which sows
good counsels, and virtuous speeches, and expositions of

doctrines profitable to life; but the reason which is considered to be classed in the light of the man receives the sacred and divine seed, unless, indeed, there is any error in the names usually given; for certainly, in the grammatical view of the words, the word reason is masculine, and the word virtue has a feminine character.

But if any one, discarding the considerations of the names which tend to throw darkness over the subject, chooses to look at the plain facts without any disguise, he will know that virtue is masculine by nature, inasmuch as it puts things in motion, and arranges them, and suggests good conceptions of noble actions and speeches; but reason is feminine, inasmuch as it is put in motion by another, and is instructed and benefited, and, in short, is altogether the patient, as its passive state is its only safety.

XXI. All men, therefore, even the most vile, in word honour and admire virtue as far as appearance goes; but it is the virtuous alone who obey its injunctions; on which account the king of Egypt, who is a figurative representation of the mind devoted to the body, as if he were acting in a theatre, assumes the character of a pretended participation in temperance though being an intemperate man, and in continence though being an incontinent man, and in justice though an unjust man, and he invites justice to himself, being eager to obtain a good report from the multitude; and the governor of the universe seeing this, for God alone has power to look into the soul, hates him and rejects him, and by the most cruel tests and powers convicts him of an utterly false disposition.

But by what instruments are these tests carried out? Surely altogether by the parts of virtue which, whenever they enter, inflict great pain and severe wounds; for a torture is a deficiency of supply to that which is insatiable, and the torture of greediness is temperance; moreover, the man who is fond of glory is tortured while simplicity and humility are in the ascendent, and so is the unjust man when justice is extolled; for it is impossible for two hostile natures to inhabit one soul, namely, for wickedness and virtue, for which reason, when they do come together, endless and irreconcilable seditions and wars are kindled between them; and yet this is the case though virtue is of a most peaceful disposition, and, as they say, is anxious whenever it is about to come to a contest of strength to make trial of its own powers first, so as only to contend if it has a prospect of being able to gain the victory; but if it finds its power unequal to the conflict, then it will never dare to descend into the arena at all, for it is not disgraceful to wickedness to be defeated, inasmuch as ingloriousness is akin to it; but it would be a shameful thing for virtue, to which glory is the most appropriate and the most peculiarly belonging of all things, on which account it is natural for virtue either to secure the victory, or else to keep itself un-conquered.

XXII. It has been said then that the disposition of the Egyptians is inhospitable and intemperate; and the human-ity of him who has been exposed to their conduct deserves admiration, for he* in the middle of the day beholding as it were three men travelling (and he did not perceive that they were in reality of a more divine nature), ran up and entreated them with great perseverance not to pass by his tent, but as was becoming to go in and receive the rites of hospitality: and they knowing the truth of the man not so much by what he said, as by his mind which they could look into, assented to his request without hesitation; and being filled as to his soul with joy, he took every possible pains to make their extemporaneous reception worthy of them; and he said to his wife, "Hasten now, and make ready quickly three measures of fine meal," and he himself went forth among the herds of oxen, and brought forth a tender and well-fed heifer, and gave it to his servant; and he having slain it, dressed it with all speed.

For no one in the house of a wise man is ever slow to perform the duties of hospitality, but both women and men, and slaves and freemen, are most eager in the performance of all those duties towards strangers; therefore, after having feasted, and being delighted, not so much with what was set before them, as with the good will of their entertainer, and with his excessive and unbounded zeal to please them, they bestow on him a reward beyond his expectation, the birth of a legitimate son in a short time, making him a promise which is to be confirmed to him by one the most

* Genesis xviii. 1, &c.

excellent of the three; for it would have been inconsistent with philosophy for them all to speak together at the same moment, but it was desirous for all the rest to assent while one spoke.

Nevertheless he did not completely believe them even when they made him this promise, by reason of the incredible nature of the thing promised; for both he and his wife, through extreme old age, were so old as utterly to have abandoned all hope of offspring; therefore the scriptures record that Abraham's wife, when she first heard what they were saying, laughed; and when they said afterwards, "Is anything impossible to God?" they were so ashamed that they denied that they had laughed; for Abraham knew that everything was possible to God, having almost learnt this doctrine as one may say from his cradle; then for the first time he appears to me to have begun to entertain a different opinion of his guests from that which he conceived at first, and to have imagined that they were either some of the prophets or of the angels who had changed their spiritual and soul-like essence, and assumed the appearance of men.

XXIII. We have now then described the hospitable temper of the man, which was as it were a sort of addition to set off his greater virtue; but his virtue was piety towards God, concerning which we have spoken before, the most evident instance of which is to be found in his conduct now recorded towards the strangers; but if any persons have fancied that house happy and blessed in which it has happened that wise men have stopped and abode, they should consider that they would not have done so, and would not even have looked into it at all, if they had seen any incurable disease in the souls of those who were therein, but I know not what excess of happiness and blessedness, I should say, existed in that house in which angels condescended to tarry and to receive the rites of hospitality from men, angels, those sacred and divine natures, the ministers and lieutenants of the mighty God, by means of whom, as of ambassadors, he announces whatever predictions he condescends to intimate to our race.

For how could they ever have endured to enter a human habitation at all, unless they had been certain that all the inhabitants within, like the well-managed and orderly crew of a ship, obeyed one signal only, namely, that of their master, as the sailors obey the command of the captain? And how would they ever have condescended to assume the appearance of guests and men feasted hospitably, if they had not thought that their entertainer was akin to them, and a fellow servant with them, bound to the service of the same master as themselves? We must think indeed that at their entrance all the parts of the house became improved and advanced in goodness, being breathed upon with a certain breeze of most perfect virtue.

And the entertainment was such as it was fitting that it should be, the persons who were being feasted displaying at the banquet their own simplicity towards their entertainer, and addressing him in a guileless manner, and all of them holding conversation suited to the occasion. And it is a thing that deserves to be looked on as a prodigy, that though they did not drink they seemed to drink, and that though they did not eat they presented the appearance of persons eating. But this was all natural and consistent with what was going on. And the most miraculous circumstance of all was, that these beings who were incorporeal presented the appearance of a body in human form by reason of their favour to the virtuous man, for otherwise what need was there of all these miracles except for the purpose of giving the wise man the evidence of his external senses by means of a more distinct sight, because his character had not escaped the knowledge of the Father of the universe.

XXIV. This then is sufficient to say by way of a literal explanation of this account: we must now speak of that which may be given if the story be looked at as figurative and symbolical.

The things which are expressed by the voice are the signs of those things which are conceived in the mind alone; when, therefore, the soul is shone upon by God as if at noonday, and when it is wholly and entirely filled with that light which is appreciable only by the intellect, and by being wholly surrounded with its brilliancy is free from all shade or darkness, it then perceives a threefold image of one subject, one image of the living God, and others of the other two, as if they were shadows irradiated by it. And some such thing as this happens to those who dwell in that light which is perceptible by the outward senses, for whether people are standing still or in motion, there is often a double shadow falling from them.

Let not any one then fancy that the word shadow is applied to God with perfect propriety. It is merely a cata-chrestical abuse of the name, by way of bringing before our eyes a more vivid representation of the matter intended to be intimated. Since this is not the actual truth, but in order that one may when speaking keep as close to the truth as possible, the one in the middle is the Father of the universe, who in the sacred scriptures is called by his proper name, I am that I am; and the beings on each side are those most ancient powers which are always close to the living God, one of which is called his creative power, and the other his royal power.

And the creative power is God, for it is by this that he made and arranged the universe; and the royal power is the Lord, for it is fitting that the Creator should lord it over and govern the creature. Therefore the middle person of the three, being attended by each of his powers as by body-guards, presents to the mind, which is endowed with the faculty of sight, a vision at one time of one being, and at another time of three; of one when the soul being completely purified, and having surmounted not only the multitudes of numbers, but also the number two, which is the neighbour of the unit, hastens onward to that idea which is devoid of all mixture, free from all combination, and by itself in need of nothing else whatever; and of three, when, not being as yet made perfect as to the important virtues, it is still seeking for initiation in those of less consequence, and is not able to attain to a comprehension of the living God by its own unassisted faculties without the aid of something else, but can only do so by judging of his deeds, whether as creator or as governor. This then, as they say, is the second best thing; and it no less partakes in the opinion which is dear to and devoted to God. But the first-mentioned disposition has no such share, but is itself the very God-loving and God-beloved opinion itself,

or rather it is truth which is older than opinion, and more
valuable than any seeming.

But we must now explain what is intimated by this
statement in a more perspicuous manner.

XXV. There are three different classes of human dispositions, each of which has received as its portion one of the
aforesaid visions. The best of them has received that vision
which is in the centre, the sight of the truly living God.
The one which is next best has received that which is on
the right hand, the sight of the beneficent power which has
the name of God. And the third has the sight of that
which is on the left hand, the governing power, which is
called lord. Therefore, the best dispositions cultivate that
being who exists of himself, without the aid of any one
else, being themselves attracted by nothing else, by reason
of all their entire attention being directed to the honour of
that one being. But of the other dispositions, some derive
their existence and owe their being recognized by the father
to his beneficent power; and others, again, owe it to his
governing power. My meaning in this statement is this:—

Men when they perceive that, under the pretext of friendship, some persons come to them, being in reality only
desirous to get what they can from them, look upon them
with suspicion, and turn away from them, fearing their
insincere, and flattering, and caressing behaviour, as very
pernicious. But God, inasmuch as he is not liable to any
injury, gladly invites all men who choose, in any way whatever to honour him, to come unto him, not choosing altogether to reject any person whatever; and, in truth, he
almost says in express words to those who have ears in the
soul, "The most valuable prizes shall be offered to those who
worship me for my own sake: the second best to those
who hope by their own efforts to be able to attain to good,
or to find a means of escape from punishments. For even
if the service of this latter class is mercenary and not
wholly incorrupt, still it nevertheless revolves within the
divine circumference, and does not stray beyond it. But
the rewards which shall be laid up for those who honour
me for my own sake are rewards of affection; while those
which are given to those who do so with a view to their

own advantage are not given through affection, but because they are not looked upon as aliens. For I receive him who wishes to be a partaker of my beneficent power to a participation in my good things, and him who out of fear seeks to propitiate my governing and despotic power, I receive so far as to avert punishment from him. For I am not unaware that, in addition to these men not becoming worse, they will become better, by gradually arriving at a sincere and pure piety by their constant perseverance in serving me. For even if the original dispositions, under the influence of which they originally endeavoured to please me, differ widely, still they must not be blamed, because they have in consequence only one aim and object, that of serving me."

But that what is seen is in reality a threefold appearance of one subject is plain, not only from the contemplation of the allegory, but also from that of the express words in which the allegory is couched. For when the wise man entreats those persons who are in the guise of three travellers to come and lodge in his house, he speaks to them not as three persons, but as one, and says, " My lord, if I have found favour with thee, do not thou pass by thy servant."* For the expressions, " my lord," and " with thee," and " do not thou pass by," and others of the same kind, are all such as are naturally addressed to a single individual, but not to many. And when those persons, having been entertained in his house, address their entertainer in an affectionate manner, it is again one of them who promises that he by himself will be present, and will bestow on him the seed of a child of his own, speaking in the following words : " I will return again and visit thee again, according to the time of life, and Sarah thy wife shall have a son."†

XXVI. And what is signified by this is indicated in a most evident and careful manner by the events which ensued. The country of the Sodomites was a district of the land of Canaan, which the Syrians afterwards called Palestine, a country full of innumerable iniquities, and especially of gluttony and debauchery, and all the great and numerous pleasures of other kinds which have been built up by men as a fortress, on which account it had been already condemned by the Judge of the whole world. And

* Genesis xviii. 3. † Genesis xviii. 10.

the cause of its excessive and immoderate intemperance was
the unlimited abundance of supplies of all kinds which its
inhabitants enjoyed.   For the land was one with a deep
soil, and well watered, and as such produced abundant crops
of every kind of fruit every year.   And he was a wise man
and spoke truly who said—

> "The greatest cause of all iniquity
> Is found in overmuch prosperity."

As men, being unable to bear discreetly a satiety of these
things, get restive like cattle, and become stiff-necked, and
discard the laws of nature, pursuing a great and intemperate indulgence of gluttony, and drinking, and unlawful
connections; for not only did they go mad after women,
and defile the marriage bed of others, but also those who
were men lusted after one another, doing unseemly things,
and not regarding or respecting their common nature, and
though eager for children, they were convicted by having
only an abortive offspring; but the conviction produced no
advantage, since they were overcome by violent desire; and
so, by degrees, the men became accustomed to be treated
like women, and in this way engendered among themselves
the disease of females, an intolerable evil; for they not only,
as to effeminacy and delicacy, became like women in their
persons, but they made also their souls most ignoble, cor-
rupting in this way the whole race of man, as far as
depended on them.   At all events, if the Greeks and barbarians were to have agreed together, and to have adopted the
commerce of the citizens of this city, their cities one after
another would have become desolate, as if they had been
emptied by a pestilence.

XXVII. But God, having taken pity on mankind, as
being a Saviour and full of love for mankind, increased, as
far as possible, the natural desire of men and women for a
connexion together, for the sake of producing children, and
detesting the unnatural and unlawful commerce of the
people of Sodom, he extinguished it, and destroyed those
who were inclined to these things, and that not by any ordinary chastisement, but he inflicted on them an astonish-
ing novelty, and unheard of rarity of vengeance; for, on a
sudden, he commanded the sky to become overclouded and

to pour forth a mighty shower, not of rain but of fire; and as the flame poured down, with a resistless and unceasing violence, the fields were burnt up, and the meadows, and all the dense groves, and the thick marshes, and the impenetrable thickets; the plain too was consumed, and all the crop of wheat, and of everything else that was sown; and all the trees of the mountain district were burnt up, the trunks and the very roots being consumed.

And the folds for the cattle, and the houses of the men, and the walls, and all that was in any building, whether of private or public property, were all burnt. And in one day these populous cities became the tomb of their inhabitants, and the vast edifices of stone and timber became thin dust and ashes. And when the flames had consumed everything that was visible and that existed on the face of the earth, they proceeded to burn even the earth itself, penetrating into its lowest recesses, and destroying all the vivifying powers which existed within it so as to produce a complete and everlasting barrenness, so that it should never again be able to bear fruit, or to put forth any verdure; and to this very day it is scorched up. For the fire of the lightning is what is most difficult to extinguish, and creeps on pervading everything, and smouldering.

And a most evident proof of this is to be found in what is seen to this day: for the smoke which is still emitted, and the sulphur which men dig up there, are a proof of the calamity which befell that country; while a most conspicuous proof of the ancient fertility of the land is left in one city, and in the land around it. For the city is very populous, and the land is fertile in grass and in corn, and in every kind of fruit, as a constant evidence of the punishment which was inflicted by the divine will on the rest of the country.

XXVIII. But I have not gone through all these particulars for the sake of showing the magnitude of that vast and novel calamity, but because I desired to prove that of the three beings who appeared to the wise Abraham in the guise of men, the scriptures only represent two as having come to the country which was subsequently destroyed for the purpose of destroying its inhabitants, since the third did not think fit to come for that purpose. Inasmuch as he, according to my conception, was the true and living God, who thought it fitting that he being present should bestow good gifts by his own power, but that he should effect the opposite objects by the agency and service of his subordinate powers, so that he might be looked upon as the cause of good only, and of no evil whatever antecedently.

And kings too appear to me to imitate the divine nature in this particular, and to act in the same way, giving their favours in person, but inflicting their chastisements by the agency of others. But since, of the two powers of God, one is a beneficent power and the other a chastising one, each of them, as is natural, is manifested to the country of the people of Sodom. Because of the five finest cities in it four were about to be destroyed by fire, and one was destined to be left unhurt and safe from every evil. For it was necessary that the calamities should be inflicted by the chastising power, and that the one which was to be saved should be saved by the beneficent power. But since the portion which was saved was not endowed with entire and complete virtues, but was blessed with kindness by the power of the living God, it was deliberately accounted unworthy to have a sight of his presence afforded to it.

XXIX. This, then, is the open explanation which is to be given of this account, and which is to be addressed to the multitude. But there is another esoteric explanation to be reserved for the few who choose for the subjects of their investigation the dispositions of the soul, and not the forms of bodies; and this shall now be mentioned.

The five cities of the land of Sodom are a figurative representation of the five outward senses which exist in us, the organs of the pleasures, by the instrumentality of which all the pleasures whether great or small are brought to perfection; for we are pleased either when we behold the varieties of colours and forms, both in things inanimate and in those endowed with vitality, or when we hear melodious sounds, or again, we are delighted by the exercise of the faculty of taste in the things which relate to eating and drinking, or by that of the sense of smell in fragrant flavours and vapours, or in accordance with our faculty of touch when conversant with soft, or hot, or smooth things.

Now of these five outward senses there are three which have

the greatest resemblance to the brute beasts and to slaves, namely the senses of taste, smell, and touch: as it is with reference to these that those species of beasts and cattle which are the most greedy and the most strongly inclined to sexual connections are the most vehemently excited. For all day and all night they are either glutting themselves insatiably with food, or else in a state of eagerness for sexual connection. But there are two of these outward senses which have something philosophical and pre-eminent in them, namely, sight and hearing. But the ears are in some degree more slow and more effeminate than the eyes, since the latter go with promptness and courage to what is to be seen, and do not wait until the objects themselves are in motion, but go forward to meet them, and desire to move themselves so as to face them.

But the sense of hearing, inasmuch as that is slow and more effeminate, may be classed in the second rank, and the sense of seeing may be allowed an especial pre-eminence and privilege: for God has made this sense a sort of queen of the rest, placing it above them all, and stationing it as it were on a citadel, has made it of all the senses in the closest connection with the soul; and any one may conjecture this from the common changes which take place in its essential organs; for when grief exists in the soul of man, the eyes are full of concern and melancholy; and on the other hand, when joy is in our heart the eyes smile and rejoice; and when fear gets the upper hand they are full of turbulent and disorderly confusion, and are subject to all kinds of irregular motions, and quiverings, and distortions.

Again, if anger occupies us, the sight becomes more fierce and bloodshot; and when we are considering or deliberating, the eyes are tranquil and motionless, and almost as intent as the mind itself; just as at moments of the relaxation and indifference of the mind, the eyes also are relaxed and indifferent; when a friend approaches the feeling of goodwill towards him is proclaimed by a calm and serene look; on the other hand, if we meet with an enemy, the eyes give an early indication of the displeasure of the soul; when our mind is inspired by boldness, our eyes bound forward and are ready to start from our heads; when we are oppressed with feelings of shame or modesty, they are gentle and repressed.

And, in short, we may say that the sight has been created to be an exact image of the soul, which is thus beautifully represented by it through the perfection of the Creator's skill, the eyes showing a visible representation of it, as in a mirror, since the soul has no visible nature in itself; but it is not in this particular alone that the beauty of the eyes exceeds the rest of the outward senses, but also because the use of the other senses is interrupted during our waking moments; for we must not include in our statement the inactivity which results from sleep; for they are at rest whenever there is not some external object to put them in motion; but the energies of the eyes when they are open are continuous and uninterrupted, as the eyes are never satiated or wearied, but continue to operate in accordance with the connection which they have with the soul; and the soul itself is everlastingly awake, and is in perpetual motion both night and day; but to the eyes, as being to a great degree partakers of the fleshly nature, a self-sufficient gift was given, to be able to continue exercising their appropriate energies during one half of the entire period of life.

XXX. But we must now proceed to speak of that which is the most necessary part of all, the advantage which we derive from the eyes. For it is to sight alone of the external senses that God has caused light to arise, which is both the most beautiful of all existing things, and is, moreover, the first thing which is pronounced in the sacred scriptures to be good. Now the nature of light is twofold: for there is one light which proceeds from the fire which we use, a perishable light proceeding from a perishable material, and one which admits of being extinguished. But the other kind is inextinguishable and imperishable, descending to us from above from heaven, as if every one of the stars was pouring down its beams upon us from an everlasting spring. And the sense of sight associates with each of these kinds of light, and through the medium of both of them does it approach the objects of sight so as to arrive at a most accurate comprehension of them. Why now need we attempt to panegyrize the eyes further by a speech, when God has engraved their true praises on pillars erected in heaven, namely, the stars? For for what purpose were the rays of the sun, and the beams of the moon, and the light of all the other planets and fixed stars called into existence, except as fields for the energies of the eyes in their service of seeing? On which account men, using the most excellent of all gifts, contemplate the things which exist in the world, the earth, the plants, the animals, the fruits of the earth, the seas, the effusion of waters springing from the earth and gushing forth in torrents and floods, and the varieties of fountains, some of which give forth cold and others hot water, and the natures of all things that exist in the air; and all the different species, of which we thus arrive at the knowlege, are innumerable and indescribable, and cannot be comprised in speech. And above all these things, the eyes can behold the heaven, which is truly a world created in another world, and it can also survey the beauties and divine images existing in heaven. Which now of the other external senses can boast that it has arrived at such a pitch of power as this?

XXXI. But now, dismissing the consideration of those of the outward senses which are in the stables, as it were, fattening up an animal which is born with us, namely, appetite, let us investigate the nature of that sense which receives speech, namely, hearing; the continued and vigorous, and most perfect course of which exists in the atmosphere which surrounds the earth, when the violence of the winds and the noise of thunder sound with a great dragging noise and terrible crash. But the eyes in a single moment can reach from earth to heaven, and taking in the extremest boundaries of the universe, reaching at the same moment to the east and to the west, and to the north and to the south, so as to survey them all at once, drag the mind towards what is visible. And the mind, at once receiving a similar impression, does not continue quiet, but being in perpetual motion, and never slumbering, receiving from the sight the power of observing the objects appreciable by the intellect, comes to consider whether these things which are brought visibly before it are uncreated, or whether they have derived their origin from creation; also, whether they are bounded or infinite. Again, whether there are many worlds or only

one; also, whether there are five elements of the whole
universe, or whether heaven and the heavenly bodies have a
peculiar and separate nature of their own, having received
a more divine conformation, differing from that of the rest
of the world.

Again, by these means it considers if the world has been
created, by whom it has been created, and who the creator
is as to his essence or quality, and with what design he
made it, and what he is doing now, and what his mode of
existence or cause of life is; and all other such questions as
the excellently-endowed mind when cohabiting with wisdom
is accustomed to examine.

These, and similar subjects, belong to philosophers, from
which it is plain that wisdom and philosophy have not derived
their origin from anything else that exists in us except from
that queen of the outward senses, the sight, which God saved
alone of the region of the body when he destroyed the other
four, because these last were slaves to the flesh and to the
passions of the flesh; but the sight alone was able to raise
its head and to look up, and to find other sources of delight
far superior to those proceeding from the bodily pleasures,
those, namely, that are derived from the contemplation of
the world and the things in it. Therefore it was appropriate for one of the five outward senses, namely, the sight,
like one city in the Pentapolis, to receive an especial reward
and honour, and to remain while the others were destroyed,
because it is not only conversant with mortal objects as
they are, but is able also to forsake such, and to depart to
the imperishable natures, and to rejoice in the sight of them.

On which account the holy scriptures very beautifully
represent it as " a little city, and yet not a little one," *
describing the power of sight under this figure. For it is
said to be little, inasmuch as it is but a small portion of the
faculties which exist in us; and yet great, inasmuch as it
desires great things, being eager to behold the entire heaven
and the whole world.

XXXII. We have now, then, given a full explanation
concerning the vision which appeared to Abraham, and concerning his celebrated and all-glorious hospitality, in which
the entertainer, who appeared to himself to be entertaining

* Genesis xix. 20.

others, was himself entertained; expounding every part of the passage with as much accuracy as we were able. But we must not pass over in silence the most important action of all, which is worthy of being listened to. For I was nearly saying that it is of more importance than all the actions of piety and religion put together. So we must say what seems to be seasonable concerning it.

A legitimate son is borne to the wise man by his wedded wife, a beloved and only son, very beautiful in his person, and very excellent in his disposition. For he was already beginning to display the more perfect exercises of his age, so that his father felt a most strong and vehement affection for him, not only from the impulse of natural regard, but also from the influence of deliberate opinion, from being, as it were, a judge of his character. To him, then, being conscious of such a disposition, an oracular command suddenly comes, which was never expected, ordering him to sacrifice this son on a certain very lofty hill, distant three days' journey from the city. And he, although attached to his child by an indescribable fondness, neither changed colour, nor wavered in his soul, but remained firm in an unyielding and unalterable purpose, as he was at first. And being wholly influenced by love towards God, he forcibly repressed all the names and charms of the natural relationship: and without mentioning the oracular command to any one of his household out of all his numerous body of servants, he took with him the two eldest, who were most thoroughly attached to their master, as if he were bent upon the celebration of some ordinary divine rite, and went forth with his son, making four in all.

And when, looking as it were from a watch-tower, he saw the appointed place afar off, he bade his servants remain there, and he gave his son the fire and the wood to carry, thinking it proper for the victim himself to be burdened with the materials for the sacrifice, a very light burden, for nothing is less troublesome than piety. And as they proceeded onwards with equal speed, not marching more rapidly with their bodies than with their minds along that short road of which holiness is the end, they at last arrive at the appointed place. And the father collected stones wherewith to build the altar; and when his son saw everything else prepared for the celebration of the sacrifice, but no animal, he looked to his father and said, "My father, behold the fire and the wood, but where is the victim for the burnt sacrifice?" * Therefore, any other father, knowing what he was about to do, and being depressed in his soul, would have been thrown into confusion by his son's words, and being filled with tears, would, out of his excessive affliction, by his silence have betrayed what was about to be done; but Abraham, betraying no alteration of voice, or countenance, or intention, looking at his son with steady eye, answered his question with a determination more steady still, "My child," said he, "God will provide himself a victim for the burnt offering," although we are in a vast desert where perhaps you despair of such a thing being found; but all things are possible to God, even all such things as are impossible and unintelligible to men. And even while saying this, he seizes his son with all rapidity, and places him on the altar, and having taken his knife in his right hand, he raised it over him as if to slay him; but God the Saviour stopped the deed in the middle, interrupting him by a voice from heaven, by which he ordered him to stay his hand, and not to touch the child: calling the father by name twice, so as to turn him and divert him from his purpose, and forbid him to complete the sacrifice.

XXXIII. And so Isaac is saved, God supplying a gift instead of him, and honouring him who was willing to make the offering in return for the piety which he had exhibited. But the action of the father, even though it was not ultimately given effect to, is nevertheless recorded and engraved as a complete and perfect sacrifice, not only in the sacred scriptures, but also in the minds of those who read them. But to those who are fond of reviling and disparaging everything, and who are by their invariable habits accustomed to prefer blaming to praising the action which Abraham was enjoined to perform, it will not appear a great and admirable deed, as we imagine it to have been. For such persons say that many other men, who have been very affectionate to their relations and very fond of their children, have given up their sons; some in order that they might be sacrificed for their country to deliver it either from war, or from drought,

* Genesis xxii. 7.

or from much rain, or from disease and pestilence; and others to satisfy the demands of some habitual religious observances, even though there may be no real piety in them.

At all events they say that some of the most celebrated men of the Greeks, not merely private individuals but kings also, caring but little for the children whom they have begotten, have, by means of their destruction secured safety to mighty and numerous forces and armies, arrayed together in an allied body, and have voluntarily slain them as if they had been enemies. And also that barbarous nations have for many ages practised the sacrifice of their children as if it were a holy work and one looked upon with favour by God, whose wickedness is mentioned by the holy Moses. For he, blaming them for this pollution, says, that "They burn their sons and their daughters to their gods."* And they say that to this very day the Gymnosophists among the Indians, when that long or incurable disease, old age, begins to attack them, before it has got a firm hold of them, and while they might still last for many years, kindle a fire and burn themselves. And, moreover, when their husbands are already dead, they say that their wives rush cheerfully to the same funeral pile, and whilst living endure to be burnt along with their husbands' bodies. One may well admire the exceeding courage of these women, who look thus contemptuously on death, and disdain it so exceedingly that they hasten and run impetuously towards it as if they were grasping immortality.

XXXIV. But why, say they, ought one to praise Abraham as the attempter of a wholly novel kind of conduct, when it is only what private men and kings, and even whole nations do at appropriate seasons? But I will make the following reply to the envy and ill-temper of these men.

Of those who sacrifice their childen, some do so out of habit, as they say some of the barbarians do; others do it because they are unable by any other means to place on a good footing some desperate and important dangers threatening their cities and countries. And of these men, some have given up their children because they have been constrained by those more powerful than themselves: and others, out of a thirst for glory, and honour, and for renown

* Deuteronomy xii. 31.

at the present moment, and celebrity in all future ages. Now those who sacrifice their children out of deference to custom, perform, in my opinion, no great exploit; for an inveterate custom is often as powerful as nature itself; so that it diminishes the terrible impression made by the action to be done, and makes even the most miserable and intolerable evils light to bear. Again: surely, they who offer up their children out of fear deserve no praise; for praise is only given to voluntary good actions, but what is involuntary, is ascribed to other causes than the immediate actors—to the occasion, or to chance, or to compulsion from men.

Again, if any one, out of a desire for glory, abandons his son or his daughter, he would justly be blamed rather than praised; seeking to acquire honour by the death of his dearest relations, while, even if he had glory, he ought rather to have risked the loss of it to secure the safety of his children. We must investigate, therefore, whether Abraham was under the influence of any one of the aforesaid motives, custom, or love of glory, or fear, when he was about to sacrifice his son.

Now Babylon, and Mesopotamia, and the nation of the Chaldæans, do not receive the custom of sacrificing their children; and these are the countries in which Abraham had been brought up and had lived most of his time; so that we cannot imagine that his sense of the misfortune that he was commanded to inflict upon himself was blunted by the frequency of such events. Again, there was no fear from men which pressed upon him, for no one knew of this oracular command which had been given to him alone, nor was there any common calamity pressing upon the land in which he was living, such as could only be remedied by the destruction of his most excellent son.

May it not have been, however, from a desire to obtain praise from the multitude that he proceeded to this action? But what praise could be obtained in the desert, when there was no one likely to be present who could possibly say anything in his favour, and when even his two servants were left at a distance on purpose that he might not seem to be hunting after praise, or to be making a display by bringing witnesses with him to see the greatness of his devotion?

XXXV. Therefore putting a barrier on their unbridled and evil-speaking mouths, let them moderate that envy in themselves which hates everything that is good, and let them forbear to attack the virtues of men who have lived excellently, which they ought rather to reward and decorate with panegyric. And that this action of Abraham's was in reality one deserving of praise and of all love, it is easy to see from many circumstances. In the first place, then, he laboured above all men to obey God, which is thought an excellent thing, and an especial object for all men's desire, by all right-minded persons, to such a degree, that he never omitted to perform anything which God commanded him, not even if it was full of arrogance and ingloriousness, or even of positive pain and misery ; for which reason he also bore, in a most noble manner, and with the most unshaken fortitude, the command given to him respecting his son.

In the second place, though it was not the custom in the land in which he was living, as perhaps it is among some nations, to offer human sacrifices, and custom, by its frequency, often removes the horror felt at the first appearance of evils, he himself was about to be the first to set the example of a novel and most extraordinary deed, which I do not think that any human being would have brought himself to submit to, even if his soul had been made of iron or of adamant ; for as some one has said,—

"'Tis a hard task with nature to contend."

In the second place, after he had become the father of this his only legitimate son, he, from the moment of his birth, cherished towards him all the genuine feelings of affection, which exceeds all modest love, and all the ties of friendship which have ever been celebrated in the world. There was added also, this most forcible charm of all, that he had become the father of this son not in the prime of his life, but in his old age. For parents become to a certain degree insane in their affection for children of their old age, either from the circumstance of their having been wishing for their birth a long time, or else because they have no longer any hope that they shall have any more ; nature having taken her stand there as at the extreme and furthest limit.

Now there is nothing unnatural or extraordinary in devoting one child to God out of a numerous family, as a sort
of first fruits of all one's children, while one still has pleasure in those who remain alive, who are no small comfort
and alleviation of the grief felt for the one who is sacrificed. But the man who gives the only beloved son that
he is possessed of performs an action beyond all powers
of language to praise, as he is giving nothing to his own
natural affection, but inclining with his whole will and
heart to show his devotion to God. Accordingly this is an
extraordinary and almost unprecedented action which was
done by Abraham.

For other men, even if they have yielded up their children to be sacrificed on behalf of the safety of their native
land or of their armies, have either remained at home themselves, or have kept at a distance from the altar of sacrifice; or at least, if they have been present they have averted
their eyes, and left others to strike the blow which they
have not endured to witness. But this man, like a priest
of sacrifice himself, did himself begin to perform the sacred
rite, although he was a most affectionate father of a son
who was in all respects most excellent. And, perhaps, according to the usual law and custom of burnt offerings he
was intending to solemnise the rite by dividing his son
limb by limb. And so he did not divide his feelings and
allot one part of his regard to his son and another part to
piety to God: but he devoted his whole soul, entire and un-
divided, to holiness; thinking but little of the kindred
blood which flowed in the victim.

Now of all the circumstances which we have enumerated
what is there which others have in common with Abraham?
What is there which is not peculiar to him, and excellent
beyond all power of language to praise? So that every
one who is not by nature envious and a lover of evil must
be struck with amazement and admiration for his excessive
piety, even if he should not call at once to mind all the
particulars on which I have been dwelling, but only some
one of the whole number; for the conception of any one of
these particulars is sufficient by a brief and faint outline to
display the greatness and loftiness of the father's soul;
though there is nothing petty in the action of the wise man.

XXXVI. But the things which we have here been saying do not appear solely in the plain and explicit language
of the text of the holy scriptures; but they appear, moreover, to exhibit a nature which is not so evident to the
multitude, but which they who place the objects of the intellect above those perceptible by the outward senses, and
who are able to appreciate them, recognise. And this
nature is of the following description.

The victim who was about to be sacrificed is called in
the Chaldæan language, Isaac; but if this name be translated into the Grecian language, it signifies "laughter;"
and this laughter is not understood to be that laughter of
the body which is frequent in childish sport, but is the
result of a settled happiness and rejoicing of the mind.
This kind of laughter the wise man is appropriately said to
offer as a sacrifice to God; showing thus, by a figure, that
to rejoice does properly belong to God alone. For the
human race is subject to sorrow and to exceeding fear,
from evils which are either present or expected, so that
men are either grieved at unexpected evils actually pressing
upon them, or are kept in suspense, and disquietude, and
fear with respect to those which are impending. But the
nature of God is free from grief, and exempt from fear, and
enjoys an immunity from every kind of suffering, and is the
only nature which possesses complete happiness and blessedness.

Now to the disposition which makes this confession in
sincerity, God is merciful, and compassionate, and kind,
driving envy to a distance from him; and to it he gives a
gift in return, to the full extent of the power of the person
benefited to receive it, and he all but gives such a person
this oracular warning, saying "I well know that the
whole species of joy and rejoicing is the possession of no
other being but me, who am the Father of the universe;
nevertheless, though it belongs to me, I have no objection
to those who deserve it enjoying a share of it. But who
can be deserving to do so, save he who obeys me and my
will? for to this man it shall be given to feel as little
grief as possible and as little fear as possible, proceeding
along that road which is inaccessible to passions and vices,
but which is frequented by excellence of soul and virtue."

And let no one fancy that that unmixed joy, which is
without any alloy of sorrow, descends from heaven to the
earth, but rather, that it is a combination of the two, that
which is the better being predominant in the mixture; in
the same manner as the light in heaven is unalloyed and
free from any admixture of darkness, but in the sublunary
atmosphere it is mingled with dark air.

For this reason, it seems to me to have been, that Sarah,*
the namesake of virtue, who had previously laughed, denied
her laughter to the person who questioned her as to the
cause of it, fearing lest she might be deprived of her
rejoicing, as belonging to no created being, but to God
alone; on which account the holy Word encouraged her,
and said, "Be not afraid," thou hast laughed a genuine
laugh, and thou hast a share in real joy; for the Father
has not permitted the race of mankind to be wholly devoured
by griefs, and sorrows, and incurable anguish, but has
mingled in their existence something of a better nature,
thinking it fitting that the soul should sometimes enjoy rest
and tranquillity; and he has also designed that the souls of
wise men should be pleased and delighted for the greater
portion of their existence with the contemplation of the soul.

XXXVII. This is enough to say about the piety of the
man, though there is a vast abundance of other things
which might be brought forward in praise of it. We must
also investigate his skill and wisdom as displayed towards
his fellow men; for it belongs to the same character to be
pious towards God and affectionate towards man; and both
these qualities, of holiness towards God and justice towards
man, are commonly seen in the same individual. Now it
would take a long time to go through all the instances and
actions which form this; but it is not out of place to record
two or three.

Abraham, being rich above most men in abundance of
gold and silver, and having numerous herds of cattle and
flocks of sheep, and being equal in his affluence and abundance to any of the men of the country, or of the original
inhabitants, who were the most wealthy, and being, in fact,
richer than any sojourner could be expected to be, was
never unpopular with any of the people among whom he

* Genesis xviii. 15.

was dwelling, but was continually praised and beloved by
all who had any acquaintance with him; and if, as is often
the case, any contention or quarrel arose between his servants and retinue and those of others, he always endeavoured to terminate it quietly by his gentle disposition,
discarding and driving to a distance from his soul all
quarrelsome, and turbulent, and disorderly things. And
there is no wonder, if he was such towards strangers, who
might have agreed together and with a heavy and powerful hand have repelled him, if he had begun acts of violence,
when he behaved with moderation towards those who were
nearly related to him in blood, but very far removed from
him in disposition, and who were desolate and isolated, and
very inferior in wealth to himself, willingly allowing himself to be inferior to them in the very things in which he
might have been superior; for there was his brother's son,
when he departed from his country, who went forth with
him, an inconstant, variable, whimsical man, inclining now
to one side and now to another; and at one time caressing
him with friendly salutations, and at another, being restive
and obstinate, by reason of the inequality of his disposition; on which account his household also was a quarrelsome and turbulent one, as it had no one to correct it, and
especially his shepherds were so, because they were removed
to a great distance from their master.

Accordingly, they, in their self-willed manner, behaving
as if they claimed complete liberty, were always quarrel-
ling with the managers of the flocks of the wise Abraham,
who yielded a great many points, because of the gentle disposition of their master; in consequence of which, the
shepherds of his nephew turned to folly and to shameless
audacity, and gave way to anger, cherishing ill-temper, and
exciting a spirit of irreconcilable enmity in their hearts,
until they compelled those whom they injured to turn to
their own defence; and when a somewhat violent battle
had taken place, the good Abraham, hearing of the attack
made by his servants on the others, though only in self-
defence, and knowing as he did that his own household
was superior both in numbers and in power, would not
allow the contest to be protracted till victory declared for
his party, in order that he might not grieve his nephew by

the defeat of his men; but standing between the two
bodies of combatants, he, by his pacific speeches, reconciled
the contending parties, and that not only for the moment,
but for all future time too; for he knew that if they
continued to dwell together, and to abide in the same
place, they would be always differing in opinion and quar-
relling with one another, and continually raising up quarrels and wars with one another. In order that this might
not be the case, he thought it desirable to abandon the
custom of dwelling together, and to separate his habitation from that of his nephew. So, sending for his nephew,
he gave him the choice of the better country, cheerfully
agreeing himself to abandon whatever portion the other
selected, as he should thus acquire the greatest of all
gains, namely, peace; and yet, what other man would ever
have yielded in any point whatever to one weaker than
himself, while he was stronger? and who that was able to
gain the victory would ever have been willing to be defeated, without availing himself of his power? But this
man alone placed the object of his desires, not in strength
and superiority, but in a life free from dissension and
blessed with tranquillity, as far as depended on himself;
for which reason he appears the most admirable of all
men.

XXXVIII. Since then this panegyric, if taken literally, is applied to Abraham as a man, and since the disposition of the soul is here intimated, it will be well for
us to investigate that also, after the fashion of those men
who go from the letter to the spirit of any statement.
Now there is an infinite variety of dispositions which arise
from different circumstances and opportunities in every
kind of action and event; but in this instance, we must
distinguish between two characters, one of which is the
elder and the other the younger.

Now the elder of the two is that disposition which
honours those things which are by nature principal and
dominant; the younger is that which regards the things
which are subject to others, and which are considered in
the lowest rank.

Now the principal and more dominant things are wisdom,
and temperance, and justice, and courage, and every descrip-

tion of virtue, and the actions in accordance with virtue; the younger things are wealth, and authority, and glory, and nobility, not real nobility, but that which the multitude think so, and all those other things which belong to the third class, next after the things of the soul, and the things of the body; the class which is in fact the last. Each then of these dispositions has, as it were, flocks and herds. The one which desires external things has for its flock, gold and silver, and all those things which are the materials and furniture of wealth; and, moreover, arms, engines, triremes, armies of infantry and cavalry, and fleets of ships, and all kinds of provisions to procure dominion, by which firm authority is secured.

But the lover of excellence has for his flock the doctrines of each individual virtue, and its speculations respecting wisdom. Moreover, there are overseers and superintendents of each of these flocks, just as there are shepherds to flocks of sheep. Of the flock of external things, the superintendents are those who are fond of money, those who are fond of glory, those who are eager for war, and all those who love authority over multitudes. And the managers of the flock of things concerning the soul are all those who are lovers of virtue and of what is honourable, and who do not prefer spurious good things to genuine ones, but genuine to spurious good. There is therefore a certain natural contest between them, inasmuch as they have no opinions in common with one another, but are always at variance and difference respecting the matter which has of all others the greatest influence in the maintenance of life as it should be, that is to say, the judgment of what things are truly good.

Now, for some time the soul was warred against by some enemy, and was full of this quarrelsome principle, inasmuch as it had not yet been completely pacified, but was still troubled by some passions and diseases which prevailed over sound reason. But from the time when it began to be more powerful, and with its superior force, to destroy the fortification of the opposite opinions, becoming elated and puffed up with pride, it in a most marvellous manner began to separate and detach the disposition in itself, which admires the external materials, and as if conversing

with man, says to him, Thou art unable to dwell with—it
is impossible that thou shouldest be connected by alliance
with—a lover, of wisdom and virtue.   Come, then, and
migrating from thy present abode, depart to a distance,
since you have no communion with me, and, indeed, cannot
possibly have any.   For all the things which you conceive to
be on the right he imagines to be on the left; and on the
contrary, whatever you think is on the left, is looked upon
by him as on the right.

XXXIX. Therefore the virtuous man was not only
peaceful and a lover of justice, but also a man of courage and
of a warlike disposition ; not for the sake of making war, for
he was not of a contentious and quarrelsome character,
but for the sake of a lasting peace for the future, which
hitherto his adversaries had destroyed. And the most convincing proof of this is to be found in what he did. Four
great kings had received for their inheritance the eastern
portion of the inhabited world ; and they were obeyed by
all the eastern nations, both on this and on the other side
of the Euphrates.   Now all the other parts remained un-
harassed by contentions, obeying the commands of these
kings, and contributing their yearly taxes and tribute without seeking for any excuses ; but the land of the inhabitants
of Sodom alone before it was destroyed by fire began to
break the peace, having been designing to revolt for a long
time.

For as it was a very rich country it was ruled by five
kings, who had divided the cities and the land among them,
though the district was not an extensive one, but fertile in
corn and trees, and abounding in all kinds of fruit.   What
then their size gives to other cities, that the excellence of
its soil gives to Sodom ; on which account it had many
princes for lovers who admired its beauty.   These, on all
other occasions, had paid the appointed revenues to the
collectors of the taxes, honouring and at the same time
fearing those more powerful sovereigns of whom they were
the viceroys.

But when they were completely sated with good things,
and when, as is ordinarily the case, satiety had begotten
insolence, they, cherishing a pride beyond their power! began
at first to lift up their heads and to become restive.   Then,

like wicked servants, they set upon their masters, trusting
more to their factious spirit than to their strength. But
their sovereigns, remembering their own nobleness and
being fortified with superior power, went against them with
great disdain, as if they would be able to defeat them by
the mere cry of battle. And having engaged them in battle,
they in a moment put some of them to flight, and others
they slew in the flight, and so they destroyed their army to
a man. And also they led away a vast multitude captive,
which they distributed among themselves with much other
booty. Moreover, they led away captive the brother's son
of the wise Abraham, who had a little while before emigrated
into one of the cities of the Pentapolis.

XL. This was communicated to Abraham by some one of
those who escaped from the defeat of his countrymen, and
it grieved him exceedingly, and he would not be quiet any
longer, being much concerned at what had happened, and
mourning more for him alive and in captivity than if he had
heard that he had been killed. For he knew that death
(τελευτή) as its very name imports, was the end (τέλος) of all
living beings, and especially of the wicked, and that there
are innumerable unexpected evils which lie, as it were, in
ambush for the living. But when he was preparing to
pursue them for the purpose of delivering his brother's son,
he found himself in want of allies, inasmuch as he himself
was a stranger and a sojourner and as no one could dare to
oppose the irresistible power of such mighty monarchs
flushed with recent victory. And he devised for himself a
most novel alliance. For necessity is the mother of invention,
and expedients are found in the most difficult circumstances
when a man has set his heart on just and humane objects.
For having collected together all his servants, and ordering
the slaves whom he had purchased to remain at home (for
he was afraid of desertion on their part), he assembled all
his domestic servants, and divided them into centuries, and
marched forward in their battalions; not, indeed, trusting
to them, for his was still a most insignificant force, in comparison with that of the king's, but placing his confidence
in the champion and defender of the just, namely in God.

Therefore putting forth all his exertions he hastened on,
in nowise relaxing his speed, until, watching his oppor-

tunity, he fell upon the enemy by night, after they had
supped, and when they were just on the point of betaking
themselves to sleep. And some he slew in their beds, and
those who were arrayed against him he utterly destroyed,
and with great vigour he defeated them all, more by the
courage of his soul than by the adequacy of his means.
And he did not cease from attacking them until he had
utterly destroyed the hostile army with their kings, and
slain them all to a man in front of their camp, and had
brought back his brother's son after this splendid and most
glorious victory, bringing back also as fair booty all their
cavalry, and all the multitude of their beasts of burden, and
a most enormous quantity of spoil.

And when the great high priest of the most high God
beheld him returning and coming back loaded with trophies,
in safety himself, with all his own force uninjured, for he
had not lost one single man of all those who went out with
him ; marvelling at the greatness of the exploit, and, as was
very natural, considering that he had never met with this
success but through the favour of the divine wisdom and
alliance, he raised his hands to heaven, and honoured him
with prayers in his behalf, and offered up sacrifices of
thanksgiving for his victory, and splendidly feasted all those
who had had a share in the expedition ; rejoicing and sym-
pathising with him as if the success had been his own, and
in reality it did greatly concern him. For as the proverb
says :—

" All that befalls from friends we common call."

And much more are all instances of good fortune common
to those whose main object it is to please God.

XLI. These things, then, are what are contained in the
plain words of the scriptures. But as many as are able to
contemplate the facts related in them in their incorporeal
and naked state, living rather in the soul than in the body,
will say that of the nine kings the four are the powers of the
four passions which exist within us, the passion of pleasure,
of desire, of fear, and of grief ; and that the other five
kings are the outward senses, being equal in number, the

* Genesis xiv. 23.

sense of sight, of hearing, of smell, of taste, and of touch. For these in some degree are sovereigns and rulers, having acquired a certain power over us, but not all to an equal extent; for the five are subordinate to the four, and are compelled to pay them taxes and tribute, such as are appointed by nature. For it is from the things which we see, or hear, or smell, or taste, or touch, that pleasures, and pains, and fears, and desires arise; as there is no one of the passions which has any power to exist of itself, if it were not supplied by the materials furnished by the outward senses.

For it is in these things that their powers consist, either in figures and in colours, or in the faculty of speaking or hearing which depends on the voice, or in flavours, or in odours, or by the subjects of touch, whether they are soft or hard, or rough, or smooth, or hot, or cold. For all these things are supplied to each of the passions by means of the outward senses. And as long as the taxes beforementioned are paid the alliance among the kings remains; but when they are no longer contributed, as they were before, then immediately do quarrels and wars arise. And this appears to happen when painful old age supervenes, in which none of the passions becomes weaker, but rather perhaps stronger than their ancient power; but the sight becomes dim, and the ears hard of hearing, and every one of the other outward senses more blunt, being no longer equally able as before to judge and decide accurately of every subject submitted to them, nor any longer to pay a tribute which will be equal to the number of the passions.

So that it happened very naturally that they being thoroughly exhausted and laid prostrate by them were easily put to flight by the adverse passions; and the statement that follows is in strict consistency with what might be naturally expected, namely, that of the five kings two fell into wells, and three took to flight. For touch and taste reach to the very deepest portions of the body, sending down into the entrails those things which are suitable for digestion; but the eyes, and the ears, and the smell, roaming abroad for the most part, escape the slavery of the body.

The good man—threatening to attack all of these, when he saw that those who had lately been friends and confederates were now in a state of disease, and that there was war instead of peace arising among the nine kingdoms, as the four kings were contending with the five for sovereignty and dominion—on a sudden, having watched his opportunity, attacked them; being desirous of the establishment of democracy in the soul, the most excellent of constitutions instead of tyrannies and absolute sovereignties, and wishing also to introduce law and justice instead of lawlessness and injustice, which had prevailed up to that time. And what is here said is not a cunningly devised fable, but is rather one of the most completely true facts, which may be seen to be true in our own selves. For it very often happens that the outward senses observe a sort of confederacy which they have formed with the passions, supplying them with objects perceptible by the outward senses; and very often also, they raise contentions, no longer choosing to pay the tribute fairly due from them, or else being unable to do so, by reason of the presence of corrective reason; which when it has taken up its complete armour, namely, the virtues, and their doctrines and contemplations, which form an irresistible power, conquers all things in the most vigorous manner. For it is not lawful for perishable things to dwell with what is immortal. Therefore the nine sovereignties of the four passions and the five outward senses are both perishable themselves and also the causes of mortality. But the truly sacred and divine word, which uses the virtues as a starting place, being placed in the number ten, that perfect number, when it descends into the contest and exerts that more vigorous power which it has in accordance with God, subdues by main force all the aforesaid powers.

XLII. And at a subsequent period his wife dies, she who was most dear to his mind and most excellent in all respects, having given innumerable proofs of her affection towards her husband in leaving all her relations together with him; and in her unhesitating migration from her own country, and in her continued and uninterrupted wanderings in a foreign land, and in her endurance of want and scarcity, and in her accompanying him in his warlike expeditions. For she was always with him at all times, and in all places, never being absent from any spot, or failing to share any of his fortune, being truly the partner of his life, and of all the circumstances of his life; judging it right equally to share all his good and evil fortune together with him. For she did not, as some persons do, shun any participation in his misfortunes, but lie in wait only for his prosperity, but with all cheerfulness took her share in both, as was fitting and becoming to a wedded wife.

XLIII. And though I might have many topics for panegyric on this woman, still I will only mention one, which shall be the most manifest possible proof of all the others. For she, being barren and childless, and fearing lest her husband's God-loving house might be left entirely destitute of offspring, came to her husband and spoke as follows:— "We have now lived together a long time mutually pleasing each; but we have no children, which is the cause for which we ourselves came together, and for which also nature designed the original connection between husband and wife; nor indeed can there be any hope of your having any offspring by me, since I am now beyond the age of childbearing; do not you then suffer for my barrenness, and do not, out of your affection for me, while you are yourself able still to become a father, be hindered from being so. For I shall not feel any jealousy towards another woman whom you may marry, not for the gratification of irrational appetite, but in order to satisfy a necessary law of nature. For which reason I will not delay to deck a new bride for you, that she may fulfil what is wanting on my part. And if the prayers which we will offer up for the birth of children be blessed with success, then the children which are born shall be your own legitimate children, but by adoption they shall be by all means mine.

"And that you may have no suspicion of any jealousy on my part, take, if you will, my own handmaid to wife; who is a slave indeed as to her body, but free and noble as to her mind; whose good qualities I have for a long time proved and experienced from the day when she was first introduced into my house, being an Egyptian by blood, and a Hebrew by deliberate choice. We have great substance and abundant wealth, not like people who are sojourners. For even already we surpass the natives themselves in the brilliancy of our prosperity, but still we have no heir or

successor, and that, too, though there might be one, if you
would be guided by my advice."

But Abraham, marvelling more and more at the love of his
wife for her husband thus continually being renewed and
gaining fresh strength, and also at her spirit of forecast so
desirous to provide for the future, takes to himself the handmaid who had been approved by her to the extent of having
a son by her; though as those who give the most clear and
probable account say he cohabited with her only till she
became pregnant; and when she conceived, which she did
after no long interval, he then desisted from all connection
with her, by reason of his natural continence, and also of
the honour in which he held his wife. So then he speedily
had a son by this handmaid, but at a very distant period
after this he had also a legitimate son, after he and his wife
had both despaired of any offspring from one another. The
bounteous God having thus bestowed on them a reward for
their excellence more perfect than their highest hopes.

XLIV. It is sufficient to mention this as a proof of the
virtue of Abraham's wife. But the topics of praise of the
wise man himself are more numerous, some of which I
have lately enumerated. Moreover I will mention also one
circumstance connected with the death of the wife, which
ought not to be buried in silence. For when Abraham had
lost such a partner of his whole life, as our account has
shown her to have been, and as the scriptures testify that
she was, he still like a wrestler prevailed over the grief
which attacked him and threatened to overwhelm his soul;
strengthening and encouraging with great virtue and resolution, reason, the natural adversary of the passions, which
indeed he had always taken as a counsellor during the whole
of his life; but at this time above all others, he thought fit
to be guided by it, when it was giving him the best and
most expedient advice. And the advice was this; not to
afflict himself beyond all measure, as if he were stricken
down with a novel and unprecedented calamity; nor, on the
other hand, to give way to indifference, as if nothing had
happened calculated to give him sorrow. But rather to
choose the middle way in preference to either extreme; and
to endeavour to grieve in a moderate degree; not being

indignant at nature for having reclaimed what belonged to her as her due ; and bearing what had befallen him with a mild and gentle spirit.

And there are evidences of these assertions to be seen in the holy scriptures ; which it is impossible should be convicted of false witness, and they tell us that Abraham, having wept a short time over his wife's body, soon rose up from the corpse ; thinking, as it should seem, that to mourn any longer would be inconsistent with that wisdom by which he had been taught that he was not to look upon death as the extinction of the soul, but rather as a separation and disjunction of it from the body, returning back to the region from whence it came ; and it came, as is fully shown in the history of the creation of the world, from God.

But just as no man of moderation or sense would be indignant at having to repay a debt to a lender or to return a deposit to the man who had deposited it ; so, in the same manner, he did not think it becoming to show impatience when nature reclaimed what belonged to her, but preferred to bear what was inevitable with cheerfulness. And when the magistrates of that country came to sympathise with him in his sorrow, seeing none of the customary signs of woe which were usually exhibited in their land by mourners, no loud wailing or howling, no beating of the breast, no loud cries of men or women, but a steady, sober depression of spirits on the part of the whole household, they marvelled exceedingly, even though they had been previously full of astonishment and admiration at all the rest of the man's way of life. And then, not concealing in their own minds their ideas of the greatness and beauty of his virtue, for it was all admirable, they approached him and addressed him thus:—"Thou art a king from God among us."* Speaking most truly, for all other kingdoms are established by man by means of wars, and military expeditions, and indescribable evils, which those persons who aim at power inflict mutually on one another, slaying one another, and raising up vast forces of infantry, and cavalry, and fleets. But the kingdom of the wise man is bestowed upon him by God ; and the virtuous man receiving it is not the cause of evil to any one, but is rather the author to all his subjects of the

* Genesis xxiii. 6.

acquisition and also of the use of good things, proclaiming
to them peace and obedience to the law.

XLV. There is also another praise of him recorded in his
honour and testified to in the holy scriptures, which Moses
has written, in which it is related of him that he believed in
God; which is a statement brief indeed in words, but of
great magnitude and importance to be confirmed in fact.
For on whom else can we believe? Are we to trust in
authorities, or in glory and honour, or in abundance of wealth
and noble birth, or in good health and a good condition of
the senses and mind, or in vigour of body and beauty of person? But in truth every kind of authority is unstable, as
it has innumerable enemies lying in wait to attack it. And
if in any instance it is firmly established, it is only so confirmed by innumerable evils and calamities which those who
are in authority both inflict and suffer. Again, honours and
glory are most unstable, being tossed about among the indiscriminate inclinations and feeble language of careless and
imprudent men; and even if they endure, their nature is
not such as to produce any genuine good. And as for riches
and illustrious birth, those things sometimes fall to the lot
of the most worthless of men. And even if they should belong only to the virtuous, still they are but the praises of
their ancestors and of fortune, and not of those who now
possess them.

Nor, again, is it right for a man to pride himself on his
personal advantages, in which other animals are superior to
him. For what man is stronger or more vigorous than a
bull among domestic animals, or than a lion among wild
beasts? And what man is more sharp-sighted than a falcon
or an eagle? And what man is so richly endowed with the
sense of hearing as that stupidest of all animals, the ass?
Also what man is more accurate in his sense of smell than a
hound, who huntsmen say can trace out by means of his
nose animals who are lying at a distance, and can run up to
them with perfect correctness, and course, though he has not
seen them; for what sight is to other animals that is the
sense of smell to hounds and to all the dogs which pursue
game.

Moreover, the greater part of the irrational animals enjoy
excellent health, and are as far as possible entirely exempt

from disease. And also in any competition in respect of beauty, some things which are even destitute of vitality, appear to me to surpass the elegance of either men or women; as, for instance, images, and statues, and pictures, and in a word all the works of either the pictorial or plastic art which arrive at excellence in either branch, and which are the objects of study and desire both to Greeks and barbarians, who erect them in the most conspicuous places for the ornament of their cities.

XLVI. Therefore, the only real, and true, and lasting good is trust in God, the comfort of life, the fulfilment of all good hopes, the absence of all evils, and the attendant source of blessings, the repudiation of all unhappiness, the recognition of piety, the inheritance of all happiness, the improvement of the soul in every respect, as it thus relies for support on the cause of all things, who is able to do everything but who wills only to do what is best. For as men who are going along a slippery road stumble and fall, but they who proceed by a dry, and level, and plain path, journey on without stumbling; so also those men who are conducting their soul through the road of bodily and external good things are only accustoming it to fall; for these things are full of stumbling and the most insecure of all. But they who by those speculations which are in accordance with virtue, hasten towards God, are guiding their souls in a safe and untroubled path. So that we may say with the most absolute truth, that the man who trusts in the good things of the body disbelieves in God, and that he who distrusts them believes in him.

But not only do the holy scriptures bear witness to the faith of Abraham in the living God, which faith is the queen of all the virtues, but moreover he is the first man whom they speak of as an elder; though there were men who had preceded him who had lived three times as many years (or even more still) as he had, not one of whom is handed down to us as worthy of the appellation. And may we not say that this is in strict accordance with natural truth? For he who is really an elder is looked upon as such, not with reference to his length of time, but to the praiseworthiness of his life. Those men, therefore, who have spent a long life in that existence which is in accordance with the body, apart from all virtue, we must call only long-lived children, having never been instructed in those branches of education which befit grey hairs. But the man who has been a lover of prudence, and wisdom, and faith in God, one may justly denominate an elder, forming his name by a slight change from the first. For in real truth the wise man is the first man in the human race, being what a pilot is in a ship, a governor in a city, a general in war, the soul in the body, or the mind in the soul; or again, what the heaven is in the world, and what God is in heaven. And God, admiring this man for his faith (πίστις) in him, gives him a pledge (πίστις) in return, namely, a confirmation by an oath of the gifts which he had promised him; no longer conversing with him as God might with man, but as one friend with another.

For he says, " By myself have I sworn,"* by him that is whose word is an oath, in order that Abraham's mind may be established still more firmly and immoveably than before. Let the virtuous man both be and be called the elder and the first, and let every fool be called the younger and the last, since he only pursues such objects as may produce revolution and as are placed in the lowest rank.

Thus much is sufficient to say on this subject. But God, adding to the multitude and magnitude of the praises of the wise man one single thing as a crowning point, says that " this man fulfilled the divine law, and all the commandments of God,"† not having been taught to do so by written books, but in accordance with the unwritten law of his nature, being anxious to obey all healthful and salutary impulses. And what is the duty of man except most firmly to believe those things which God asserts?

Such is the life of the first author and founder of our nation ; a man according to the law, as some persons think, but, as my argument has shown, one who is himself the unwritten law and justice of God.

* Genesis xv. 6.   † Genesis xxvi. 5.

A TREATISE

ON

THE MIGRATION OF ABRAHAM.

I. AND the Lord said to Abraham, " Depart from thy land, and from thy kindred, and from thy father's house, to a land which I will show thee; and I will make thee into a great nation. And I will bless thee, and I will magnify thy name, and thou shalt be blessed. And I will bless them that bless thee, and I will curse them that curse thee; and in thy name shall all the nations of the earth be blessed."*

God, wishing to purify the soul of man, first of all gives it an impulse towards complete salvation, namely, a change of abode, so as to quit the three regions of the body, the outward sense and speech according to utterance; for his country is the emblem of the body, and his kindred are the symbol of the outward sense, and his father's house of speech. Why so? Because the body derives its composition from the earth, and is again dissolved into earth; and Moses is a witness of this when he says, " Dust thou art, and unto dust shalt thou return."† For he says, that man was compounded by God fashioning a lump of clay into the form of a man; and it follows of necessity that, a composite being, when dissolved, must be dissolved into its component parts. But the outward sense is nearly con- nected with and akin to the mind, the irrational part to the rational, since they are both parts of one soul: but speech is the abode of the father, because our father is the mind, which im- plants in each of its parts its own powers, and distributes its energies among them, undertaking the care and superinten- dence of them all; and the abode in which it dwells is speech, a dwelling separated from all the rest of the house; for as the hearth is the abode of a man, so is speech of the mind : at all

* Genesis xii. 1—3.   † Genesis iii. 19.

events, it displays itself, and all the notions which it conceives, arranging them and setting them in order in speech, as if in a house.

And you must not wonder that Moses has called speech in man the abode of the mind, for he also says, that the mind of the universe, that is to say, God, has for his abode his own word.   And the practiser of virtue, Jacob, seizing on this apprehension, confesses in express words that, "This is no other than the house of God,"* an expression equivalent to, The house of God is not this thing, or anything which can be made the subject of ocular demonstration, or, in short, anything which comes under the province of the outward senses, but is invisible, destitute of all specific form, only to be comprehended by the soul as soul.   What, then, can it be except the Word, which is more ancient than all the things which were the objects of creation, and by means of which it is that the Ruler of the universe, taking hold of it as a rudder, governs all things.   And when he was fashioning the world, he used this as his instrument for the blameless arrangement of all the things which he was completing.

II. That he means by Abraham's country the body, and by his kindred the outward senses, and by his father's house uttered speech, we have now shown.   But the command, "Depart from them, " is not like or equivalent to, Be separated from them according to your essence, since that would be the injunction of one who was pronouncing sentence of death. But it is the same as saying, Be alienated from them in your mind, allowing none of them to cling to you, standing above them all ; they are your subjects, use them not as your rulers ; since you are a king, learn to govern and not to be governed ; know yourself all your life, as Moses teaches us in many passages where he says, "Take heed to thyself."†   For thus you will perceive what you ought to be obedient to, and what you ought to be the master of.   Depart therefore from the earthly parts which envelop you, O my friend, fleeing from that base and polluted prison house the body, and from the keepers as it were of the prison, its pleasures and appetites, putting forth all your strength and all your power so as to suffer none of thy good things to come to harm, but improving all your good faculties together and unitedly.   Depart also from thy

* Genesis xxviii. 17.   † Exodus xxxiv. 12.

kindred, outward senses; for now indeed you have given yourself up to each of them to be made use of as it will, and you have become a good, the property of others who have borrowed you, having lost your own power over yourself. But you know that, even though all men are silent on the subject, your eyes lead you, and so do your ears, and all the rest of the multitude of that kindred connection, towards those objects which are pleasing to themselves. But if you choose to collect again those portions of yourself which you have lent away, and to invest yourself with the possession of yourself, without separating off or alienating any part of it, you will have a happy life, enjoying for ever and ever the fruit of good things which belong not to strangers but to yourself.

But now rise up also and quit speech according to utterance, which Moses here represents God as calling your father's house, that you may not be deceived by the specious beauty of words and names, and so be separated from that real beauty which exists in the things themselves which are intended by these names. For it is absurd for a shadow to be looked upon as of more importance than the bodies themselves, or for an imitation to carry off the palm from the model. Now the interpretation resembles a shadow and an imitation, but the natures of things signified under these expressions, thus interpreted, resemble the bodies and original models which the man who aims at being such and such rather than at appearing so must cling to, removing to a distance from the other things.

III. When therefore the mind begins to become acquainted with itself, and to dwell among the speculations which come under the province of the intellect, all the inclinations of the soul for the species which is comprehensible by the intellect will be repelled, which inclination is called by the Hebrews, Lot; for which reason the wise man is represented as distinctly saying, "Depart, and separate yourself from me;"* for it is impossible for a man who is overwhelmed with the love of incorporeal and imperishable objects to dwell with one, whose every inclination is towards the mortal objects of the outward senses.

Very beautifully therefore has the sacred interpreter of God's will entitled one entire holy volume of the giving of the

* Genesis xiii. 9.

law, the Exodus, having thus found out an appropriate name
for the oracles contained therein. For being a man desirous
of giving instruction and exceedingly ready to admonish and
correct, he desires to remove the whole of the people of the
soul as a multitude capable of receiving admonition and
correction from the country of Egypt, that is to say, the body,
and to take them out from among its inhabitants, thinking it
a most terrible and grievous burden that the mind which is
endowed with the faculty of sight should be oppressed by the
pleasures of the flesh, and should obey whatever commands
the relentless desires choose to impose upon it.

Therefore, after the merciful God has instructed this people,
groaning and bitterly weeping for the abundance of the things
concerning the body, and the exceeding supply of external
things (for it is said, "The children of Israel groaned by
reason of the works ")* when, God, I say, had instructed them
about their going out, the prophet himself led them forth in
safety.

But there are some persons who have made a treaty with the
body to last till the day of their death, and who have buried
themselves in it as in a chest or coffin or whatever else you
like to call it, of whom all the parts which are devoted to the
slavery of the body and of the passions are consigned to
oblivion and buried. But if anything well affected towards
virtue has shot up by the side of it, that is preserved in the
recollection, by means of which good things are naturally
destined to be kept alive.

IV. Accordingly, the sacred scriptures command the bones
of Joseph—I mean by this the only parts of such a soul as
were left behind, being species which know no corruption and
which deserve to have mention made of them—to be preserved,
thinking it preposterous for pure things not to be united to
pure things.   And what is especially worthy of being mentioned
is this, that he believed that God would visit †the race which
"was capable of seeing," and would not give it up for ever and
ever to ignorance, that blind mistress, but would distinguish
between the immortal and the mortal parts of the soul, and
leave in Egypt those parts which were conversant about the
pleasures of the body and the other immoderate indulgences of
the passions ; but with respect to those parts which are im-

* Exodus ii. 23.   † Genesis l. 24.

perishable, would make a covenant that they should be conducted onwards with those persons who were going up to the cities of virtue and would further ratify this covenant with an oath.

What then are the parts which are imperishable? In the first place, a perfect alienation from pleasure which says, " Let us lie down together,"* and let us enjoy human enjoyments; secondly, presence of mind combined with fortitude, by means of which the soul separates and distinguishes from one another those things which by vain opinions are accounted good things, as so many dreams, confessing that " the only true and accurate explanations of things are to be found with God ; "† and that all those imaginings, which exist in the unsteady, puffed up, and arrogant life of those men who are not yet purified, but who delight in those pleasures which proceed from bakers, and cooks, and wine-bearers, are uncertain and indistinct ; so that such a man is not a subject but a ruler of Egypt, that is to say, of the whole region of the body ; so that " he boasted of being of the race of the Hebrews,"‡ who were accustomed to rise up and leave the objects of the outward senses, and to go over to those of the intellect ; for the name Hebrew, being interpreted, means " one who passes over, " because he boasted that " here he had done nothing."§

For to do nothing of those things which are thought much of among the wicked, but to hate them all and reject them, is praiseworthy in no slight degree ; as it is to despise immoderate indulgence of the desires and all other passions ; to fear God, if a man is not yet capable of loving him, and even while in Egypt to have a desire for real life.

V. Which he who sees, marvelling at (and indeed it was enough ‖ to cause astonishment), says, " It is a great thing for me if my son Joseph is still alive,"¶ and has not died at the same time with vain opinions and the body which is but a lifeless carcass ; and he also confessed that " it was the work of God, "** and not of any created being, that he was recognised by his brethren, and so could put into commotion and agitation, and put to the rout by force, all the dispositions devoted to the

---

* Genesis xxxix. 7. † Genesis xl. 8.
‡ Genesis xl. 15. § Genesis xl. 15.
‖ Genesis xlii. 18. ¶ Genesis xlv. 28.
** Genesis l. 19.

body which flattered themselves that they could stand firmly on their own doctrines; he also said that "he had not been sent away by men, but had been appointed by God"* for the legitimate overseeing of the body and of all external things; but there are many other things also resembling these, being of a superior and more sacred kind of order; and they do not endure to abide in Egypt, the house of the body, and are never buried in a coffin at all, but depart to a distance outside of every thing mortal, and follow the words of the lawgiver, namely, Moses, who is the guide of their path.

For Moses, being the nurse as it were and tutor of good works, and good expressions, and good intentions, which, even if at times they are mingled with those of an opposite character by reason of the somewhat confused medley which exists in mortal man; are nevertheless distinguished when they have passed, so that all the seeds and plants of excellence may not be destroyed and perish for ever and ever. And he exhorts men very vigorously to quit that which is called the mother of every thing that is absurd, without any delay or sluggishness, but rather using exceeding swiftness; for he says that men "must sacrifice the *pascha*, in haste,"† and the word *pascha*, being interpreted, means a "passing over," in order that the mind, exerting its reasonings without any doubt, and also an energetic willingness and promptness, may, without ever turning back make a passing over from the passions, to gratitude to God the Saviour, who has led it forth beyond all its expectations to freedom.

VI. And why do we wonder if he exhorts the man who is led away by the force of unreasonable passions, neither to yield, nor to allow himself to be carried away by the impetuosity of its onward course, but to exert all his strength, to resist, and if he is unable to resist effectually, then to flee. For the second advance towards safety on the part of those who are unable to make a good resistance is flight. When the occasion does not permit the man who is a combatant by nature, and who has never been a slave of the passions, but who is always undergoing the toil of resistance to every separate one of them, to put forth all his powers of antagonism at all times, lest from the continuance of his struggles against them he may gradually contract a painful infection from them; for there

* Genesis xlv. 5. † Exodus xii. 11.

have before now been many instances of men having become imitators of the wickedness to which they were previously antagonists, as, on the other hand, some opposers of virtue have become copiers of that.

And for this reason the following scripture has been given to men, " Return to the land of thy father and to thy family, and I will be with thee ;"* which is equivalent to saying, you have been a perfect wrestler for me, and you have been thought worthy of the prize and crown of victory, virtue having been the establisher of the contest and proposing to give prizes of victory; and now get rid of your fondness for contention, that you may not be always labouring but that you may be able to enjoy the fruit of your labours, which will never happen to you if you remain here dwelling among the objects of the external senses, and wasting your time among the distinctive qualities of the body, of which Laban is the leader (and this name means " distinctive quality"); but you must be an emigrant and must return to your native land, the land of the sacred word, and in some sense of the father of all those who practise virtue, which is wisdom, the best possible abiding place for those souls which love virtue.

In this country you have a race which learns everything of itself, and is self-taught, which has no share in the infantine food of milk, but which by the divine oracle " has been forbidden to go down to Egypt, "† and to put itself in the way of the attractive pleasures of the flesh, surnamed Isaac ; and if you receive his inheritance, you will of necessity discard labour, for excessive abundance of things ready prepared, and of good things offered to your hand, will be the causes of cessation from toil. And the fountain from which good things are poured forth is the presence of the bounteous and beneficent God ; on which account setting the seal to his loving kindnesses he says, " I will be with thee."

VII. How then should any good thing be wanting when the all-accomplishing God is at all times present with his graces, which are his virgin daughters, which he, the Father, who begot them, always cherishes as virgins, free from all impure contact and pollution? Then all cares, and labours, and exercises of practice, have a respite ; and everything that is useful is at the same time given to everybody without the em-

* Genesis xxxi. 3.   † Genesis xxvi. 2.

ployment of art, by the prescient care of nature; and the rapid influx of all these spontaneous blessings is called relaxation, since the mind is then relaxed and released from its energies as to its own peculiar objects, and is as it were emancipated from its yearly burdens,* by reason of the multitude of the things which are incessantly showered and rained upon it; and these things are in their own nature most admirable and most beautiful; for of the things of which the soul is in travail by herself, the greater part are premature and abortive progeny; but those on which God pours his showers and which he waters, are produced in a perfect, and entire, and most excellent state.

I am not ashamed to relate what has happened to me myself, which I know from having experienced it ten thousand times. Sometimes, when I have desired to come to my usual employment of writing on the doctrines of philosophy, though I have known accurately what it was proper to set down, I have found my mind barren and unproductive, and have been completely unsuccessful in my object, being indignant at my mind for the uncertainty and vanity of its then existing opinions, and filled with amazement at the power of the living God, by whom the womb of the soul is at times opened and at times closed up; and sometimes when I have come to my work empty I have suddenly become full, ideas being, in an invisible manner, showered upon me, and implanted in me from on high; so that, through the influence of divine inspiration, I have become greatly excited, and have known neither the place in which I was nor those who were present, nor myself, nor what I was saying, nor what I was writing; for then I have been conscious of a richness of interpretation, an enjoyment of light, a most penetrating sight, a most manifest energy in all that was to be done, having such an effect on my mind as the clearest ocular demonstration would have on the eyes.

VIII. That then which is shown is that thing so worthy of being beheld, so worthy of being contemplated, so worthy of being beloved, the perfect good, the nature of which is to change and sweeten the bitternesses of the soul, the most

* Here again Mangey supposes the text to be hopelessly corrupt. The word there is ἑκουσίων, for which he proposes and translates φόρτων τῶν ἐτησίων.

beautiful additional seasoning, full of all kinds of sweetnesses, by the addition of which, even those things which are not nutritious become salutary food; for it is said, that "the Lord showed him (Moses) a tree, and he cast it into the water,"* that is to say, into the mind, dissolved, and relaxed, and full of bitterness, that it might become sweetened and serviceable. But this tree promises not only food but likewise immortality; for Moses tells us, that the tree of life was planted in the midst of the paradise, being, in fact, goodness surrounded as by a body-guard by all the particular virtues, and by the actions in accordance with them; for it is virtue which has received the inheritance of the most central and excellent place in the soul.

And he who sees is the wise man; for the foolish are blind, or at best dim sighted. On this account I have before mentioned, that the then prophets were called seers;† and Jacob, the practiser of virtue, was desirous to give his ears in exchange for his eyes, if he could only see what he had previously heard described, and accordingly he receives an inheritance according to sight, having passed over that which was derived from hearing; for the coin of learning and instruction, which is synonymous with Jacob, is re-coined into the seeing Israel, in consequence of which he, the faculty of seeing, beholds the divine light, which is in no respect different from knowledge, which opens the eye of the soul, and leads it on to embrace the most conspicuous and manifest comprehension of existing things :‡ for as it is through music that the principles of music are understood, and through each separate art that its principles are comprehended, so also it is owing to wisdom that what is wise is contemplated : but not only is wisdom like light, the instrument of seeing, but it does also behold itself. This, in God, is the light which is the archetypal model of the sun, and the sun itself is only its image and copy; and he who shows each thing is the only all-knowing being, God; for men are called knowing only because they appear to know; but God, who really does know, is spoken of, as to his knowledge, in a manner inferior to its

---

* Exodus xv. 25.   † 1 Samuel ix. 9.

‡ This again is Mangey's emendation. The Greek text has ὠτίον, which is either nonsense, or at least the opposite of what must be meant.

real nature, for everything that is ever spoken in his praise
comes short of the real power of the living God.

And he recommends his wisdom, not merely by the fact
that it was he who created the world, but also by that of his
having established the knowledge of everything that has happened, or that has been created in the firmest manner close
to himself; for it is said, that " God saw all the things that
he had made,"* which is an expression equivalent not to, He
directed his sight towards each thing, but to, He conceived a
knowledge, and understanding, and comprehension, of all the
things that he had made.   It was very proper, therefore, to
teach and to instruct, and to point out to the ignorant, each
separate thing, but it was unnecessary to do so to the all-
knowing God, who is not like a man, benefited by art, but
who is himself confessed to be the beginning and source of all
arts and sciences.

IX. And Moses speaks very cautiously, inasmuch as he
defines not the present time but the future in the promise
which he records, when he says, " Not that which I *do* show
you, but that which I *will* show you;"† as a testimony to the
faith with which the soul believed in God, showing its gratitude
not by what had been already done, but by its expectation of
the future; for, being kept in a state of suspense and eagerness by good hope, and thinking that even what was not
present would beyond all question be present immediately, on
account of its most certain faith in him who had promised,
it found a reward, the perfect good; for in another passage it
is said that Abraham believed in God.

And in the same way, God, when showing Moses all the
land, says that, " I have shown it to thy eyes; but thou shalt
not enter therein."‡   Do not then fancy that this is spoken
of the death of the all-wise Moses, as some inconsiderate
persons believe; for it is a piece of folly to think that slaves
should have the country of virtue assigned to them in
preference to the friends of God.   But first of all, God wishes
to make it understood by you that there is one place for
infants and another for full-grown men, the one being called
practice and the other wisdom; and secondly, that the most
beautiful of all the things in nature are rather such as can be
seen than such as can be acquired; for how can it be possible

* Genesis i. 31.   † Genesis xv. 5.   ‡ Deut. xxxiv. 4.

to acquire possession of those things which are endowed in the same degree with the diviner attributes? But it is not impossible to see them, though it may not be given to all men to do so, for this may be permitted only to the purest and most acute-sighted race, to whom the father of the universe, when he displays his own works, is giving the greatest of all gifts.

For what life can be better than that which is devoted to speculation, or what can be more closely connected with rational existence; for which reason it is that though the voices of mortal beings are judged of by the faculty of hearing, nevertheless the scriptures present to us the words of God, to be actually visible to us like light; for in them it is said that, "All the people saw the voice of God;"* they do not say, "heard it," since what took place was not a beating of the air by means of the organs of the mouth and tongue, but a most exceedingly brilliant ray of virtue, not different in any respect from the source of reason, which also in another passage is spoken of in the following manner, "Ye have seen that I spake unto you from out of heaven,"† not "Ye have heard," for the same reason.

But there are passages where he distinguishes between what is heard and what is seen, and between the sense of seeing and that of hearing, as where he says, " Ye, heard the sound of the words, but ye saw no similitude, only ye heard a voice ;"‡ speaking here with excessive precision; for the discourse which was divided into nouns and verbs, and in short into all the different parts of speech, he has very appropriately spoken of as something to be heard; for in fact that is examined by the sense of hearing; but that which has nothing to do with either nouns or verbs, but is the voice of God, and seen by the eye of the soul, he very properly represents as visible; and having previously reminded them, " Ye saw no similitude," he proceeds to say, " Only ye heard a voice, which ye all saw;" for this must be what is understood as implied in those words. So that the words of God have for their tribunal and judge the sense of sight, which is situated in the soul; but those which are subdivided into nouns, and verbs, and other parts of speech, have for their judge the sense of hearing.

But as the writer being new in all kinds of knowledge, has

* Exodus xx. 18.   † Exodus xx. 22.   ‡ Deut. iv. 12.

also introduced this novelty both in his accounts of domestic and of foreign matters, saying that the voice is a thing to be judged of by the sight, which in point of fact is almost the only thing in us which is not an object of sight, with the single exception of the mind; for the things which are the objects of the rest of the outward senses are, every one of them, visible to the sight, such as colours, tastes, smells, things that are hot or cold, things that are smooth or rough, things that are soft or hard, inasmuch as they are substantial bodies. And what is meant by this I will explain more distinctly: a flavour is appreciable by the sight, not inasmuch as it is flavour, but so far as it is a mere substance, for in so far as it is flavour the sense of taste will judge of it; again a smell, in so far as it is a smell, will be decided upon by the nostrils, but inasmuch as it is a bodily substance, it will also be judged of by the eyes: and the other objects of sense will be tested in this manner; but voice is not appreciable by the sense of sight, neither inasmuch as it is a body, if indeed it is a body at all, nor inasmuch as it can be heard; but there are these two things in us which are wholly invisible—mind and speech; but the sound that proceeds from us does not the least resemble the divine organ of voice; for one organ of voice is mingled with the air, and flies to a kindred region with itself, namely to the ears; but the divine organ consists of unmixed and unalloyed speech, which outstrips the sense of hearing by reason of its fineness, and which is discerned by a pure soul, by means of its acuteness in the faculty of sight.

X. Therefore, after having left all mortal things, God, as I have said before, gives, as his first gift to the soul, an exhibition and an opportunity of contemplating mortal things: and in the second place he gives it an improvement in the doctrines of virtue, in respect both of their numbers and of their importance; for he says, "And I will make thee into a mighty nation," using this expression with reference to the multitude of the nation, and with reference to the increase and improvement of what was already great; and that this quantity in each kind, that is to say, both as to magnitude and as to number, was greatly increased, is pointed out by the king of Egypt, where he says, "For behold," says he, "the race of the children of Israel is a great multitude."*

* Exodus i. 9.

Since both these facts bear witness to the race which had the power of beholding the living God, that it had derived increase both in number and in magnitude, and as having done so, had met with prosperity, both in its life and in its language; for he does not say here (as any one would say who paid attention to the connection of the words which he was using), a numerous multitude, but he says, "A great multitude," knowing that the word numerous by itself implies an imperfect multitude, unless in addition to its numbers it has the attributes of intelligence and knowledge; for what advantage is it to comprehend many subjects of speculation, unless each of them receives a power of growth to a suitable size; for in like manner a field is not perfect in which there are innumerable plants growing on the ground, and no plant has grown up by means of the skill of the husbandman so as to arrive at perfection, unless it is now able to produce fruit.

But the beginning and the end of the greatness and numerousness of good things is the ceaseless and uninterrupted recollection of God, and an invocation of his assistance in the civil and domestic, confused and continual, warfare of life; for Moses says, "Behold, the people is wise and full of knowledge; this is a mighty nation; for what nation is there so great, that has God so near, as the Lord our God is to us in all the circumstances in which we call upon him?"* Therefore it has been plainly shown that there is power with God, which is a suitable and useful helper and defender, and the ruler himself comes nearer to the assistance of those persons who are worthy to be assisted.

XI. But who are they who are worthy to obtain such a mercy as this? It is plain that they are all lovers of wisdom and knowledge; for these are the wise people and the people of knowledge of whom he speaks, each of whom may naturally be called great, since he aims at great things, and at one great thing with excessive earnestness and eagerness, namely, at never being separated from the Almighty God, but at being able to endure his approach when he comes near steadily, and without any amazement or display.

This is the definition of great, to be near to God, or at least to be near to that thing to which God is near; forsooth the world and the wise citizen of the world are both full of many

* Deuteronomy iv. 6.

and great good things, but all the rest of the multitude of
men is involved in numerous evils, and in but few good things;
for the good is rare in the agitated and confused life of man.
On which account it is said in the sacred scriptures, " It is not
because you are numerous beyond all the nations that the
Lord has selected you above them all, and has chosen you out;
for in truth you are but few in comparison of all nations, but it
is because the Lord loves you;"* for if any one were to choose
to distribute the multitude of one soul as if according to
nations, he would find a great many ranks totally destitute of
all order, of which pleasures, or appetites or griefs, or fears, or
again follies and iniquities, and all the other vices which are
connected with or akin to them, are the leaders, and he would
find but one rank alone well regulated, that namely which is
under the leadership of right reason,

Among men, then, the unjust multitude is usually honoured
more than one single just person; but in the eye of God a
small company that is good is preferred to an infinite number
of persons who are unjust. And, on that account, he warns
men never to consent to a multitude of such a character;
" For," says he, " thou shalt not join with a multitude to do
evil."† May one, then, join a few to do so? One may never
join a single bad man. But a bad man, though he be but a
single individual, is a multitude in wickedness, and it is the
greatest possible evil to join with him; for, on the contrary, it
is becoming rather to oppose him and to make war upon him
with fearless energy. " For if," says Moses, " you go forth to
war against your enemies and see a horse," the emblem of arrogant and restive passion which scorns all control, " and a rider,"
the symbol of the mind devoted to the service of the passions,
riding upon it, " and a great body of your people," admirers of
those before-mentioned passions, and following in a solid
phalanx, " you shall not be terrified so as to flee from them,"
for you, though only a single person, shall have a single being
for your ally, " because the Lord your God is on your side;"‡
for his advance to battle puts an end to war, builds up peace
again, overthrows numbers of long-accustomed evils, preserves
the scanty race which loves God, to whom every one who becomes subject hates and abominates the ranks of the more
earthly armies.

* Deut. vii. 7.   † Exodus xxiii. 2.   ‡ Deut. xx. 1.

XII. "For," says Moses, "you shall not eat those animals which have a multitude of feet, being numbered among all the reptiles that are upon the earth ; because they are an abomination."* But the soul is not deserving of being hated which goes upon the earth in one part of itself, but only that which does so with all or with the greatest proportion of its parts, and which is exceedingly greedy about the things of the body, and which, in short, is unable to penetrate into and contemplate the divine revolutions of the heaven. And, moreover, as the animal with many feet is accursed among reptiles, so also is that which has no feet at all; the one for the cause already mentioned, and the other because it entirely falls upon the ground in all its parts, not being supported off the ground by anything, not even for the briefest minute.

For Moses says that, "Everything which goes upon its belly is unclean ;"† meaning, under this figurative expression, to point out those who pursue the pleasures of the belly. But some going far beyond these persons in wickedness, not only indulge in every description of desire, but also acquire that passion which is akin to desire, namely, anger, wishing to excite the whole of the irrational part of the soul and to destroy the mind. For what has been said in words, indeed, is applicable to the serpent, but in reality it is meant to apply to every man who is irrational and a slave to his passions, being truly a divine oracle, "Upon thy breast and upon thy belly shalt thou go ;"‡ for anger has its abode about the breast, and the seat of desire is in the belly. But the foolish man proceeds always by means of the two passions together, both anger and desire, omitting no opportunity, and discarding reason as his pilot and judge.

But the man who is contrary to him has extirpated anger and desire from his nature, and has enlisted himself under divine reason as his guide ; as also Moses, that faithful servant of God, did. Who, when he is offering the burnt offerings of the soul, "washes out the belly ;"§ that is to say, he washes out the whole seat of desires, and he takes away "the breast of the ram of the consecration ;"‖ that is to say, the whole of the warlike disposition, that so the remainder, the better portion of the soul, the rational part, having no longer anything to draw

* Leviticus xi. 42.   † Leviticus xi. 43.   ‡ Genesis iii. 14.
§ Leviticus viii. 21.   ‖ Leviticus viii. 29.

it in a different direction or to counteract its natural impulses, may indulge its own free and noble inclinations towards everything that is beautiful ; for, in this way, it will improve both in quantity and in magnitude. For it is said, "How long shall this people exasperate me ? and till what time will they refuse to believe me in all the signs which I have done among them ? I will smite them with death and I will destroy them, and I will make thee and thy father's house into a mighty nation, greater and mightier than this."*

For when the great multitude of the passions which indulge in anger and desire in the soul is put to the rout, then immediately those affections which depend on its rational nature rise up and become brilliant ; for as the reptile with many feet and that with no feet at all, though they are exactly opposite to one another in the race of reptiles, are both pronounced unclean, so also the opinion which denies any God, and that which worships a multitude of Gods, though quite opposite in the soul, are both profane. And a proof of this is that the law banishes them both " from the sacred assembly,"† forbidding the atheistical opinion, as a eunuch and mutilated person, to come into the assembly ; and the polytheistic, inasmuch as it prohibits any one born of a harlot from either hearing or speaking in the assembly. For he who worships no God at all is barren, and he who worships a multitude is the son of a harlot, who is in a state of blindness as to his true father, and who on this account is figuratively spoken of as having many fathers, instead of one.

XIII. There have now been two gifts of God already mentioned : the hope of a life devoted to contemplation, and an improvement in good things in respect both of quantity and of magnitude. The third gift is blessing, without which it is not possible that the graces already mentioned can be confirmed ; for the scripture says, "And I will bless thee ;" that is to say, I will give thee a word which shall be praised ; for the portion εὖ (in εὐλογήσω, I will bless), is always applicable to virtue. And of speech, one kind is like a spring and another kind is like a stream ; that which is in the mind being like the spring, and the utterance through the medium of the mouth and tongue resembling a stream. And it is great riches for either species of speech to be improved, for the mind to be so by exerting

* Numbers xiv. 11. † Deuteronomy xxiii. 2.

soundness of reason in everything, whether important or unimportant, or for the utterance to be so when under the guidance of right instruction ; for many men think, indeed, most excellently, but are betrayed by a bad interpreter, namely, speech, because they have not throughly worked up the whole course of encyclical instruction. Others, again, have been exceedingly skilful in explaining their ideas, but very bad hands at forming intentions, as, for instance, those who are called sophists, for the mind of these sophists is destitute of all harmony and of all real learning; but their speeches, which are uttered by the organs of their voice, are full of music and beauty.

But God gives no imperfect gifts to his subjects, but all his presents are complete and perfect. On which account he now dispenses blessing not to one section only, that of speech, but to both portions ; thinking it proper that the man who has received a benefit should also conceive the most excellent notions, and should also be able to explain what he has conceived in a powerful manner; for perfection, as it seems, consists in the two points, of being able to form clear and just conceptions and intentions, and also of being able to interpret them correctly. Do'you not see that Abel (and the name Abel is the name of one who mourns over mortal things, and attributes happiness to immortal things), has a mind wholly free from all liability to reproach ? And yet, from not being practised in discussions, he is defeated by one who is clever as an antagonist in such things, Cain being able to get the better of him more through superiority of skill than of strength ; for which reason, though I admire him on account of the good fortune with which he was endowed by nature, I nevertheless blame the disposition in him that, when he was challenged to a contest of discussion, he came forward to contend, when he ought to have abided by his usual tranquillity, discarding all love for contention. But if he was determined by all means to enter into such a contest, then still he ought not to have engaged in it until he had sufficiently practised himself in the exercises of the art ; for men who have been long versed in political strife are usually accustomed to get the better of men of uncultivated acuteness.

XIV. For this reason also the all-accomplished Moses deprecates coming to a consideration of reasonable looking and plausible arguments, from the time that God began to cause the light of truth to shine upon him through the immortal words of his knowledge and wisdom. But he is not the less led on to the contemplation of these arguments, not for the sake of becoming skilful in many things (for the contemplation of God himself and of his most sacred powers, are quite sufficient for a man who is fond of contemplation), but with a view to get the better of the sophists in Egypt, where fabulous and plausible inventions are looked upon as entitled to higher honour than a clear statement of truth.

When, therefore, the mind walks abroad among the affairs of the ruler of the universe, it requires nothing further as an object of contemplation, since the mind alone is the most piercing of all eyes as applied to the objects of the intellect; but when it is directed towards those things which are properly objects of the outward senses, or to any passion, or substance, of which the land of Egypt is the emblem, then it will have need of skill and power in argument. On which account Moses is directed also to take Aaron with him as an addition, Aaron being the symbol of uttered speech, "Behold," says God, "is not Aaron thy brother?"* For one rational nature being the mother of them both, it follows of course that the offspring are brothers, "I know that he will speak." For it is the office of the mind to comprehend, and of utterance to speak. "He," says God, "will speak for thee." For the mind not being able to give an adequate exposition of the part which is assigned to it, uses its neighbour speech as an interpreter, for the purpose of explaining what it feels.

Presently he further adds, "Behold he will come to meet thee," since in truth speech when it meets the conceptions, and embodies them in words, and names stamps what had before no impression on it, so as to make it current coin. And further on he says, "And when he seeth thee he will rejoice in himself;" for speech rejoices and exults when the conception is not indistinct, because it being clear and evident employs speech as an unerring and fluent expositor of itself, having a full supply of appropriate and felicitous expressions full of abundant distinctness and intelligibility.

XV. At all events when the conceptions are at all indistinct and ambiguous, speech is the treading as it were on empty air, and often stumbles and meets with a severe fall, so as never to be able to rise again. "And thou shalt speak to

* Exodus iv. 14.

him, and thou shalt give my words into his mouth," which is equivalent to, Thou shalt suggest to him conceptions which are in no respect different from divine language and divine arguments. For without some one to offer suggestions, speech will not speak; and the mind is what suggests to speech, as God suggests to the mind. "And he shall speak for thee to the people, and he shall be thy mouth, and thou shalt be to him as God." And there is a most emphatic meaning in the expression, "He shall speak for thee," that is to say, He shall interpret thy conceptions, and "He shall be thy mouth." For the stream of speech being borne through the tongue and mouth conveys the conceptions abroad. But speech is the interpreter of the mind to men, while again mind is by means of speech the interpreter to God; but these thoughts are those of which God alone is the overseer.

Therefore it is necessary for any one who is about to enter into a contest of sophistry, to pay attention to all his words with such vigorous earnestness, that he may not only be able to escape from the manœuvres of his adversaries, but may also in his turn attack them, and get the better of them, both in skill and in power. Do you not see that conjurors and enchanters, who attempting to contend against the divine word with their sophistries, and who daring to endeavour to do other things of a similar kind, labour not so much to display their own knowledge, as to tear to pieces and turn into ridicule what was done? For they even transform their rods into the nature of serpents, and change water into the complexion of blood, and by their incantations they attract the remainder of the frogs to the land,*and, like miserable men as they are, they increase everything for their own destruction, and while thinking to deceive others they are deceived themselves. And how was it possible for Moses to encounter such men as these unless he had prepared speech, the interpreter of his mind, namely Aaron? who now indeed is called his mouth; but in a subsequent passage we shall find that he is called a prophet, when also the mind, being under the influence of divine inspiration, is called God.

"For," says God, "I give thee as a God to Pharaoh, and Aaron thy brother shall be thy prophet."† O the harmonious and well-organised consequence! For that which interprets

* Exodus vii. 12.   † Exodus vii. 1.

the will of God is the prophetical race, being under the influence of divine possession and frenzy. Therefore " the rod of Aaron swallowed up their rods,"* as the holy scripture tells us. For all sophistical reasons are swallowed up and destroyed by the varied skilfulness of nature ; so that they are forced to confess that what is done is "the finger of God,"† an expression equivalent to confessing the truth of the divine scripture which asserts that sophistry is always subdued by wisdom. For the sacred account tells us that " the tables" on which the commandments were engraved as on a pillar, "were also written by the finger of God."‡ On which account the conjurors were not able to stand before Moses, but fell down as in a wrestling match, being overcome by the superior strength of their antagonist.

XVI. What then is the fourth gift? The having a great name, for God says, " I will magnify thy name;"§ and the meaning of this, as it appears to me, is as follows ; as to be good is honourable, so also to appear to be so is advantageous. And truth is better than appearance, but perfect happiness is when the two are combined. For there are great numbers of people who apply themselves to virtue in genuine honesty and sincerity, and who admire its genuine beauty, having no regard to the reputation which they may have with the multitude, and who in consequence have been plotted against, being thought wicked though in reality they are good. And indeed there is no advantage whatever in seeming, unless being has also been added long before, as is the case with respect to bodies ; for if all men were to fancy that one who was labouring under a disease was in good health, or that one in good health was labouring under a disease, still their opinion would not of itself create either disease or good health. But the man to whom God has given both things, namely both to be good and virtuous and also to appear so, that man is truly happy, and has a name which is really magnified. And one must have a prudent regard for a good reputation as a thing of great importance, and one which greatly benefits the life which is dependent on the body. And it falls to the lot of every one who, rejoicing with contentment, changes none of the

* Exodus vii. 12.   † Exodus viii 15.
‡ Exodus xxxii. 16.   § Genesis xii. 2.

existing laws, but zealously preserves the constitution of his native land.

For there are some men, who, looking upon written laws as symbols of things appreciable by the intellect, have studied some things with superfluous accuracy, and have treated others with neglectful indifference; whom I should blame for their levity; for they ought to attend to both classes of things, applying themselves both to an accurate investigation of invisible things, and also to an irreproachable observance of those laws which are notorious. But now men living solitarily by themselves as if they were in a desert, or else as if they were mere souls unconnected with the body, and as if they had no knowledge of any city, or village, or house, or in short of any company of men whatever, overlook what appears to the many to be true, and seek for plain naked truth by itself, whom the sacred scripture teaches not to neglect a good reputation, and not to break through any established customs which divine men of greater wisdom than any in our time have enacted or established. For although the seventh day is a lesson to teach us the power which exists in the uncreated God, and also that the creature is entitled to rest from his labours, it does not follow that on that account we may abrogate the laws which are established respecting it, so as to light a fire, or till land, or carry burdens, or bring accusations, or conduct suits at law, or demand a restoration of a deposit, or exact the repayment of a debt, or do any other of the things which are usually permitted at times which are not days of festival. Nor does it follow, because the feast is the symbol of the joy of the soul and of its gratitude towards God, that we are to repudiate the assemblies ordained at the periodical seasons of the year; nor because the rite of circumcision is an emblem of the excision of pleasures and of all the passions, and of the destruction of that impious opinion, according to which the mind has imagined itself to be by itself competent to produce offspring, does it follow that we are to annul the law which has been enacted about circumcision. Since we shall neglect the laws about the due observance of the ceremonies in the temple, and numbers of others too, if we exclude all figurative interpretation and attend only to those things which are expressly ordained in plain words.

But it is right to think that this class of things resembles the body, and the other class the soul; therefore, just as we take care of the body because it is the abode of the soul, so also must we take care of the laws that are enacted in plain terms : for while they are regarded, those other things also will be more clearly understood, of which these laws are the symbols, and in the same way one will escape blame and accusation from men in general. Do you not see that Abraham also says, that both small and great blessings fell to the share of the wise man, and he calls the great things, " all that he had," and his possessions, which it is allowed to the legitimate son alone to receive as his inheritance ; but the small things he calls gifts, of which the illegitimate children and those born of concubines, are also accounted worthy. The one, therefore, resemble those laws which are natural, and the other those which derive their origin from human enactment.

XVII. I also admire Leah, that woman endued with all virtue, who, at the birth of Asher, who is the symbol of that bastard wealth, which is perceptible by the outward senses, says, " Blessed am I, because all women shall call me happy."*
For she sees plainly that she will have a favourable reputation, thinking that she deserves to be praised, not only by those reasonings which are really masculine and manly, which have a nature free from all spot and stain, and which honour that which is really honest and incorrupt, but also by those more feminine reasonings which are in every respect overcome by those things which are visible, and which are unable to comprehend any object of contemplation which is beyond them. But it is the part of a perfect soul to set up a claim, not only to be, but also to appear to be, and, to labour earnestly not merely to have a good reputation in the houses of the men, but also in the secret chambers of the women.

On which account Moses also committed the preparation of the sacred works of the tabernacle not only to men, but also to women, who were to aid in making them ; for all " the woven works of hyacinthine colour, and of purple and of scarlet work, and of fine linen, and of goats' hair, do the women make;" and they also contribute their own ornaments without hesitation, " seals, and ear-rings, and finger-rings, and armlets, and tablets, all jewels of gold,"†—everything, in short, of which gold was the material, gladly giving up the ornaments of their

* Genesis xxx. 13. † Exodus xxxv. 22.

person in exchange for piety; and, moreover, carrying their zeal to a still higher degree, they likewise consecrated even their mirrors, that a laver might be made of them,"* in order that those who were about to assist at the sacrifices, washing their hands and their feet, that is to say, those works about which the mind is occupied and on which it is fixed, may have a view of themselves in a mirror according to the recollection of those mirrors of which the laver was made; for in this way they will never permit anything disgraceful to remain in any portion of the soul. And now they will dedicate the offering of fasting and patience, the most beautiful and sacred, and perfect of offerings.

But these real citizens and virtuous women are really as it were the outward senses, by whom Leah, that is virtue, desires to be honoured. But they who kindle an additional fire against the miserable mind are destitute of any city. For we read in the scripture that even, "women still burnt additional fire to Moab."† But may we not in this way say that so each of the outward senses of the foolish man when set on fire by the appropriate objects of outward sense, does also set fire to the mind, spreading over it an exceeding and interminable flame with irresistible vigour and impetuosity. At all events it is best to propitiate the array of women, that is to say, of the outward senses in the soul, just as it is desirable to do so with respect to the men, that is to say, with respect to the particular reasonings. For in this manner we shall arrange a more excellent system of life in a very beautiful manner.

XVIII. On this account also the self-instructed Isaac prays to the lover of wisdom, that he may be able to comprehend both those good things which are perceptible by the outward senses, and those which are appreciable only by the intellect. For he says, "May God give thee of the dew of heaven, and of the fatness of the earth,"‡ a prayer equivalent to, May he in the first place pour upon thee a continual and heavenly rain appreciable by the intellect, not violently so as to wash thee away, but mildly and gently like dew, so as to benefit thee. And in the second place, may he bestow upon thee that earthly wealth which is perceptible by the outward senses, fat and fertile, having drained off its opposite, namely poverty, from the soul and from all its parts.

* Exodus xxxviii. 8.   † Numbers xxi. 30.   ‡ Genesis xxvii. 28.

But if you examine the great high priest, that is to say reason, you will find him entertaining ideas in harmony with these, and having his sacred garments richly embroidered by all the powers which are comprehensible either by the outward senses or by the intellect; the other portion of which clothing would require a more prolix explanation than is practicable on the present occasion, and we must pass it by for the present. But the extreme portions, those namely at the head and at the feet, we will examine,

There is then on the head " a golden leaf,"* pure, having on it the impression of a seal, " Holiness to the Lord." And on the feet there are, " on the fringe of the inner garment, bells and small flowerets."† But this seal is an idea of ideas, according to which God fashioned the world, being an incorporeal idea, comprehensible only by the intellect. And the flowerets and the bells are symbols of distinctive qualities perceptible by the outward senses; of which the faculties of hearing and of seeing are the judges. And he adds, with exceeding accuracy of investigation, " The voice of him shall be heard as he enters into the holy place," in order that when the soul enters into the places appreciable by the intellect, and divine, and truly holy, the very outward senses may likewise be benefited, and may sound in unison, in accordance with virtue ; and our whole system, like a melodious chorus of many men, may sing in concert one well-harmonised melody composed of different sounds well combined, the thoughts inspiring the leading notes (for the objects of intellect are the leaders of the chorus) ; and the objects of the external senses, singing in melodies, accord the symphonies which follow, which are compared to individual members of the chorus.

For, in short, as the law says, it was not right for the soul to be deprived of " its necessaries, and its garments, and its place of abode,"‡ these three things; but it ought rather to have had each of them allotted to it in a durable manner. Now the necessaries of the soul are those good things which are perceptible only by the intellect, which ought, and indeed are bound by the law of nature, to be attached to it ; and the clothing means those things which relate to the exterior and visible ornament of human life ; and the place of abode is continued diligence and care respecting each of the species

* Exodus xxviii. 36.   † Exodus xxviii. 34.   ‡ Exodus xxi. 10.

before mentioned, in order that the objects of the outward senses may appear as the invisible objects of the intellect do also.

XIX. There is, also, a fifth gift, which consists only in the bare fact of existence; and it is mentioned after all the pre- vious ones, not because it is inferior to them, but rather because it overtops and excels them all; for what can be a greater blessing than to be formed by nature, and to be, without any falsehood or fictitious pretence, really good and worthy of the most perfect praise? "For," says God, "thou shalt be blessed"* (εὐλογητὸς); not merely a person who is blessed (εὐλογημένος), for this latter fact is estimated by the opinions and report of the multitude, but the other depends on a person being, in real truth, deserving of blessings; for as the being praiseworthy (τὸ ἐπαινετὸν εἶναι) differs from being praised, being superior to it; and as the being blameworthy differs from being blamed, in being worse; for the one depends upon a person's natural character, while the other is affirmed only with refer- ence to his being considered such and such. And real genuine nature is a more reliable thing than opinion; so, also, to be blessed by men, that is to say, to be celebrated by their praises and benedictions, is of less value than to be formed by nature so as to be worthy of blessing, even though all men should be silent respecting one, and this last is what is meant in the scriptures by the term blessed (εὐλογητὸς).

XX. These are the good things which are given to him who is about to be wise. But let us now examine what God, for the sake of the wise man, bestows on the rest of mankind also. He says, "I will bless those who bless thee, and curse those who curse thee."† Now that this is said by way of doing honour to the good man, is plain to every one. And this, too, is not the only reason why it is said, but it is said also on account of the harmonious consequence which exists in things; for he who praises a good man is himself worthy of encomium, and he who blames him is, on the other hand, deserving of blame. But it is not so much the power of those who utter or who write praise or blame that is trusted to, as the real character of what is due; so that those persons would not really appear to praise or to blame at all who, in either case, adopt or intro- duce any falsehood of their own. Do you not see flatterers who,

* Genesis xii. 2.   † Genesis xii. 3.

day and night, weary and annoy the ears of those to whom
they address their flatteries, and who not only nod assent to
every word that they say, but who also string together long
sentences, and connect rhapsodies, and often pray to them with
their mouths, but who are continually cursing them in their
hearts? What, then, would any one in his senses say? Would
he not pronounce that those who speak thus are, in reality,
enemies rather than friends, and do in reality blame them
rather than praise them, even if they put together whole dramas
full of panegyric and sing them in their honour?

Therefore, the vain Balaam, although he sang hymns of
exceeding sublimity to God, among which, also, is that one
beginning, "God is not as a man,"* the most beautiful of all
songs, and who uttered panegyrics on the seeing multitude,
Israel, going through a countless body of particulars, is rightly
judged by the wise lawgiver to have been an impious man and
accursed, and to have been cursing rather than blessing; for
he says that he was hired for money by the enemy, and so became an evil prophet of evil things, bearing in his soul most
bitter curses against the God loving nature, but being compelled to utter prophetically with his mouth and tongue the
most exquisite and sublime prayers in their favour; for the
things that he said, being very excellent, were, in fact, suggested
by the God who loves virtue; but the curses which he conceived
in his mind (for they were wicked) were the offspring of his
mind, which hated virtue.

And the sacred scripture bears testimony to this fact; for it
says, "God did not grant to Balaam leave to curse thee, but
turned his curses into blessing;"† though, in fact, all the
words that he uttered were full of good omen. But he who
looks into all that is laid up in the recesses of the heart, and
who alone has the power to see those things which are invisible
to created beings, from these secret things has passed a con-
demnatory decree, being in his own person at once the most
indubitable of witnesses and the most incorruptible of judges,
since even the contrary thing is praised, namely, for a man
who appears to calumniate and to accuse with his mouth, in
his heart to be blessing, and praising, and speaking words of
good omen. This, as it would seem, is the custom of those
who correct youth, and of preceptors, and of parents, and of

* Numbers xxiii. 19.   † Deuteronomy xxiii. 6.

elders, and of rulers, and of laws; for they, at times, do each of
them reprove and punish, and by these means render the souls
of those who are under their instruction better. And of these
men no one is an enemy to his pupil, but they are all of them
friendly to all of them; but it is the office of friends who have
a genuine and unalloyed good will to others to speak freely,
without any unfriendly purpose.

Therefore, as far as blessings, and praises, and prayers, or, on
the other hand, reproaches and curses are concerned, one
must not so much be guided by what proceeds out of the mouth
by utterance, as by what is in the heart, by which, as by the
original source of them all, both kinds of speeches are estimated.

XXI. These, then, are the things which, he says, happen in
the first instance to others on account of the good man, when
they seek to load him with either praise or blame, or with
blessings or curses. But that which comes next in order is the
most important thing; that when they are silent, still no
portion of the rational nature is left without a participation in
the benefits; for God says that, " In thee shall all the nations
of the world be blessed." And this is a promise exceedingly full
of doctrine; for if the mind is always free from disease and
from injury, it then exerts all the tribes of feelings which
affect it, and all its powers in a state of sound health, namely,
its powers of seeing and of hearing, and all those which belong
to the outward senses; and, moreover, all its appetites which
are conversant about pleasures and desires, and all those feelings likewise which being reduced from a state of agitation to
one of tranquillity, receive a better character from the change.

Before now, indeed, cities, and countries, and peoples, and
nations of the earth, have enjoyed the greatest happiness and
prosperity in consequence of the virtue and prudence of the
individual; especially so when, in addition to a good disposition
and wisdom, God has also given him irresistible power, as he
may have given to a musician or to any artist the proper
instruments for music, or for carrying out any other art, or as
wood is supplied as a material for fire; for in good truth the
just man is the prop of all the human race; and he, bringing all
that he has into the common stock for the advantage of these
who can use it, bestows his treasures ungrudgingly, and what-

ever he finds that he has not got in himself, he prays for to the only giver of all wealth, the all-bounteous God.

And God, opening the treasures of heaven, pours forth and showers down upon him all kinds of good things together; so that all the channels on earth are filled with them to over-flowing. And these blessings he at all times freely bestows, never rejecting the prayer of supplication which is addressed to him; for it is said in another passage, when Moses addresses him with supplication: " I am favourable to them according to thy word."* And this expression, as it seems, is equivalent to the other: " In thee all the nations of the earth shall be blessed." On which account also the wise Abraham, who had had experience of the goodness of God in all things, believes that even if all other things are destroyed, still a small fragment of virtue would be preserved, like a spark of fire, and that for the sake of this little spark, he pities those other things also, so as to raise them up when fallen, and re-kindle them when extinct.

For even the slightest spark of fire that is still smouldering, when it is fanned and re-kindled will set fire to a large pile : and so too the smallest spark of virtue, when it beams up, being wakened into life by good hopes, gives light to what has previously been dim-sighted and blind, and causes what has been withered to shoot up again, and whatever is barren and unproductive it transforms and brings to abundance of prolific power. Thus a good, which is but rare, is, by the kindness of God, made abundant and showered upon men, making everything else to resemble itself.

XXII. Let us therefore pray that the mind may be in the soul like a pillar in a house, and, in like manner, that the just man may be firmly established in the human race for the relief of all diseases; for while he is in vigorous health, one must not abandon all hope of complete safety, as through the medium of him, I imagine God the Saviour extending his all-healing medicine, that is to say, his propitious and merciful power to his suppliants and worshippers, bids them employ it for the salvation of those who are sick; spreading it like a salve over the wounds of the soul, which folly, and injustice, and all the other multitude of vices, being sharpened up, have

* Numbers xiv. 20.

grievously inflicted upon it. And a most visible example of this is the righteous Noah, who, when so many portions of the soul were swallowed up in the great deluge, himself vigorously overtopped the waves and floated on their surface, and so rose above all the dangers which threatened him; and when he had escaped in safety, he sent out great and beautiful roots from himself, from which, like a tree, the whole crop of wisdom sprang up, which, bearing useful fruit, put forth the three fruits of the seeing creature, Israel, the measures of time, Abraham, Isaac, and Jacob.

For, virtue is, and will be, and has been in everything; which virtue perhaps is at times obscured among men by the want of opportunity, but which opportunity the minister of God again brings to light. Since Sarah, that is to say, prudence, brings forth a male child, flourishing, not according to the periodical seasons of the year, but according to those seasons and felicitous occasions which have no connection with time; for it is said, "I will surely return and visit thee according to the time of life; and Sarah, thy wife, shall have a son."*

XXIII. We have now, then, said enough about the gifts which God is accustomed to bestow on those who are to become perfect, and through the medium of them on others also.

In the next passage it is said, that "Abraham went as the Lord commanded him."† And this is the end which is celebrated among those who study philosophy in the best manner, namely, to live in accordance with nature. And this takes place when the mind, entering into the path of virtue, treads in the steps of right reason, and follows God, remembering his commandments, and at all times and in all places confirming them both by word and deed; for "he went as the Lord commanded him." And the meaning of this is, as God commands (and he commands in a beautiful and praiseworthy manner), in that very manner does the virtuous man act, guiding the path of his life in a blameless way, so that the actions of the wise man are in no respect different from the divine commands. At all events, God is represented in another passage as saying, "Abraham has kept all my law."‡ And law is nothing else but the word of God, enjoining what

* Genesis xviii. 10. † Genesis xii. 4. ‡ Genesis xxvi. 5.

is right, and forbidding what is not right, as he bears witness, where he says, " He received the law from his words."*

If, then, the divine word is the law, and if the righteous man does the law, then by all means he also performs the the word of God. So that, as I said before, the words of God are the actions of the wise man. Accordingly, the end is, according to the most holy Moses, to follow God ; as he says also in another passage, " Thou shalt walk after the Lord thy God ; "† not meaning that he should employ the motion of his legs ; for the earth is the support of a man, but whether the whole world is sufficient to be the support of God, I do not know ; but he seems here to be speaking allegorically, intending to represent the way in which the soul follows the divine doctrines, which has a direct reference to the honour due to the great cause of all things.

XXIV. And he also, with a wish further to excite an irresistible desire of what is good, enjoins one to cleave to it ; for he says, " Thou shalt fear the Lord thy God, and him only shalt thou serve ; and thou shalt cleave to him."‡ What, then, is this cleaving ? What ? Surely it is piety and faith ; for these virtues adapt and invite the mind to incorruptible nature. For Abraham also, when he believed, is said to have " come near to God."§ If, therefore, while you are walking you are neither fatigued, so as to give way and stumble, nor are so careless as to turn to either the right hand or to the left hand, and so to stray and miss the direct road which lies between the two ; but if, imitating good runners, you finish the course of life without stumbling or error, you will deservedly obtain the crown and worthy prize of victory when you have arrived at your desired end.

For is not this the crown and the prize of victory not to miss the proposed end of one's labours, but to arrive at that goal of prudence which is so difficult to be reached ? What, then, is the object of having right wisdom ? To be able to condemn one's own folly and that of every created being. For to be aware that one knows nothing is the end of all knowledge, since there is only one wise being, who is also the only God. On which account Moses very beautifully has represented the father of the universe as being also the inspector and superin-

* Deut. xxxiii. 4.   † Deut. xiii. 4.
‡ Deut. x. 20.   § Genesis xviii. 23.

tendent of all that he has created, saying, " God saw all that he had made, and behold it was very good."* For it was not possible for any one to have an accurate view of all that had been created, except for the Creator.

Come, then, ye who are full of arrogance, and ignorance, and of exceeding insolence, ye that are wise in your own conceit, and who say not only that ye know accurately what each thing is, but that you are also able to explain the causes why it is so, showing daring with great rashness, as if ye had either been present at the creation of the world, and had actually seen how and from what each separate thing was made, or had been counsellors of the Creator concerning the things which were created. Come, and at once abandoning all other things, learn to know yourselves, and tell us plainly what ye yourselves are in respect of your bodies, in respect of your souls, in respect of your external senses, and in respect of your reason.

Tell us now with respect to one, and that the smallest, perhaps, of the senses, what sight is, and how it is that you see ; tell us what hearing is, and how is it that you hear ; tell us what taste is, what touch is, what smell is, and how it is that you exercise the energies of each of these faculties ; and what the sources of them are from which they originate. For do not tell me long stories about the moon and the sun, and all the other things in heaven and in the world, which are at such a distance from us and which are so different in their natures, empty-minded creatures that you are, before you examine into and become acquainted with yourselves ; for when you have learnt to understand yourselves, then perhaps one may believe you when you enter into explanations respecting other things. But till you are able to tell what you yourselves are, do not expect ever to be looked upon as truth-telling judges or witnesses with respect to others.

XXV. Since, then, these things are in this state, the mind, when it is rendered perfect, will pay its proper tribute to the God who causes perfection, according to that most sacred scripture, " For the law is, that tribute belongs to the Lord." † When does the mind pay it ? When ? " On the third day it comes to the place which God has told it of,"‡ having passed by the greater portions of the differences of time, and being now passing over to that nature which has no connection with

* Genesis i. 31.   † Numbers xxxi. 40.   ‡ Genesis xxii. 4.

time; for then it will sacrifice its beloved son, not a man (for the wise man is not a slayer of his children), but the male off-spring of a virtuously living soul, the fruit which germinates from it, as to which it knows not how it bore it, the divine shoot, which, when it appears, the soul then having appeared to be pregnant, confesses that it does not understand the good which has happened to it, saying, " Who will tell to Abraham ?"* as if, in fact, he would refuse to believe about the rising up of the self-taught race, that " Sarah was suckling a child," not that the child was being suckled by Sarah.   For the self-taught offspring is nourished by no one, but is itself the nourishment of others as being competent to teach, and having no need to learn ; for " I have brought forth a son, " not like the Egyptian women, in the flower of my age and in the height of my bodily vigour, but like the Hebrew souls, " in my old age," † when all the objects of the outward senses and all mortal things are faded, and when the objects of the intel-lect and immortal things are in their full vigour and worthy of all estimation and honour.

And I have brought forth, too, without requiring the aid of the midwife's skill ; for we bring forth even before any skill or knowledge of man can come to us, without any of the ordi-nary means of assistance to help us, God having sown and generated an excellent offspring, which, in accordance with the law made concerning gratitude, very properly requites its creator with gratitude and honour.   For, says God, " My gifts, and my offerings, and my first fruits, you have taken care to bring to me." ‡

XXVI. This is the end of the path of those who follow the arguments and injunctions contained in the law, and who walk in the way which God leads them in ; but he who falls short of this, on account of his hunger after pleasure and his greedi-ness for the indulgence of his passions, by name Amalek ; § for the interpretation of the name Amalek is, " the people that licks up " shall be cut off.   And the sacred scriptures teach us that this disposition is an insidious one ; for when it per-ceives that the most vigorous portion of the power of the soul has passed over, then, " rising up from its ambuscade, it cuts to pieces the fatigued portion like a rearguard."

* Genesis xxi. 7.   † Genesis xxi. 7.
‡ Numbers xxviii. 2.   § Deuteronomy xxv. 17.

And of fatigue there is one kind which easily succumbs through the weakness of its reason which is unable to support the labours, which are to be encountered in the cause of virtue, and so, like those who are surprised in the rearguard, it is easily overcome. But the other kind is willing to endure honourable toil, vigorously persevering in all good things, and not choosing to bear anything whatever that is bad, not even though it be ever so trifling, but rejecting it as though it were the heaviest of burdens.

On which account, the law has also, by a very felicitous appellation, called virtue Leah, which name, being interpreted, means " wearied ; " for she very naturally thought the life of the wicked heavy and burdensome, and in its own nature wearisome ; and did not choose even to look upon it, turning her eyes only on what is beautiful; and let the mind labour not only to follow God without any relaxation or want of vigour, but also to walk onwards by the straight path, turning to neither side, neither to the right nor yet to the left, as the earthly Edom did, seeking out of the way lurking places, at one time being full of excesses and superfluities, and at another of differences and short comings ; for it is better to proceed along the middle road, which is that which is really the royal road, and which the great and only King, God, has widened to be a most suitable abode for the souls that love virtue. On which account some also of those who prosecute a gentle kind of philosophy, which is conversant chiefly about the society of mankind, have pronounced the virtues to be means, placing them on the confines between two extremes. Since, on the one hand, excessive pride, being full of much insolence is an evil, and to take up with a humble and self-abasing demeanour is to expose one's self to be trampled upon; but the mean, which is compounded of both, in a gentle manner is advantageous.

XXVII. We must also inquire what the meaning of the expression, " He went with Lot," * is. Now, the name Lot, being interpreted, means " declination ;" and the mind declines or inclines, at one time rejecting what is good, and at another time what is evil. And both these declinations are often seen in one and the same thing. For there are some hesitating and wavering people who incline to both sides in turn, like a

* Genesis xii. 4.

ship which is tossed about by different winds, or like the
different sides of a scale, being unable to rest firmly on one
thing ; people whom one cannot praise even when they turn to
the better side, for they are influenced by impulse, and not by
deliberate meaning.   Now, of these men Lot is a spectator,
who Moses here says went with the lover of wisdom.   But it
was very well that when he began to accompany him he should
unlearn ignorance, and should never again return to it.   But
still he goes with him, not in the hope of deriving improvement from an imitation of a better man, but with a view of
persecuting him also with a counter attraction and allurements
in an opposite direction, and of leading him where there was a
chance of his falling.

And a proof of this is, that the one, having fallen back again
into his ancient disease, departs, having been taken prisoner by
those enemies who are in the soul; but the other, having guarded
against all his designs, concealed in ambuscade, took every imaginable care to live at a distance from him.   But the separate
habitation he will arrange hereafter, but not yet.   For at present, his speculations, as would be likely to be the case with a
man who has but lately begun to apply himself to divine contemplation, have a want of solidity and steadiness in them.   But
when they have become more compact, and are established on a
firmer footing, then he will be able to separate from himself the
alluring and flattering disposition as an irreconcileable enemy,
and one difficult to subdue : for this is that disposition which
attaches itself to the soul in such a manner as to be difficult to
shake off, hindering it from proceeding swiftly on its progress
towards virtue.

This, too, when we leave Egypt, that is to say, the whole of the
district connected with the body, being anxious to unlearn our
subjection to the passions, in accordance with the language and
precepts of the prophet Moses, follows us close, checking and
impeding our zeal in the departure, and out of envy causing
delay to the rapidity of setting forth ; for it is said, " And a
great mixed multitude went up with them, and sheep, and oxen,
and very much cattle."*   But this mixed multitude, if one
is to speak the plain truth, are the cattle-like and irrational
doctrines of the soul.

XXVIII. And it is with particular beauty and propriety that

* Exodus xii. 38.

he calls the soul of the wicked man a mixed multitude : for it
is truly a company which has been collected and brought together from all quarters, and composed of a promiscuous body of
numerous and antagonist opinions, being, though only one in
point of number, of infinite variety by reason of its versatility
and diversity ; on which account, besides the word " mixed,"
there is also added the epithet " great :" for he who looks at one
end only is truly simple, and unmixed, and plain ; but he who
proposes to himself many objects of life is manifold, and mixed,
and rough, in real truth : on which account the sacred scriptures say, that that practiser of virtue, Jacob, was a smooth man,
and that Esau, the practiser of what is shameful, was a hairy or
rough man.

On account, then, of this mixed and rough multitude collected
together from mixed opinions collected from all imaginable
quarters, the mind which was able to exert great speed when it
was fleeing from the country of the body, that is, from Egypt,
and which was able in those days to receive the inheritance of
virtue, being assisted by a threefold light, the memory of past
things, the energy of present things, and the hope of the future,
passed that exceeding length of time, forty years, in going up
and down, and all around, wandering in every direction by reason
of the diversity of manners, when it ought rather to have proceeded by the straight and most advantageous way.

This is he who not only rejoiced in a few species of desire, but
who also chose to pass by none whatever entirely, so that he
might obtain the whole entire genus in which every species is
included ; for it is said that, " the mixed multitude that was
among them desired all kinds of concupiscence,"* that is to say,
the very genus of concupiscence itself, and not some one species;
and sitting down they wept.   For the mind is conscious that it
is possessed of but slight power, and when it is not able to obtain what it desires, it weeps and groans ; and yet it ought to
rejoice when it fails to be able to indulge its passions, or to become infected with diseases, and it ought to think their want and
absence a very great piece of good fortune.   But it very often
happens to the followers of virtue, also, to become languid and
to weep, either because they are bewailing the calamities of
the foolish, on account of their participation in their common

* Numbers xi. 4.

nature, and their natural love for their race, or through excess of joy.

And this excess of joy arises whenever on a sudden an abundance of all kinds of good coming together are showered down to overflowing, without having been previously expected; in reference to which kind of joy it is that the poet appears to me to have used the expression—

Smiling amid her tears.*

For exceeding joy, the best of all feelings, falling on the soul when completely unexpected, makes it greater than it was before, so that the body can no longer contain it by reason of its bulk and magnitude; and so, being closely packed and pressed down, it distils drops which it is the fashion to call tears, concerning which it is said in the Psalms, "Thou shalt give me to eat bread steeped in tears;"† and again, "My tears have been my bread day and night;"‡ for the food of the mind are tears such as are visible, proceeding from laughter seated internally and excited by virtuous causes, when the divine desire instilled into our hearts changes the song which was merely the lament of the creature into the hymn of the uncreated God.

XXIX. Some persons then repudiate this mixed and rough multitude, and raise a wall of fortification to keep it from them, rejoicing only in the race which loves God; but some, on the other hand, form associations with it, thinking it desirable to arrange their own lives according to such a system that they can place them on the confines between human and divine virtues, in order that they may touch both those which are virtues in truth and those which are such in appearance.

Now the disposition which concerns itself in the affairs of state adheres to this opinion, which disposition it is usual to call Joseph, with whom, when he is about to bring his father, there go up "all the servants of Pharaoh, and the elders of his house, and all the elders of the land of Egypt, and all the whole family of Joseph, himself, and his brothers, and all his father's house."§ You see here that this disposition which is conversant about affairs of state is placed between the house of Pharaoh and his father's house, in order that it might equally reach the affairs of the body, that is to say, of Egypt;

---

* Homer's Iliad, vi. 484. † Psalm lxxx. 6.
‡ Psalm xlii. 4. § Genesis l. 7.

and those of the soul, which are all laid up in his father's
house as in a treasury; for when he says, "I am of God,"*
and all the other things which are akin to or connected with
him abide among the established laws of his father's house;
and when he mounts up into the second chariot of the mind,
which appears to bear sovereign sway, namely Pharaoh, he is
again establishing Egyptian pride. And he is more miserable
who is looked upon as a king of considerable renown, and who
is borne along in the chariot which has the precedence; for to
be pre-eminent in what is not honourable is the most conspicuous disgrace, just as it is a lighter evil to come off second
best in such a contest.

But you may learn to perceive how wavering a disposition
such a man has from the oaths which he swears, swearing at
one time "by the health of Pharaoh,"† and then again, on the
contrary, "not by the health of Pharaoh." But this latter
formula of oath, which contains a negation, looks as if it were
the injunction of his father's house, which is always medi-
tating the destruction of the passions, and wishing that they
should die; but the other brings us back to the discipline of
Egypt, which desires that these passions should be preserved;
on which account, although so great a multitude went up
together, he still does not call it a mixed multitude, since to a
person who is endowed with a real power of seeing, and who
is a lover of virtue, every thing which is not virtue nor an
action of virtue, appears to be mixed and confused; but to him
who still loves the things of earth, the prizes of earth do by
themselves seem to be worthy of love and worthy of honour.

XXX. Accordingly, as I have already said, the lovers of
wisdom will raise a wall of exclusion against the man who,
like a drone, has resolved to injure his profitable labours, and
who follows him with this object, and he will receive those who,
out of their admiration of what is honourable, follow him
with a view to imitating him; assigning to each of them that
portion which is suited to them; for, says he, "of the
men who went with me, Eschol, Annan, and Mamre shall
receive a share."‡ And by these names of persons he means
dispositions which are good by nature and fond of contemplation; for Eschol is an emblem of a good disposition, having a
name of fire, since a good disposition is full of good daring

* Genesis l. 19.　　　† Genesis xlii. 16.　　　‡ Genesis xiv. 24.

and fervour, and adheres to what it has ever applied itself. And Annan is the symbol of a man fond of contemplation; for the name, being interpreted, means "the eyes," from the fact that the eyes of the soul also are opened by cheerfulness; and of both these persons a life of contemplation is the inheritance, which is entitled Mamre, which name is derived from seeing; and to the contemplative man, the faculty of seeing is most appropriate and most peculiarly belonging.

But when the mind, having been under the tuition of these trainers, finds nothing wanting for practice, it then proceeds onwards with and accompanies perfect wisdom, not outstripping it nor being outstripped by it, but marching alongside of it step by step, with equal pace. And the words of scripture show this, in which it is distinctly stated that "they both of them went together, and came to the plain which God had mentioned to them:"* a most excellent equality of virtues, better than any rivalry, an equality of labour with a natural good condition of body, and an equality of art with self-instructed nature, so that both of them are able to carry off equal prizes of virtue; as if the arts of painting and statuary were not only able, as they are at present, to make representations devoid of motion or animation, but were able also to invest the objects which they paint or form with motion and life; for in that case the arts which were previously imitative of the works of nature would appear now to have become the natures themselves.

XXXI. But whoever is raised on high to such a sublime elevation will never any more allow any of the portions of his soul to dwell below among mortal men, but will draw them all up to himself as if they were suspended by a rope; for which reason a sacred injunction of the following purport was given to the wise man, "Go thou up to thy Lord, thou, and Aaron, and Nadab, and Abihu, and seventy of the elders of Israel."† And the meaning of this injunction is as follows, "Go up, O soul, to the view of the living God, in an orderly manner, rationally, voluntarily, fearlessly, lovingly, in the holy and perfect numbers of seven multiplied tenfold." For Aaron is described in the law as the prophet of Moses, being loudly uttered speech prophesying to the mind. And Nadab is interpreted "voluntary," that is to say, the man who honours the

* Genesis xxii. 3.   † Exodus xxiv. 1.

Deity without compulsion; and the interpretation of the name Abihu is, "my father." This man is one who has not need of a master by reason of his folly, more than of a father by reason of his wisdom, namely such a father as God the ruler of the world. And these powers are the body-guards of the mind which is worthy to bear sovereign sway, which ought also to attend upon the king, and conduct him on his way.

But the soul is afraid by itself to rise up to the contemplation of the living God, if it does not know the road, from being lifted up by a union of ignorance and audacity; and the falls which are caused by such a union of ignorance and great rashness are very serious; on which account Moses prays that he may have God himself as his guide to the road which leads to him. For he says, "If thou wilt not thyself go with me, then do not thou lead me hence."* Because every motion which is without the divine approbation is mischievous, and it is better for men to remain here wandering about in this mortal life, as the greater portion of the human race does, than raising themselves up to heaven in pride and arrogance, to encounter an overthrow, as has happened to countless numbers of sophists, who have looked upon wisdom as only a discovery of plausible arguments, and not, as it is, a certain belief in and well-assured knowledge of facts. And perhaps too there is some such meaning as this intended to be conveyed by these words,—do not raise me up on high, bestowing on me riches, or glory, or honours, or authority, or any other of those things which are usually ranked as good, unless you intend also to go with them and me yourself; for these things are often calculated to cause either great mischief, or great advantage to their possessors; advantage when God is the guide of their mind; injury when the contrary is the case. For to great numbers of people the things which are called good not being so in reality have been the causes of irremediable evils, but the man who follows God does of necessity have for his fellow travellers all those reasons which are the attendants of God, which we are accustomed to call angels.

At all events, it is said that "Abraham went with them conducting them on their way."† Oh the admirable praise! according to which, he who was conducting others was himself conducted by them, only giving what he was receiving; not

* Exodus xxxiii. 15.   † Genesis xviii. 16.

giving one thing instead of another, but only that one single
thing, which was prepared as a retributory gift, for until a man
is made perfect he uses divine reason as the guide of his path,
for that is the sacred oracle of scripture : " Behold, I send my
angel before thy face that he may keep thee in the road, so as
to lead thee into the land which I have prepared for thee.
Attend thou to him, and listen to him ; do not disobey him ; for
he will not pardon your transgressions, for my name is in
him."* But when he has arrived at the height of perfect
knowledge, then, running forward vigorously, he keeps up with
the speed of him who was previously leading him in his way;
for in this way they will both become attendants of God who
is the guide of all things ; no one of those who hold erroneous
opinions accompanying them any longer, and even Lot himself,
who turned on one side the soul, which might have been
upright and inflexible, removing and living at a distance.

XXXII. And " Abraham," says Moses, " was seventy-five
years of age, when he departed out of Charran." Now concerning the number of seventy-five years (for this contains a
calculation corresponding to what has been previously advanced), we will enter into an accurate examination hereafter.
But first of all we will examine what Charran is, and what is
meant by the departure from this country to go and live
in another. Now it is not probable that any one of those persons
who are acquainted with the law are ignorant that Abraham
had previously migrated from Chaldæa when he came to live
in Charran. But after his father died he then departed from
this land of Chaldæa, so that he had now migrated from two
different places. What then shall we say ?

The Chaldeans appear beyond all other men to have devoted
themselves to the study of astronomy and of genealogies;
adapting things on earth to things sublime, and also adapting
the things of heaven to those on earth, and like people who,
availing themselves of the principles of music, exhibit a most
perfect symphony as existing in the universe by the common
union and sympathy of the parts for one another, which though
separated as to place, are not disunited in regard of kindred.
These men, then, imagined that this world which we behold
was the only world in the existing universe, and was either
God himself, or else that it contained within itself God, that

* Exodus xxiii. 20.

is, the soul of the universe. Then, having erected fate and necessity into gods, they filled human life with excessive impiety, teaching men that with the exception of those things which are apparent there is no other cause whatever of anything, but that it is the periodical revolutions of the sun, and moon, and other stars, which distribute good and evil to all existing beings.

Moses indeed appears to have in some degree subscribed to the doctrine of the common union and sympathy existing between the parts of the universe, as he has said that the world was one and created (for as it is a created thing and also one, it is reasonable to suppose that the same elementary essences are laid as the foundations of all the particular effects which arise, as happens with respect to united bodies that they reciprocally contain each other); but he differs from them widely in their opinion of God, not intimating that either the world itself, or the soul of the world, is the original God, nor that the stars or their motions are the primary causes of the events which happen among men; but he teaches that this universe is held together by invisible powers, which the Creator has spread from the extreme borders of the earth to heaven, making a beautiful provision to prevent what he has joined together from being dissolved; for the indissoluble chains which bind the universe are his powers.

On which account even though it may be said somewhere in the declaration of the law, " God is in the heaven above, and in the earth beneath," let no one suppose that God is here spoken of according to his essence. For the living God contains everything, and it is impiety to suppose that he is contained by any thing, but what is meant is, that his power according to which he made, and arranged, and established the universe, is both in heaven and earth. And this, to speak correctly, is goodness, which has driven away from itself envy, which hates virtue and detests what is good, and which generates those virtues by which it has brought all existing things into existence and exhibited them as they are.

Since the living God is indeed conceived of in opinion everywhere, but in real truth he is seen nowhere; so that divine scripture is most completely true in which it is said, " Here am I," speaking of him who cannot be shown as if he were being shown, of " him who is invisible as if he were

visible, before thou existedst." * For he proceeds onward before
the created universe, and outside of it, and not contained or
borne onward in any of the things whose existence began after
his.

XXXIII. These things then having been now said for the
purpose of overturning the opinions of the Chaldeans ; he
thinks that it is desirable to lead off and invite away those
who are still Chaldaizing in their minds to the truth of his
teaching, and he begins thus :—

"Why," says he, " my excellent friends do you raise yourselves up in such a sudden manner from the earth, and soar to
such a height? and why do ye rise above the air, and tread the
ethereal expanse, investigating accurately the motions of the
sun, and the periodical revolutions of the moon, and the
harmonious and much-renowned paths of the rest of the stars?
for these things are too great for your comprehension, inasmuch
as they have received a more blessed and divine position.
Descend therefore from heaven, and when you have come down,
do not, on the other hand, employ yourselves in the investigation
of the earth and the sea, and the rivers, and the natures of
plants and animals, but rather seek to become acquainted with
yourselves and your own nature, and do not prefer to dwell
anywhere else, rather than in yourselves. For by contemplating
the things which are to be seen in your own dwelling, that
which bears the mastery therein, and that which is in subjection ;
that which has life, and that which is inanimate ; that which is
endowed with and that which is destitute of reason ; that which
is immortal, and that which is mortal ; that which is better,
and that which is worse ; you will at once arrive at a correct
knowledge of God and of his works. For you will perceive
that there is a mind in you and in the universe ; and that your
mind, having asserted its authority and power over all the things
in you, has brought each of the parts into subjection to himself.
In like manner also, the mind of the universe being invested
with the supremacy, governs the world by independent law and
justice, having a providential regard not only for those things
which are of more importance, but also for those which appear
to be somewhat obscure."

XXXIV. Abandoning therefore your superfluous anxiety to

* Exodus xvii. 6.

investigate the things of heaven, dwell, as I said just now within yourselves, forsaking the land of the Chaldeans, that is, opinion, and migrating to Charran the region of the outward sense, which is the corporeal abode of the mind. For the name Charran, being interpreted, means "a hole;" and holes are the emblems of the places of the outward sense. For in some sense they are all holes and caves, the eyes being the caves in which the sight dwells, the ears those of hearing, the nostrils those of smelling, the throat the cavern of taste, and the whole frame of the body, being the abode of touch. Do ye therefore, dwelling among these things, remain tranquil and quiet, and investigate with all the exactness in your power the nature of each, and when you have learnt what there is good and bad in each part, avoid the one and choose the other.

And when you have thoroughly and perfectly considered the whole of your own habitation, and have understood what relative importance each of its parts possesses, then rouse yourselves up and seek to accomplish a migration from hence, which shall announce to you, not death, but immortality; the evident proofs of which you will see even while involved in the corporeal cares perceptible by the outward senses, sometimes while in deep slumber (for then the mind, roaming abroad, and straying beyond the confines of the outward senses, and of all the other affections of the body, begins to associate with itself, looking on truth as at a mirror, and discarding all the imaginations which it had contracted from the outward senses, becomes inspired by the truest divination respecting the future, through the instrumentality of dreams), and at other times in your waking moments. For when, being under the influence of some philosophical speculations, you are allured onwards, then the mind follows this, and forgets all the other things which concern its corporeal abode; and if the external senses prevent it from arriving at an accurate sight of the objects of the intellect, then those who are fond of contemplation take care to diminish the impetuosity of its attack, for they close their eyes and stop up their ears, and check the rapid motion of the other organ, and choose to abide in tranquillity and darkness, that the eye of the soul, to which God has granted the power of understanding the objects of the intellect, may never be overshadowed by any of those objects appreciable only by the outward senses.

XXXV. Having then in this manner learnt to accomplish the abandonment of mortal things, you shall become instructed in the proper doctrines respecting the uncreated God, unless indeed you think that our mind, when it has put off the body, the external senses, and reason, can, when destitute of all these things and naked, perceive existing things, and that the mind of the universe, that is to say, God, does not dwell outside of all material nature, and that he contains everything and is not contained by anything; and further, he does not penetrate beyond things by his intellect alone, like a man, but also by his essential nature, as is natural for a God to do; for it is not our mind which made the body, but that is the work of something else, on which account it is contained in the body as in a vessel; but the mind of the universe created the universe, and the Creator is better than the created, therefore it can never be contained in what is inferior to itself; besides that it is not suitable for the father to be contained in the son, but rather for the son to derive increase from the love of the father.

And in this manner the mind, migrating for a short time, will come to the father of piety and holiness, removing at first to a distance from genealogical science, which originally did erroneously persuade it to fancy that the world was the primary god, and not the creature of the first God, and that the motions and agitations of the stars were the causes to men of disaster, or, on the contrary, of good fortune. After that the mind, coming to a due consideration of itself, and studying philosophically the things affecting its own abode, that is the things of the body, the things of the outward sense, the things of reason, and knowing, as the line in the poet has it—

That in those halls both good and ill are planned ;*

Then, opening the road for itself, and hoping by travelling along it to arrive at a notion of the father of the universe, so difficult to be understood by any guesses or conjectures, when it has come to understand itself accurately, it will very likely be able to comprehend the nature of God ; no longer remaining in Charran, that is in the organs of outward sense, but returning to itself. For it is impossible, while it is still in a state of motion, in a manner appreciable by the outward sense rather

* Homer. Odyssey, iv. 392.

than by the intellect, to arrive at a proper consideration of the living God.

XXXVI. On which account also that disposition which is ranked in the highest class by God, by name Samuel, does not explain the just precepts of kingly power to Saul, while he is still lying among the pots, but only after he has drawn him out from thence: for he inquires whether the man is still coming hither, and the sacred oracle answers, "Behold, he is hidden among the stuff." * What, then, ought he who hears this answer, and who is by nature inclined to receive instruction, to do, but to draw him out at once from thence? Accordingly, we are told, " He ran up and took him out from thence,"because he who was abiding among the vessels of the soul, that is, the body and the outward senses, was not worthy to hear the doctrines and laws of the kingdom (and by the kingdom, we mean wisdom, since we call the wise man a king); but when he has risen up and changed his place, then the mist around him is dissipated, and he will be able to see clearly.

Very appropriately, therefore, does the companion of knowledge think it right to leave the region of the outward sense, by name Charran; and he leaves it when he is seventy-five years old; and this number is on the confines of the nature discernible by the outward senses, and of that intelligible by the intellect, and of the older and younger, and also of perishable and imperishable nature; for the elder, the imperishable ratio, that comprehensible by the intellect, exists in the seventy; the younger ratio, discernible by the outward senses, is equal in number to the five outward senses. In this latter also the practiser of virtue is seen exercising himself when he has not yet been able to carry off the perfect prize of victory;— for, it is said, that all the souls which came out of Jacob were seventy and five; †—for to him, while wrestling, and not shrinking at all from the truly sacred contest, for the acquisition of virtue, belong the souls which are the offspring of the body, and which have not yet acquired reason, but are still attracted by the multitude of the outward senses.

For Jacob is the name of one who is wrestling and engaged in a contest and trying to trip up his antagonist, not of one who has gained the victory. But when he appeared to have gained ability to behold God, his name was changed to Israel, and

* 1 Samuel x. 22.　　　　　　　† Exodus i. 5.

then he uses only the computation of seventy, having extirpated the number five, the number of the outward senses ; for
it is said, that " thy fathers went down to Egypt, being seventy
souls."* This is the number which is familiar to Moses the
wise man : for it happened that those who were selected as
carefully picked men out of the whole multitude, were seventy
in number; and those all elders, not only in point of age, but
also in wisdom and counsel, and in prudence, and in ancient
integrity of manners. And this number is consecrated and
dedicated' to God when the perfect fruits of the soul are
offered up.

For, on the feast of tabernacles, besides all other sacrifices,
it is ordered that the priest should offer up seventy heifers for
a burnt offering. Again, it is in accordance with the computation of seventy that the phials of the princes are provided,
for each of them is of the weight of seventy shekels ; since
whatever things are associated and confederate together in the
soul, and dear to one another, have a power which is truly attractive, namely, the sacred computation of seventy, which
Egypt, the nature which hates virtue, and loves to indulge the
passions, is introduced as lamenting; for mourning among
them is computed at seventy days.†

XXXVII. This number, therefore, as I have said before, is
familiar to Moses, but the number of the five outward senses is
familiar to him who embraces the body and external things,
which it is customary to call Joseph ; for he pays such attention
to those things, that he presents his own uterine brother,‡ the
offspring of the outward sense, for he had no acquaintance at all
with those who were only his brothers as sons of the same father,
with five exceedingly beautiful garments, thinking the outward
senses things of exceeding beauty, and worthy of being adorned
and honoured by him. Moreover, he also enacts laws for the
whole of Egypt, that they should honour them, and pay taxes
and tribute to them every year as to their kings ; for he commands them to take a fifth§ part of the corn, that is to say, to
store up in the treasury abundant materials and nourishment
for the five outward senses, in order that each of them might
rejoice while filling itself unrestrainedly with suitable food, and
that it might weigh down and overwhelm the mind with the

* Deuteronomy x. 22.   † Genesis l. 8.
‡ Genesis xlv. 22.   § Genesis xlvii. 24.

multitude of things which were thus brought upon it; for during the banquet of the outer senses, the mind is labouring under a famine, as, on the contrary, when the outward senses are fasting, the mind is feasting.

Do you not see that the five daughters of Salpaad, which we, using allegorical expressions, call the outward senses, were born of the tribe of Manasseh, who is the son of Joseph, the elder son in point of time, but the younger in rank and power? and very naturally, for he is so called from forgetfulness, which is a thing of equal power with an outward sense. But recollection is placed in the second rank, after memory, of which Ephraim is the namesake; and the interpretation of the name of Ephraim is, " bearing fruit;" and the most beautiful and nutritious fruit in souls is a memory which never forgets; therefore the virgins speak to one another in a becoming manner, saying, " Our father is dead." Now the death of recollection is forgetfulness: " And he has died not for his own sin,"* speaking very righteously, for forgetfulness is not a voluntary affection, but is one of those things which are not actually in us, but which come upon us from without. And they were not his sons, but his daughters; since the power of memory, as being what has its existence by its own nature, is the parent of male children; but forgetfulness, arising from the slumber of reason, is the parent of female children, for it is destitute of reason; and the outward senses are the daughters of the irrational part of the soul.

But if any one has outrun him in speed, and has become a follower of Moses, though he is not yet able to keep pace with him, he will use a compound and mixed number, namely, that of five and seventy, which is the symbol of the nature which is both perceptible by the outward senses and intelligible by the intellect, the two uniting together for the production of one irreproachable species.

XXXVIII. I very much admire Rebecca, who is patience, because she, at that time, recommends the man who is perfect in his soul, and who has destroyed the roughnesses of the passions and vices, to flee and return to Charran; for she says, " Now, therefore, my child, hear my voice, and rise up and depart, and flee away to Laban, my brother, to Charran, and dwell with him certain days, until the anger and rage of thy

* Numbers xxvii. 3.

brother is turned from being against thee, and till he forgets what thou hast done to him."* And it is with great beauty that she here calls going by the road, which leads to the outward senses, a fleeing away; for, in truth, the mind is then a fugitive, when, having left its own appropriate objects which are comprehensible to the understanding, it turns to the opposite rank of those which are perceptible by the outward senses. And there are cases in which to run away is useful, when a person adopts this line of conduct, not out of hatred to his superior, but in order to avoid the snares which are laid for him by his inferior.

What, then, is the recommendation of patience? A most admirable and excellent one. If ever, she says, you see the passion of rage and anger highly provoked and excited to ferocity either in thyself or in any one else, which is nourished by irrational and unmanageable nature, do not excite it further and make it more savage, for then perhaps it will inflict incurable wounds; but cool its fervour, and pacify its too highly inflamed disposition, for if it be tamed and rendered tractable it will do you less injury.

What, then, are the means by which it can be tamed and pacified? Having, as far as appearance goes, assumed another form and another character, follow it, first of all, wherever it pleases, and, opposing it in nothing, admit that you have the same objects of love and hatred with itself, for by these means it will be rendered propitious; and, when it is pacified, then you may lay aside your pretence, and, not expecting any longer to suffer any evil at its hand, you may with indifference return to the care of your own objects; for it is on this account that Charran is represented as full of cattle, and as having tenders of flocks for its inhabitants. For what region could be more suitable for irrational nature, and for those who have undertaken the care and superintendence of it, than the external senses which exist in us? Accordingly, when the practiser of virtue asks, "From whence come ye?" the shepherds answer him truly, that they come "from Charran."† For the irrational powers come from the external sense, as the rational ones come from the mind. And when he further inquires whether they know Laban, they very naturally assert that they do know him, for the outward sense is acquainted with complexion and

* Genesis xxvii. 43.   † Genesis xxix. 4.

with every distinctive quality, as it thinks; and of complexion and distinctive qualities Laban is the symbol.

And he himself, when at last he is made perfect, will quit the abode of the outward senses, and will set up the abode of the soul as belonging to the soul, which, while still among labours and among the external senses, he gives a vivid description of; for he says, "When shall I make myself, also, a house?"* When, disregarding the objects of the external senses and the external senses themselves, shall I dwell in mind and intellect, being, in name, going to and fro among and dwelling among the objects of contemplation, like those souls which are fond of investigating invisible objects, which it is usual to call midwives? For they also make suitable coverings and phylacteries for souls which are devoted to virtue; but the strongest and most defensible abode was the fear of God, to those, at least, who have him for an impregnable fortress and wall. "For," says Moses, "when the midwives feared God they made themselves houses."†

XXXIX. The mind, therefore, going forth out of the places which are in Charran, is said "to have travelled through the land until it came to the place of Sichem, to a lofty oak."‡ And let us now consider what this travelling through the land means. The disposition which is fond of learning is inquisitive and exceedingly curious by nature, going everywhere without fear or hesitation and prying into every place, and not choosing to leave anything in existence, whether person or thing, not thoroughly investigated; for it is by nature extraordinarily greedy of everything that can be seen or heard, so as not only not to be satisfied with the things of its own country, but even to desire foreign things which are established at a great distance. At all events, they say that it is an absurd thing for merchants and dealers to cross the seas for the sake of gain, and to travel all round the habitable world, not allowing any considerations of summer, or winter, or violent gales, or contrary winds, or old age, or bodily sickness, or the society of friends, or the unspeakable pleasures arising from wife, or children, or one's other relations, or love of one's country, or the enjoyment of political connections, or the safe fruition of one's money and other possessions, or, in fact, anything whatever, whether great or small, to be any hindrance to them; and

* Genesis xxx. 30.   † Exodus i. 21.   ‡ Genesis xii. 6.

yet for men, for the sake of that most beautiful and desirable of all possessions, the only one which is peculiar to the human race, namely, wisdom, to be unwilling to cross over every sea and to penetrate every recess of the earth, inquiring whenever they can find anything beautiful either to see or to hear, and tracing out such things with all imaginable zeal and earnestness, until they arrive at the enjoyment of the things which are thus sought for and desired.

Do thou then, O my soul, travel through the land, and through man, bringing if you think fit, each individual man to a judgment of the things which concern him ; as, for instance, what the body is, and under what influences, whether active or passive, it co-operates with the mind ; what the external sense is, and in what manner that assists the dominant mind ; what speech is, and of what it becomes the interpreter so as to contribute to virtue; what are pleasure and desire ; what are pain and fear ; and what art is capable of supplying a remedy for these things ; by the aid of which a man when infected with these feelings may easily escape, or else perhaps may never be infected at all : what folly is, what intemperance, what committing injustice, what the whole multitude of other diseases, which it is the nature of all destructive vice to engender; and also what are the means by which they can be averted. And also, on the contrary, what justice is, what prudence is, and temperance, and manly courage, and deliberate wisdom, and in short what each virtue is, and what the mastery over the passions is, and in what way each of these virtues is usually produced.

Travel also through the greatest and most perfect being, namely this world, and consider all its parts, how they are separated in respect of place and united in respect of power ; and also what is this invisible chain of harmony and unity, which connects all those parts ; and if while considering these matters, thou canst not easily comprehend what thou seekest to know, persevere and be not wearied ; for these matters are not attainable without a struggle, but they are only found out with difficulty and by means of much and great labour ; on which account the man fond of learning is taken up to the field of Sichem ; and the name Sichem, being interpreted means, "a shoulder," and intimates labour, since it is on the shoulders that men are accustomed to bear burdens. As Moses also mentions in another passage, when speaking of a certain athlete he proceeds in this manner, " He put his shoulder to the labour and became a husbandman."*

So that never, O my mind, do thou become effeminate and yield; but even if any thing does appear difficult to be discovered by contemplation, still opening the seeing faculties that are in thyself, look inwards and investigate existing things more accurately, and never close thy eyes whether intentionally or unintentionally; for sleep is a blind thing as wakefulness is a sharp-sighted thing. And it is well to be content if by assiduity in investigation it is granted to thee to arrive at a correct conception of the objects of thy search. Do you not see that the scripture says that a lofty oak was planted in Sichem? meaning under this figurative expression to represent the labour of instruction which never gives in, and never bends through weariness, but is solid, firm, and invincible, which the man who wishes to be perfect must of necessity exert, in order that the tribunal of the soul, by name Dinah, for the interpretation of the name Dinah is "judgment" may not be seized by the exertions of that man who, being a plotter against prudence, is labouring in an opposite direction.

For he who bears the same name as this place, namely Sichem, the son of Hamor, that is, of irrational nature; for the name Hamor means " an ass; " giving himself up to folly and being bred up with shamelessness and audacity, infamous man that he was, attempted to pollute and to defile the judicial faculties of the mind; if the pupils and friends of wisdom, Sichem and Levi, had not speedily come up, having made the defences of their house safe, and destroyed those who were still involved in the labour devoted to pleasure and to the indulgence of the passions and uncircumcised. For though there was a sacred scripture that, " There should be no harlot among the daughters of the seer, Israel,"† these men, having ravished a virgin soul, hoped to escape notice; for there is never a scarcity of avengers against those who violate treaties; but even though some persons fancy there may be, they will only fancy it, and will in the reality of the fact be proved to entertain a false opinion.

For justice hates the wicked, and is implacable, and a relentless avenger of all unrighteous actions, overthrowing the ranks of those who defile virtue, and when they are overthrown, then

* Genesis xlix. 15.   † Deuteronomy xxiii. 18.

again the soul, which before appeared to be defiled, changes and returns to its virgin state. I say, which appeared to be defiled, because, in fact, it never was defiled; for of involuntary accidents that which affects the patient is not in reality his suffering, just as what is done by a person who does wrong unintentionally, the wrong is not really his action.

A TREATISE

ON THE

LIFE OF MOSES,

THAT IS TO SAY,

ON THE THEOLOGY AND PROPHETIC OFFICE OF MOSES.

BOOK I.

I. I HAVE conceived the idea of writing the life of Moses, who, according to the account of some persons, was the lawgiver of the Jews, but according to others only an interpreter of the sacred laws, the greatest and most perfect man that ever lived, having a desire to make his character fully known to those who ought not to remain in ignorance respecting him, for the glory of the laws which he left behind him has reached over the whole world, and has penetrated to the very furthest limits of the universe; and those who do really and truly understand him are not many, perhaps partly out of envy, or else from the disposition so common to many persons of resisting the commands which are delivered by lawgivers in different states, since the historians who have flourished among the Greeks have not chosen to think him worthy of mention, the greater part of whom have both in their poems and also in their prose writings, disparaged or defaced the powers which they have received through education, composing comedies and works full of Sybaritish profligacy and licentiousness to their everlasting shame, while they ought rather to have employed their natural endowments and abilities in preserving a record of virtuous men and praiseworthy lives, so that honourable actions, whether ancient or modern, might not be buried in silence, and thus have all recollection of them lost, while they might shine gloriously if duly celebrated; and that they might not themselves have seemed to pass by more appropriate subjects, and to prefer such as were unworthy of being mentioned at all, while they were eager to give a specious appearance to infamous actions, so as to secure notoriety for disgraceful deeds.

But I disregard the envious disposition of these men, and shall proceed to narrate the events which befell him, having learnt them both from those sacred scriptures which he has left as marvellous memorials of his wisdom, and having also heard many things from the elders of my nation, for I have continually connected together what I have heard with what I have read, and in this way I look upon it that I am acquainted with the history of his life more accurately than other people.

II. And I will begin first with that with which it is necessary to begin.

Moses was by birth a Hebrew, but he was born, and brought up, and educated in Egypt, his ancestors having migrated into Egypt with all their families on account of the long famine which oppressed Babylon and all the adjacent countries; for they were in search of food, and Egypt was a champaign country blessed with a rich soil, and very productive of every thing which the nature of man requires, and especially of corn and wheat, for the river of that country at the height of summer, when they say that all other rivers which are derived from winter torrents and from springs in the ground are smaller, rises and increases, and overflows so as to irrigate all the lands, and make them one vast lake. And so the land, without having any need of rain, supplies every year an unlimited abundance of every kind of good food, unless sometimes the anger of God interrupts this abundance by reason of the excessive impiety of the inhabitants.

And his father and mother were among the most excellent persons of their time, and though they were of the same time, still they were induced to unite themselves together more from an unanimity of feeling than because they were related in blood; and Moses is the seventh generation in succession from the original settler in the country who was the founder of the whole race of the Jews.

III. And he was thought worthy of being bred up in the royal palace, the cause of which circumstance was as follows. The king of the country, inasmuch as the nation of the Hebrews kept continually increasing in numbers, fearing lest gradually the settlers should become more numerous than the original inhabitants, and being more powerful should set upon them and subdue them by force, and make themselves their masters, conceived the idea of destroying their strength by impious devices, and ordered that of all the children that were born the females only should be brought up (since a woman, by reason of the weakness of her nature, is disinclined to and unfitted for war), and that all the male children should be destroyed, that the population of their cities might not be increased, since a power which consists of a number of men is a fortress difficult to take and difficult to destroy.

Accordingly as the child Moses, as soon as he was born, displayed a more beautiful and noble form than usual, his parents resolved, as far as was in their power, to disregard the proclamations of the tyrant. Accordingly they say that for three months continuously they kept him at home, feeding him on milk, without its coming to the knowledge of the multitude; but when, as is commonly the case in monarchies, some persons discovered what was kept secret and in darkness, of those persons who are always eager to bring any new report to the king, his parents being afraid lest while seeking to secure the safety of one individual, they who were many might become involved in his destruction, with many tears exposed their child on the banks of the river, and departed groaning and lamenting, pitying themselves for the necessity which had fallen upon them, and calling themselves the slayers and murderers of their child, and commiserating the infant too for his destruction, which they had hoped to avert.

Then, as was natural for people involved in a miserable misfortune, they accused themselves as having brought a heavier affliction on themselves than they need have done. "For why," said they, "did we not expose him at the first moment of his birth?" For people in general do not look upon one who has not lived long enough to partake of salutary food as a human being at all. "But we, in our superfluous affection, have nourished him these three entire months, causing ourselves by such conduct more abundant grief, and inflicting upon him a heavier punishment, in order that he, having at last attained to a great capacity for feeling pleasures and pains, should at last perish in the perception of the most grievous evils."

IV. And so they departed in ignorance of the future, being wholly overwhelmed with sad misery; but the sister of the

infant who was thus exposed, being still a maiden, out of the
vehemence of her fraternal affection, stood a little way off
watching to see what would happen, and all the events which
concerned him appear to me to have taken place in accordance
with the providence of God, who watched over the infant.
Now the king of the country had an only daughter, whom he
tenderly loved, and they say that she, although she had been
married a long time, had never had any children, and therefore, as was natural, was very desirous of children, and
especially of male offspring, which should succeed to the noble
inheritance of her father's prosperity and imperial authority,
which was otherwise in danger of being lost, since the king
had no other grandsons.

And as she was always desponding and lamenting, so especially on that particular day was she overcome by the weight
of her anxiety, that, though it was her ordinary custom to stay
in doors and never to pass over the threshold of her house,
yet now she went forth with her handmaidens down to the
river, where the infant was lying. And there, as she was
about to indulge in a bath and purification in the thickest part
of the marsh, she beheld the child, and commanded her handmaidens to bring him to her. Then, after she had surveyed
him from head to foot, and admired his elegant form and
healthy vigorous appearance, and saw that he was crying, she
had compassion on him, her soul being already moved within
her by maternal feelings of affection as if he had been her own
child.

And when she knew that the infant belonged to one of the
Hebrews who was afraid because of the commandment of the
king, she herself conceived the idea of rearing him up, and
took counsel with herself on the subject, thinking that it was
not safe to bring him at once into the palace; and while she
was still hesitating, the sister of the infant, who was still
looking out, conjecturing her hesitation from what she beheld,
ran up and asked her whether she would like that the child
should be brought up at the breast by some one of the Hebrew
women who had been lately delivered; and as she said that
she wished that she would do so, the maiden went and fetched
her own mother and that of the infant, as if she had been a
stranger, who with great readiness and willingness cheerfully
promised to take the child and bring him up, pretending to be

tempted by the reward to be paid, the providence of God thus making the original bringing up of the child to accord with the genuine course of nature.   Then she gave him a name, calling him Moses with great propriety, because she had received him out of the water, for the Egyptians call water " mos."

V. But when the child began to grow and increase, he was weaned, not in accordance with the time of his age, but earlier than usual; and then his mother, who was also his nurse, came to bring him back to the princess who had given him to her, inasmuch as he no longer required to be fed on milk, and as he was now a fine and noble child to look upon.   And when the king's daughter saw that he was more perfect than could have been expected at his age, and when from his appearance she conceived greater good will than ever towards him, she adopted him as her son, having first put in practice all sorts of contrivances to increase the apparent bulk of her belly, so that he might be looked upon as her own genuine child, and not as a supposititious one; but God easily brings to pass whatever he is inclined to effect, however difficult it may be to bring to a successful issue.

Therefore the child being now thought worthy of a royal education and a royal attendance, was not, like a mere child, long delighted with toys and objects of laughter and amusement, even though those who had undertaken the care of him allowed him holidays and times for relaxation, and never behaved in any stern or morose way to him ; but he himself exhibited a modest and dignified deportment in all his words and gestures, attending diligently to every lesson of every kind which could tend to the improvement of his mind.   And immediately he had all kinds of masters, one after another, some coming of their own accord from the neighbouring countries and the different districts of Egypt, and some being even procured from Greece by the temptation of large presents. But in a short time he surpassed all their knowledge, anticipating all their lessons by the excellent natural endowments of his own genius ; so that everything in his case appeared to be a recollecting rather than a learning, while he himself also, without any teacher, comprehended by his instinctive genius many difficult subjects; for great abilities cut out for themselves many new roads to knowledge.

And just as vigorous and healthy bodies which are active and quick in motion in all their parts, release their trainers from much care, giving them little or no trouble and anxiety, and as trees which are of a good sort, and which have a natural good growth, give no trouble to their cultivators, but grow finely and improve of themselves, so in the same manner the well disposed soul, going forward to meet the lessons which are imparted to it, is improved in reality by itself rather than by its teachers, and taking hold of some beginning or principle of knowledge, bounds, as the proverb has it, like a horse over the plain.

Accordingly he speedily learnt arithmetic, and geometry, and the whole science of rhythm and harmony and metre, and the whole of music, by means of the use of musical instruments, and by lectures on the different arts, and by explanations of each topic; and lessons on these subjects were given him by Egyptian philosophers, who also taught him the philosophy which is contained in symbols, which they exhibit in those sacred characters or hieroglyphics, as they are called, and also that philosophy which is conversant about that respect which they pay to animals which they invest with the honours due to God.

And all the other branches of the encyclical education he learnt from Greeks; and the philosophers from the adjacent countries taught him Assyrian literature and the knowledge of the heavenly bodies so much studied by the Chaldæans. And this knowledge he derived also from the Egyptians, who study mathematics above all things, and he learnt with great accuracy the state of that art among both the Chaldæans and Egyptians, making himself acquainted with the points in which they agree with and differ from each other—making himself master of all their disputes without encouraging any disputatious disposition in himself—but seeking the plain truth, since his mind was unable to admit any falsehood, as those are accustomed to do who contend violently for one particular side of a question; and who advocate any doctrine which is set before them, whatever it may be, not inquiring whether it deserves to be supported, but acting in the same manner as those lawyers who defend a cause for pay, and are wholly indifferent to the justice of their cause.

VI. And when he had passed the boundaries of the age of

infancy he began to exercise his intellect; not, as some people
do, letting his youthful passions roam at large without restraint,
although in him they had ten thousand incentives by reason of
the abundant means for the gratification of them which royal
places supply; but he behaved with temperance and fortitude,
as though he had bound them with reins, and thus he restrained
their onward impetuosity by force. And he tamed, and appeased, and brought under due command every one of the other
passions which are naturally and as far as they are themselves
concerned frantic, and violent, and unmanageable. And if
any one of them at all excited itself and endeavoured to get free
from restraint he administered severe punishment to it, reprov-
ing it with severity of language; and, in short, he repressed all
the principal impulses and most violent affections of the soul,
and kept guard over them as over a restive horse, fearing lest
they might break all bounds and get beyond the power of
reason which ought to be their guide to restrain them, and so
throw everything everywhere into confusion.

For these passions are the causes of all good and of all evil;
of good when they submit to the authority of dominant reason,
and of evil when they break out of bounds and scorn all
government and restraint.

Very naturally, therefore, those who associated with him
and every one who was acquainted with him marvelled at him,
being astonished as at a novel spectacle, and inquiring what
kind of mind it was that had its abode in his body, and that
was set up in it like an image in a shrine; whether it was a
human mind or a divine intellect, or something combined of
the two; because he had nothing in him resembling the many,
but had gone beyond them all and was elevated to a more sublime height. For he never provided his stomach with any
luxuries beyond those necessary tributes which nature has appointed to be paid to it, and as to the pleasures of the organs
below the stomach he paid no attention to them at all, except as
far as the object of having legitimate children was concerned.

And being in a most eminent degree a practiser of abstinence and self-denial, and being above all men inclined to
ridicule a life of effeminacy and luxury (for he desired to live
for his soul alone, and not for his body), he exhibited the
doctrines of philosophy in all his daily actions, saying precisely what he thought, and performing such actions only as

were consistent with his words, so as to exhibit a perfect harmony between his language and his life, so that as his words were such also was his life, and as his life was such likewise was his language, like people who are playing together in tune on a musical instrument.

Therefore men in general, even if the slightest breeze of prosperity does only blow their way for a moment, become puffed up and give themselves great airs, becoming insolent to all those who are in a lower condition than themselves, and calling them dregs of the earth, and annoyances, and sources of trouble, and burdens of the earth, and all sorts of names of that kind, as if they had been thoroughly able to establish the undeviating character of their prosperity on a solid foundation, though, very likely, they will not remain in the same condition even till to-morrow, for there is nothing more inconstant than fortune, which tosses human affairs up and down like dice. Often has a single day thrown down the man who was previously placed on an eminence, and raised the lowly man on high. And while men see these events continually taking place, and though they are well assured of the fact, still they overlook their relations and friends, and transgress the laws according to which they were born and brought up ; and they overturn their national hereditary customs to which no just blame whatever is attached, dwelling in a foreign land, and by reason of their cordial reception of the customs among which they are living, no longer remembering a single one of their ancient usages.

VII. But Moses, having now reached the very highest point of human good fortune, and being looked upon as the grandson of this mighty king, and being almost considered in the expectations of all men as the future inheritor of his grandfather's kingdom, and being always addressed as the young prince, still felt a desire for and admiration of the education of his kinsmen and ancestors, considering all the things which were thought good among those who had adopted him as spurious, even though they might, in consequence of the present state of affairs, have a brilliant appearance; and those things which were thought good by his natural parents, even though they might be for a short time somewhat obscure, at all events akin to himself and genuine good things.

Accordingly, like an uncorrupt judge both of his real parents

and of those who had adopted him, he cherished towards the
one a good will and an ardent affection, and he displayed gratitude towards the others in requital of the kindness which he
had received at their hands, and he would have displayed the
same throughout his whole life if he had not beheld a great and
novel iniquity wrought in the country by the king; for, as I
have said before, the Jews were strangers in Egypt, the
founders of their race having migrated from Babylon and the
upper satrapies in the time of the famine, by reason of their
want of food, and come and settled in Egypt, and having in a
manner taken refuge like suppliants in the country as in a
sacred asylum, fleeing for protection to the good faith of the
king and the compassion of the inhabitants; for strangers, in
my opinion, should be looked upon as refugees, and as the suppliants of those who receive them in their country; and,
besides, being suppliants, these men were likewise sojourners
in the land, and friends desiring to be admitted to equal honours
with the citizens, and neighbours differing but little in their
character from original natives.

The men, therefore, who had left their homes and come
into Egypt, as if they were to dwell in that land as in a second
country in perfect security, the king of the country reduced to
slavery, and, as if he had taken them prisoners by the laws of
war, or had bought them from masters in whose house they had
been bred, he oppressed them and treated them as slaves,
though they were not only free men, but also strangers, and
suppliants, and sojourners, having no respect for nor any awe
of God, who presides over the rights of free men, and of strangers, and of suppliants, and of hospitality, and who beholds all
such actions as his. Then he laid commands on them beyond
their power to fulfil, imposing on them labour after labour;
and, when they fainted from weakness, the sword came upon
them.

He appointed overseers over their works, the most pitiless
and inhuman of men, who pardoned and made allowance for no
one, and whom they from the circumstances and from their
behaviour called persecutors of work. And they wrought with
clay, some of them fashioning it into bricks, and others collect-
ing straw from all quarters, for straw is the bond which binds
bricks together; while others, again, had the task allotted to
them of building up houses, and walls, and gates, and cutting

trenches, bearing wood themselves day and night without interruption, having no rest or respite, and not even being allowed
time so much as to sleep, but being compelled to perform all
the works not only of workmen but also of journeymen, so that
in a short time their bodies failed them, their souls having
already fainted beneath their afflictions.

And so they died, one after another, as if smitten by a pesti-
lential destruction, and then their taskmasters threw their
bodies away unburied beyond the borders of the land, not
suffering their kinsmen or their friends to sprinkle even a little
dust on their corpses, nor to weep over those who had thus
miserably perished; but, like impious men as they were, they
threatened to extend their despotism over the passions of
the soul (that cannot be enslaved, and which are nearly the
only things which nature has made completely free), oppressing them with the intolerable weight of a necessity beyond
their powers.

VIII. At all these events Moses was greatly grieved and
indignant, not being able either to chastise the unjust oppressors of his people nor to assist those who were oppressed, but
he gave them all the assistance that was in his power, by
words, recommending their overseers to treat them with moderation, and to relax and abate somewhat of the oppressive nature
of their commands, and exhorting the oppressed who were
labouring thus to bear their present distresses with a noble
spirit and to be men in their minds, and not to let their souls
faint as well as their bodies, but to hope for good fortune after
their present adversity; for that all things in this world have
a tendency to change to the opposite, cloudy weather to fine,
violent gales to calm and absence of wind, storms and heavy
billows at sea to fair weather and an unruffled surface of the
water; and much more are human affairs likely to change, inasmuch as they are more unstable than anything.

By using these charms, as it were, like a good physician, he
thought he should be able to alleviate their afflictions, although
they were most grievous. But whenever their distress abated,
then again their taskmasters returned and oppressed them
with increased severity, always after the respite adding some
new evil which should be even more intolerable than their previous sufferings; for some of their overseers were very savage
and furious men, being, as to their cruelty, not at all different

from poisonous serpents or carnivorous beasts—wild beasts in human form—being clothed with the form of a human body so as to give an appearance of gentleness in order to deceive and catch their victim, but in reality being harder than iron or adamant.

One of these men, then, the most violent of them, when, in addition to yielding nothing of his purpose, he was even exasperated at the exhortations of Moses and rendered more savage by them, beating those who did not labour with energy and unremittingly at the work which was imposed upon them, and insulting them and subjecting them to every kind of ill-treatment, so as even to be the death of many, Moses slew, thinking the deed a pious action ; and, indeed, it was a pious action to destroy one who only lived for the destruction of others.

When the king heard of this action he was very indignant, thinking it an intolerable thing, not for one man to be dead, or for another to have killed him, whether justly or unjustly, but for his grandson not to agree with him, and not to look upon his friends or his enemies as his own, but to hate persons whom the king loved, and to love persons whom the king looked upon as outcasts, and to pity those whom he regarded with unchangeable and implacable aversion.

IX. But when the Egyptian authorities had once got an opportunity of attacking the young man, having already reason for looking upon him with suspicion (for they well knew that he would hereafter bear them ill-will for their evil practices, and would revenge himself on them when he had an opportunity) they poured in, at all times and from all quarters, thousands and thousands of calumnies into the willing ears of his grandfather, so that they even implanted in his mind an apprehension that Moses was plotting to deprive him of his kingdom, saying to him: "He will strip you of your crown. He has no humble designs or notions. He is continually seeking to busy himself in what does not concern him, and to acquire some additional power. He is eager for the kingdom before his time. He caresses some people ; he threatens others ; he kills others without a trial ; he hates all those who are the best affected towards you. Why do you delay ? Why do you not cut short all his designs and machinations ? Delay on the part of those against whom they are plotting is of the greatest advantage to those who wish to attack them."

As they urged these arguments to the king he retreated to the contiguous country of Arabia, where it was safe to abide, entreating God that he would deliver his countrymen from inextricable calamities, and would worthily chastise their oppressors who omitted no circumstance of insolence and tyranny, and would double his joy by allowing him to behold the accomplishment of both these prayers. And God heard his prayers, looking favourably on his disposition, so devoted to what is good, and so hostile to what is evil, and not long after he pronounced his decision upon the affairs of that land as became a God. But while he was preparing to display the decision which he was about to pronounce, Moses was devoting himself to all the labours of virtue, having a teacher within himself, virtuous reason, by whom he had been trained to the most virtuous pursuits of life, and had learnt to apply himself to the contemplation and practice of virtue and to the continual study of the doctrines of philosophy, which he easily and thoroughly comprehended in his soul, and committed to memory in such a manner as never to forget them; and, moreover, he made all his own actions, which were intrinsically praiseworthy, to harmonise with them, desiring not to seem wise and good, but in truth and reality to be so, because he made the right reason of nature his only aim; which is, in fact, the only first principle and fountain of all the virtues.

Any one else, perhaps, fleeing from the implacable fury of the king, and coming now for the first time into a foreign land, when he had not as yet associated with or learnt the customs of the natives, and not knowing with any accuracy the objects in which they delighted or which they regarded with aversion, would have been desirous to enjoy tranquillity and to live in obscurity, escaping the notice of men in general; or else, if he had wished to come forward in public, he would have endeavoured by all means to propitiate the powerful men and those in the highest authority in the country by persevering attentions, as men from whom some advantage or assistance might be expected, if any pursuers should come after him and endeavour to drag him away by force. But this man proceeded by the path which was the exact opposite of that which was the probable one for him to take, following the healthy impulses of his soul, and not allowing any one of them to be impeded in its progress. On which account, at times, with the fervour of youth, he attempted things beyond his existing strength; looking upon justice as an irresistible power, by which he was encouraged so as to go spontaneously to the assistance of the weaker side.

X. I will also mention one action which was done by him at that time, even although it may be but a trifling one in appearance, but still it proceeded from a lofty spirit. The Arabs are great breeders of cattle, and they all feed their flocks together, not merely men, but also women, and youths, and maidens with them, and this, too, not merely in the obscurer classes and lower ranks of life, but also among the most eminent persons of the nation.

Now there were seven damsels, whose father was the priest, and they all came to a certain fountain leading their flocks, and having loosened their vessels and let them down by thongs they succeeded one another in drawing up the water, so as for them all to have an equal share in the work; and in this way they cheerfully and rapidly filled the troughs which were at hand. And when other shepherds came up they disregarded the weakness of the damsels and endeavoured to drive them away with their flocks, and then brought their own herds to the drink that was prepared, desiring to reap the fruits of the labour of others. But Moses, seeing what was done, for he was at no great distance, hastened and ran up; and, when he had come near to them, he said: "Will not you desist from behaving thus unjustly, thinking this solitary place a fitting field for the exercise of your covetousness? Are you not ashamed to have such cowardly arms and hands? You are long-haired people, female flesh, and not men. The damsels behave like vigorous youths, hesitating about nothing that they ought to do; but you, young men, are now behaving lazily, like girls. Will you not depart? Will you not be off and give place to those who arrived first, to whom the water belongs, and who are entitled to it; when you ought rather to have drawn water for them, that so they might have had it in greater abundance? And are you, on the contrary, endeavouring to to take away from them what they themselves have got ready?

"But I swear, by the celestial eye of justice, which sees what is done even in the most solitary places, that you shall not take it from them. And at all events, now justice has sent me and appointed me to bring them assistance who never expected such an officer; for I am an ally to these damsels who are thus injured by violence, and I come with a might which you evil-doers and covetous people cannot face, but you shall feel it wounding you in an invisible manner, if you do not change your ways." He said this; and they, being alarmed at his words, since while he was speaking he appeared inspired, and his appearance became changed, so that he looked like a prophet, and fearing lest he might be uttering divine oracles and predictions, they obeyed and became submissive, and brought back the flock of the maidens to the troughs, first of all removing their own cattle.

XI. So the damsels went home exceedingly delighted, and they related all that had happened to them beyond their hopes, so that they wished their father with an earnest desire to see the stranger. At all events he blamed them for their ingratitude, speaking as follows: "What were ye about, that ye let him go, when you ought at once to have brought him hither, and to have entreated him to come if he declined? Or when did you see any inhospitality in me? Or do you expect never again to fall into difficulties? Those who are forgetful of services must needs lack defenders, but nevertheless hasten after him, for as yet the error which you have committed may be repaired; and go with haste and invite him first of all to a hospitable reception, and then endeavour to requite his service, for great thanks are due to him."

So they made haste, and went after him, and overtook him at no great distance from the fountain; and when they had delivered their father's message to him, they persuaded him to return home with them. And their father was at once greatly struck by his appearance, and soon afterwards he learnt to admire his wisdom, for great natures are very easily discovered, and do not require a length of time to be appreciated, and so he gave him the most beautiful of his daughters to be his wife, conjecturing by that one action of his how completely good and excellent he was, and testifying that what is good is the only thing which deserves to be loved, and that it does not require any external recommendation, but bears in itself proofs by which it may be known and understood.

And after his marriage, Moses took his father-in-law's herds and tended them, being thus instructed in the lessons proper to qualify him for becoming the leader of a people, for the business of a shepherd is a preparation for the office of a king to any one who is destined to preside over that most manageable of all flocks, mankind, just as hunting is a good training-school for men of warlike dispositions; for they who are practising with a view to learning the management of an army, previously study the science of hunting, brute animals being as some raw material exposed to their attacks in order for them to practise the art of commanding on each occasion of war or of peace, for the pursuit of wild beasts is a training-school of strategy to be developed against enemies, and the care and management of tame animals is a royal training for the government of subjects; for which reason kings are called shepherds of their people, not by way of reproach, but as a most especial and pre-eminent honour.

And it appears to me, who have examined the matter not with any reference to the opinions of the many, but solely with regard to truth (and he may laugh who pleases), that that man alone can be a perfect king who is well skilled in the art of the shepherd, being thus instructed as to more important matters by experience of the inferior animals; for it is impossible for great things to be brought to perfection before small ones.

XII. Therefore Moses, having become the most skilful herdsman of his time, and the most prudent provider of all the necessary things for his flock, and of all things which tended to their advantage, because he never delayed or hesitated, but exerted a voluntary and spontaneous cheerfulness in all things necessary for the animals under his charge, saw his flocks increase with great joy and guileless good faith, so that he soon incurred the envy of the other herdsmen, who saw nothing in their own flocks resembling the condition of his; but they thought themselves well off if they continued as before, while the flock of Moses would have been thought to be falling off if it had not improved, every day, by reason of the vast augmentations that it was in the habit of receiving in beauty from its high condition and fatness, and in number from the prolific character of the females, and the wholesome way in which it was fed and managed.

And when Moses was leading his flock into a situation full of good water and good grass, where there was also a great deal of herbage especially suitable for sheep, he came upon a certain grove in a valley, where he saw a most marvellous sight. There was a bush or briar, a very thorny plant, and very weak and supple. This bush was on a sudden set in a blaze without any one applying any fire to it, and being entirely enveloped from the root to the topmost branch by the abundant flame, as though it had proceeded from some fountain showering fire over it, it nevertheless remained whole without being consumed, like some impassible essence, and not as if it were itself the natural fuel for fire, but rather as if it were taking the fire for its own fuel. And in the middle of the flame there was seen a certain very beautiful form, not resembling any visible thing, a most Godlike image, emitting a light more brilliant than fire, which any one might have imagined to be the image of the living God. But let it be called an angel, because it merely related (διηγγέλλετο) the events which were about to happen in a silence more distinct than any voice by reason of the marvellous sight which was thus exhibited.

For the burning bush was a symbol of the oppressed people, and the burning fire was a symbol of the oppressors; and the circumstance of the burning bush not being consumed was an emblem of the fact that the people thus oppressed would not be destroyed by those who were attacking them, but that their hostility would be unsuccessful and fruitless to the one party, and the fact of their being plotted against would fail to be injurious to the others. The angel, again, was the emblem of the providence of God, who mitigates circumstances which appear very formidable, so as to produce from them great tranquillity beyond the hopes or expectation of any one.

XIII. But we must now accurately investigate the comparison here made. The briar, as has been already said, is a most weak and supple plant, yet it is not without thorns, so that it wounds one if one only touches it. Nor was it consumed by fire, which is naturally destructive, but on the contrary it was preserved by it, and in addition to not being consumed, it continued just as it was before, and without undergoing any change whatever itself, acquired additional brilliancy.

All these circumstances are an allegory to intimate the suggestions given by the other notions which at that time prevailed, almost crying out in plain words to persons in affliction, " Do not faint; your weakness is your strength, which shall pierce and wound innumerable hosts. You shall be saved rather than destroyed, by those who are desirous to destroy your whole race against their will, so that you shall not be overwhelmed by the evils with which they will afflict you, but when your enemies think most surely that they are destroying you, then you shall most brilliantly shine out in glory."

Again, the fire, which is a destructive essence, convicting the men of cruel dispositions, says, Be not elated so as to rely on your own strength; be admonished rather when you see irresistible powers destroyed. The consuming power of flame is itself consumed like firewood, and the wood, which is by its intrinsic nature capable of being burnt, burns other things visibly like fire.

XIV. God, having shown this prodigious and miraculous sight to Moses, gave him, in this way, a most visible lesson as to the events which are about to be accomplished; and he begins to exhort him, by divine admonitions and predictions, to apply himself to the government of his nation, as one who was to be not only the author of its freedom, but also its leader in its migration from Egypt, which should take place at no distant period; promising to be present with him as his coadjutor in every thing. For says God, " I myself have had compassion for a long time on them while ill-treated and subjected to insolence hard to be borne, while there was no man to lighten their sufferings, nor to pity their calamities; for I have seen them all, each individual privately and the whole nation, with one accord turning to address supplications and prayers to me, and hoping for assistance from me. And I am by nature merciful, and propitious to all sincere suppliants. But go thou to the king of the country, without fearing any thing whatever; for the former king is dead from whom you fled for fear of his plotting against thee. And another king now governs the land, who has no ill-will against thee on account of any thing, and who has taken the elders of the nation into his council; tell him that the whole nation is called forth by me, by my divine oracle, that in accordance with the customs of their ancestors they may depart three days' journey out of the country, and there may sacrifice unto me."

But Moses, not being ignorant that even his own country-men would distrust his word, and also that every one else would do so, said, " If then they ask what is the name of him who sent thee, and if I know not what to reply to them, shall I not seem to be deceiving them?" And God said, "At first say unto them, I am that I am, that when they have learnt that there is a difference between him that is and him that is not, they may be further taught that there is no name whatever that can properly be assigned to me, who am the only being to whom existence belongs. And if, inasmuch as they are weak in their natural abilities, they shall inquire further about my appellation, tell them not only this one fact that I am God, but also that I am the God of those men who have derived their names from virtue, that I am the God of Abraham, and the God of Isaac, and the God of Jacob, one of whom is the rule of that wisdom which is derived from teaching, another of natural wisdom, and the third of that which is derived from practice. And if they are still distrustful they shall be taught by these tokens, and then they shall change their dispositions, seeing such signs as no man has hitherto either seen or heard."

Now the tokens were as follows. The rod which Moses held in his hand God ordered him to throw down on the ground; and immediately it received life, and crawled along, and speedily became the most powerful of all the animals which want feet, namely an immense serpent, complete in all its parts. And when Moses retreated from the beast, and out of fear was on the point of taking to flight, he was called back again; and when God laid his commands upon him, and inspired him with courage, he laid hold of it by the tail; and the serpent, though still crawling onwards, stopped at his touch, and being stretched out at its full length again returned to its original elements and became the same rod as before, so that Moses marvelled at both the changes, not knowing which was the most wonderful; as he was unable to decide between them, his soul being overwhelmed with these appearances of equal strangeness.

This now was the first sign.

The second miraculous token was afforded to him at no great distance of time. God commanded him to put one of his hands in his bosom and hide it there, and a moment afterwards to draw it out again. And when he had done what he was commanded, his hand in a moment appeared whiter than snow. Again, when he had put his hand a second time into his bosom, and had a second time drawn it forth, it returned to its original complexion, and resumed its proper appearance. These two lessons he was taught in solitude, when he was alone with God, like a pupil alone with his master, and having about him the instruments with which these wonders were worked, namely, his hand and his rod, with which indeed he walked along the road.

But the third he could not carry about with him, nor could he be instructed as to that beforehand; but it was destined to astonish him not less than the others, deriving the origin of its existence from Egypt. And this was its character. God said, " The water of the river, as much as you can take up in your hand and pour upon the ground shall be dark blood, being both in colour and in power transformed with a complete transformation." And, as was natural, this also appeared credible to Moses, not merely by reason of the truth-telling nature of the speaker, but also because of the marvels that had already been shown to him, with respect to his hand and to his rod.

But though he believed the words of God, nevertheless he tried to avoid the office to which God was appointing him, urging that he was a man of a weak voice, and slow of speech, and not eloquent, and especially so ever since he had heard God himself speaking. For judging the greatest human eloquence to be mere speechlessness in comparison with the truth, and being also prudent and cautious by nature, he shrunk from the undertaking, thinking such great matters proper for proud and bold men and not for him. And he entreated God to choose some one else who would be able easily to accomplish all the commands which he thus laid upon him. But he approved of his modesty, and said, " Art thou ignorant who it is that giveth to man a mouth, and who has formed his windpipe and his tongue, and all the apparatus of the articulate voice? I am he. Therefore, fear thou nothing. For when I approve, every thing will become articulate and clear, and will change for the better, and improve; so that no one shall hinder thee, but the stream of thy words shall flow forth in a rapid and smooth current as if from a pure fountain. And if there is any need of an interpreter, thou shalt have thy brother, who will be a subordinate mouthpiece for thee, that he may utter to the multitude the words which he receives from thee, while thou utterest to him the words that thou receivest from God."

XV. Having heard these things (for it was not at all safe or free from danger to oppose the commands of God), he departed and proceeded with his wife and children by the road leading to Egypt, on which he met with his brother and persuaded him to accompany him, announcing to him the oracular commands which he had received from God. And his brother's soul was already wrought up to obedience by divine providence, so that he, without hesitation, agreed to his proposal and readily followed him. And when they thus arrived in Egypt with one mind and soul, they first of all collected together the elders of the nation in a secret place, and there they laid the commands of God before them, and told them how God had conceived pity and compassion for them, promised them freedom and a departure from thence to a better country, promising also that he himself would be their guide on their road.

And after these events, they take courage now to converse with the king with respect to sending forth their people from his territories that they might sacrifice to God; for they said, "That it was necessary that their national sacrifices should be accomplished in the wilderness, inasmuch as they were not performed in the same manner as the sacred rites of other nations, but according to a system and law removed from the ordinary course, on account of the special peculiarities of their habits." But the monarch, who from his cradle had had his soul filled with all the arrogance of his ancestors, and who had no notion in the world of any God appreciable only by the intellect apart from those objects which are visible to the sight, answered them with insolence, saying, "Who is it whom I am to obey? I know not this new Lord of whom you are speaking. I will not let the nation go to be disobedient and headstrong under pretence of fasts and sacrifices."

And then, like a man of cruel and passionate disposition and implacable in his anger, he commanded the overseers of the works to oppress them still more, because they had previously given them some relaxation and leisure, saying that, it was from this relaxation and leisure that their forming designs of feasting and sacrifice had arisen; for that men who were in great straits did not think of these things, but only those whose life had been spent in much ease and luxury.

Therefore the Jews had now to endure more terrible afflictions than before, and were indignant at Moses and his brother as deceivers, and accused them, sometimes secretly and sometimes openly, and charged them with impiety in appearing to have spoken falsely against God ; and accordingly Moses began to exhibit the marvellous wonders which he had been previously taught, thinking that thus he should be able to bring over those who saw them from their former incredulity to believe all that he said. And this exhibition of prodigies was carefully displayed before the king and magistrates of the Egyptians.

XVI. Therefore, when all the powerful men of the state were assembled round the king, the brother of Moses taking his rod, and shaking it in a very remarkable and demonstrative manner, threw it on the ground, and it immediately became a serpent. And all those who were standing around saw it, and marvelled, and, in alarm and terror, withdrew, and fled. But all the sophists and magicians who were present said, "Why are you thus alarmed ? we also are not unpractised in such tricks as these, and we are skilled in an art which can produce similar effects." And then each of them threw down the rod which he held in his hand, and so there was a multitude of serpents which went crawling about that rod which had first been changed. And that serpent, with the excess of his power, raised himself up on high, and dilated his chest, and opened his mouth, and with the violent impulse of an attractive drawing in of his breath, drew them all towards him as if he had surrounded a large cast of fishes in a net cast around them, and then, when he had swallowed them all, he returned to his original nature of a stick.

So now the marvellous sight thus exhibited to them wrought a fear in the soul of every one of these wicked and malicious men, so that they no longer fancied that what was done was the trick or artifice of men, devised merely for deceit ; but they saw that it was a more divine power which was the cause of these things, to which all things are easy. But when by the evident might of what was done they were compelled to confess this, they still were not the less audacious, clinging to their original inhumanity and impiety as to some inalienable

virtue, and not pitying those who were unjustly enslaved, nor
doing any such things as they were commanded by the word
of God.   And though God himself had declared his will to
them by demonstrations clearer than any verbal commands,
namely, by signs and wonders, still they required a yet more
severe impression to be made upon them, and it was necessary
for him to rise up against them with still greater power ; and
accordingly, those foolish men, whom reason and command
could not influence, are corrected by a series of afflictions ;
and ten punishments were inflicted on the land ; so that the
number of the chastiseménts might be complete which was inflicted upon those who had completed their sins ; and the
punishment far transcended all ordinary visitations.

XVII. For the elements of the universe, earth, water, air,
and fire, of which the world was made, were all by the command of God, brought into a state of hostility against them,
so that the country of those impious men was destroyed, in
order to exhibit the height of the authority which God
wielded.

XXVII. And of those who now went forth out of Egypt and
left their abodes in that country, the men of age to bear arms
were more than six hundred thousand men, and the other multitude of elders, and children, and women were so great that it
was not easy to calculate it.   Moreover, there also went forth
with them a mixed multitude cf promiscuous persons collected
from all quarters, and servants, like an illegitimate crowd with
a body of genuine citizens.   Among these were those who had
been born to Hebrew fathers by Egyptian women, and who
were enrolled as members of their father's race.   And, also, all
those who had admired the decent piety of the men, and therefore joined them ; and some, also, who had come over to them,
having learnt the right way, by reason of the magnitude and
multitude of the incessant punishments which had been inflicted
on their own countrymen.

Of all these men, Moses was elected the leader ; receiving
the authority and sovereignty over them, not having gained it
like some men who have forced their way to power and supremacy by force of arms and intrigue, and by armies of cavalry
and infantry, and by powerful fleets, but having been appointed
for the sake of his virtue and excellence and that benevolence
towards all men which he was always feeling and exhibiting ;

and, also, because God, who loves virtue, and piety, and excellence, gave him his authority as a well-deserved reward. For, as he had abandoned the chief authority in Egypt, which he might have had as the grandson of the reigning king, on account of the iniquities which were being perpetrated in that country, and by reason of his nobleness of soul and of the greatness of his spirit, and the natural detestation of wickedness, scorning and rejecting all the hopes which he might have conceived from those who had adopted him, it seemed good to the Ruler and Governor of the universe to recompense him with the sovereign authority over a more populous and more powerful nation, which he was about to take to himself out of all other nations and to consecrate to the priesthood, that it might for ever offer up prayers for the whole universal race of mankind, for the sake of averting evil from them and procuring them a participation in blessings.

And when he had received this authority, he did not show anxiety, as some persons do, to increase the power of his own family, and promote his sons (for he had two) to any great dignity, so as to make them at the present time partakers in, and subsequently successors to, his sovereignty; for as he always cherished a pure and guileless disposition in all things both small and great, he now subdued his natural love and affection for his children, like an honest judge, making these feelings subordinate to his own incorruptible reason ; for he kept one most invariable object always steadily before him, namely, that of benefiting those who were subjected to his authority, and of doing everything both in word and deed, with a view to their advantage, never omitting any opportunity of doing anything that might tend to their prosperity.

Therefore he alone of all the persons who have ever enjoyed supreme authority, neither accumulated treasures of silver and gold, nor levied taxes, nor acquired possession of houses, or property, or cattle, or servants of his household, or revenues, or anything else which has reference to magnificence and superfluity, although he might have acquired an unlimited abundance of them all.

But as he thought it a token of poverty of soul to be anxious about material wealth, he despised it as a blind thing, but he honoured the far-sighted wealth of nature, and was as great an admirer as any one in the world of that kind of riches,

as he showed himself to be in his clothes, and in his food, and
in his whole system and manner of life, not indulging in any
theatrical affectation of pomp and magnificence, but cultivating
the simplicity and unpretending affable plainness of a private
individual, but a sumptuousness which was truly royal, in
those things which it is becoming for a ruler to desire and to
abound in; and these things are, temperance, and fortitude,
and continence, and presence of mind, and acuteness, and
knowledge, and industry, and patience under evil, and con-
tempt of pleasure, and justice, and exhortations to virtue and
blame, and lawful punishment of offenders, and, on the contrary, praise and honour to those who did well in accordance
with law.

XXVIII. Therefore, as he had utterly discarded all desire
of gain and of those riches which are held in the highest
repute among men, God honoured him, and gave him instead the greatest and most perfect wealth; and this is the
wealth* of all the earth and sea, and of all the rivers, and of
all the other elements, and all combinations whatever; for
having judged him deserving of being made a partaker with
himself in the portion which he had reserved for himself, he
gave him the whole world as a possession suitable for his heir:
therefore, every one of the elements obeyed him as its master,
changing the power which it had by nature and submitting to
his commands.   And perhaps there was nothing wonderful in
this; for if it be true according to the proverb,—

"That all the property of friends is common;"

and if the prophet was truly called the friend of God, then it
follows that he would naturally partake of God himself and of
all his possessions as far as he had need; for God possesses
everything and is in need of nothing; but the good man has
nothing which is properly his own, no, not even himself; but
he has a share granted to him of the treasures of God as far
as he is able to partake of them.   And this is natural enough;
for he is a citizen of the world; on which account he is not
spoken of as to be enrolled as a citizen of any particular city
in the habitable world, since he very appropriately has for his
inheritance not a portion of a district, but the whole world.

What more shall I say?   Has he not also enjoyed an even

* The text here is very corrupt.

greater communion with the Father and Creator of the universe, being thought unworthy of being called by the same appellation? For he also was called the god and king of the whole nation, and he is said to have entered into the darkness where God was; that is to say, into the invisible, and shapeless, and incorporeal world, the essence, which is the model of all existing things, where he beheld things invisible to mortal nature; for, having brought himself and his own life into the middle, as an excellently wrought picture, he established himself as a most beautiful and God-like work, to be a model for all those who were inclined to imitate him.

And happy are they who have been able to take, or have even diligently laboured to take, a faithful copy of this excellence in their own souls; for let the mind, above all other parts, take the perfect appearance of virtue, and if that cannot be, at all events let it feel an unhesitating and unvarying desire to acquire that appearance; for, indeed, there is no one who does not know that men in a lowly condition are imitators of men of high reputation, and that what they see, these last chiefly desire, towards that do they also direct their own inclinations and endeavours.

Therefore, when the chief of a nation begins to indulge in luxury and to turn aside to a delicate and effeminate life, then the whole of his subjects, or very nearly the whole, carry their desire for indulging the appetites of the belly and the parts below the belly beyond all reasonable bounds, except that there may be some persons who, through the natural goodness of their disposition, have a soul far removed from treachery, being rather merciful and kind.

If, on the other hand, the chief of a people adopts a more austere and dignified course of life, then even those of his subjects, who are inclined to be very incontinent, change and become temperate, hastening, either out of fear or out of shame, to give him an idea that they are devoted to the same pursuits and inclinations that he is; and, in fact, the lower orders will never, no, nor will mad men even, reject the customs and habits of their superiors: but, perhaps, since Moses was also destined to be the lawgiver of his nation, he was himself long previously, through the providence of God, a living and reasonable law, since that providence appointed him to be the lawgiver, when as yet he knew nothing of his appointment.

XXIX. When then he received the supreme authority, with
the good will of all his subjects, God himself being the regulator and approver of all his actions, he conducted his people
as a colony into Phœnicia, and into the hollow Syria (Cœle-
syria), and Palestine, which was at that time called the land
of the Canaanites, the borders of which country were three
days' journey distant from Egypt. Then he led them forward,
not by the shortest road, partly because he was afraid lest the
inhabitants should come out to meet and to resist him in his
march, from fear of being overthrown and enslaved by such a
multitude, and so, if a war arose, they might be again driven
back into Egypt, falling from one enemy to another, and
being driven by their new foes upon their ancient tyrants, and
so become a sport and a laughing-stock to the Egyptians, and
have to endure greater and more grievous hardships than
before.

He was also desirous, by leading them through a desolate
and extensive country, to prove them, and see how obedient
they would be when they were not surrounded by any abundance of necessaries, but were but scantily provided and nearly
in actual want.

Therefore, turning aside from the direct road he found an
oblique path, and thinking that it must extend as far as the
Red Sea, he began to march by that road, and, they say, that
a most portentous miracle happened at that time, a prodigy
of nature, which no one anywhere recollects to have ever happened before; for a cloud, fashioned into the form of a vast
pillar, went before the multitude by day, giving forth a light
like that of the sun, but by night it displayed a fiery blaze, in
order that the Hebrews might not wander on their journey,
but might follow the guidance of their leader along the road,
without any deviation. Perhaps, indeed, this was one of the
ministers of the mighty King, an unseen messenger, a guide
of the way enveloped in this cloud, whom it was not lawful for
men to behold with the eyes of the body.

XXX. But when the king of Egypt saw them proceeding
along a pathless track, as he fancied, and marching through a
rough and untrodden wilderness, he was delighted with the
blunder they were making respecting their line of march, thinking that now they were hemmed in, having no way of escape
whatever. And, as he repented of having let them go, he

determined to pursue them, thinking that he should either subdue the multitude by fear, and so reduce them a second time to slavery, or else that if they resisted he should slay them all from the children upwards.   Accordingly, he took all his force of cavalry, and his darters, and his slingers, and his equestrian archers, and all the rest of his light-armed troops, and he gave his commanders six hundred of the finest of his scythe-bearing chariots, that with all becoming dignity and display they might pursue these men, and join in the expedition and so using all possible speed, he sallied forth after them and hastened and pressed on the march, wishing to come upon them suddenly before they had any expectation of him.

For an unexpected evil is at all times more grievous than one which has been looked for, in proportion as that which has been despised finds it easier to make a formidable attack than that which has been regarded with care.

The king, therefore, with these ideas, pursued after the Hebrews, thinking that he should subdue them by the mere shout of battle.   And, when he overtook them, they were already encamped along the shore of the Red Sea.   And they were just about to go to breakfast, when, at first, a mighty sound reached them, as was natural from such a host of men and beasts of burden all proceeding on with great haste, so that they all ran out of their tents to look round, and stood on tip-toes to see and hear what was the matter.   Then, a short time afterwards, the army of the enemy came in sight as it rose over a hill, all in arms, and ready arranged in line of battle.

XXXI. And the Hebrews, being terrified at this extraordinary and unexpected danger, and not being well prepared for defence, because of a scarcity of defensive armour and of weapons (for they had not marched out for war, but to found a colony), and not being able to escape, for behind was the sea, and in front was the enemy, and on each side a vast and pathless wilderness, reviled against Moses, and, being dismayed at the magnitude of the evils that threatened them, began, as is very common in such calamities, to blame their governors, and said : " Because there were no graves in Egypt in which we could be buried after we were dead, have you brought us out hither to kill and bury us here ?   Or, is not even slavery a lighter evil than death ?   Having allured the multitude with the hope of liberty, you have caused them to incur a still more

grievous danger than slavery, namely, the risk of the loss of
life. Did you not know our simplicity, and the bitterness
and cruel anger of the Egyptians? Do you not see the magnitude of the evils which surround us, and from which we cannot
escape? What are we to do? Are we, unarmed, to fight
against men in complete armour? or shall we flee now that we
are hemmed in as by nets cast all around us by our pitiless
enemies—hemmed in by pathless deserts and impassable seas?
Or, even, if the sea was navigable, how are we to get any
vessels to cross over it?"

Moses, when he heard these complaints, pardoned his people,
but remembered the oracles of God. And, at the same time, he
so divided and distributed his mind and his speech, that with
the one he associated invisibly with God, in order that God
might deliver him from otherwise inextricable calamities; and,
with the other, he encouraged and comforted those who cried
out to him, saying: "Do not faint and despair. God does not
deliver in the same way that man does. Why do you only
trust such means of deliverance as seem probable and likely?
God, when he comes as an assistant, stands in need of no
adventitious preparations. It is his peculiar attribute to find
a path amid inextricable perplexities. What is impossible to
every created being is possible and easy to him above."

Thus he spoke to them while yet standing still. But after a
short time he became inspired by God, and being full of the
divine spirit and under the influence of that spirit which was
accustomed to enter into him, he prophesied and animated
them thus: "This army which you behold so splendidly
equipped with arms, you shall no more see arrayed against
you; for it shall fall, utterly and completely overthrown, so
that not a relic shall be seen any more upon the earth, and
that not at any distance of time, but this very next night."

XXXII. He then spoke thus. But when the sun had set,
immediately a most violent south wind set in and began to
blow, under the influence of which the sea retreated; for, as it
was accustomed to ebb and flow, on this occasion it was driven
back much further towards the shore, and drawn up in a heap
as if into a ravine or a whirlpool. And no stars were visible,
but a dense and black cloud covered the whole of the heaven,
so that the night became totally dark, to the consternation of

the pursuers. And Moses, at the command of God, smote the sea with his staff. And it was broken and divided into two parts, and one of the divisions at the part where it was broken off, was raised to a height and mounted up, and being thus consolidated like a strong wall, stood quiet and unshaken; and the portion behind the Hebrews was also contracted and raised in, and prevented from proceeding forwards, as if it were held back by invisible reins. And the intermediate space, where the fracture had taken place, was dried up and became a broad, and level, and easy road.

When Moses beheld this he marvelled and rejoiced; and, being filled with joy, he encouraged his followers and exhorted them to march forward with all possible speed. And when they were about to pass over, a most extraordinary prodigy was seen; for the cloud, which had been their guide, and which during all the rest of the period of their march had gone in front of them, now turned back and placed itself at the back of the multitude to guard their rear; and, being situated between the pursuers and the pursued, it guided the one party so as to keep them with safety and perfect freedom from danger, and it checked and embarrassed the others, who were hastening on to pursue them. And, when the Egyptians saw this, they were entirely filled with disorder and confusion, and through their consternation they threw all their ranks into disorder, falling upon one another and endeavouring to flee, when there was no advantage to be derived from flight.

For, at the first appearance of morning, the Hebrews passed over by a dry path, with their wives, and families, and infant children. But the portions of the sea which were rolled up and consolidated on each side overwhelmed the Egyptians with their horses and chariots, the tide being brought back by a strong north wind and poured over them, and coming upon them with vast waves and overpowering billows, so that there was not even a torchbearer left to carry the news of this sudden disaster back to Egypt.

Then the Hebrews, being amazed at this great and wonderful event, gained a victory which they had never hoped for without bloodshed or loss; and, seeing the instantaneous and complete destruction of the enemy, formed two choruses, one of men and the other of women, on the sea shore, and sang hymns of

gratitude to God, Moses leading the song of the men, and his
sister that of the women; for these two persons were the
leaders of the choruses.

XXXIII. And when they had departed from the sea they
went on for some time travelling, and no longer feeling any
apprehension of their enemies. But when water failed them,
so that for three days they had nothing to drink, they were
again reduced to despondency by thirst, and again began to
blame their fate as if they had not enjoyed any good fortune
previously; for it always happens that the presence of an existing and present evil takes away the recollection of the pleasure
which was caused by former good. At last, when they beheld
some fountains, they ran up full of joy with the idea that they
were going to drink, being deceived by ignorance of the truth;
for the springs were bitter.

Then when they had tasted them they were bowed down by
the unexpected disappointment, and fainted, and yielded both
in body and soul, lamenting not so much for themselves as for
their helpless children, whom they could not endure without
tears to behold imploring drink ; and some of those who were
of more careless dispositions, and of no settled notions of
piety, blamed all that had gone before, as if it had turned out
not so as to do them any good, but rather so as to lead them
to a suffering of more grievous calamities than ever; saying
that it was better for them to die, not only once but three
times over, by the hands of their enemies, than to perish with
thirst; for they affirmed that a quick and painless departure
from life did in no respect differ from freedom from death in
the opinion of wise men, but that that was real death which
was slow and accompanied by pain ; that what was fearful was
not to be dead but only to be dying.

When they were lamenting and bewailing themselves in
this manner, Moses again besought God, who knew the weakness of all creatures, and especially of men, and the necessary
wants of the body which depends for its existence on food,
and which is enslaved by those severe task-mistresses, eating
and drinking, to pardon his desponding people, and to relieve
their want of everything, and that too not after a long interval
of time, but by a prompt and undeferred liberality, since by
reason of the natural impotency of their mortal nature, they
required a very speedy measure of assistance and deliverance.

But he, by his bountiful and merciful power, anticipated their wishes, sending forth and opening the watchful, anxious eye of the soul of his suppliant, and showed him a piece of wood which he bade him take up and throw into the water, which indeed had been made by nature with such a power for that purpose, and which perhaps had a quality which was previously unknown, or perhaps was then first endowed with it, for the purpose of effecting the service which it was then about to perform : and when he had done that which he was commanded to do, the fountains became changed and sweet and drinkable, so that no one was able to recognise the fact of their having been bitter previously, because there was not the slightest trace or spark of their ancient bitterness left to excite the recollection.

XXXIV. And so having appeased their thirst with double pleasure, since the blessing of enjoyment when it comes beyond one's hopes delights one still more, and having also replenished their ewers, they departed as from a feast, as if they had been entertained at a luxurious banquet, and as if they were intoxicated not with the drunkenness which proceeds from wine, but with a sober joy which they had imbibed purely, while pledging and being pledged by the piety of the ruler who was leading them ; and so they arrive at a second halting place, well supplied with water, and well shaded with trees, called Aileem, irrigated with twelve fountains, near which were young and vigorous trunks of palm trees to the number of seventy, a visible indication and token of good to the whole nation, to all who were gifted with a clear-sighted intellect.

For the nation itself was divided into twelve tribes, each of which, if pious and religious, would be looked upon in the light of a fountain, since piety is contniually pouring forth everlasting and unceasing springs of virtuous actions. And the elders and chiefs of the whole nation were seventy in number, being therefore very naturally likened to palm trees which are the most excellent of all trees, being both most beautiful to behold, and bearing the most exquisite fruit, which has also its vitality and power of existence, not buried in the roots like other trees, but situated high up like the heart of a man, and lodged in the centre of its highest branches, by which it is attended and guarded like a queen as it really is, they being spread all round it. And the intellect too of those persons who have tasted of holiness has a similar nature; for it has learned to look upwards and to soar on high, and is continually keeping its eye fixed on sublime objects, and investigating divine things, and ridiculing, and scorning all earthly beauty, thinking the last only toys, and divine things the only real and proper objects worthy of its attention.

XXXV. But after these events only a short time elapsed, when they became oppressed by famine through the scarcity of provisions, as if one necessary thing after another was to foil them in succession: for thirst and hunger are very cruel and terrible mistresses, and having portioned out the afflictions between them, attacked them by turns; and it so fell out that when the first calamity was relaxed the second came on, which was most intolerable to those who had to bear it, inasmuch as having only just fancied that they were delivered from thirst, they now found another evil, namely famine, lying in ambush to attack them; and not only was their present scarcity terrible, but they were also in despair as to the supply of necessary food for the future; for when they saw the vast and extensive desert around them, so utterly unproductive of any kind of crop, their hearts sank within them.

For all around were rugged and precipitous rocks, or else a salt and brackish plain, and stony mountains, or deep sands reaching up and forming mountains of inaccessible height; and moreover there was no river, neither winter torrent nor ever-flowing stream; there were no springs, no plant growing from seed, no tree whether for fruit or timber, no animal whether flying or terrestrial, except some few poisonous reptiles born for the destruction of mankind, and serpents, and scorpions. So then the Hebrews, remembering the plenty and luxury which they had enjoyed in Egypt, and the abundance of all things which was bestowed upon them there, and contrasting it with the universal want of all things which they were now experiencing, were grieved and indignant, and talked the matter over with one another, saying:—

"We left our former abodes and emigrated, from a hope of freedom, happy only in the promises of our leader; as far as his actions go, we are of all men the most miserable. What will be the end of this long and interminable journey? Every-one else, whether sailing over the sea or marching on foot, has some limit before him at which he will eventually arrive ; some being bound for marts and harbours, others for some city or country ; but we alone have nothing to look forward to but a pathless desert, and a difficult journey, and terrible hopelessness, and despair ; for as we advance, the desert lies before us like an ever open, vast, and pathless sea which widens and increases every day. But Moses having raised our expectations, and puffed us up with fine speeches, and filled our ears with vain hopes, racks our bodies with hunger, and does not give us even necessary food. He has deceived this vast multitude with the name of a settlement in a colony ; having first of all led us out of an inhabited country into an uninhabitable district, and now sending us down to the shades below, which is the last journey of life."

XXXVI. Moses, being reviled in this way, was nevertheless not so much grieved at their accusations which they brought against himself, as at the inconstancy of their own resolutions and minds. For though they had already experienced an infinite number of blessings which had befallen them unexpectedly and out of the ordinary course of affairs, they ought, in his opinion, not to have allowed themselves to be led away by any specious or plausible complaints, but to have trusted in him, as they had already received the clearest possible proofs that he spoke truly about everything.

But again, when he came to take into consideration the want of food, than which there is no more terrible evil which can afflict mankind, he pardoned them, knowing that the multitude is by nature inconstant and always moved by present circumstances, which cause it to forget what has gone before, and despair of the future. Therefore, as they were all in the extremity of suffering, and expecting the most fearful misery which they fancied was lying in ambush for them and close at hand, God, partly by reason of his natural love and compassion for man, and partly because he desired to honour the commander whom he had appointed to govern them, and still more to show his great piety and holiness in all matters whether visible or invisible, pitied them and relieved their distress.

Therefore he now devised an entirely new kind of benefit, that they, being taught by manifest signs and displays of his power, might feel reverence for him, and learn for the future not to be impatient if anything turned out contrary to their wishes, but to endure present evils with fortitude, in the expectation of future blessings.

What then happened? The very next day, about sun-rise, a dense and abundant dew fell in a circle all round about the camp, which rained down upon it gently and quietly in an unusual and unprecedented shower; not water, nor hail, nor snow, nor ice, for these are the things which the changes of the clouds produce in the winter season; but what was now rained down upon them was a very small and light grain, like millet, which, by reason of its incessant fall, rested in heaps before the camp, a most extraordinary sight. And the Hebrews marvelled at it, and inquired of the commander what this rain was, which no man had ever seen before, and for what it was sent.

And he was inspired, and full of the spirit of prophecy, and spoke to them as follows: " A fertile plain has been granted to mortal men, which they cut up into furrows, and plough, and sow, and do everything else which relates to agriculture, providing the yearly fruits so as to enjoy abundance of necessary food. But it is not one portion only of the universe, but the whole world that belongs to God, and all its parts obey their master, supplying everything which he desires that they should supply. Now therefore, it has seemed good to him that the air should produce food instead of water, since the earth has often brought forth rain; for when the river in Egypt every year overflows with inundations and irrigates all the fields, what else is that but a rain which is showered up from below?" That other would have been indeed a most surprising fact if it had stopped there; but now he wrought wonders with still more surprising circumstances; for all the population bringing vessels one after another, collected what fell, some putting them upon beasts of burden, others loading themselves and taking them on their shoulders, being prudently eager to provide themselves with necessary food for a longer time. But it was something that would bear to be stored up and dispensed gradually, since God is accustomed always to give his gifts fresh.

Accordingly, they now prepared enough for their immediate necessities and present use, and ate it with pleasure. But of what was left till the next day they found not a morsel unhurt, but it was all changed and fetid, and full of little animals of the kind which usually cause putrefaction. So this they naturally threw away, but they found fresh quantities of it ready for food, so that it fell out that this food was carried down every day with the dew. But the holy seventh day had an especial honour; for, as it is not permitted to do anything whatever on that day (and it is expressly commanded that men are then to abstain from every work, great or little), so that they were not able to collect food that day, instead of food for one day, God rained upon them a double quantity, and ordered them to collect what shall be food enough for two days. And what was then collected remained sound, no portion of it becoming spoiled as it had before.

XXXVII. I will also relate a circumstance which is more marvellous than even this one; for, though they were travelling for forty years, yet during all this long period of time they had an abundant supply of all necessary things in their appointed order, as is the case in clubs and messes which are regularly measured out with a view to the distribution of what is required by each individual. And, at the same time, they learnt the value of that long-wished for day; for, having inquired for a long time what the day of the creation of the world was, the day on which the universe was completely finished, and, having received this question from their fathers and their ancestors undecided, they at last, though with great difficulty, did ascertain it, not being taught only by the sacred scriptures, but also by a certain proof which was very distinct; for, as that portion of the manna (as has been already said) which was more than was wanted on the other days of the week was spoiled, still that portion which was rained down on the day before the seventh not only did not change its nature, but was dispensed in a twofold quantity. And the use was as follows.

At dawn they collected what had been showered down, and then they ground or pounded it; and then they roasted it and made a very sweet food of it, like honey cheesecake, and so they ate it, without requiring any exceeding skill on the part of the preparers of the food. But they also had no scarcity of, nor any great distance to go for, the means of making life even luxurious, as if they had been in a populous and productive land, since God had determined out of his great abundance to supply them with plenty of all things which they required even

in the wilderness; for, in the evenings, there was an uninterrupted cloud of quails borne to them from the sea, which overshadowed the whole camp, flying very near the ground so as to
be easily caught. Therefore, the Hebrews, taking them and
preparing them as each individual liked, enjoyed the most
exquisite meat, pleasing themselves and varying their food
with this necessary and delicious addition.

XXXVIII. Accordingly, they had a great abundance of
these birds, as they never failed. But, a second time, a terrible
scarcity of water came upon them and afflicted them; and, as
they again speedily began to despair of their safety, Moses,
taking his sacred rod with which he had wrought the signs in
Egypt, being inspired by God, smote the precipitous rock.
And the rock being struck this seasonable blow, whether it was
that there was a spring previously concealed beneath it, or
whether water was then for the first time conveyed into it by
invisible channels pouring in all together and being forced out
with violence, at all events the rock, I say, was cleft open by
the force of the blow and poured forth water in a stream, so
that it not only then furnished a relief from thirst, but also
supplied for a long time an abundance of drink for so many
myriads of people.

For they filled all their water vessels, as they had done
before, from the fountains which were bitter by nature, but
which, by divine providence, were changed to sweet water.
And, if any one disbelieves these facts, he neither knows God
nor has he ever sought to know him; for, if he had, he would
have instantly known, he would have known and surely comprehended, that all these unexpected and extraordinary things
are the amusement of God; looking at the things which are
really great and deserving of serious attention, namely, the
creation of the heaven, and the revolutions of the planets and
fixed stars, and the shining of light—of the light of the sun by
day and that of the moon by night—and the position of the
earth in the most centre spot of the universe, and the vast
dominions of the different continents and islands, and the
innumerable varieties of animals and plants, and the effusion of
the sea, andt he rapid courses of the ever-flowing rivers and
winter mountain torrents, and the streams of everlasting
springs, some of which pour forth cold and others hot water,

and the various changes and alterations of the air and climate, and the different seasons of the year, and an infinite number of other beautiful objects.

And the whole of a man's life would be too short if he wished to enumerate all the separate instances of such things, or even to detail fully all that is to be seen in one complete portion of the world; aye, if he were to be the most long-lived man that has ever been seen. But all these things, though they are in truth really wonderful, are despised by us by reason of our familiarity with them. But the things to which we are not accustomed, even though they may be unimportant, still make an impression upon us from our love of novelty, while we yield to strange ideas concerning them.

XXXIX. And now, as they had gone over a vast tract of land previously untravelled, there appeared some boundaries of habitable country and some suburbs, as it were, of the land to which they were proceeding, and the Phœnicians inhabited it. But they, hoping that a tranquil and peaceable life would now be permitted to them, were deceived in their expectation; for the king of the country, being afraid lest he might be destroyed, roused up all the youth of his cities, and collected an army, and went forth to meet them to keep them from his borders. And if they attempted to force their way, he showed that he would proceed to repel them with all his forces, his army being fresh, and now for the first time levied and marshalled for battle, while the Hebrews were wearied and worn out with their long travelling and with the scarcity of meat and drink which had in turns oppressed them,

But when Moses had learnt from his scouts that the army of the enemy was marshalled at no great distance, he chose out those men who were in the flower of their youth, and appointed one of his subordinate officers, named Joshua, to be their general, while he himself went to procure a more powerful alliance; for, having purified himself with the customary purification, he rode up with speed to a neighbouring hill, and there he besought God to hold his shield over the Hebrews and to give them the victory and the mastery, as he had delivered them before from more formidable dangers and from other evils, not only dissipating the calamities with which they were threatened at the hands of men, but also all those which the transformation of the elements so wonderfully caused in the land of Egypt, and from those which the long scarcity inflicted upon them in their travels.

And just as the two armies were about to engage in battle, a most marvellous miracle took place with respect to his hands; for they became by turns lighter and heavier. Then, whenever they were lighter, so that he could hold them up on high, the alliance between God and his people was strengthened, and waxed mighty, and became more glorious. But whenever his hands sank down the enemy prevailed, God showing thus by a figure that the earth and all the extremities of it were the appropriate inheritance of the one party, and the most sacred air the inheritance of the other. And as the heaven is in every respect supreme to and superior over the earth, so also shall the nation which has heaven for its inheritance be superior to their enemies.

For some time, then, his hands, like the balances in a scale, were by turns light, and by turns descended as being heavy; and, during this period, the battle was undecided. But, on a sudden, they became quite devoid of weight, using their fingers as if they were wings, and so they were raised to a lofty height, like winged birds who traverse the heaven, and they continued at this height until the Hebrews had gained an unquestionable victory, their enemies being slain to a man from the youth upward, and suffering with justice what they had endeavoured to inflict on others, contrary to what was befitting.

Then Moses erected an altar, which from the circumstances that had taken place he named the refuge of God, on which he offered sacrifices in honour of his victory, and poured forth prayers of gratitude to God.

successful issue, and of the inheritances which he distributed in portions to his soldiers.

But the book which we are now about to compose relates to the affairs which follow those others in due order, and bear a certain correspondence and connection with them.

For some persons say, and not without some reason and propriety, that this is the only way by which cities can be expected to advance in improvement, if either the kings culti- vate philosophy, or if philosophers exercise the kingly power. But Moses will be seen not only to have displayed all these powers—I mean the genius of the philosopher and of the king —in an extraordinary degree at the same time, but three other powers likewise, one of which is conversant about legislation, the second about the way of discharging the duties of high priest, and the last about the prophetic office; and it is on these subjects that I have now been constrained to choose to enlarge; for I conceive that all these things have fitly been united in him, inasmuch as in accordance with the providential will of God he was both a king and a lawgiver, and a high priest and a prophet, and because in each office he displayed the most eminent wisdom and virtue.

We must now show how it is that every thing is fitly united in him. It becomes a king to command what ought to be done, and to forbid what ought not to be done; but the com manding what ought to be done, and the prohibition of what ought not to be done, belongs especially to the law, so that the king is at once a living law, and the law is a just king. But a king and a lawgiver ought to pay attention not only to human things, but also to divine ones, for the affairs of neither kings nor subjects go on well except by the intervention of divine providence; on which account it was necessary that such a man as Moses should enjoy the first priesthood, in order that he might with perfectly conducted sacrifices, and with a perfect knowledge of the proper way to serve God, entreat for a deliverance from evil and for a participation in good, both for himself and for the people whom he was governing, from the merciful God who listens favourably to prayers.

But since there is an infinite variety of both human and divine circumstances which are unknown both to king, and lawgiver, and chief priest, for a man is no less a created and mortal being from having all these offices, or because he is

clothed with such a vast and boundless inheritance of honour
and happiness, he was also of necessity invested with the gift
of prophecy, in order that he might through the providence of
God learn all those things which he was unable to comprehend
by his own reason; for what the mind is unable to attain to,
that prophecy masters. Therefore the connection of these
four powers is beautiful and harmonious, for being all connected together and united one to another, they unite in concert,
receiving and imparting a reciprocity of benefits from and to
one another, imitating the virgin graces with whom it is an
immutable law of their nature that they cannot be disunited,
with respect to whom one might fairly say, what is habitually
said of the virtues, that he who has one has them all.

II. And first of all we must speak of the matters which
relate to his character and conduct as a lawgiver.

I am not ignorant that the man who desires to be an excellent and perfect lawgiver ought to exercise all the virtues in
their complete integrity and perfection, since in the houses of
his nation some are near relations and some distant, but still
they are all related to one another. And in like manner we
must look upon some of the virtues as connected more closely
with some matters, and on others as being more removed from
them. Now these four qualities are closely connected with
and related to the legislative power, namely, humility, the love
of justice, the love of virtue, and the hatred of iniquity; for
every individual who has any desire for exercising his talents
as a lawgiver is under the influence of each of these feelings.
It is the province of humanity to prepare for adoption such
opinions as will benefit the common weal, and to teach the
advantages which will proceed from them. It is the part of
justice to point out how we ought to honour equality, and to
assign to every man his due according to his deserts. It is the
part of the love of virtue to embrace those things which are by
nature good, and to give to every one who deserves them
facilities without limit for the most unrestrained enjoyment of
happiness. It is also the province of the hatred of iniquity to
reject all those who dishonour virtue, and to look upon them
as common enemies of the human race.

Therefore it is a very great thing if it has fallen to the lot of
any one to arrive at any one of the qualities before mentioned,
and it is a marvellous thing, as it should seem, for any one

man to have been able to grasp them all, which in fact Moses appears to have been the only person who has ever done, having given a very clear description of the aforesaid virtues in the commandments which he established. And those who are well versed in the sacred scriptures know this, for if he had not had these principles innate within him he would never have compiled those scriptures at the promptings of God. And he gave to those who were worthy to use them the most admirable of all possessions, namely, faithful copies and imitations of the original examples which were consecrated and enshrined in the soul, which became the laws which he revealed and established, displaying in the clearest manner the virtues which I have enumerated and described above.

III. But that he himself is the most admirable of all the lawgivers who have ever lived in any country either among the Greeks or among the barbarians, and that his are the most admirable of all laws, and truly divine, omitting no one particular which they ought to comprehend, there is the clearest proof possible in this fact, the laws of other lawgivers, if any one examines them by his reason, he will find to be put in motion in an innumerable multitude of pretexts, either because of wars, or of tyrannies, or of some other unexpected events which come upon nations through the various alterations and innovations of fortune; and very often luxury, abounding in all kind of superfluity and unbounded extravagance, has overturned laws, from the multitude not being able to bear unlimited prosperity, but having a tendency to become insolent through satiety, and insolence is in opposition to law.

But the enactments of this lawgiver are firm, not shaken by commotions, not liable to alteration, but stamped as it were with the seal of nature herself, and they remain firm and lasting from the day on which they were first promulgated to the present one, and there may well be a hope that they will remain to all future time, as being immortal, as long as the sun and the moon, and the whole heaven and the whole world shall endure. At all events, though the nation of the Hebrews experienced so many changes both in the direction of prosperity and of the opposite destiny, no one, no not even the very smallest and most unimportant of all his commandments was changed, since every one, as it seems, honoured their venerable and godlike character; and what neither famine, nor

pestilence, nor war, nor sovereign, nor tyrant, nor the rise of
any passions or evil feelings against either soul or body, nor
any other evil, whether inflicted by God or deriving its rise
from men, ever dissolved, can surely never be looked upon by
us in any other light than as objects of all admiration, and
beyond all powers of description in respect of their excellence.

IV. But this is not so entirely wonderful, although it may
fairly by itself be considered a thing of great intrinsic importance, that his laws were kept securely and immutably from all
time ; but this is more wonderful by far, as it seems, that not
only the Jews, but that also almost every other nation, and
especially those who make the greatest account of virtue,
have dedicated themselves to embrace and honour them, for
they have received this especial honour above all other codes
of laws, which is not given to any other code. And a proof of
this is to be found in the fact that of all the cities in Greece
and in the territory of the barbarians, if one may so say,
speaking generally, there is not one single city which pays any
respect to the laws of another state. In fact, a city scarcely
adheres to its own laws with any constancy for ever, but continually modifies them, and adapts them to the changes of
times and circumstances.

The Athenians rejected the customs and laws of the Lacedæmonians, and so did the Lacedæmonians repudiate the laws
of the Athenians. Nor, again, in the countries of the barbarians do the Egyptians keep the laws of the Scythians, nor do
the Scythians keep the laws of the Egyptians ; nor, in short,
do those who live in Asia attend to the laws which obtain in
Europe, nor do the inhabitants of Europe respect the laws of
the Asiatic nations.

And, in short, it is very nearly an universal rule, from the
rising of the sun to its extreme west, that every country, and
nation, and city, is alienated from the laws and customs of
foreign nations and states, and that they think that they are
adding to the estimation in which they hold their own laws
by despising those in use among other nations. But this is
not the case with our laws which Moses has given to us ; for
they lead after them and influence all nations, barbarians, and
Greeks, the inhabitants of continents and islands, the eastern
nations and the western, Europe and Asia ; in short, the
whole habitable world from one extremity to the other.

For what man is there who does not honour that sacred seventh day, granting in consequence a relief and relaxation from labour, for himself and for all those who are near to him, and that not to free men only, but also to slaves, and even to beasts of burden; for the holiday extends even to every description of animal, and to every beast whatever which performs service to man, like slaves obeying their natural master, and it affects even every species of plant and tree; for there is no shoot, and no branch, and no leaf even which it is allowed to cut or to pluck on that day, nor any fruit which it is lawful to gather; but everything is at liberty and in safety on that day, and enjoys, as it were, perfect freedom, no one ever touching them, in obedience to a universal proclamation.

Again, who is there who does not pay all due respect and honour to that which is called "the fast," and especially to that great yearly one which is of a more austere and venerable character than the ordinary solemnity at the full moon? on which, indeed, much pure wine is drunk, and costly entertainments are provided, and everything which relates to eating and drinking is supplied in the most unlimited profusion, by which the insatiable pleasures of the belly are inflamed and increased. But on this fast it is not lawful to take any food or any drink, in order that no bodily passion may at all disturb or hinder the pure operations of the mind; but these passions are wont to be generated by fulness and satiety, so that at this time men feast, propitiating the Father of the universe with holy prayers, by which they are accustomed to solicit pardon for their former sins, and the acquisition and enjoyment of new blessings.

V. And that beauty and dignity of the legislation of Moses is honoured not among the Jews only, but also by all other nations, is plain, both from what has been already said and from what I am about to state. In olden time the laws were written in the Chaldæan language, and for a long time they remained in the same condition as at first, not changing their language as long as their beauty had not made them known to other nations; but when, from the daily and uninterrupted respect shown to them by those to whom they had been given, and from their ceaseless observance of their ordinances, other nations also obtained an understanding of them, their reputation spread over all lands; for what was really good, even though it may through envy be overshadowed for a short time, still in time shines again through the intrinsic excellence of its nature.

Some persons, thinking it a scandalous thing that these laws should only be known among one half portion of the human race, namely, among the barbarians, and that the Greek nation should be wholly and entirely ignorant of them, turned their attention to their translation.

And since this undertaking was an important one, tending to the general advantage, not only of private persons, but also of rulers, of whom the number was not great, it was entrusted to kings and to the most illustrious of all kings. Ptolemy, surnamed Philadelphus, was the third in succession after Alexander, the monarch who subdued Egypt; and he was, in all virtues which can be displayed in government, the most excellent sovereign, not only of all those of his time, but of all that ever lived; so that even now, after the lapse of so many generations, his fame is still celebrated, as having left many instances and monuments of his magnanimity in the cities and districts of his kingdom, so that even now it is come to be a sort of proverbial expression to call excessive magnificence, and zeal, for honour and splendour in preparation, Philadelphian, from his name; and, in a word, the whole family of the Ptolemies was exceedingly eminent and conspicuous above all other royal families, and among the Ptolemies, Philadelphus was the most illustrious; for all the rest put together scarcely did as many glorious and praiseworthy actions as this one king did by himself, being, as it were, the leader of the herd, and in a manner the head of all the kings.

VI. He, then, being a sovereign of this character, and having conceived a great admiration for and love of the legislation of Moses, conceived the idea of having our laws translated into the Greek language; and immediately he sent out ambassadors to the high-priest and king of Judea, for they were the same person. And having explained his wishes, and having requested him to pick him out a number of men, of perfect fitness for the task, who should translate the law, the high-priest, as was natural, being greatly pleased, and thinking that the king had only felt the inclination to undertake a work of such a character from having been influenced by the providence of' God, considered, and with great care selected the most respectable of the Hebrews whom he had about him, who in addition to their knowledge of their national scriptures, had also been well instructed in Grecian literature, and cheerfully sent them.

And when they arrived at the king's court they were hospitably received by the king; and while they feasted, they in return feasted their entertainer with witty and virtuous conversation; for he made experiment of the wisdom of each individual among them, putting to them a succession of new and extraordinary questions; and they, since the time did not allow of their being prolix in their answers, replied with great propriety and fidelity as if they were delivering apophthegms which they had already prepared. So when they had won his approval, they immediately began to fulfil the objects for which that honourable embassy had been sent; and considering among themselves how important the affair was, to translate laws which had been divinely given by direct inspiration, since they were not able either to take away anything, or to add anything, or to alter anything, but were bound to preserve the original form and character of the whole composition, they looked out for the most completely purified place of all the spots on the outside of the city.

For the places within the walls, as being filled with all kinds of animals, were held in suspicion by them by reason of the diseases and deaths of some, and the accursed actions of those who were in health. The island of Pharos lies in front of Alexandria, the neck of which runs out like a sort of tongue towards the city, being surrounded with water of no great depth, but chiefly with shoals and shallow water, so that the great noise and roaring from the beating of the waves is kept at a considerable distance, and so mitigated. They judged this place to be the most suitable of all the spots in the neighbourhood for them to enjoy quiet and tranquillity in, so that they might associate with the laws alone in their minds; and there they remained, and having taken the sacred scriptures, they lifted up them and their hands also to heaven, entreating of God that they might not fail in their object. And he assented to their prayers, that the greater part, or indeed the universal race of mankind might be benefited, by using these philosophical and entirely beautiful commandments for the correction of their lives.

VII. Therefore, being settled in a secret place, and nothing ever being present with them except the elements of nature, the earth, the water, the air, and the heaven, concerning the creation of which they were going in the first place to explain the sacred account; for the account of the creation of the world is the beginning of the law; they, like men inspired, prophesied, not one saying one thing and another another, but every one of them employed the self-same nouns and verbs, as if some unseen prompter had suggested all their language to them. And yet who is there who does not know that every language, and the Greek language above all others, is rich in a variety of words, and that it is possible to vary a sentence and to paraphrase the same idea, so as to set it forth in a great variety of manners, adapting many different forms of expression to it at different times.

But this, they say, did not happen at all in the case of this translation of the law, but that, in every case, exactly corresponding Greek words were employed to translate literally the appropriate Chaldaic words, being adapted with exceeding propriety to the matters which were to be explained; for just as I suppose the things which are proved in geometry and logic do not admit any variety of explanation, but the proposition which was set forth from the beginning remains unaltered, in like manner I conceive did these men find words precisely and literally corresponding to the things, which words were alone, or in the greatest possible degree, destined to explain with clearness and force the matters which it was desired to reveal. And there is a very evident proof of this; for if Chaldæans were to learn the Greek language, and if Greeks were to learn Chaldæan, and if each were to meet with those scriptures in both languages, namely, the Chaldaic and the translated version, they would admire and reverence them both as sisters, or rather as one and the same both in their facts and in their language; considering these translators not mere interpreters but hierophants and prophets to whom it had been granted with their honest and guileless minds to go along with the most pure spirit of Moses.

On which account, even to this very day, there is every year a solemn assembly held and a festival celebrated in the island of Pharos, to which not only the Jews but a great number of persons of other nations sail across, reverencing the place in which the first light of interpretation shone forth, and thanking

God for that ancient piece of beneficence which was always
young and fresh.

And after the prayers and the giving of thanks some of
them pitched their tents on the shore, and some of them lay
down without any tents in the open air on the sand of the
shore, and feasted with their relations and friends, thinking
the shore at that time a more beautiful abode than the furniture of the king's palace.

In this way those admirable, and incomparable, and most
desirable laws were made known to all people, whether private
individuals or kings, and this too at a period when the nation
had not been prosperous for a long time.   And it is generally
the case that a cloud is thrown over the affairs of those who
are not flourishing, so that but little is known of them; and
then, if they make any fresh start and begin to improve, how
great is the increase of their renown and glory?   I think that
in that case every nation, abandoning all their own individual
customs, and utterly disregarding their national laws, would
change and come over to the honour of such a people only; for
their laws shining in connection with, and simultaneously with,
the prosperity of the nation, will obscure all others, just as the
rising sun obscures the stars.

VIII. Now what has been here said is quite sufficient for
the abundant praise of Moses as a lawgiver.   But there is
another more extensive praise which his own holy writings
themselves contain, and it is to them that we must now turn
for the purpose of exhibiting the virtue of him who compiled
them.

Now these writings of Moses may be divided into several
parts; one of which is the historical part, another is occupied
with commands and prohibitions, respecting which part we will
speak at some other time when we have first of all accurately
examined that part which comes first in the order of our division.   Again, the historical part may be subdivided into the
account of the creation of the world, and the genealogical part.
And the genealogical part, or the history of the different
families, may be divided into the accounts of the punishment
of the wicked, and of the honours bestowed on the just; we
must also explain on what account it was that he began his
history of the giving of the law with these particulars, and
placed the commandments and prohibitions in the second

order; for he was not like any ordinary compiler of history, studying to leave behind him records of ancient transactions as memorials to future ages for the mere sake of affording pleasure without any advantage; but he traced back the most ancient events from the beginning of the world, commencing with the creation of the universe, in order to make known two most necessary principles. First, that the same being was the father and creator of the world, and likewise the lawgiver of truth; secondly, that the man who adhered to these laws, and clung closely to a connection with and obedience to nature, would live in a manner corresponding to the arrangement of the universe with a perfect harmony and union, between his words and his actions and between his actions and his words.

IX. Now of all other lawgivers, some the moment that they have promulgated positive commands as to what it is right to do and what it is right not to do, proceed to appoint punishments for those who transgress those laws; but others, who appear to have proceeded on a better plan, have not begun in this manner, but, having first of all built and established their city in accordance with reason, have then adapted to this city which they have built, that constitution which they have considered the best adapted and most akin to it, and have confirmed this constitution by the giving of laws. But he, thinking the first of the two courses above mentioned to be tyrannical and despotic, as indeed it is, namely, that of laying positive commands on persons as if they were not free men but slaves, without offering them any alleviation; and that the second course was better indeed, but was not entirely to be commended, must appear to all judges to be superior in each of the above considerations.

For both in his commandments and also in his prohibitions he suggests and recommends rather than commands, endeavouring with many prefaces and perorations to suggest the greater part of the precepts that he desires to enforce, desiring rather to allure men to virtue than to drive them to it, and looking upon the foundation and beginning of a city made with hands, which he has made the commencement of his work a commencement beneath the dignity of his laws, looking rather with the most accurate eye of his mind at the importance and beauty of his whole legislative system, and thinking it too excellent and too divine to be limited as it were by any circle of things on earth; and therefore he has related the creation of that great metropolis, the world, thinking his laws the most fruitful image and likeness of the constitution of the whole world.

X. At all events if any one were inclined to examine with accuracy the powers of each individual and particular law, he will find them all aiming at the harmony of the universe, and corresponding to the law of eternal nature : on which account those men who have had unbounded prosperity bestowed upon them, and all things tending to the production of health of body, and riches, and glory, and all other external parts of good fortune, but who have rejected virtue, and have chosen crafty wickedness, and all other kinds of vice, not through compulsion, but of their own spontaneous free will, looking upon that which is the greatest of all evils as the greatest possible advantage, he looks upon as enemies not of mankind only, but of the entire heaven and world, and says that they are awaiting, not any ordinary punishments, but new and extraordinary ones, which that constant assessor of God, justice, who detests wickedness, invents and inflicts terribly upon them, turning against them the most powerful elements of the universe, water and fire, so that at appointed times some are desroyed by deluges, others are burnt with fire, and perish in that manner.

The seas were raised up, and the rivers both such as flow everlastingly, and the winter torrents were swollen and washed away, and carried off all the cities in the plain ; and those in the mountain country were destroyed by incessant and irresistible impetuosity of rain, ceasing neither by day nor by night, and when at a subsequent period the race of mankind had again increased from those who had been spared, and had become very numerous, since the succeeding generations did not take the calamities which had befallen their ancestors as a lesson to teach themselves wisdom and moderation, but turned to acts of intemperance and became studiers of evil practices, God determined to destroy them with fire. Therefore on this occasion, as the holy scriptures tell us, thunderbolts fell from heaven, and burnt up those wicked men and their cities ; and even to this day there are seen in Syria monuments of the unprecedented destruction that fell upon them, in the ruins, and ashes, and sulphur, and smoke, and dusky flame which still is sent up from the ground as of a fire smouldering beneath; and in this way it came to pass that those wicked men were punished with the aforesaid chastisements, while those who were eminent for virtue and piety were well off, receiving rewards worthy of their virtue.

But when the whole of that district was thus burnt, inhabitants and all, by the impetuous rush of the heavenly fire, one single man in the country, a sojourner, was preserved by the providence of God because he had never shared in the transgressions of the natives, though sojourners in general were in the habit of adopting the customs of the foreign nations, among which they might be settled, for the sake of their own safety, since, if they despised them, they might be in danger from the inhabitants of the land. And yet this man had not attained to any perfection of wisdom, so as to be thought worthy of such an honour by reason of the perfect excellence of his nature; but he was spared only because he did not join the multitude who were inclined to luxury and effeminacy, and who pursued every kind of pleasure and indulged every kind of appetite, gratifying them abundantly, and inflaming them as one might inflame fire by heaping upon it plenty of rough fuel.

XI. But in the great deluge I may almost say that the whole of the human race was destroyed, while the history tells us that the house of Noah alone was preserved free from all evil, inasmuch as the father and governor of the house was a man who had never committed any intentional or voluntary wickedness. And it is worth while to relate the manner of his preservation as the sacred scriptures deliver it to us, both on account of the extraordinary character of it, and also that it may lead to an improvement in our own dispositions and lives.

For he, being considered a fit man, not only to be exempted from the common calamity which was to overwhelm the world, but also to be himself the beginning of a second generation of men, in obedience to the divine commands which were conveyed to him by the word of God, built a most enormous fabric of wood, three hundred cubits in length, and fifty in width, and thirty in height, and having prepared a number of connected chambers within it, both on the ground floor and in the upper story, the whole building consisting of three, and in some parts of four stories, and having prepared food, brought into it some of every description of animals, beasts and also birds, both male and female, in order to preserve a means of propagating the different species in the times that should come hereafter; for he knew that the nature of God was merciful, and that even if the subordinate species were destroyed, still there would be a germ in the entire genus which should be safe from destruction, for the sake of preserving a similitude to those animals which had hitherto existed, and of preventing anything that had been deliberately called into existence from being utterly destroyed.

XII. On which account everything was now made obedient to Noah; and even beasts, which up to that time had been savage, became gentle, and being tamed, followed him as their shepherd and superintendent; and after they had all entered into the ark, if any one had beheld the entire collection, he would not have been wrong if he had said that it was a representation of the whole earth, containing, as it did, every kind of animal, of which the whole earth had previously produced innumerable species, and will hereafter produce such again.

And what was expected happened at no long period after; for the evil abated, and the destruction caused by the deluge was diminished every day, the rain being checked, and the water which had been spread over the whole earth, being partly dried up by the flame of the sun, and partly returning into the chasms and rivers, and other channels and receptacles in the earth; for, as if God had issued a command to that effect, every nature received back, as a necessary repayment of a loan, what it had lent, that is, every sea, and fountain, and river, received back their waters; and every stream returned into its appropriate channel.

But after the purification, in this way, of all the things beneath the moon, the earth being thus washed and appearing new again, and such as it appeared to be when it was at first created, along with the entire universe, Noah came forth out of his wooden edifice, himself and his wife, and his sons and their wives, and with his family there came forth likewise, in one company, all the races of animals which had gone in with them, in order to the generation and propagation of similar creatures in future.

These are the rewards and honours for pre-eminent excellence given to good men, by means of which, not only did they themselves and their families obtain safety, having escaped from the greatest dangers which were thus aimed against all men all over the earth, by the change in the character of the elements; but they became also the founders of a new generation, and the chiefs of a second period of the world, being left behind as sparks of the most excellent kind of creatures, namely, of men, man having received the supremacy over all earthly creatures whatsoever, being a kind of copy of the powers of God, a visible image of his invisible nature, a created image of an uncreated and immortal original.

A TREATISE

ON THE

LIFE OF MOSES,

THAT IS TO SAY,

ON THE THEOLOGY AND PROPHETIC OFFICE OF MOSES.

BOOK III.

I. WE have already, then, gone through two parts of the life of Moses, discussing his character in his capacity of a king and of a lawgiver. We must now consider him in a third light, as fulfilling the office of the priesthood.

Now this man, Moses, practised beyond all other men that which is the most important and most indispensable virtue in a chief priest, namely, piety, partly because he was endowed with most admirable natural qualities; and philosophy, receiving his nature like a fertile field, cultivated and improved it by the contemplation of excellent and beautiful doctrines, and did not dismiss it until all the fruits of virtue were brought to perfection in him, in respect of words and actions. Therefore he, with a few other men, was dear to God and devoted to God, being inspired by heavenly love, and honouring the Father of the universe above all things, and being in return honoured by him in a particular manner. And it was an honour well adapted to the wise man to be allowed to serve

the true and living God.   Now the priesthood has for its duty
the service of God.   Of this honour, then, Moses was thought
worthy, than which there is no greater honour in the whole
world, being instructed by the sacred oracles of God in everything that related to the sacred offices and ministrations.

II. But, in the first place, before assuming that office, it
was necessary for him to purify not only his soul but also his
body, so that it should be connected with and defiled by no
passion, but should be pure from everything which is of a
mortal nature, from all meat and drink, and from all connection with women. And this last thing, indeed, he had despised
for a long time, and almost from the first moment that he
began to prophesy and to feel a divine inspiration, thinking
that it was proper that he should at all times be ready to give
his whole attention to the commands of God.   And how he
neglected all meat and drink for forty days together, evidently
because he had more excellent food than that in those contemplations with which he was inspired from above from
heaven, by which also he was improved in the first instance in
his mind, and, secondly, in his body, through his soul, increasing in strength and health both of body and soul, so that
those who saw him afterwards could not believe that he was
the same person.

For, having gone up into the loftiest and most sacred mountain in that district in accordance with the divine commands,
a mountain which was very difficult of access and very hard to
ascend, he is said to have remained there all that time without
eating any of that food even which is necessary for life ; and, as
I said before, he descended again forty days afterwards, being
much more beautiful in his face than when he went up, so that
those who saw him wondered and were amazed, and could no
longer endure to look upon him with their eyes, inasmuch as
his countenance shone like the light of the sun.

III. And while he was still abiding in the mountain he was
initiated in the sacred will of God, being instructed in all the
most important matters which relate to his priesthood, those
which come first in order being the commands of God respecting the building of a temple and all its furniture. If, then,
they had already occupied the country into which they were
migrating, it would have been necessary for them to have
erected a most magnificent temple of the most costly stone in

some place unincumbered with wood, and to have built vast walls around it, and abundant and well-furnished houses for the keepers of the temple, calling the place itself the holy city. But, as they were still wandering in the wilderness, it was more suitable for people who had as yet no settled habitation to have a moveable temple, that so, in all their journeyings, and military expeditions, and encampments, they might be able to offer up sacrifices, and might not feel the want of any of the things which related to their holy ministrations, and which those who dwell in cities require to have.

Therefore Moses now determined to build a tabernacle, a most holy edifice, the furniture of which he was instructed how to supply by precise commands from God, given to him while he was on the mount, contemplating with his soul the incorporeal patterns of bodies which were about to be made perfect, in due similitude to which he was bound to make the furniture, that it might be an imitation perceptible by the outward senses of an archetypal sketch and pattern, appreciable only by the intellect; for it was suitable and consistent for the task of preparing and furnishing the temple to be entrusted to the real high priest, that he might with all due perfection and propriety make all his ministrations in the performance of his sacred duties correspond to the works which he was now to make.

IV. Therefore the general form of the model was stamped upon the mind of the prophet, being accurately painted and fashioned beforehand invisibly without any materials, in species which were not apparent to the eye; and the completion of the work was made in the similitude of the model, the maker giving an accurate representation of the impression in material substances corresponding to each part of the model, and the fashion of the building was as follows.

There were eight and forty pillars of cedar, which is the most incorruptible of all woods, cut out of solid trunks of great beauty, and they were all veneered with gold of great thickness. Then under each pillar there were placed two silver pedestals to support it, and on the top of each was placed one golden capital; and of these pillars the architect arranged forty along the length of the tabernacle, one half of them, or twenty, on each side, placing nothing between them, but arranging them and uniting them all in regular order, and

close together, so that they might present the appearance of
one solid wall ; and he ranged the other eight along the inner
breadth, placing six in the middle space, and two at the
extreme corners, one on each side at the right and left of the
centre. Again, at the entrance he placed four others, like
the first in all other respects except that they had only one
pedestal instead of two, as those opposite to them had, and
behind them he placed five more on the outside differing only
in the pedestals, for the pedestals of these last were made of
brass.

So that all the pillars of the tabernacle taken together,
besides the two at the corners which could not be seen, were
fifty-five in number, all conspicuous, being the number made
by the addition of all the numbers from the unit to the complete and perfect decade.

And if any were inclined to count those five pillars of the
outer vestibule in the open air separately, as being in the
outer court as it was called, there will then be left that most
holy number of fifty, being the power of a rectangular triangle,
which is the foundation of the creation of the universe, and is
here entirely completed by the pillars inside the tabernacle;
there being first of all forty, twenty on either side, and those
in the middle being six, without counting those which were out
of sight and concealed at the corners, and those opposite to the
entrance, from which the veil was suspended, being four; and
the reason for which I reckon the other five with the first fifty,
and again why I separate them from the fifty, I will now
explain.

The number five is the number of the external senses, and
the external sense in man at one time inclines towards external
things, and at another time comes back again upon the mind,
being as it were a kind of handmaid of the laws of its nature;
on which account it is that the architect has here allotted a
central position to the five pillars, for those which are inside
of them leant towards the innermost shrine of the tabernacle,
which under a symbol is appreciable only by the intellect;
and the outermost pillars, which are in the open air, and in
the outer courtyard, and which are also perceptible by the
external senses, in reference to which fact it is that they are
said to have differed from the others only in the pedestals,
for they were made, of brass. But since the mind is the

principal thing in us, having an authority over the external
senses, and since that which is an object of the external senses
is the extremity, and as it were the pedestal or foundation of
it, the architect has likened the mind to gold, and the object
of the external sense to brass.

And these are the measures of the pillars, they are ten
cubits in length, and five cubits and a half in width, in order
that the tabernacle may be seen to be of equal dimensions in
all its parts.

V. Moreover the architect surrounded the tabernacle with
very beautiful woven work of all kinds, employing work of
hyacinth colour, and purple, and scarlet, and fine linen for the
tapestry ; for he caused to be wrought ten cloths, which in the
sacred scriptures he has called curtains, of the kinds which I
have just mentioned, every one of them being eight and twenty
cubits in length, and extending four cubits in width, in order
that the complete number of the decade, and also the number
four, which is the essence of the decade, and also the number
twenty-eight, which is likewise a perfect number, being equal
to its parts ; and also the number forty, the most prolific and
productive of all numbers, in which number they say that man
was fashioned in the workshop of nature.

Therefore the eight and twenty cubits of the curtains have
this distribution : there are ten along the roof, for that is the
width of the tabernacle, and the rest are placed along the
sides, on each side nine, which are extended so as to cover and
conceal the pillars, one cubit from the floor being left uncovered
in order that the beautiful and holy looking embroidery might
not be dragged. And of the forty which are included in the
calculation and made up of the width of the ten curtains, the
length takes thirty, for such is the length of the tabernacle,
and the chamber behind takes nine. And the remaining one
is in the outer vestibule, that it may be the bond to unite the
whole circumference.

And the outer vestibule is overshadowed by the veil; and
the curtains themselves are nearly the same as veils, not only
because they cover the roof and the walls, but also because
they are woven and embroidered by the same figures, and with
hyacinth colour, and purple, and scarlet, and fine linen. And
the veil, and that thing, too, which was called the covering,
was made of the same things   That which was within was

placed along the five pillars, that the innermost shrine might be concealed; and that which was outside being placed along the five pillars, that no one of those who were not holy men might be able from any secret or distant place to behold the holy rites and ceremonies.

VI. Moreover, he chose the materials of this embroidery, selecting with great care what was most excellent out of an infinite quantity, choosing materials equal in number to the elements of which the world was made, and having a direct relation to them; the elements being the earth and the water, and the air and the fire. For the fine flax is produced from the earth, and the purple from the water, and the hyacinth colour is compared to the air (for, by nature, it is black), and the scarlet is likened to fire, because each is of a red colour; for it followed of necessity that those who were preparing a temple made by hands for the Father and Ruler of the universe must take essences similar to those of which he made the universe itself.

Therefore the tabernacle was built in the manner that has been here described, like a holy temple. And all around it a sacred precinct extended a hundred cubits in length and fifty cubits in width, having pillars all placed at an equal distance of five cubits from one another, so that there were in all sixty pillars; and they were divided so that forty were placed along the length and twenty along the breadth of the tabernacle, one half on each side.

And the material of which the pillars were composed was cedar within, and on the surface without silver; and the pedestals of all of them were made of brass, and the height was equal to five cubits. For it seemed to the architect to be proper to make the height of what was called the hall equal to one half of the entire length, that so the tabernacle might appear to be elevated to double its real height. And there were thin curtains fitted to the pillars along their entire length and breadth, resembling so many sails, in order that no one might be able to enter in who was not pure.

VII. And the situation was as follows. In the middle was placed a tent, being in length thirty cubits and in width ten cubits, including the depth of the pillars. And it was distant from the centre space by three intervals of equal distance, two being at the sides and one along the back chamber. And the interval between was by measurement twenty cubits. But along the vestibule, as was natural, by reason of the number of those who entered, the distance between them was increased and extended to fifty cubits and more; for in this way the hundred pillars of the hall were intended to be made up, twenty being along the chamber behind, and those which the tent contained, thirty in number, being included in the same calculation with the fifty at the entrances; for the outer vestibule of the tabernacle was placed as a sort of boundary in the middle of the two fifties, the one, I mean, towards the east where the entrance was, and the other being on the west, in which direction the length of the tabernacle and the surrounding wall behind was.

Moreover, another outer vestibule, of great size and exceeding beauty, was made at the beginning of the entrance into the hall, by means of four pillars, along which was stretched the embroidered curtain in the same manner as the inner curtains were stretched along the tabernacle, and wrought also of similar materials; and with this there were also many sacred vessels made, an ark, and a candlestick, and a table, and an altar of incense, and an altar of sacrifice. Now, the altar of sacrifice was placed in the open air, right opposite to the entrances of the tabernacle, being distant from it just so far as was necessary to give the ministering officers room to perform the sacrifices that were offered up every day.

VIII. But the ark was in the innermost shrine, in the inaccessible holy of holies, behind curtains; being gilded in a most costly and magnificent manner within and without, the covering of which was like to that which is called in the sacred scriptures the mercy-seat. Its length and width are accurately described, but its depth is not mentioned, being chiefly compared to and resembling a geometrical superficies; so that it appears to be an emblem, if looked at physically, of the merciful power of God; and, if regarded in a moral point of view, of a certain intellect spontaneously propitious to itself, which is especially desirous to contract and destroy, by means of the love of simplicity united with knowledge, that vain opinion which raises itself up to an unreasonable height and puffs itself up without any grounds.

But the ark is the depository of the laws, for in that are placed the holy oracles of God, which were given to Moses;

and the covering of the ark, which is called the mercy-seat, is a foundation for two winged creatures to rest upon, which are called, in the native language of the Hebrews, cherubim, but as the Greeks would translate the word, vast knowledge and science. Now some persons say, that these cherubim are the symbols of the two hemispheres, placed opposite to and fronting one another, the one beneath the earth and the other above the earth, for the whole heaven is endowed with wings.

But I myself should say, that what is here represented under a figure are the two most ancient and supreme powers of the divine God, namely, his creative and his kingly power; and his creative power is called God; according to which he arranged, and created, and adorned this universe, and his kingly power is called Lord, by which he rules over the beings whom he has created, and governs them with justice and firmness; for he, being the only true living God, is also really the Creator of the world; since he brought things which had no existence into being; and he is also a king by nature, because no one can rule over beings that have been created more justly than he who created them.

IX. And in the space between the five pillars and the four pillars, is that space which is, properly speaking, the space before the temple, being cut off by two curtains of woven work, the inner one of which is called the veil, and the outer one is called the covering: and the remaining three vessels, of those which I have enumerated, were placed as follows:—The altar of incense was placed in the middle, between earth and water, as a symbol of gratitude, which it was fitting should be offered up, on account of the things that had been done for the Hebrews on both these elements, for these elements have had the central situation of the world allotted to them. The candlestick was placed on the southern side of the tabernacle, since by it the maker intimates, in a figurative manner, the motions of the stars which give light; for the sun, and the moon, and the rest of the stars, being all at a great distance from the northern parts of the universe, make all their revolutions in the south. And from this candlestick there proceeded six branches, three on each side, projecting from the candlestick in the centre, so as altogether to complete the number of seven; and in all the seven there were seven candles and seven lights, being symbols of those seven stars which are called planets by those men who are versed in natural philosophy; for the sun, like the candlestick, being placed in the middle of the other six, in the fourth rank, gives light to the three planets which are above him, and to those of equal number which are below him, adapting to circumstances the musical and truly divine instrument.

X. And the table, on which bread and salt are laid, was placed on the northern side, since it is the north which is the most productive of winds, and because too all nourishment proceeds from heaven and earth, the one giving rain, and the other bringing to perfection all seeds by means of the irrigation of water; for the symbols of heaven and earth are placed side by side, as the holy scripture shows, the candlestick being the symbol of heaven, and that which is truly called the altar of incense, on which all the fumigatory offerings are made, being the emblem of the things of earth.

But it became usual to call the altar which was in the open air the altar of sacrifice, as being that which preserved and took care of the sacrifices; intimating, figuratively, the consuming power of these things, and not the lambs and different parts of the victims which were offered, and which were naturally calculated to be destroyed by fire, but the intention of him who offered them; for if the man who made the offerings was foolish and ignorant, the sacrifices were no sacrifices, the victims were not sacred or hallowed, the prayers were ill-omened, and liable to be answered by utter destruction, for even when they appear to be received, they produce not remission of sins but only a reminding of them.

But if the man who offers the sacrifice be holy and just, then the sacrifice remains firm, even if the flesh of the victim be consumed, or rather, I might say, even if no victim be offered up at all; for what can be a real and true sacrifice but the piety of a soul which loves God? The gratitude of which is blessed with immortality, and without being recorded in writing is engraved on a pillar in the mind of God, being made equally everlasting with the sun, and moon, and the universal world.

XI. After these things the architect of the tabernacle next prepared a sacred dress for him who was to be appointed high priest, having in its embroidery a most exceedingly beautiful and admirable work; and the robe was two-fold; one part of which was called the under-robe, and the other the robe over the shoulders. Now the under-robe was of a more simple form and character, for it was entirely of hyacinthine colours, except the lowest and exterior portions, and these were ornamented with golden pomegranates, and bells, and wreaths of flowers; but the robe over the shoulders or mantle was a most beautiful and skilful work, and was made with most perfect skill of all the aforesaid kinds of material, of hyacinth colour, and purple, and fine linen, and scarlet, gold thread being entwined and embroidered in it.

For the leaves were divided into fine hairs, and woven in with every thread, and on the collar stones were fitted in, two being costly emeralds of exceeding value, on which the names of the patriarchs of the tribes were engraved, six on each, making twelve in all; and on the breast were twelve other precious stones, differing in colour like seals, in four rows of three stones each, and these were fitted in what was called the logeum and the logeum was made square and double, as a sort of foundation, that it might bear on it, as an image, two virtues, manifestation and truth ; and the whole was fastened to the mantle by fine golden chains, and fastened to it so that it might never get loose; and a golden leaf was wrought like a crown, having four names engraved on it which may only be mentioned or heard by holy men having their ears and their tongues purified by wisdom, and by no one else at all in any place whatever.

And this holy prophet Moses calls the name, a name of four letters, making them perhaps symbols of the primary numbers, the unit, the number two, the number three, the number four : since all things are comprised in the number four, namely, a point, and a line, and a superficies, and a solid, and the measures of all things, and the most excellent symphonies of music, and the diatessaron in the sesquitertial proportion, and the chord in fifths, in the ratio of one and a half to one, and the diapason in the double ratio, and the double diapason in the fourfold ratio. Moreover, the number four has an innumerable list of other virtues likewise, the greater part of which we have discussed with accuracy in our dissertation on numbers.

And in it there was a mitre, in order that the leaf might not touch the head ; and there was also a cidaris made, for the kings of the eastern countries are accustomed to use a cidaris, instead of a diadem.

XII. Such, then, is the dress of the high priest. But we must not omit to mention the signification which it conceals beneath both in its whole and in its parts. In its whole it is a copy and representation of the world ; and the parts are a representation of the separate parts of the world.

And we must begin with the long robe reaching down to the feet of the wearer. This tunic is wholly of the colour of a hyacinth, so as to be a representation of the air; for by nature the air is black, and in a measure it reaches down from the highest parts to the feet, being stretched from the parts about the moon, as far as the extremites of the earth, and being diffused everywhere. On which account also, the tunic reaches from the chest to the feet, and is spread over the whole body, and unto it there is attached a fringe of pomegranates round the ankles, and flowers, and bells. Now the flowers are an emblem of the earth ; for it is from the earth that all flowers spring and bloom ; but the pomegranates (ῥοΐσκοι) are a symbol of water, since, indeed, they derive their name from the flowing (ῥύσις) of water, being very appropriately named ; and the bells are the emblem of the concord and harmony that exist between these things ; for neither is the earth without the water, nor the water without the earthly substance, suf- ficent for the production of anything ; but that can only be effected by the meeting and combination of both.

And the place itself is the most distinct possible evidence of what is here meant to be expressed ; for as the pomegranates, and the flowers, and the bells, are placed in the hem of the garment which reaches to the feet, so likewise the things of which they are the symbols, namely, the earth and water, have had the lowest position in the world assigned to them, and being in strict accord with the harmony of the universe, they display their own particular powers in definite periods of time and suitable seasons.

Now of the three elements, out of which and in which all the different kinds of things which are perceptible by the out- ward senses and perishable are formed, namely, the air, the water and the earth, the garment which reached down to the feet in conjunction with the ornaments which were attached to that part of it which was about the ankles have been plainly shown to be appropriate symbols; for as the tunic is one, and as the aforesaid three elements are all of one species, since they all have all their revolutions and changes beneath the moon, and as to the garment are attached the pomegranates, and the flowers; so also in a certain manner the earth and the water may be said to be attached to and suspended from the air, for the air is their chariot.

And our argument will be able to bring forth twenty probable reasons that the mantle over the shoulders is an emblem of heaven. For in the first place, the two emeralds on the shoulder-blades, which are two round stones, are, in the opinion of some persons who have studied the subject, emblems of those stars which are the rulers of night and day, namely, the sun and moon; or rather, as one might argue with more correctness and a nearer approach to truth, they are the emblems of the two hemispheres; for, like those two stones, the portion below the earth and that over the earth are both equal, and neither of them is by nature adapted to be either increased or diminished like the moon. And the colour of the stars is an additional evidence in favour of my view; for to the glance of the eye the appearance of the heaven does resemble an emerald; and it follows necessarily that six names are engraved on each of the stones, because each of the hemispheres cuts the zodiac in two parts, and in this way comprehends within itself six animals.

Then the twelve stones on the breast, which are not like one another in colour, and which are divided into four rows of three stones in each, what else can they be emblems of, except of the circle of the zodiac? For that also is divided into four parts, each consisting of three animals, by which divisions it makes up the seasons of the year, spring, summer, autumn, and winter, distinguishing the four changes, the two solstices, and the two equinoxes, each of which has its limit of three signs of this zodiac, by the revolutions of the sun, according to that unchangeable, and most lasting, and really divine ratio which exists in numbers; on which account they attached it to that which is with great propriety called the logeum. For all the changes of the year and the seasons are arranged by well-defined, and stated, and firm reason; and, though this seems a most extraordinary and incredible thing, by their seasonable

changes they display their undeviating and everlasting per-
manence and durability.

And it is said with great correctness, and exceeding beauty
also, that the twelve stones all differ in their colour, and that
no one of them resembles the other; for also in the zodiac
each animal produces that colour which is akin to and belongs
to itself, both in the air, and in the earth, and in the water;
and it produces it likewise in all the affections which move
them, and in all kinds of animals and of plants.

XIII. And this logeum is described as double with great
correctness; for reason is double, both in the universe and
also in the nature of mankind, in the universe there is that
reason which is conversant about incorporeal species which
are like patterns as it were, from which that world which is
perceptible only by the intellect was made, and also that which
is concerned with the visible objects of sight, which are copies
and imitations of those species above mentioned, of which the
world which is perceptible by the outward senses was made.

Again, in man there is one reason which is kept back, and
another which finds vent in utterance: and the one is, as it
were a spring, and the other (that which is uttered) flows
from it; and the place of the one is the dominant part, that
is, the mind; but the place of the one which finds vent in
utterance is the tongue, and the mouth, and all the rest of the
organs of the voice.

And the architect assigned a quadrangular form to the
logeum, intimating under an exceedingly beautiful figure, that
both the reason of nature, and also that of man, ought to
penetrate everywhere, and ought never to waver in any case;
in reference to which, it is that he has also assigned to it the
two virtues that have been already enumerated, manifestation and truth; for the reason of nature is true, and calculated
to make manifest, and to explain everything; and the reason
of the wise man, imitating that other reason, ought naturally,
and appropriately to be completely sincere, honouring truth, and
not obscuring anything through envy, the knowledge of which
can benefit those to whom it would be explained; not but what
he has also assigned their two appropriate virtues to those
two kinds of reason which exist in each of us, namely, that
which is uttered and that which is kept concealed, attributing clearness of manifestation to the uttered one, and truth to

that which is concealed in the mind; for it is suitable to the mind that it should admit of no error or falsehood, and to explanation that it should not hinder anything that can conduce to the most accurate manifestation.

Therefore there is no advantage in reason which expends itself in dignified and pompous language, about things which are good and desirable, unless it is followed by consistent practice of suitable actions; on which account the architect has affixed the logeum to the robe which is worn over the shoulder, in order that it may never get loose, as he does not approve of the language being separated from the actions; for he puts forth the shoulder as the emblem of energy and action.

XIV. Such then are the figurative meanings which he desires to indicate by the sacred vestments of the high priest; and instead of a diadem he represents a cidaris on the head, because he thinks it right that the man who is consecrated to God, as his high priest, should, during the time of his exercising his office be superior to all men, not only to all private individuals, but even to all kings; and above this cidaris is a golden leaf, on which an engraving of four letters was impressed; by which letters they say that the name of the living God is indicated, since it is not possible that anything that is in existence, should exist without God being invoked; for it is his goodness and his power combined with mercy that is the harmony and uniter of all things.

The high priest, then, being equipped in this way, is properly prepared for the performance of all sacred ceremonies, that, whenever he enters the temple to offer up the prayers and sacrifices in use among his nation, all the world may likewise enter in with him, by means of the imitations of it which he bears about him, the garment reaching to his feet, being the imitation of the air, the pomegranate of the water, the flowery hem of the earth, and the scarlet dye of his robe being the emblem of fire; also, the mantle over his shoulders being a representation of heaven itself; the two hemispheres being further indicated by the round emeralds on the shoulder-blades, on each of which were engraved six characters equivalent to six signs of the zodiac; the twelve stones arranged on the breast in four rows of three stones each, namely the logeum, being also an emblem of that reason which holds together and regulates the universe.

For it was indispensable that the man who was consecrated to the Father of the world, should have as a paraclete, his son, the being most perfect in all virtue, to procure forgiveness of sins, and a supply of unlimited blessings ; perhaps, also, he is thus giving a previous warning to the servant of God, even if he is unable to make himself worthy of the Creator, of the world, at least to labour incessantly to make himself worthy of the world itself; the image of which he is clothed in, in a manner that binds him from the time that he puts it on, to bear about the pattern of it in his mind, so that he shall be in a manner changed from the nature of a man into the nature of the world, and, if one may say so (and one may by all means and at all times speak the plain truth in sincerity), become a little world himself.

XV. Again, outside the outer vestibule, at the entrance, is a brazen laver ; the architect having not taken any mere raw material for the manufacture of it, as is very common, but having employed on its formation vessels which had been constructed with great care for other purposes ; and which the women contributed with all imaginable zeal and eagerness, in rivalry of one another, competing with the men themselves in piety, having determined to enter upon a glorious contest, and to the utmost extent of their power to exert themselves so as not to fall short of their holiness.

For though no one enjoined them to do so, they, of their own spontaneous zeal and earnestness, contributed the mirrors with which they had been accustomed to deck and set off their beauty, as the most becoming first fruits of their modesty, and of the purity of their married life, and as one may say of the beauty of their souls. The maker then thought it well to accept these offerings, and to melt them down, and to make nothing except the laver of them, in order that the priests who were about to enter the temple might be supplied from it, with water of purification for the purpose of performing the sacred ministrations which were appointed for them ; washing their feet most especially, and their hands, as a symbol of their irreproachable life, and of a course of conduct which take itself pure in all kinds of praiseworthy actions, proceeding not along the rough road of wickedness which one may more properly call no road at all, but keeping straight along the level and direct path of virtue.

Let him remember, says he, let him who is about to be sprinkled with the water of purification from this laver, remember that the materials of which this vessel was composed were mirrors, that he himself may look into his own mind as into a mirror; and if there is perceptible in it any deformity arising from some agitation unconnected with reason or from any pleasure which would excite us, and raise us up in hostility to reason, or from any pain which might mislead us and turn us from our purpose of proceeding by the straight road, or from any desire alluring us and even dragging us by force to the pursuit of present pleasures, he seeks to relieve and cure that, desiring only that beauty which is genuine and unadulterated.

For the beauty of the body consists in symmetry of parts, and in a good complexion, and a healthy firmness of flesh, having also but a short period during which it is in its prime ; but the beauty of the mind consists in a harmony of doctrines and a perfect accord of virtues, which do not fade away or become impaired by lapse of time, but as long as they endure at all are constantly acquiring fresh vigour and renewed youth, being set off by the pre-eminent complexion of truth, and the agreement of its words with its actions, and of its actions with its words, and also of its designs with both.

XVI. And when he had been taught the patterns of the sacred tabernacle, and had in turn himself taught those who were gifted with acute comprehension, and well-qualified by nature for the comprehension and execution of those works, which it was indispensably necessary should be made; then, as was natural, when the temple had been built and finished, it was fitting also, that most suitable persons should be appointed as priests, and should be instructed in what manner it was proper for them to offer up their sacrifices, and perform their sacred ministrations.

Accordingly, Moses selected his brother, choosing him out of all men, because of his superior virtue, to be high priest, and his sons he appointed priests, not giving precedence to his own family, but to the piety and holiness which he perceived to exist in those men ; and what is the clearest proof of this is, that he did not think either of his sons worthy of this honour (and he had two); while he must inevitably have appointed both of them, if he had attached any importance to love for his family; and he appointed them with the unanimous consent of the whole nation, as the sacred scriptures have recorded, which was a most novel mode of proceeding, and one especially worthy of being mentioned; and, in the first place, he washed them all over with the most pure and vivifying water of the fountain; and then he gave them their sacred vestments, giving to his brother the robe which reached down to his feet, and the mantle which covered the shoulders, as a sort of breast-plate, being an embroidered robe, adorned with all kinds of figures, and a representation of the universe. And to all his nephews he gave linen tunics, and girdles, and trowsers; the girdles, in order that the wearers might be unimpeded and ready for all their sacred ministrations, were fastened up tight round the loose waists of the tunics; and the breeches, that nothing which ought to be hidden might be visible, especially when they were going up to the altar, or coming down from the high place, and doing everything with earnestness and celerity.

For if their equipment had not been so accurately attended to for the sake of guarding against the uncertain future, and for the sake of providing for an energetic promptness in the sacred ministrations, the men would have appeared naked, not being able to preserve the becoming order necessary to holy men dedicated to the service of God.

XVII. And when he had thus furnished them with proper vestments, he took very fragrant ointment, which had been made by the skill of the perfumer, and first of all he anointed the altar in the open air, and the laver, sprinkling it with the perfume seven times; after that he anointed the tabernacle and every one of the sacred vessels, the ark, and the candlestick, and the altar of incense, and the table, and the censers, and the vials, and all the other things which were either necessary or useful for the sacrifices; and last of all bringing the high priest close to himself, he anointed his head with abundant quantities of oil.

When he had done all this, he then, in strict accordance with what was holy, commanded a heifer and two rams to be brought; the one that he might sacrifice it for the remission of sins, intimating by a figure that to sin is congenital with every created being, however good it may be, inasmuch as it is created, and that therefore it is indispensable that God should be propitiated in its behalf by means of prayers and sacrifices, that he may not be provoked to chastise it. And of the rams, one he required for a whole burnt-offering of gratitude for the successful arrangement of all those things, of which every individual has such a share as is suited to him, deriving benefit from all the elements, enjoying the earth for his abode and in respect of the nourishment which is derived from it; the water for drinking, and washing, and sailing on; the air for breathing and for the comprehension of those things which are the objects of our outward senses (since the air is the medium in which they all are exerted), and for the seasons of the year; enjoying fire both of that kind which is used for cooking food and for warming one's self, and also that heavenly kind which is serviceable for light and for all the objects of sight. The other ram he employed for the complete accomplishment of the purification of the priests, which he appropriately called the ram of perfection, since the priests were intended to exercise their office in teaching proper and convenient rites and ceremonies to the servants and ministers of God. And he took the blood, and with some of it he poured a libation all round the altar, and part he took, holding a vial under it to catch it, and with it he anointed three parts of the body of the initiated priests, the tip of the ear, the extremity of the hand, and the extremity of the foot, all on the right side, signifying by this action that the perfect man must be pure in every word and action, and in his whole life, for it is the hearing which judges of his words, and the hand is the symbol of action, and the foot of the way in which a man walks in life; and since each of these members is an extremity of the body, and is likewise on the right side, we must imagine that it is here indicated by a figure that improvement in every thing is to be arrived at by a certain dexterity, being a portion of supreme felicity, and being the true aim in life, which a man must necessarily labour to attain, and to which he ought to refer all his actions, aiming at them in his life, as in the practice of archery men aim at a target.

XVIII. Accordingly, he first of all anointed the three parts before mentioned of the bodies of the priests with the unmixed blood of one of the victims, that, namely, which was called the ram of perfection; and afterwards, taking some of the blood which was upon the altar, being the blood of all the victims

mingled together, and some also of the unguent which has
already been mentioned, which the ointment makers had prepared, and mixing some of the oil with the mingled blood of
the different victims, he sprinkled some upon the priests and
upon their garments, with the intention that they should have
a share not only in that purity which was external and in the
open air, but also of that which was in the inmost shrine, since
they were about to minister within the temple. And all the
things within the temple were anointed with oil.

And when they had brought forward other sacrifices in addition to the former ones, partly the priests sacrificing for themselves, and partly the elders sacrificing on behalf of the whole
nation, then Moses entered into the tabernacle, leading his
brother by the hand (and it was the eighth and last day of the
festival, for the seven previous days had been devoted to the
initiation of the hierophants), he now initiated both him and
his nephews. And when he had entered in he taught him as
a learned teacher might instruct an ignorant pupil, in what
way the high priest ought to perform the ministrations which
are performed inside the temple.

Then, when they had both come out and held up their hands
in front of their head, they, with a pure and holy mind, offered
up such prayers as were suitable and becoming for the nation.
And while they were still praying a most marvellous prodigy
happened; for from out of the inmost shrine, whether it was a
portion of the purest possible æther, or whether the air, according to some natural change of the elements, had become dissolved with fire, on a sudden a body of flame shone forth, and
with impetuous violence descended on the altar and consumed
all that was thereon, with the view, as I imagine, of showing
in the clearest manner that none of the things which had
been done had been done without the especial providence of
God.

For it was natural that an especial honour should be assigned
to the holy place, not only by means of those things in which
men are the workmen employed, but also by that purest of all
essences, fire, in order that the ordinary fire which is used by
men might not touch the altar; perhaps by reason of its being
defiled by ten thousand impurities. For it is concerned not
only with irrational animals when they are roasted or boiled
for the unjust appeasing of our miserable bellies, but also in the

case of men who are slain by hostile attack, not merely in a small body of three or four, but in numerous hosts.

At all events, before now, arrows charged with fire have been aimed at vast naval fleets and have burnt them; and fire has destroyed whole cities, which have blazed away till they have been consumed down to their very foundations and reduced to ashes, so that no trace whatever has remained of their former situation.

It appears to me that this was the reason for which God rejected from his sacred altar the fire which is applied to common uses, as being defiled; and that, instead of it, he rained down celestial flame from heaven, in order to make a distinction between holy and profane things, and to separate the things belonging to man from the things belonging to God; for it was fitting that a more incorruptible essence of fire than that which served the common purposes of life should be set apart for sacrifices.

XIX. And as many sacrifices were of necessity offered up every day, and especially on all days of solemn assembly and festival, both on behalf of each individual separately and in common for the whole nation, for innumerable and various reasons, inasmuch as the nation was very populous and very pious, there was a need also of a multitude of keepers of the temple for the sacred and subordinate ministrations. And, again, the election of these officers was conducted in a novel and not in the ordinary manner. God chose out one of the twelve tribes, having selected it for its superior excellence, and appointed that to furnish the keepers of the temple, giving it rewards and peculiar honours in return for its pious acting. And the action which it had to perform was of this kind.

When Moses had gone up into the neighbouring mountain and had remained several days alone with God, the fickle-minded among the people, thinking that his absence was a favourable opportunity, as if they had no longer any ruler at all, rushed unrestrainedly to impiety, and, forgetting the holiness of the living God, became eager imitators of the Egyptian inventions. Then, having made a golden calf in imitation of that which appeared to be the most sacred animal in that district, they offered up unholy sacrifices, and instituted blasphemous dances, and sang hymns which differed in no respect from dirges, and, being filled with strong wine, gave themselves up to a two-fold intoxication, the intoxication of wine and that of folly, revelling and devoting the night to feasting, and, having no foresight as to the future, they spent their time in pleasant sins, though justice had her eye upon them, who saw them while they could not see, and decided what punishments they deserved.

But when the continued outcries in the camp, from men collected in numerous and dense crowds, reached over a great distance, so that the sound penetrated even to the summit of the mountain, Moses, hearing the uproar, was in great perplexity, as being at the same time a devout worshipper of God and a friend to mankind, not being able to bring his mind to quit the society of God with whom he was conversing, and in which he, being alone with him, was conferring with him by himself, nor, on the other hand, could he be indifferent to the multitude thus full of anarchy and wickedness; for he recognised the tumult, since he was a very shrewd man at conjecturing, from inarticulate sounds of no distinct meaning, the passions of the soul which were inaccessible to and out of the reach of the conjectures of others, because he perceived at once that the noise proceeded partly from intoxication, since intemperance had produced satiety and a disposition to insult the law.

And being drawn both ways, and under strong attraction in both directions, he fluctuated this way and that way, and did not know what he ought to do; and while he was considering the matter the following command was given to him, " Go down quickly; descend from this place, the people have turned with haste to lawlessness, having fashioned a god made with hands in the form of a bull, they are falling down before that which is no god, and sacrificing unto him, forgetting all the things that they have seen, and all that thay have heard, which might lead them to piety." So Moses, being amazed, and being also constrained by this command, believes those incredible events, and sprung down to be a mediator and reconciler; not however, in a moment, for first of all he addressed supplications and prayers on behalf of his nation to God, entreating God that he would pardon these their sins; then, this governor of and intercessor for his people, having appeased the Ruler of the universe, went down at the same time rejoicing and feeling sorrowful; he rejoiced indeed that God had admitted his supplication, but he was full of anxiety and depression, being greatly indignant at the lawless transgression of the multitude.

XX. And when he came into the middle of the camp, and marvelled at the sudden way in which the multitude had forsaken all their ancient habits, and at the vast amount of falsehood which they had embraced instead of truth, he, seeing that the disease had not extended among them all, but that some were still sound, and still cherished a disposition which loathed wickedness; wishing to distinguish those who were incurable from those who felt indignation at what had taken place, and to know also whether any of those who had offended repented them of their sin, caused a proclamation to be made; and it was indeed a shrewd test of the inclination of each individual, to see how he was disposed to holiness, or to the contrary.

"Whoever," said he, "is on the side of the Lord, let him come to me." It was but a brief sentence which he thus uttered, but the meaning concealed under it was important; for what was intimated by his words was the following sense: "If any one does not think anything whatever that is made by hands, or anything that is created, a god, but believes that there is one ruler of the universe only, let him come to me."

Now of the others, some resisted by reason of the admiration which they had conceived for the Egyptian pride, and they did not attend to what he said; others wanted courage to come nearer to him, perhaps out of fear of punishment; or else perhaps they dreaded punishment at the hand of Moses, or a rising up against them on the part of the people; for the multitude invariably attack those who do not share in their frenzy.

But that single tribe of the whole number which was called the tribe of Levi, when they heard the proclamation, as if by one preconcerted agreement, ran with great haste, displaying their earnestness by their promptness and rapidity, and proving the keenness of the desire of their soul for piety; and, when Moses saw them rushing forward as if starting from the goal in a race, he said, "Surely it is not with your bodies alone that you are hastening to come unto me, but you shall soon bear witness with your minds to your eagerness; let every one of you take a sword, and slay those men who have done things worthy of ten thousand deaths, who have forsaken the true God, and made for themselves false gods, of perishable and created substances, calling them by the name which belongs only to the uncreated and everlasting God; let every one, I say, slay those men, whether it be his own kinsmen or his friends, looking upon nothing to be either friendship or kindred but the holy fellowship of good men."

And the tribe of Levi, outrunning his command with the most eager readiness, since they were already alienated from those men in their minds, almost from the first moment that they beheld the beginning of their lawless iniquity, killed them all to a man, to the number of three thousand, though they had been but a short time before their dearest friends; and as the corpses were lying in the middle of the place of the assembly of the people, the multitude beholding them pitied them, and fearing the still fervid, and angry, and indignant disposition of those who had slain them, reproved them out of fear; but Moses, gladly approving of their exceeding virtue, devised in their favour and confirmed to them an honour which was appropriate to their exploit, for it was fitting that those who had undertaken a voluntary war for the sake of the honour of God, and who had carried it out successfully in a short time, should be thought worthy to receive the priesthood and charge of officiating in his service.

XXI. But, since there is not one order only of consecrated priests, but since to some of them the charge is committed of attending to all the prayers, and sacrifices, and other most sacred ceremonies, being allowed to enter into the inmost and most holy shrine; while others are not permitted to do any of these things, but have the duty of taking care of and guarding the temple and all that is therein, both day and night, whom some call keepers of the temple; a sedition arose respecting the precedency in honour, which was to many persons in many ways the cause of infinite evils, and it broke out now from the keepers of the temple attacking the priests, and endeavouring to deprive them of the honour which belonged to them; and they thought that they should be able easily to succeed in their object, since they were many times more numerous than the others.

But for the sake of not appearing to be planning any innovations of their own heads, they persuaded also the eldest of the twelve tribes to embrace their opinions, which last tribe was followed by many of the more fickle of the populace, as thinking it entitled to the precedence and to the principal share of authority over the whole host

Moses now knew that a great plot was in agitation against him; for he had appointed his brother high priest in accordance with the will of God, which had been declared to him. And now false accusations were brought against him, as if he had falsified the oracles of God, and as if he had done so and made the appointment by reason of his family affection and goodwill towards his brother. And he, being very naturally grieved at this, inasmuch as he was not only distrusted by such accusations while exhibiting his own good faith in a most genuine manner, but he was also grieved at those actions of his being calumniated which had for their object the honour of God, and which were of such a nature as to deserve by themselves that even such a man who had in other respects shown an insincere disposition should be looked upon as behaving in this case with truth; for truth is the invariable attendant of God.

But he did not think fit to give any explanation by words respecting his appointment of his brother, knowing that it was difficult to endeavour to persuade those who were previously possessed by contrary opinions to change their minds; but he besought God to give the people a visible demonstration that he had in no respect behaved with dishonesty respecting the appointment to the priesthood. And he, therefore, commanded that twelve rods should be taken, so as to be equal in number to the tribes of the nation; and he commanded further that the names of the other patriarchs of the tribes should be written on eleven of the rods, but on the remaining one the name of his brother, the high priest, and then that they should all be carried into the temple as far as the inmost shrine; and the officer who did what he had been commanded waited in expectation to see the result.

And on the next day, in obedience to a command from God, he went into the temple, while all the people were standing around, and brought out the rods, the others differing in no respect from the state in which they were when they were put in; but the one on which the name of his brother was written had undergone a miraculous change; for like a fine plant it suddenly put forth shoots all over, and was weighed down with the abundance of its crop of fruit.

XXII. And the fruit were almonds, which is a fruit of a different character from any other. For in most fruit, such as grapes, olives, and apples, the seed and the eatable part differ from one another, and being different are separated as to their position, for the eatable part is outside, and the seed is shut up within; but in the case of this fruit the seed and the eatable part are the same, both of them being comprised in one species, and their position is one and the same, being without strongly protected and fortified with a twofold fence, consisting partly of a very thick bark, and partly of what appears in no respect short of a wooden case, by which perfect virtue is figuratively indicated.

For as in the almond the beginning and the end are the same, the beginning as far as it is seed, and the end as far as it is fruit; so also is it the case with the virtues; for each one of them is at the same time both beginning and end, a beginning, because it proceeds not from any other power, but from itself; and an end, because the life in accordance with nature hastens towards it. This is one reason; and another is also mentioned, more clear and emphatic than the former; for the part of the almond which looks like bark is bitter, but that which lies inside the bark, like a wooden case, is very hard and impenetrable, so that the fruit, being enclosed in these two coverings, is not very easily to be got at.

This is an emblem of the soul which is inclined to the practice of meditation, from which he thinks it is proper to turn it to virtue by showing it that it is necessary first of all to encounter danger. But labour is a bitter, and distasteful, and harsh thing, from which good is produced, for the sake of which one must not yield to effeminate indolence; for he who seeks to avoid labour is also avoiding good. And he, again, who encounters what is disagreeable to be borne with fortitude and manly perseverance, is taking the best road to happiness; for it is not the nature of virtue to abide with those who are given up to delicacy and luxury, and who have become effeminate in their souls, and whose bodies are enervated by the incessant luxury which they practise every day; but it is subdued by such conduct, and determined to change its abode, having first of all arranged its departure so as to depart to, and abide with, the ruler of right reason.

But, if I must tell the truth, the most sacred company of

prudence, and temperance, and courage, and justice seeks the
society of those who practise virtue, and of those who admire
a life of austerity and rigid duty, devoting themselves to fortitude and self-denial, with wise economy and abstinence ; by
means of which virtues the most powerful of all the principles
within us, namely, reason, improves and attains to a state of
perfect health and vigour, overthrowing the violent attacks of
the body, which the moderate use of wine, and epicurism, and
licentiousness, and other insatiable appetites excite against it,
engendering a fulness of flesh which is the direct enemy of
shrewdness and wisdom.

Moreover, it is said, that of all the trees that are accustomed
to blossom in the spring, the almond is the first to flourish,
bringing as it were good tidings of abundance of fruit; and
that afterwards it is the last to lose its leaves, extending the
yearly old age of its verdure to the longest period; in each of
which particulars it is an emblem of the tribe of the priesthood,
as Moses intimates under the figure of this tree that this tribe
shall be the first of the whole human race to flourish, and likewise the last; as long as it shall please God to liken our life to
the revolutions of the spring, destroying covetousness that most
treacherous of passions, and the fountain of all unhappiness.

XXXIX. And some time afterwards, when he was about
to depart from hence to heaven, to take up his abode·there,
and leaving this mortal life to become immortal, having been
summoned by the Father, who now changed him, having
previously been a double being, composed of soul and body,
into the nature of a single body, transforming him wholly
and entirely into a most sun-like mind; he then, being
wholly possessed by inspiration, does not seem any longer
to have prophesied comprehensively to the whole nation
altogether, but to have predicted to each tribe separately
what would happen to each of them, and to their future
generations, some of which things have already come to
pass, and some are still expected, because the accomplishment of those predictions which have been fulfilled is the
clearest testimony to the future.

For it was very appropriate that those who were different
in the circumstances of their birth and in the mothers, from
whom they were descended, should differ also in the variety
of their designs and counsels, and also in the excessive
diversity of their pursuits in life, and should therefore have
for their inheritance, as it were, a different distribution of

oracles and predictions. These things, therefore, are wonderful; and most wonderful of all is the end of his sacred writings, which is to the whole book of the law what the head is to an animal.

For when he was now on the point of being taken away, and was standing at the very starting-place, as it were, that he might fly away and complete his journey to heaven, he was once more inspired and filled with the Holy Spirit, and while still alive, he prophesied admirably what should happen to himself after his death, relating, that is, how he had died when he was not as yet dead, and how he was buried without any one being present so as to know of his tomb, because in fact he was entombed not by mortal hands, but by immortal powers, so that he was not placed in the tomb of his forefathers, having met with particular grace which no man ever saw; and mentioning further how the whole nation mourned for him with tears a whole month, displaying the individual and general sorrow on account of his unspeakable benevolence towards each individual and towards the whole collective host, and of the wisdom with which he had ruled them.

Such was the life and such was the death of the king, and lawgiver, and high priest, and prophet, Moses, as it is recorded in the sacred scriptures.

The tenth is the feast of tabernacles, which is the last of all the annual festivals, ending so as to make the perfect number of ten. We must now begin with the first festival.

THE FIRST FESTIVAL.

I. The law sets down every day as a festival, adapting itself to an irreproachable life, as if men continually obeyed nature and her injunctions. And if wickedness did not prosper, subduing by their predominant influence all those reasonings about what things might be expedient, which they have driven out of the soul of each individual, but if all the powers of the virtues remained in all respects unsubdued, then the whole time from a man's birth to his death would be one uninterrupted festival, and all houses and every city would pass their time in continual fearlessness and peace, being full of every imaginable blessing, enjoying perfect tranquillity. But, as it is at present, covetousness and the system of mutual hostility and retaliation with which both men and women are continually forming designs against one another, and even against themselves, have destroyed the continuity of cheerfulness and happiness.

And the proof of what I have just asserted is visible to all men ; for all those men, whether among the Greeks or among the barbarians, who are practisers of wisdom, living in a blameless and irreproachable manner, determining not to do any injustice, nor even to retaliate it when done to them, shunning all association with busy-bodies, in all the cities which they inhabit, avoid all courts of justice, and council halls, and marketplaces, and places of assembly, and, in short, every spot where any band or company of precipitate headstrong men is collected, admiring, as it were, a life of peace and tranquillity, being the most devoted contemplators of nature and of all the things in it. Investigating earth and sea, and the air, and the heaven, and all the different natures in each of them ; dwelling, if one may so say, in their minds, at least, with the moon, and the sun, and the whole company of the rest of the stars, both planets and fixed stars. Having their bodies, indeed, firmly planted on the earth, but having their souls furnished with wings, in order that thus hovering in the air they may closely survey all the powers above, looking upon them as in reality the most excellent of cosmopolites, who consider the whole world as their native city, and all the devotees of wisdom as their fellow citizens, virtue herself having enrolled them as such, to whom it has been entrusted to frame a constitution for their common city.

II. Being, therefore, full of all kinds of excellence, and being accustomed to disregard all those good things which affect the body and external circumstances, and being inured to look upon things indifferent as really indifferent, and being armed by study against the pleasures and appetites, and, in short, being always labouring to raise themselves above the passions, and being instructed to exert all their power to pull down the fortification which those appetites have built up, and being insensible to any impression which the attacks of fortune might make upon them, because they have previously estimated the power of its attacks in their anticipations (for anticipation makes even those things light which would be most terrible if unexpected), their minds in this manner calculating that nothing that happens is wholly strange, but having a kind of faint perception of everything as old and in some degree blunted. These men, being very naturally rendered cheerful by their virtues, pass the whole of their lives as a festival.

These men, however, are therefore but a small number, kindling in their different cities a sort of spark of wisdom, in order that virtue may not become utterly extinguished, and so be entirely extirpated from our race. But if men everywhere agreed with this small number, and became, as nature originally designed that they should, all blameless and irreproachable, lovers of wisdom, delighting in all that is virtuous and honourable, and thinking that and that alone good, and looking on everything else as subordinate and slaves, as if they themselves were the masters of them, then all the cities would be full of happiness, being wholly free from all the things which are the causes of pain or fear, and full of all those which produce joy and cheerfulness. So that no time would ever cease to be the time of a happy life, but that the whole circle of the year would be one festival.

III. Wherefore, if truth were to be the judge, no wicked or worthless man can pass a time of festival, no not even for the briefest period, inasmuch as he must be continually pained by the consciousness of his own iniquities, even though, with his soul, and his voice, and his countenance, he may pretend to

smile ; for how can a man who is full of the most evil counsels, and who lives with folly, have any period of genuine joy?
A man who is in every respect unfortunate and miserable, in
his tongue, and his belly, and all his other members, since he
uses the first for the utterance of things which ought to be
secret and buried in silence, and the second he fills full of
abundance of strong wine and immoderate quantities of food
out of gluttony, and the rest of his members he uses for the indulgence of unlawful desires and illicit connections, not only
seeking to violate the marriage bed of others, but lusting un-
naturally, and seeking to deface the manly character of the
nature of man, and to change it into a womanlike appearance, for
the sake of the gratification of his own polluted and accursed
passions.

On which account the all-great Moses, seeing the pre-
eminence of the beauty of that which is the real festival, looked
upon it as too perfect for human nature and dedicated it to
God himself, speaking thus, in these very words : "The feast
of the Lord."* In considering the melancholy and fearful
condition of the human race, and how full it is of innumerable
evils, which the covetousness of the soul begets, which the
defects of the body produce, and which all the inequalities of
the soul inflict upon us, and which the retaliations of those
among whom we live, both doing and suffering innumerable
evils, are continually causing us, he then wondered whether
any one being tossed about in such a sea of troubles, some
brought on deliberately and others unintentionally, and never
being able to rest in peace nor to cast anchor in the safe haven
of a life free from danger, could by any possibility really keep
a feast, not one in name, but one which should really be so,
enjoying himself and being happy in the contemplation of the
world and all the things in it, and in obedience to nature, and
in a perfect harmony between his words and his actions, between
his actions and his words.

On which account he necessarily said that the feasts belonged
to God alone ; for he alone is happy and blessed, having no
participation in any evil whatever, but being full of all perfect
blessings. Or rather, if one is to say the exact truth, being
himself the good, who has showered all particular good things
over the heaven and earth. In reference to which fact, a cer-

* Leviticus xxiii. 2.

tain pre-eminently virtuous mind among the people of old, when all its passions were tranquil, smiled, being full of and completely penetrated with joy, and reasoning with itself whether perhaps to rejoice was not a peculiar attribute of God, and whether it might not itself miss this joy by pursuing what are thought delights by men, was timorous, and denied the laughter of her soul until she was comforted.

For the merciful God lightened her fear, bidding her by his holy word confess that she did laugh, in order to teach us that the creature is not wholly and entirely deprived of joy; but that joy is unmingled and the purest of all which can receive nothing of an opposite nature, the chosen peculiar joy of God. But the joy which flows from that is a mingled one, being alloyed, being that of a man who is already wise, and who has received as the most valuable gift possible such a mixture as that in which the pleasant are far more numerous than the unpleasant ingredients. And this is enough to say on this subject.

THE SECOND FESTIVAL.

I. BUT after this continued and uninterrupted festival which thus lasts through all time, there is another celebrated, namely, that of the sacred seventh day after each recurring interval of six days, which some have denominated the virgin, looking at its exceeding sanctity and purity. And others have called the motherless, as being produced by the Father of the universe alone, as a specimen of the male kind unconnected with the sex of women; for the number seven is a most brave and valiant number, well adapted by nature for government and authority. Some, again, have called it the occasion, forming their conjectures of that part of its essence which is appreciable only by the intellect, from the objects intelligible to their outward senses. For whatever is best among the objects of the external senses, the things by means of which the seasons of the year and the revolutions of time are brought to perfection in their appointed order, partake of the number seven. I mean that there are seven planets; that the stars of the Bear are seven, that the Pleiads are seven, and the revolutions of the moon when increasing and waning, and the orderly well-regulated circuits of the other bodies, the beauty of which exceeds all description.

But Moses, from a most honourable cause, called it consummation and perfection; attributing to the number six the origination of all the parts of the world, and to the number seven their perfection; for the number six is an odd-even number, being composed of twice three, having the odd number for the male and the even number for the female, from the union of which, production takes place in accordance with the unalterable laws of nature. But the number seven is free from all such commixture, and is, if one must speak plainly, the light of the number six; for what the number six engendered, that the number seven displayed when brought to perfection. In reference to which fact it may properly be called the birthday of the world, as the day in which the work of the Father, being exhibited as perfect with all its parts perfect, was commanded to rest and abstain from all works.

Not that the law is the adviser of idleness, for it is always accustoming its followers to submit to hardships, and training them to labour, and it hates those who desire to be indolent and idle; at all events, it expressly commands us to labour diligently for six days,* but in order to give some remission from uninterrupted and incessant toil, it refreshes the body with seasons of moderate relaxation exactly measured out, so as to renew it again for fresh works. For those who take breath in this way, I am speaking not merely about private individuals but even about athletes, collect fresh strength, and with more vigorous power, without any shrinking and with great endurance, encounter everything that must be done. And the works meant are those enjoined by precepts and doctrines in accordance with virtue.

And in the day he exhorts us to apply ourselves to philosophy, improving our souls and the dominant part of us, our mind. Accordingly, on the seventh day there are spread before the people in every city innumerable lessons of prudence, and temperance, and courage, and justice, and all other virtues; during the giving of which the common people sit down, keeping silence and pricking up their ears, with all possible attention, from their thirst for wholesome instruction; but some of those who are very learned explain to them what is of great importance and use, lessons by which the whole of their lives may be improved.

* Exodus xx. 9.

And there are, as we may say, two most especially important heads of all the innumerable particular lessons and doctrines; the regulating of one's conduct towards God by the rules of piety and holiness, and of one's conduct towards men by the rules of humanity and justice; each of which is subdivided into a great number of subordinate ideas, all praiseworthy. From which considerations it is plain that Moses does not leave those persons at any time idle who submit to be guided by his sacred admonitions; but since we are composed of both soul and body, he has allotted to the body such work as is suited to it, and to the soul also such tasks as are good for that. And he has taken care that the one shall succeed the other, so that while the body is labouring the soul may be at rest, and when the body is enjoying relaxation the soul may be labouring; and so the best lives with the contemplative and the active life, succeed to one another in regular alternations. The active life having received the number six, according to the service appointed for the body; and the contemplative life the number seven, as tending to knowledge and to the perfecting of the intellect

II. It is forbidden also on this day to kindle a fire, as being the beginning and seed of all the business of life; since without fire it is not possible to make any of the things which are indispensably necessary for life, so that men in the absence of one single element, the highest and most ancient of all, are cut off from all works and employments of art, especially from all handicraft trades, and also from all particular services. But it seems likely that it was on account of those who were less obedient, and who were the least inclined to attend to what was done, that Moses gave additional laws, besides, thinking it right, not only that those who were free should abstain from all works on the seventh day, but also that their servants and handmaids should have a respite from their tasks, proclaiming a day of freedom to them also after every space of six days, in order to teach both classes this most admirable lesson; so that the masters should be accustomed to do some things with their own hands, not waiting for the services and ministrations of their servants, in order that if any unforeseen necessities came upon them, according to the changes which take place in human affairs, they might not, from being wholly unaccustomed to do anything for themselves, faint at what they had to do; but, finding the different parts of the body active and handy, might work with ease and cheerfulness; and teaching the servants not to despair of better prospects, but having a relaxation every six days as a kind of spark and kindling of freedom, to look forward to a complete relaxation hereafter, if they continued faithful and attached to their masters.

And from the occurrence of the free men at times submitting to the tasks of servants, and of the servants enjoying a respite and holiday, it will arise that the life of mankind advances in improvement towards perfect virtue, from their being thus reminded of the principles of equality, and repaying each other with necessary services, both those of high and those of obscure rank.

But the law has given a relaxation, not to servants only on the seventh day, but also to the cattle. And yet by nature the servants are born free; for no man is by nature a slave. But other animals are expressly made for the use and service of man, and are therefore ranked as slaves; but, nevertheless, those that ought to bear burdens, and to endure toil and labour on behalf of their owners, do all find a respite on the seventh day. And why need I mention other particulars? The ox, the animal who is born for the most important and most useful of all the purposes of life, namely, for the plough, when the earth is already prepared for seed; and again, when the sheaves are brought into the barn, for threshing in order to the purification of the crop, is on this day unharnessed, keeping as a festival that day which is the birthday of the year. And thus its holiness pervades every thing and affects every creature.

III. And Moses thinks the number seven worthy of such reverence that even all other things which at all partake of it are honoured by him; at all events, on every seventh year he ordains a remission of debts, assisting the poor, and inviting the rich to humanity;* that so they, from their abundance, giving to those that are in want, may also look forward to receiving services from them in the case of any disaster happening to them. For the accidents of human life are numerous, and life is not always anchored on the same bottom, but is apt to change like the fickle wind which blows in different

* Deuteronomy xv. 1.

directions at different times.   It is well, therefore, that the kindness shown by the creditors should extend to all the debtors.   But since all men are not naturally inclined to magnanimity, but some men are the slaves of money, or perhaps not very rich, the law has appointed that they should contribute what will not inconvenience them when parted with.

For while it does not permit them to lend on usury to their fellow countrymen, it has allowed them to receive interest from foreigners; calling the former, with great felicity of expression, their brothers, in order to prevent any one's grudging to give of his possessions to those who are as if by nature joint inheritors with themselves; but those who are not their fellow countrymen are called strangers, as is very natural. For the being a stranger shows that a person has no right to a participation in any thing, unless, indeed, any one out of an excess of virtue should treat even those in the conditions of strangers as kindred and related, from having been bred up under a virtuous state of things, and under virtuous laws which look upon what is virtuous alone as good.

But the action of lending on usury is blameable; for a man who lends on usury has not abundant means of living, but is clearly in some want; and he does so as being compelled to add the interest to his principal in order to subsist, and so he at last becomes of necessity very poor; and while he thinks that he is deriving advantage he is in reality injured, just as foolish animals are when they are deceived by a present bait.   But I should say to such persons, " O you who lend on usury, why do you seek to disguise your unsociable disposition by an apparent pretence of good fellowship?   And why do you in words, indeed, pretend to be a humane and considerate person, while in your actions you exhibit a want of humanity and a terrible hardness of heart, exacting more than you gave, and sometimes even doubling your original loan, so as to make the poor man an absolute beggar?   Therefore no one sympathises with you in your distress, when, having endeavoured to obtain more, you fail to do so, and besides lose even what you had before.   But, on the contrary, all men are glad of your misfortunes, calling you a usurer, and a skinflint, and all kinds of names like those, looking on you as one who lies in wait for human misfortunes, and who esteems the misfortunes of others his own prosperity."

But, as some have said, wickedness is a most laborious thing; and he who lends on usury is blind, not seeing the time of repayment, in which he will scarcely, or perhaps not at all, receive the things which in his covetousness he had hoped to gain. Let such a man pay the penalty of his avaricious disposition, not recovering back what he has expended, so as to make a gain of the misfortunes of men, deriving a revenue from unbecoming sources. But let the debtors be thought worthy of a humanity enjoined by the law, not paying back their loans and usurious interest upon them, but paying back merely the original sum lent. For again, at a proper season, they will give the same assistance to those who have aided them, requiting those who set the example of kindness with equal services.

IV. After having given these commandments, Moses proceeds in regular order to establish a law full of all gentleness and humanity. " If," says this law, " one of thy brethren be sold to thee, let him serve thee for six years; and in the seventh year let him be set free without any payment,"* Here again Moses calls their fellow countrymen their brothers, implanting in the soul of the owner by this appellation an idea of relationship to his servant, that he may not neglect him as a stranger, towards whom he has no bond of goodwill. But that, yielding to a feeling of affection for him as a relation, in consequence of the lesson which the holy scripture thus suggests, he may not feel indignant when his servant is about to recover his freedom. For it has come to pass that such men are called slaves (δοῦλοι), but they are in reality only servants (θῆτες), serving their masters for the sake of their necessities. And even though they had a thousand times over given their masters absolute power and authority over them, still their masters ought to be gentle to them, considering these beautiful injunctions of the law. O man, he is a hireling who is called a slave, and he also is a man, having a most sublime relationship to you, inasmuch as he is of the same nation as yourself; and perhaps he is even of the same tribe and the same borough as yourself, and is now reduced to this condition through want. Do you, therefore, casting out of your soul that treacherous evil, insolence, behave to him as if he were a hireling, giving some things and receiving others. And so he will, with all

* Deuteronomy xv. 12.

energy and cheerfulness perform the services due to you, at all times and in all places, never delaying, but by his speed and willingness anticipating your commands. And do you, in return, provide him with food and raiment, and take all other necessary care of him; not yoking him to the plough like a brute beast, and not oppressing him with heavy burdens beyond his power to bear, nor treating him with insolence, nor reducing him to painful despondency by threats and infliction of punishment; but giving him proper relaxation and well-regulated periods of rest; for the precept, "Let nothing be too much," applies to every case, and especially to the conduct of masters to their servants.

Therefore, when he has served you for a very sufficient time, for six years, then, when the most sacred number, the seventh year is about to arrive, let him who is free by nature depart in freedom; and grant him this kindness without hesitating as to your part, my good man, but joyfully, because you have now an opportunity of doing a service to that most excellent of all animals, man, in the most important of all matters; for there is no blessing to a slave greater than freedom. Do you, therefore, set him free joyfully; and, moreover, make him a present from your own property, from each portion of your possessions, giving to him who has served you faithfully means to support himself on his journey. For it will tend to your credit if he does not leave your house in poverty but having a plentiful supply for all his necessities, so that he may not again, through want, fall into his previous calamity, namely, slavery, being compelled through want of his daily food to sell himself, and so your kindness will be lost. This, then, is enough to say about the poor.

V. In the next place Moses commands the people to leave the land fallow and untilled every seventh year, for many reasons;* first of all, that they may honour the number seven, or each period of days, and months, and years; for every seventh day is sacred, which is called by the Hebrews the sabbath; and the seventh month in every year has the greatest of the festivals allotted to it, so that very naturally the seventh year also has a share of the veneration paid to this number, and receives especial honour.

And the second reason is this, "Be not," says the lawgiver,

* Leviticus xxv. 4.

" wholly devoted to gain, but even willingly submit to some loss," that so you may bear with the more indifference involuntary calamity if it should ever fall upon you, and not grieve and despond, as if at some new and strange occurrence; for there are some rich men so unfortunate in their dispositions, as, when want comes upon them, to groan and despond no less than they might do if they were deprived of all their substance. But of the followers of Moses, all who are true disciples, being practised in good laws, are accustomed, from their earliest age, to bear want with patience, by the custom of leaving their fertile land fallow; and being also taught magnanimity, and one may almost say, to let slip out of their hands, from deliberate intention, revenues of admitted certainty.

The third reason appears to me to be thus, which is intimated in a somewhat figurative manner, namely, to show that it does not become any one whatever to weigh down and oppress men with burdens; for if one is to allow a period of rest to the portions of the earth which cannot by nature have any share in the feelings of pleasure or of pain, how much the more must men be entitled to a similar relaxation, who have not only these outward senses, which are common to the brute beasts, but also the especial gift of reason, by which the painful feelings which arise from toil and fatigue, are more vividly imprinted on their imaginations?

Cease, therefore, ye who are called masters, from imposing harsh and intolerable commands on your slaves, which break the strength of the body by their compulsion, and compel the souls to faint even before the bodies; for there is no objection to your exerting a moderate degree of authority, giving orders by which you will receive the services to which you are entitled, and in consequence of which your servants will cheerfully do what they are desired; and then they will discharge their duties but for a short period, as if early exhausted, and, if one must say the truth, brought by their labours to old age before their time; but like athletes, preserving their youthful vigour for a long time, who do not become fat and corpulent, but who are accustomed, by exertion and sweat, to train themselves, so as to be able to acquire the things which are necessary and useful for life.

Moreover let the governors of cities cease to oppress them

with continual and excessive taxes and tributes, filling their own stores with money, and in preserving as a treasure the illiberal vices which defile their whole lives; for they do, on purpose, select as collectors of their revenues the most pitiless of men, persons full of all kinds of inhumanity, giving them abundant opportunity for the exercise of their covetousness; and they, in addition to their own innate severity of temper, receiving free license from the commands of their masters, and having determined to do everything so as to please them, practise all the harshest measures which they can imagine, having no notion of gentleness or humanity, not even in their dreams; therefore they throw everything into disorder and confusion, levying their exactions, not only on the possessions of the citizens, but also on their persons, with insults and violence, and the invention of new and unprecedented torture.

And before now I have heard of some persons who, in their ferocity and unequalled fury, have not spared even the dead; but have been so brutal as even to venture to beat the dead corpses with goads; and when some one blamed their brutality, in that not even death, that relief and real end of all miseries, could prevent their victims from being insulted by them, but that, instead of a grave and the customary funeral rites, they were exposed to continued insult, they made a defence worse even than the accusation brought against them, saying that they were insulting the dead, not for the sake of abusing the dumb and senseless dust, for there was no advantage in that, but for the sake of making those who through ties of blood or of friendship were nearly connected with them feel compassion for them, and so inducing them to pay a ransom for their bodies, thus doing them the last service in their power.

VI, Then, O you most worthless of all men! I would say to them, have you not first learnt what you are now teaching? or do you know how to invite other people to compassion even by the most inhuman actions, and yet have you eradicated all merciful and humane feelings from your own souls? And do you act in this way in spite of not being in want of good advisers, and especially of our laws, which have released even the earth from its yearly burdens, giving it a relaxation and a respite? and it, although it seems to be inanimate, is nevertheless fully prepared to make a requital and to recompence favours, hastening to pay back any gift which it has received;

for as it receives an exemption every seventh year, and is not forced to exert itself that year, but is set wholly free for the whole circle of the year, in the subsequent year produces double, or sometimes, many times, larger crops than usual from its great productiveness.

And in like manner you may see the trainers acting in the same way towards the athletes ; for when they are exercising them with continual and uninterrupted practice, before they are wholly knocked up, they refresh them, giving a respite not only from their exertions in training, but also from their strict regimen of eating and drinking, relaxing the severity of their diet so as to produce a cheerfulness of soul and good condition of body. And yet they are not to be looked upon as teachers of indolence and luxury, inasmuch as their professed business is to train men to the endurance of labours, but by a certain method and artificial system they add to their natural strength a strength more powerful still, and to their innate vigour a more energetic vigour still, increasing their previous powers by reciprocal remission and exertion, as by a well-regulated harmony.

And I have learnt all this from all-wise nature, which, knowing the industrious and laborious condition of our race, has distributed them into day and night, giving to us the one for wakefulness, and the other for sleep : for she felt a natural anxiety, like a careful mother, that her offspring should not be worn out with toil ; for by day she excites our bodies, and rouses them up to all the necessities and duties belonging to life, compelling those to work who would gladly be accustomed to cultivate the leisure of idleness, and an effeminate and luxurious life. But by night, as if she were sounding a retreat in time of war, she invites us to rest, and to take care of our bodies. And those men who have laid aside a heavy weight of business, which has lasted from morning till evening, do now lay their burdens aside and return home and devote themselves to ease, and indulging in profound sleep, refresh themselves after the labours of the day. This long interval between sleeping and waking nature has allotted to men, that they may by turns labour diligently and by turns rest, so as to have all the parts of their bodies more ready for action, and more active and powerful.

VII. And the lawgiver, who is a prophetic spirit, gave us our laws, having a regard to these things, and proclaimed a holiday to the whole country, restraining the farmers from cultivating the land after each six years' incessant industry. But it was not only on account of the motives which I have mentioned that he gave these injunctions, but also because of his innate humanity, which he thinks fit to weave in with every part of his legislation, stamping on all who study the holy scriptures a sociable and humane disposition.

For he commands his people every seventh year to forbear to enclose any piece of land, but to let all the olive gardens and vineyards remain open, and all their other possessions, whether they be seed-land or trees, that so the poor may be able to enjoy the spontaneously growing crops without fear, in a greater, or at all events not in a less degree than the owners themselves. On which account he does not allow the masters to cultivate the land, having in view the object of not causing them any annoyance from the feeling that they are at all the expense, but that they do not receive any revenue from their lands to make up for the expense, while the poor enjoy all the crops as their own ; and he permits those who appear to be strangers to enjoy all these things, raising them from their apparent lowly condition, and from the reproach of being beggars.

Is it not then fit to love these laws which are full of such abundant humanity? by which the rich men are taught to share the blessings which they have with and to communicate them to others : and the poor are comforted, not being for ever compelled to frequent the houses of the indigent to supply the deficiencies by which they themselves are oppressed ; but there are times when the widows and orphan children, as if they had been deriving a revenue from their own properties, namely the spontaneously growing crops, as I have said before, and all other classes of persons who are disregarded from not being wealthy, do at last find themselves in the possession of plenty, being on a sudden enriched by the gift of God, who has called them to share with the possessors themselves in the number of the sacred seven.

And all those who breed flocks and herds lend their own cattle with fearlessness and impunity to graze on the land of others, choosing the most fertile plains, and the lands most suitable for the feeding of their cattle, availing themselves of the license of the jubilee ; and they are not met by any ill-will or illiberality on the part of the masters, as having the property in these lands by old custom, which having prevailed for a very long time, so as to become familiar, has now prevailed even over nature.

VIII. Having laid down these principles as a kind of foundation of gentleness and humanity, he then puts together seven sevens of years, and so makes the fiftieth year an entirely sacred year, enacting with reference to it some ordinances of especial honour beyond those which relate to the ordinary years of communication of property.

In the first place he gives this commandment. He thinks it fitting that all property that has been alienated should now be restored to its original masters in order that the inheritances originally apportioned to the different tribes may be preserved, and that no one who originally received an allotment may be wholly deprived of his possessions. Since it often happens that unforeseen circumstances come upon men by which they are compelled to sell what belongs to them. And so he provided in a suitable manner for their necessities, and prevented those who purchased the lands from being deceived, allowing the one to sell their lands, and teaching the others very plainly the conditions on which they are going to purchase. For the law says Do not give a price as if for an everlasting possession, but only for a definite number of years, which must be less than fifty; for the sale effected ought not to be a sale of the lands owned, but a sale of the crops, for two most weighty reasons; one, that the whole country is called the possession of God, and it is impious for any one else to be recorded as the masters of the possessions of God; and secondly, because a separate allotment has been assigned to each land-owner, of which the law does not choose the man who originally received the allotment to be deprived. Therefore, the law invites the man who is able to recover his original property within the period of fifty years, or any one of his nearest relations, to use every exertion to repay the price which he received, and not to be the cause of loss to the man who purchased it, and who served him at a time when he was in need of assistance. And at the same time it sympathises with the man who is in too great a state of indigence to do so, and bestows its compassion on him, giving him back his former property with the exception of any fields which have been

consecrated by a vow, and are so placed in the class of offerings to God. And it is contrary to divine law that any thing
which has been offered to God should ever by lapse of time
become profane. On which account it is commanded that the
accurate value of those fields shall be fully exacted, without
showing any favour to the man who dedicated the offering.

IX. These are the commandments which are given with
respect to the divisions of the land and the inheritances so
portioned out. There are others also enacted with respect to
houses. And since of houses some are in cities, being within
walls; while others are open abodes in the country, and not
within any walls; the law has directed that those in the
country shall always be redeemed with money, and that those
which are not redeemed before the fiftieth year shall be
restored without any payment to their original owners, just as
their other possessions;* for the houses are a portion of the
man's possessions. But those which are within walls shall be
liable to be redeemed by those who have sold them for a full
year;† but if they be not redeemed within that year, then
after that year they shall be confirmed to those who had bought
them, the jubilee of the fiftieth year not injuring the claim of
the purchasers.

And the reason of these enactments is that God wills to
give even to strangers an opportunity of becoming firmly
established in the land. For since they have no participation
in the land, inasmuch as they are not numbered among those
to whom the inheritances have been apportioned, the law has
allotted to them a property in houses, being desirous that they
who have come as suppliants to the laws, and who have taken
refuge under their protection, should not be homeless wander-
ers in the land. For the cities, when the land was originally
portioned out in inheritances, were not divided among the
tribes, nor indeed were they originally built together in streets,
but the inhabitants of the land preferred to make their abode
in their open houses in the fields. But afterwards they quitted
these houses and came together, the feeling of a love of fellowship and communication, as was natural, becoming stronger
after a lapse of time, and so they build houses in the same
place, and cities, of which they allowed a share also to the

* Leviticus xxv. 31.   † Leviticus xxv. 19.

strangers, that they might not be destitute of every thing both in the country and in the cities.

X. And concerning the tribe which was set apart as consecrated for the priesthood, the following laws are established. The law did not bestow upon the keepers of the temple any portion of the land, considering the first fruits of it a sufficient revenue for them. But it allotted them eight and forty cities to dwell in, and a suburb of two thousand cubits around each city.* Therefore, it did not confirm the houses in these cities in the same manner that it did those in the other cities which are built within walls, to the purchasers, if those who had sold them were not able to redeem them within the year, but it permitted them to be redeemed at any time, like the open houses in the country taken from the gentiles, to which they corresponded. Since the Levites had received only houses in this district, of which the lawgiver did not think it fit that those who received them should be deprived any more than those to whom the allotments of the open houses in the country had fallen. And this is enough to say about the houses.

XI. But the laws established with respect to those who owed money to usurers, and to those who had become servants to masters, resemble those already mentioned; that the usurers shall not exact usurers' interest from their fellow countrymen, but shall be contented to receive back only what they lent; and that the masters shall behave to those whom they have bought with their money not as if they were by nature slaves, but only hirelings, giving them immunity and liberty, at once, indeed, to those who can pay down a ransom for themselves, and at a subsequent period to the indigent, either when the seventh year from the beginning of their slavery arrives, or when the fiftieth year comes, even if a man happen to have fallen into slavery only the day before. For this year both is and is looked upon as a year of remission; every one retracing his steps and turning back again to his previous state of prosperity.

But the law permits the people to acquire a property in slaves who are not of their own countrymen, but who are of different nations; intending in the first place that there should be a difference between one's own countrymen and strangers, and secondly, not desiring completely to exclude from the

* Numbers xxxv. 1—8.

constitution that most entirely indispensable property of slaves ; for there are an innumerable host of circumstances in life which require the ministrations of servants.

THE THIRD FESTIVAL.

Following the order which we have adopted, we proceed to speak of the third festival, that of the new moon. First of all, because it is the beginning of the month, and the beginning, whether of number or of time, is honourable. Secondly, because at this time there is nothing in the whole of heaven destitute of light. Thirdly, because at that period the more powerful and important body gives a portion of necessary assistance to the less important and weaker body ; for, at the time of the new moon, the sun begins to illuminate the moon with a light which is visible to the outward senses, and then she displays her own beauty to the beholders. And this is, as it seems, an evident lesson of kindness and humanity to men, to teach them that they should never grudge to impart their own good things to others, but, imitating the heavenly bodies, should drive envy away and banish it from the soul.

THE FOURTH FESTIVAL.

And after the feast of the new moon comes the fourth festival, that of the passover, which the Hebrews call pascha, on which the whole people offer sacrifice, beginning at noon-day and continuing till evening. And this festival is instituted in remembrance of, and as giving thanks for, their great migration which they made from Egypt, with many myriads of people, in accordance with the commands of God given to them ; leaving then, as it seems, a country full of all inhumanity and practising every kind of inhospitality, and (what was worst of all) giving the honour due to God to brute beasts ; and, therefore, they sacrificed at that time themselves out of their exceeding joy, without waiting for priests. And what was then done the law enjoined to be repeated once every year, as a memorial of the gratitude due for their deliverance.

These things are thus related in accordance with the ancient historic accounts. But those who are in the habit of turning plain stories into allegory, argue that the passover figuratively represents the purification of the soul; for they say that the lover of wisdom is never practising anything else except a pass-

ing over from the body and the passions.   And each house is
at that time invested with the character and dignity of a
temple, the victim being sacrificed so as to make a suitable
feast for the man who has provided it and of those who are
collected to share in the feast, being all duly purified with holy
ablutions.

And those who are to share in the feast come together not
as they do to other entertainments, to gratify their bellies with
wine and meat, but to fulfil their hereditary custom with prayer
and songs of praise.   And this universal sacrifice of the whole
people is celebrated on the fourteenth day of the month, which
consists of two periods of seven, in order that nothing which is
accounted worthy of honour may be separated from the number
seven.   But this number is the beginning of brilliancy and
dignity to everything.

THE FIFTH FESTIVAL.

And there is another festival combined with the feast of the
passover, having a use of food different from the usual one,
and not customary ; the use, namely, of unleavened bread, from
which it derives its name.   And there are two accounts given
of this festival, the one peculiar to the nation, on account of
the migration already described; the other a common one, in
accordance with conformity to nature and with the harmony of
the whole world.   And we must consider how accurate the
hypothesis is.

This month, being the seventh both in number and order,
according to the revolutions of the sun, is the first in power ;
on which account it is also called the first in the sacred scriptures.   And the reason, as I imagine, is as follows.   The vernal
equinox is an imitation and representation of that beginning
in accordance with which this world was created.   Accordingly,
every year, God reminds men of the creation of the world, and
with this view puts forward the spring, in which season all
plants flourish and bloom; for which reason this is very correctly set down in the law as the first month, since, in a
manner, it may be said to be an impression of the first beginning of all, being stamped by it as by an archetypal seal.   And
this feast is begun on the fifteenth day of the month, in the
middle of the month, on the day on which the moon is full of

---

* Exodus xii. 1.

light, in consequence of the providence of God taking care that there shall be no darkness on that day.

And, again, the feast is celebrated for seven days, on account of the honour due to that number, in order that nothing which tends to cheerfulness and to the giving of. thanks to God may be separated from the holy number seven. And of the seven days, Moses pronounces two, the first and the last, holy; giving, as is natural, a pre-eminence to the beginning and to the end; and wishing, as if in the case of a musical instru. ment, to unite the two extremities in harmony.

And the unleavened bread is ordained because their ances- tors took unleavened bread with them when they went forth out of Egypt, under the guidance of the Deity; or else, because at that time (I mean at the spring season, during which this festival is celebrated) the crop of wheat is not yet ripe, the plains being still loaded with the corn, and it not being as yet the harvest time, and therefore the lawgiver has ordained the use of unleavened food with a view to assimilating it to the state of the crops. For unleavened food is also imperfect or unripe, as a memorial of the good hope which is entertained; since nature is by this time preparing her annual gifts for the race of mankind, with an abundance and plenteous pouring forth of necessaries.

The interpreters of the holy scriptures do also say that the unleavened food is a gift of nature, but that barmed bread is a work of art. Since, therefore, the vernal festival is a com- memoration of the creation of the world, and since that it was inevitable that the most ancient persons, those formed out of the earth, must have used the gifts of the world without altera- tion, pleasure not having as yet obtained the dominion, the lawgiver ordained that food which was the most suitable to the occasion, wishing to kindle every year a desire to walk in the paths of a holy and rigid way of life.

THE SIXTH FESTIVAL.

There is also a festival on the day of the paschal feast, which succeeds the first day, and this is named the sheaf, from what takes place on it; for the sheaf is brought to the altar as a first fruit both of the country which the nation has received for its own, and also of the whole land; so as to be an offering both for the nation separately, and also a common

one for the whole race of mankind ; and so that the people by
it worship the living God; both for themselves and for all the
rest of mankind, because they have received the fertile earth
for their inheritance ; for in the country there is no barren soil
but even all those parts which appear to be stony and rugged
are surrounded with soft veins of great depth, which, by reason
of their richness, are very well suited for the production of
living things.

And there are many meanings intended by this offering of
the first fruits. In the first place they are a memorial of God ;
secondly, they are a most just requital to be offered to him
who is the real cause of all fertility ; and the sheaf of the first
fruits is barley, calculated for the innocent and blameless use
of the inferior animals ; for since it is not consistent with
holiness to offer first fruits of everything, since most things
are made rather for pleasure than for any actually indispensable use, it is also not consistent with holiness to enjoy and
partake of any thing which is given for food, without first giving
thanks to that being to whom it is becoming and pious to
offer them.

That portion of the food which was honoured with the
second place, namely, barley, was ordered by the law to be
offered as first fruits ; for the first honours were assigned to
wheat, of which it has deferred the offering of the first fruits,
as being more honourable, to a more suitable season.

THE SEVENTH FESTIVAL.

The solemn assembly on the occasion of the festival of the
sheaf having such great privileges, is the prelude to another
festival of still greater importance ; for from this day the
fiftieth day is reckoned, making up the sacred number of
seven sevens, with the addition of a unit as a seal to the whole ;
and this festival, being that of the first fruits of the corn, has
derived its name of pentecost from the number of fifty,
(πεντηκοστὸς). And on it it is the custom to offer up two
leavened loaves made of wheat, as a first fruit of the best kind
of food made of corn ; either because, before the fruit of the
year is converted to the use of man, the first produce of the
new crop, the first gathered corn that appears is offered as a
first fruit, in order that by an insignificant emblem the people
may display their grateful disposition [. . .]

THE EIGHTH FESTIVAL.

Immediately after comes the festival of the sacred moon; in which it is the custom to play the trumpet in the temple at the same moment that the sacrifices are offered. From which practice this is called the true feast of trumpets, and there are two reasons for it, one peculiar to the nation, and the other common to all mankind. Peculiar to the nation, as being a commemoration of that most marvellous, wonderful, and miraculous event that took place when the holy oracles of the law were given; for then the voice of a trumpet sounded from heaven, which it is natural to suppose reached to the very extremities of the universe, so that so wondrous a sound attracted all who were present, making them consider, as it is probable, that such mighty events were signs betokening some great things to be accomplished. And what more great or more beneficial thing could come to men than laws affecting the whole race?

And what was common to all mankind was this: the trumpet is the instrument of war, sounding both when commanding the charge and the retreat. . . .

There is also another kind of war, ordained of God, when nature is at variance with itself, its different parts attacking one another. And by both these kinds of war the things on earth are injured. They are injured by the enemies, by the cutting down of trees, and by conflagrations; and also by natural injuries, such as droughts, heavy rains, lightning from heaven, snow and cold; the usual harmony of the seasons of the year being transformed into a want of all concord.

On this account it is that the law has given this festival the name of a warlike instrument, in order to show the proper gratitude to God as the giver of peace, who has abolished all seditions in cities, and in all parts of the universe, and has produced plenty and prosperity, not allowing a single spark that could tend to the destruction of the crops to be kindled into flame.

THE NINTH FESTIVAL.

And after the feast of trumpets the solemnity of the fast is celebrated, and this Moses has called the greatest of the festivals, denominating it in his national language the sabbath of sabbaths, or, as the Greeks would style it, the week of weeks, the most holy of all holy times. And it has this title for many reasons.

The first reason is the temperance which the lawgiver is continually exhorting men to display at all times, both in their language and in their appetites, both in and below the belly. And he most especially enjoins them to display it now, when he devotes a day to the particular observances of it. For when a person has once learnt to be indifferent to meat and drink, those very necessary things, what can there be of things which are superfluous that he would find any difficulty in disregarding?

The second reason is, that every one is at this time occupied in prayers and supplications, and since they all devote their entire leisure to nothing else from morning till evening, except to most acceptable prayers by which they endeavour to gain the favour of God, entreating pardon for their sins and hoping for his mercy, not for their own merits but through the compassionate nature of that Being who will have forgiveness rather than punishment.

The third is an account of the time at which this fast is fixed to take place; for by this season all the fruits which the earth has produced during the whole year are gathered in. And therefore to proceed at once to devour what has been produced Moses looked upon as an act of greediness; but to fast, and to abstain from touching food, he considered a mark of perfect piety which teaches the mind not to trust to the food which it may have prepared as the cause of health or life. Therefore those who, after the gathering in of the harvest, abstain from the food, do almost declare in express words, "We have with joy received, and we shall cheerfully store up the bounteous gifts of nature; but we do not ascribe to any corruptible thing the cause of our own durable existence, but we attribute that to the Saviour, to the God who rules in the world, and who is able, either by means of these things or without them, to nourish and to preserve us. At all events, behold, he nourished our forefathers even in the desert for forty years."*

And this day of the fast is celebrated in the tenth month, because the number ten is a perfect number. Therefore God has ordained that abstinence from food should take place in

* Deuteronomy viii. 2.

accordance with the perfect number, for the sake of affording the best nourishment to the best thing which is in us; that no one may suppose that the interpreter of God's word is enjoining hunger, the most intolerable of all evils, but only a brief cutting off of the stream which flows into the channels of the body. For thus the clear stream which proceeds from the fountain of reason was likely to be borne smoothly and evenly to the soul, since the uninterrupted use of food inundating the body contributes also to confuse the reason. But if the supply of food be checked, then the reason getting a firm footing as it in a dry road, will be able to proceed in safety without stumbling; and besides it was fitting that when the supply of all things had turned out according to the wishes of the people and become completed, they should, amid the abundance of their harvest, preserve a commemoration of their previous want by abstinence from food, and should offer up prayers, in order that they might never come to a real experience of a want of necessary food.

THE TENTH FESTIVAL.

The last of all the annual festivals is that which is called the feast of tabernacles, which is fixed for the season of the autumnal equinox. And by this festival the lawgiver teaches two lessons, both that it is necessary to honour equality, the first principle and beginning of justice, the principle akin to unshadowed light; and that it is becoming also, after witnessing the perfection of all the fruits of the year, to give thanks to that Being who has made them perfect. For the autumn (μετόπωρον), as its very name shows is the season which comes after (μετὰ) the fruits of the year (τὴν ὀπώραν) are now gathered into the granaries, on account of the providence of nature which loves the living creatures upon the earth.

And indeed, the people are commanded to pass the whole period of the feast under tents, either because there is no longer any necessity for remaining in the open air labouring at the cultivation of the land, since there is nothing left in the land, but all . . . is stored up in the barns, on account of the injuries which otherwise might be likely to visit it from the burning of the sun or the violence of the rains.

It is also intended as a commemoration of the long journeying of their ancestors, while making which through the desert they lodged in numerous tents for many years, while stopping at each halting place. And it is proper in the time of riches to remember one's poverty, and in an hour of glory to recollect the days of one's disgrace, and at a season of peace to think upon the dangers that are past.

Again, the beginning of this festival is appointed for the fifteenth day of the month, on account of the reason which has already been mentioned respecting the spring season, also that the world may be full, not by day only but also by night, of the most beautiful light, the sun and moon on their rising opposite to one another with uninterrupted light, without any darkness interposing itself between so as to divide them. And after the festival has lasted seven days, he adds an eighth as a seal, calling it a kind of crowning feast, not only as it would seem to this festival, but also to all the feasts of the year which we have enumerated; for it is the last feast of the year, and is a very stable and holy sort of conclusion, befitting men who have now received all the produce from the land, and who are no longer in perplexity and apprehension respecting any barrenness or scarcity.

I have spoken in this way about the sacred week and the sacred number seven at more than usual length, wishing to show that all the feasts of the year are, as it were, the offspring of the number seven, which stands in the relation of a mother.

taking its beginning in the account of the creation of the heaven, and ending with that of the formation of man; the first of which things is the most perfect of all imperishable things, and the other of all corruptible and perishable things. And the Creator, connecting together immortal and mortal things at the creation, made the world, making what he had already created the dominant parts, and what he was about to create the subject parts.

The historical part is a record of the lives of different wicked and virtuous men, and of the rewards, and honours, and punishments set apart for each class in each generation.

The legislative part is sub-divided into two sections, one of which has a more general object proposed to it, laying down accordingly a few general comprehensive laws; the other part consists of special and particular ordinances. And the general heads of these special ordinances are ten, which are said not to have been delivered to the people by an interpreter, but to have been fashioned in the lofty region of the air, and to have been connected by a rational distinctness and utterance. While the others, I mean the particular and minute laws, were delivered by the prophet.

And as, in my former treatises, I have dwelt upon each of these to as great an extent as the time permitted me, and as I have also enlarged upon all the different virtues which the lawgiver has assigned to peace and war, I will now proceed in regular order to mention the rewards which have been proposed for virtuous men, and the punishments threatened to the wicked; for, after he had trained all those who are living under his constitution and laws by gentle precepts, and admonitions, and expectations, and subsequently by more severe threats and warnings, he summoned them all to hear the promulgation of the law; and they all, coming as to a sacred meeting, displayed their own eager choice and approbation of those laws in such a way as to give a most convincing proof of their truth. And then some of them were found to be diligent labourers in the practice of virtue, not disappointing the good hopes which were formed of them, nor dishonouring the laws which were their instructors. Others were found to be unmanly, and effeminate, and cowardly, out of the innate weakness and imbecility of their souls, who, fainting before any real danger or trouble came upon them, disgraced themselves and became the ridicule of

the spectators. On which account the one class received decisions in their favour, and proclamations in their honour, and
all such rewards as are usually given to conquerors; while the
others departed not only without the garlands of victory, but
even after having sustained a most disgraceful defeat, more
grievous than any which befalls a man in the gymnastic contests. For there the bodies, indeed, of the athletes are overthrown, but so that they can be easily raised again; but in this
case it is the whole life which falls, which, when once it is
overthrown, it is scarcely possible to raise again.

And our lawgiver announces a very suitable arrangement
and appointment of privileges and honours for the one; and,
on the contrary, of punishments for the others, as affecting
individuals, and houses, and cities, and countries, and nations,
and vast regions of the earth.

II. And, first of all, we must investigate the subject of
honours, since that is both more profitable and more pleasant
to hear of, taking our commencement from the particular instances of individuals.

The Greeks say that in ancient times the famous Triptolemus
was raised aloft and borne on winged dragons, and that while
flying along in this manner he sowed the grains of wheat over
the whole of the earth, in order that, instead of eating acorns,
the human race might for the future have wholesome, and
advantageous, and most pleasant food. This story, then, like
many other tales, being, as it were, a fabulous fiction, may well
be left to those who are accustomed to study sophistry rather
than wisdom, and juggling tricks in preference to the truth;
for originally and simultaneously with the first creation of the
universe, God supplied all living creatures with necessary
food, producing it out of the earth, and, above all things,
providing the race of mankind with all that was requisite,
to whom also he gave the supremacy over every animal born
of the earth. For, among the works of the Deity, there is
nothing posthumous, but all those things which appear
to be brought to perfection at a subsequent time by the care,
and diligence, and skill of men are in all cases previously produced in a half-finished state by the provident care of nature,
so that it is not a wholly absurd statement that all learning is
only recollection.

However, these questions may be postponed for subsequent

discussion.   But we must now consider that most necessary of all things, the sowing of seed, which the Creator has sown in a very excellent soil, namely, in the rational soul.   Now, of this the most important seed is hope, the fountain of all men's lives; for it is by the hope of gain that the money-changer applies himself to many kinds of traffic; and it is through hope of a favourable voyage that the sailor passes over long seas ; and it is from hope of glory that the ambitious man applies himself to public affairs, and to the superintendance of the commonwealth and matters of state.   It is through hope of decisions in their favour and of crowns, that those who exercise their bodies in athletic labours enter the gymnastic contests. Hope is the source of all happiness; hope excites those persons who are filled with an admiration of virtue to study philosophy, under the idea that by her means they will be able to obtain a clear sight of the nature of all existing things, and to do things which are in accordance with and consistent with the perfection of those two most excellent modes of life—the contemplative and the practical, which he who attains to is at once truly happy.

Now some persons have either, like enemies, stifled and destroyed all the seeds of hope by kindling all the vices in the soul, or else, like persons ignorant of and indifferent to the skill of the husbandman, they have allowed them to perish through neglect.   There are also some persons who, appearing to be diligent husbandmen, but who yet, esteeming self-love above piety, have attributed the causes of their successes to themselves.   And all these men are very blameable, and he alone is worthy of being accepted who attributes his hope to God, both as being the author of his birth and as being alone able to keep him free from injury and free from utter destruction.

What reward, then, is assigned to the man who is crowned as conqueror in this contest?   Man is a compound animal, made up of a mortal and immortal nature, not being the same with nor yet entirely different from the one who has obtained the prize.   This man the Chaldæans name Enos, but this name, when translated into the Grecian language, means "a man," he having received the common name of the whole race for his own name, as an especial honour; as if it was not right for any one to be considered as a man at all who does not hope in God.

III. And after the victory of hope there is another contest in which repentance contends for the prize; having, indeed, no share in that nature which is invincible, and which never changes its purpose, and which is always of the same character, entertaining the same disposition, but which is on a sudden seized with an admiration for and love of the better part, and which is anxious to leave the covetousness and injustice in which it has been bred up, and to go over to moderation and justice, and the other virtues; for these are twofold prizes, which are proposed for twofold successes, first of all for the abandonment of what is disgraceful, and, secondly, for the choice of what is excellent; and the prizes are a departure from home, and solitude.

For Moses says, with reference to one who fled from the audacious innovations of the body, and who came over to the interests of the soul, " He was not found because God changed his place;"* and by this enigmatical expression the two things are clearly intimated, the migration by the change of place, and the solitude by his not being found. And very appropriately is this stated; for if in real truth man had resolved at all times to show himself really superior to the passions, despising all pleasures and all appetites, then he would require to prepare himself diligently, fleeing without ever turning his head round, and forsaking his home, and his country, and his relations, and his friends; for familiar custom is an attractive thing, so that there is reason to fear that if a man remains behind he may be taken prisoner, being caught by such powerful charms all round, the appearances of which will again rouse up the disgraceful though at present dormant appetites for evil pursuits, and will restore to vitality those recollections which it was creditable to have forgotten.

Accordingly, many persons have become corrected and improved by migrations from their native land, having been cured by such means of their frenzied and wicked desires, by reason of the sight no longer being able to furnish to the passion the images of pleasure. For in consequence of the separation which has taken place, this passion has only a

* Genesis v. 24.

vacuum through which to rove, since there is no longer any object present by which it can be inflamed. And if it does rise up and quit its former abode, still let it avoid the assemblies of the multitude, embracing solitude; for there are snares in a foreign land resembling those, which are found in a man's own country into which those men must fall who are careless and do not look before them, and who rejoice in the society of the multitude; for the multitude is a very concentration of every thing that is irregular, disorderly, improper, and blameable, with which it is a most mischievous thing for the man who is now for the first time passing over to the ranks of virtue to proceed. For as the bodies of those men who are only just beginning to recover from a long attack of sickness are very subject to a relapse; so the soul which is just recovering its health finds its intellectual vigour weak and wavering, so that there is room to apprehend that the evil passions may return which were wont to be excited in it by a habit of living in the society of inconsiderate men.

IV. Then, after these contests in which repentance is concerned, he proposes a third class of prizes, relating to justice, which every one who practises obtains a twofold reward; in the first place, that of preservation at the time of general destruction; and secondly, that of being the steward and guardian of every description of animal which is coupled in pairs for the purpose of raising a second stock instead of that which from time to time perishes; for the Creator provided that the same being should be both the end of the generation which is condemned and the beginning of that which is irreproachable, teaching those who say that the world is destitute of all providence by works and not by words, that in accordance with the law which he promulgated and established in the nature of things, all the innumerable multitudes of men which live in obedience to injustice are not to be compared to one single individual who lives as a follower of justice.

Now this man the Greeks call Deucalion, but the Chaldæans name him Noah; and it was in his time that the great deluge took place. And after this triad there was a second triad still more holy and more pious, of one family. For father, and son, and grandson all directed all their views to the same end of life, namely, to please the Creator and Father of the universe, despising all those objects which the generality of men admire; glory, and riches, and pleasure, and laughing at that pride which is continually being put together and set forth with all kinds of fictitious ornaments in order to deceive the spectators. This is that which makes gods of inanimate things, a great and almost impregnable fortification by the sophistries and manœuvres of whom every city is allured, and since it takes especial hold on the souls of the young. For having entered into them it establishes itself and dwells in them from the earliest infancy to old age, subduing all those on whom God has not poured the beams of his truth. But pride is the adversary of truth, and is hard to be removed, though when it is subdued by a stronger power than itself then it does depart.

And this class of men is small, indeed, in number; but in power it is very numerous and very great, so that even the whole circle of the earth cannot contain it. And it reaches even to heaven; for as it is possessed of an indescribable love of contemplation and of being always among divine objects, when it has thoroughly investigated and explained all that nature which is perceptible to the sight, it immediately proceeds onwards to that which is incorporeal and appreciable only by the intellect, without requiring the assistance of any one of the outward senses, indeed discarding even the irrational parts of the soul, and employing those parts only which are called mind and reason.

Therefore, the first establisher of the sentiments devoted to God, namely, Abraham, the first person who passed over from pride to truth, employing that virtue which proceeds from instruction as a means towards perfection, chooses as his reward faith in God. And because he, by the innate goodness of his natural dispositions, had acquired a spontaneous, self-taught, and self-implanted virtue, joy was given to him as a prize. Again, to his grandson, the meditator on and practiser of virtue, who attained to what was good by indefatigable and incessant labours, the crown which was given was the sight of God. And what can any one conceive to be either more useful or more respectable than to believe in God and throughout one's whole life to be continually rejoicing and beholding the living God?

V. And let us now perceive each of these things more accurately, without allowing ourselves to be led away by names, but investigating them in their inmost parts, and going deep into them with our minds. Therefore, he who has in all sincerity believed God has by so doing received a disbelief in all other things which are created and perishable, beginning with those things in himself which exalt themselves very highly, namely, reason and the outward sense. For each of these things has a private consistory and tribunal of its own, which is erected in the one in order to ensure the proper consideration of the objects appreciable only by the intellect, the end of which is truth; and in the other for the perception of visible things, the end of which is opinion. Therefore, the unstable, and erroneous, and untrustworthy character of opinion is plain from this circumstance; for it anchors upon images and probabilities. And every image is deceitful, exhibiting itself by a certain attractive similarity in lieu of the original thing itself.

But reason, which is the leader of the outward sense, thinking that the decision about all things which are perceptible only by the intellect, and which are always the same and in the same condition, belongs to itself, is convicted of being in error on many points. For when it directs its view to particucular instances which are innumerable, it finds itself powerless, and unequal to the task, and faints under it, like a wrestler who is tripped up by some more mighty power; but the man to whom it has been granted to see and thoroughly examine all corporeal and all incorporeal things, and to lean upon and to found himself upon God alone, with firm and steadfast reason and unalterable and sure confidence, is truly happy and blessed.

After faith the next prize which is offered as destined for the man who acquires virtue by the gift of nature, as being victorious without a struggle, is joy. For this man is named as the Greeks would call him, Laughter, but as the Chaldæans would entitle him, Isaac. And laughter is an emblem in the body of that unseen joy which exists in the mind. And joy is the most excellent and the most beautiful of all the pleasant affections of the mind, by means of which the whole soul is in every part entirely filled with cheerfulness, rejoicing in the Father and Creator of all men and things, namely, in God, and rejoicing also in those things which are done without wickedness, even though they may not be pleasant, as being done virtuously, and as contributing to the duration of the universe.

For as in great and dangerous sicknesses a physician sometimes actually takes away parts of the body, aiming at ensuring the sound health of the rest, and as when storms arise the pilot often throws overboard the cargo, out of a prudent regard to the safety of the men sailing in the ship; and yet the physician is not blamed for the mutilation of the body, nor the pilot for the loss of the cargo, but on the contrary both of them are praised as having seen and ensured what was advantageous in preference to what was pleasant; so in the same manner we must always look with proper admiration at the nature of the entire universe, and we must be pleased with all things which are done in the world without intentional wickedness, inquiring not whether any thing has been done which is not altogether pleasant, but whether the world, like a city enjoying good laws, is guided and governed in a manner calculated to ensure its safety. This man, therefore, is happy in no less a degree than the one whom I mentioned before, inasmuch as he is free from all depression or melancholy, and as he enjoys a life exempt from sorrow and exempt from fear, having no connection, not even in a dream, with any painful or austere plans of life, because every part of his soul is wholly occupied by joy.

VI. And next to the man who has acquired self-taught virtue, and who has availed himself of the riches of nature, the third person who is made perfect is the meditator on and practiser of virtue, who receives as his especial reward the sight of God; for as he has had experience of all the things which can occur in human life, and as he has attained to a most intimate understanding of them, and has shrunk from no labour and from no danger which might enable him to track out and overtake that most desirable thing, truth, he has found in connection with human life and with the human race a great deal of darkness both by land and sea, and in the air, and in the atmosphere. For the atmosphere and the whole of heaven has presented to him the appearance of night, since every nature which is discernible by the outward senses is indefinite; and what is indefinite is akin to and closely resembling darkness.

Accordingly, he who had during the preceding periods of his life had the eyes of his soul closed, now began, though with

difficulty, to open them for the continual labours which were
before him, and to pierce through and dissipate the mist
which had overshadowed him.　For an incorporeal ray of
light, purer than the atmosphere, suddenly beaming upon him,
displayed to him the fact of the world appreciable only by the
intellect being guided by a regular governor.　But that
governor or guider, being surrounded on all sides by unalloyed
light, was difficult to be perceived and difficult to be understood by conjecture, since the power of sight was obscured by
the brilliancy of those beams.　But nevertheless the sight,
although a great violence of fire was poured upon it, held out
against it out of an immense desire of seeing what was before
it.　And the Father pitied its sincere desire and eagerness to
see, and gave it power, and did not grudge the acuteness of
the sight thus directed a perception of himself, as far at least
as a created and mortal nature could attain to such a thing,
not indeed such a perception as should show him what God is,
but merely such as should prove to him that he exists; for
even this, which is better than good, and more ancient than
the unit, and more simple than one, cannot possibly be contemplated by any other being; because, in fact, it is not possible for God to be comprehended by any being but himself.

VII.　But the fact that he does exist, though it is comprehensible from the mere name of existence, is nevertheless not
understood by every one, or at all events not in the best way by
every one; but some men have expressly and wholly denied
that there is any deity at all; while others have doubted and
hesitated, as if they were unable to affirm with certainty
whether he has any existence or not.　Others again, who have
more through habit than from any exertion of their reason,
received ideas about the existence of God from those who have
brought them up, have seemed to be pious by a sort of felicity
of conjecture, if they have stamped their piety with an impression of superstition.　But if any men, by a great depth of real
knowledge, have been able to represent to themselves the
Creator and Governor of this universe, they, according to the
common phrase, have advanced upwards from below; for
having entered into this world as into a city regulated by
admirable laws, and having beheld the earth consisting of
mountains, and of plains, and full of seed-crops, and of trees,
and of fruits, and also of all kinds of animals; and beholding

also seas, and ports, and lakes, and rivers of all sorts, whether proceeding from winter floods, or from everlasting springs, diffused over the surface of it, and the admirable temperature of the breezes and of the atmosphere, and the harmonious changes and well-ordered revolutions of the seasons of the year, and beyond all these things, the sun and moon, the planets and fixed stars, and the whole heaven, and all the host of heaven in its proper arrangement, and, in fact, the whole real world revolving in admirable order and regularity : admiring, and being struck with awe and amazement at these things, they are come to form notions consistent with what they behold, that all these beautiful things, excessive as they are, and of such admirable arrangement and contrivance, were not produced spontaneously but were the work of some maker, the Creator of the whole world, and therefore that there must of necessity be a superintending providence.

For it is a law of nature, that the Creator must take care of what he has created. But these admirable men, so superior to all others, have, as I said, raised themselves upwards from below, ascending as if by some ladder reaching to heaven, so as, through the contemplation of his works, to form a conjectural conception of the Creator by a probable train of reasoning. And if any persons have been able to comprehend him by himself, without employing any other reasonings as assistants towards their perception of him, they deserve to be recorded as holy and genuine servants of his, and sincere worshippers of God. In this company is the man who in the Chaldæan language is denominated Israel, but in the Greek "seeing God;" not meaning by this expression seeing what kind of being God is, for that is impossible, as I have said before, but seeing that he really does exist ; not having learnt this fact from any one else, nor from anything on earth, nor from anything in heaven, nor from any one of the elements, nor from anything compounded of them, whether mortal or immortal, but being instructed in the fact by God himself, who is willing to reveal his own existence to his suppliant.

And how this impression was made, it is worth while to see by the observation of some similitude. Take this sun, which is perceptible by our outward senses, do we see it by any other means than by the aid of the sun? And do we see the stars by any other light than that of the stars? And, in short, is not all light seen in consequence of light ? And in the same manner God, being his own light, is perceived by himself alone, nothing and no other being co-operating with or assisting him, or being at all able to contribute to the pure comprehension of his existence ; therefore those persons are mere guessers who are anxious to contemplate the uncreated God through the medium of the things which he created, acting like those persons who seek to ascertain the nature of the unit through the number two, when they ought, on the other hand, to employ the investigation of the unit itself to ascertain the nature of the number two ; for the unit is the first principle.

But these men have arrived at the real truth, who form their ideas of God from God, of light from light.

VIII. We have now described the greatest prize of all : but in addition to these prizes, the meditator on virtue receives another prize, not well-sounding indeed as to name, but very excellent to be conceived of ; and this prize is called " the torpor of breadth," speaking figuratively. Now by breadth haughtiness and arrogance are typified ; the soul, in those conditions, pouring forth an immoderate effusion over objects which are not desirable : and by torpor is typified the contraction of conceit, an elated and puffed-up thing. But nothing is so expedient, as that unrestrained and unlimited impulses should be repressed and reduced to torpor, through the spirit of the mind being extinguished : so that the immoderate violence of the passions having become enfeebled, it may give breadth to the better part of the soul. And we must also consider how exceedingly suitable a prize has thus been assigned to each of the three individuals ; for to him who has been made perfect by education, faith is given as his reward ; since it is necessary that he who learns must trust the man who teaches him in the matters concerning which he is instructing him ; for it is difficult, or rather I might say impossible, for a man to be instructed who distrusts his teacher.

Again : to him who arrives at virtue by his own good natural disposition, joy is given ; for a good natural disposition is a thing to be rejoiced at, and so are the gifts of nature ; since the mind derives enjoyment from all displays of acuteness and felicitous inventions, by which it finds the object which it is seeking without trouble ; as if there was some prompter within enriching it with inventions ; for the prompt discovery of matters previously, not certainly understood, is a subject of joy.

Again : to him who has acquired wisdom by meditation and practice, sight is given.   For after the practical life of youth comes the contemplative life of old age, which is the most excellent and the most sacred, which God has sent down from above to take its place in the stern like a pilot, and has given the helm into his hand as being able to guide the course of all earthly things ; for without contemplation based on knowledge, there is nothing whatever that is good done.

IX. Having thus mentioned one man of each class, since I am anxious not to be prolix, I will proceed to what comes next in the order of discussion.   Now, this man was proclaimed as conqueror, and crowned as such in the sacred contests.   And when I speak of sacred contests, I do not mean those which are accounted such by other nations, for they are in reality unholy, affixing, as they do, rewards and honours to acts of violence, and insolence, and injustice, instead of the very extremity of punishment, which of right belongs to them : but I mean rather such as the soul is by nature formed to go through, which, by means of prudence, drives away folly and wicked cunning, and by temperance drives away prodigality and stinginess, and by courage drives away both rashness and cowardice, and the other vices which are in direct opposition to the respective virtues, and which are of no use either to themselves or to any one else ; therefore all the virtues are represented as virgins.

And the most excellent of all, having taken the post of leader as if in a chorus, is piety and righteousness, which Moses, the interpreter of the will of God, possessed in a most eminent degree.   On which account, besides an innumerable host of other circumstances which are recorded of him in the accounts which have come down to us of his life, he has received also four most especial prizes, in being invested with sovereign power, with the office of lawgiver, with the power of prophecy, and with the office of high priest.   For he was a king, not indeed acording to the usual fashion with soldiers and arms, and forces of fleets, and infantry, and cavalry, but as having been appointed by God, with the free consent of the people who were to be governed by him, and who wrought in his subjects a willingness to make such a voluntary choice.

For he is the only king of whom we have any mention as
being neither a speaker nor one frequently heard, nor possessed of wealth or riches, since he was anxious rather about
the wealth which sees than about that which is blind, and, if
one is to speak the truth without any concealment, one who
looked upon the inheritance of God as his peculiar property.
And this same man was likewise a lawgiver; for a king must
of necessity both command and forbid, and law is nothing
else but a discourse which enjoins what is right and forbids
what is not right; but since it is uncertain what is expedient
in each separate case (for we often out of ignorance command
what is not right to be done, and forbid what is right), it was
very natural for him also to receive the gift of prophecy, in
order to ensure him against stumbling; for a prophet is an
interpreter, God from within prompting him what he ought to
say; and with God nothing is blameable.

In the fourth place he received the high priesthood, by means
of which he, prophesying in accordance with knowledge, worships the living God, and by which also he will bring before
him in a propitiating manner, the thanksgivings of his subjects when they do well, and their prayers and supplications
if at any time they are unfortunate; now since all these things
belong to one class, they ought to be held together and united
by mutual bonds, and to be perceived in the same man,
since he who is deficient in any one of the four is imperfect
in his authority, as he is consequently invested with but a
crippled authority over the common interests.

A TREATISE

ON A CONTEMPLATIVE LIFE,

OR

ON THE VIRTUES OF SUPPLIANTS.

I. HAVING mentioned the Essenes, who in all respects selected for their admiration and for their especial adoption the practical course of life, and who excel in all, or what perhaps may be a less unpopular and invidious thing to say, in most of its parts, I will now proceed, in the regular order of my subject, to speak of those who have embraced the speculative life, and I will say what appears to me to be desirable to be said on the subject, not drawing any fictitious statements from my own head for the sake of improving the appearance of that side of the question which nearly all poets and essayists are much accustomed to do in the scarcity of good actions to extol, but with the greatest simplicity adhering strictly to the truth itself, to which I know well that even the most eloquent men do not keep close in their speeches.

Nevertheless we must make the endeavour and labour to attain to this virtue ; for it is not right that the greatness of the virtue of the men should be a cause of silence to those who do not think it right that anything which is creditable should be suppressed in silence ; but the deliberate intention of the philosopher is at once displayed from the appellation given to them ; for with strict regard to etymology, they are called therapeutæ and therapeutrides,* either because they profess an art of medicine more excellent than that in general use in cities (for that only heals bodies, but the other heals souls which are under the mastery of terrible and almost incurable diseases, which pleasures and appetites, fears and griefs, and covetousness, and follies, and injustice, and all the rest of the innumerable multitude of other passions and vices, have inflicted upon them), or else because they have been instructed by nature and the sacred laws to serve the living God, who is

* From θεραπεύω, "to heal."

superior to the good, and more simple than the one, and more
ancient than the unit; with whom, however, who is there of
those who profess piety that we can possibly compare? Can
we compare those who honour the elements, earth, water, air,
and fire? to whom different nations have given different
names, calling fire Hephæstus, I imagine because of its kindling,* and the air Hera, I imagine because of its being raised
up,† and raised aloft to a great height, and water Poseidon,
probably because of its being drinkable,‡ and the earth Demeter, because it appears to be the mother § of all plants and of
all animals.

But these names are the inventions of sophists: but the
elements are inanimate matter, and immovable by any power
of their own, being subjected to the operator on them to
receive from him every kind of shape or distinctive quality
which he chooses to give them. But what shall we say of
those men who worship the perfect things made of them,
the sun, the moon, and the other stars, planets, or fixed-stars,
or the whole heaven, or the universal world? And yet even
they do not owe their existence to themselves, but to some
creator whose knowledge has been most perfect, both in mind
and degree. What, again, shall we say of the demi-gods?
This is a matter which is perfectly ridiculous : for how can the
same man be both mortal and immortal, even if we leave out
of the question the fact that the origin of the birth of all these
beings is liable to reproach, as being full of youthful intemperance, which its authors endeavour with great profanity to
impute to blessed and divine natures, as if they, being madly
in love with mortal women, had connected themselves with
them ; while we know gods to be free from all participation in
and from all influence of passion, and completely happy.

Again, what shall we say of those who worship carved
works and images? the substances of which, stone and wood,
were only a little while before perfectly destitute of shape,

---

* The Greek is ἕξαψις, as if Ἥφαιστος were also derived from
ἅπτομαι, being akin to ἀφή.

† The Greek word is αἴρεσθαι, to which Ἥρα has some similarity in
sound.

‡ The Greek word is πότον, derived from 3rd sing. perf. pass. of
πίνω πέποται, from the 2nd sing. of which Πέποσαι, ποσειδῶν may
probably be derived.

§ The Greek word is μητήρ, evidently the root of Δημητήρ.

before the stone-cutters or wood-cutters hewed them out of the
kindred stuff around them, while the remainder of the material,
their near relation and brother as it were, is made into ewers,
or foot-pans, and other common and dishonoured vessels, which
are employed rather for uses of darkness than for such as will
bear the light; for as for the customs of the Egyptians, it is
not creditable even to mention them, for they have introduced
irrational beasts, and those not merely such as are domestic and
tame, but even the most ferocious of wild beasts to share the
honours of the gods, taking some out of each of the elements
beneath the moon, as the lion from among the animals which
live on the earth, the crocodile from among those which live
in the water, the kite from such as traverse the air, and the
Egyptian ibis. And though they actually see that these animals
are born, and that they are in need of food, and that they are
insatiable in voracity and full of all sorts of filth, and moreover
poisonous and devourers of men, and liable to be destroyed by
all kinds of diseases, and that in fact they are often destroyed
not only by natural deaths, but also by violence, still they,
civilised men, worship these untameable and ferocious beasts;
though rational men, they worship irrational beasts; though
they have a near relationship to the Deity, they worship
creatures unworthy of being compared even to some of the
beasts; though appointed as rulers and masters, they worship
creatures which are by nature subjects and slaves.

II. But since these men infect not only their fellow
countrymen, but also all that come near them with folly, let
them remain uncovered, being mutilated in that most indispensable of all the outward senses, namely, sight. I am
speaking here not of the sight of the body, but of that of the
soul, by which alone truth and falsehood are distinguished from
one another. But the therapeutic sect of mankind, being continually taught to see without interruption, may well aim at
obtaining a sight of the living God, and may pass by the sun,
which is visible to the outward sense, and never leave this
order which conducts to perfect happiness. But they who
apply themselves to this kind of worship, not because they are
influenced to do so by custom, nor by the advice or recommendation of any particular persons, but because they are carried
away by a certain heavenly love, give way to enthusiasm,
behaving like so many revellers in bacchanalian or corybantian

mysteries, until they see the object which they have been earnestly desiring.

Then, because of their anxious desire for an immortal and blessed existence, thinking that their mortal life has already come to an end, they leave their possessions to their sons or daughters, or perhaps to other relations, giving them up their inheritance with willing cheerfulness ; and those who know no relations give their property to their companions or friends, for it followed of necessity that those who have acquired the wealth which sees, as if ready prepared for them, should be willing to surrender that wealth which is blind to those who themselves also are still blind in their minds.

The Greeks celebrate Anaxagoras and Democritus, because they, being smitten with a desire for philosophy, allowed all their estates to be devoured by cattle. I myself admire the men who thus showed themselves superior to the attractions of money ; but how much better were those who have not permitted cattle to devour their possessions, but have supplied the necessities of mankind, of their own relations and friends, and have made them rich though they were poor before ? For surely that was inconsiderate conduct (that I may avoid saying that any action of men whom Greece has agreed to admire was a piece of insanity) ; but this is the act of sober men, and one which has been carefully elaborated by exceeding prudence.

For what more can enemies do than ravage, and destroy, and cut down all the trees in the country of their antagonists, that they may be forced to submit by reason of the extent to which they are oppressed by want of necessaries ? And yet Democritus did this to his own blood relations, inflicting artificial want and penury upon them, not perhaps from any hostile intention towards them, but because he did not foresee and provide for what was advantageous to others. How much better and more admirable are they who, without having any inferior eagerness for the attainment of philosophy, have nevertheless preferred magnanimity to carelessness, and, giving presents from their possessions instead of destroying them, so as to be able to benefit others and themselves also, have made others happy by imparting to them of the abundance of their wealth, and themselves by the study of philosophy ? For an undue care for money and wealth causes great waste

of time, and it is proper to economise time, since, according
to the saying of the celebrated physician Hippocrates, life is
short but art long. And this is what Homer appears to me to
imply figuratively in the Iliad, at the beginning of the
thirteenth book, by the following lines,—

> "The Mysian close-fighting bands,
> And dwellers on the Scythian lands,
> Content to seek their humble fare
> From milk of cow and milk of mare,
> The justest of mankind." *

As if great anxiety concerning the means of subsistence and
the acquisition of money engendered injustice by reason of
the inequality which it produced, while the contrary disposition and pursuit produced justice by reason of its equality,
according to which it is that the wealth of nature is defined,
and is superior to that which exists only in vain opinion.

When, therefore, men abandon their property without being
influenced by any predominant attraction, they flee without
even turning their heads back again, deserting their brethren,
their children, their wives, their parents, their numerous
families, their affectionate bands of companions, their native
lands in which they have been born and brought up, though
long familiarity is a most attractive bond, and one very well
able to allure any one. And they depart, not to another city
as those do who entreat to be purchased from those who at
present possess them, being either unfortunate or else worthless servants, and as such seeking a change of masters rather
than endeavouring to procure freedom (for every city, even
that which is under the happiest laws, is full of indescribable
tumults, and disorders, and calamities, which no one would
submit to who had been even for a moment under the influence of wisdom), but they take up their abode outside of
walls, or gardens, or solitary lands, seeking for a desert place,
not because of any ill-natured misanthropy to which they
have learnt to devote themselves, but because of the associations with people of wholly dissimilar dispositions to which
they would otherwise be compelled, and which they know to
be unprofitable and mischievous.

III. Now this class of persons may be met with in many
places, for it was fitting that both Greece and the country

* II. xiii. 5.

of the barbarians should partake of whatever is perfectly
good ; and there is the greatest number of such men in Egypt,
in every one of the districts, or nomi as they are called, and
especially around Alexandria ; and from all quarters those
who are the best of these therapeutæ proceed on their pil-
grimage to some most suitable place as if it were their country,
which is beyond the Mareotic lake, lying in a somewhat level
plain a little raised above the rest, being suitable for their
purpose by reason of its safety and also of the fine temperature of the air.

For the houses built in the fields and the villages which
surround it on all sides give it safety ; and the admirable temperature of the air proceeds from the continual breezes which
come from the lake which falls into the sea, and also from the
sea itself in the neighbourhood, the breezes from the sea
being light, and those which proceed from the lake which falls
into the sea being heavy, the mixture of which produces a
most healthy atmosphere.

But the houses of these men thus congregated together are
very plain, just giving shelter in respect of the two things
most important to be provided against, the heat of the sun,
and the cold from the open air ; and they did not live near to one
another as men do in cities, for immediate neighbourhood to
others would be a troublesome and unpleasant thing to men
who have conceived an admiration for, and have determined to
devote themselves to, solitude ; and, on the other hand, they
did not live very far from one another on account of the
fellowship which they desire to cultivate, and because of the
desirableness of being able to assist one another if they
should be attacked by robbers.

And in every house there is a sacred shrine which is called
the holy place, and the monastery in which they retire by
themselves and perform all the mysteries of a holy life, bringing in nothing, neither meat, nor drink, nor anything else
which is indispensable towards supplying the necessities of
the body, but studying in that place the laws and the sacred
oracles of God enunciated by the holy prophets, and hymns,
and psalms, and all kinds of other things by reason of which
knowledge and piety are increased and brought to perfection.

Therefore they always retain an imperishable recollection of
God, so that not even in their dreams is any other object ever

presented to their eyes except the beauty of the divine virtues and of the divine powers. Therefore many persons speak in their sleep, divulging and publishing the celebrated doctrines of the sacred philosophy. And they are accustomed to pray twice every day, at morning and at evening ; when the sun is rising entreating God that the happiness of the coming day may be real happiness, so that their minds may be filled with heavenly light, and when the sun is setting they pray that their soul, being entirely lightened and relieved of the burden of the outward senses, and of the appropriate object of these outward senses, may be able to trace out truth existing in its own consistory and council chamber. And the interval between morning and evening is by them devoted wholly to meditation on and to practice of virtue, for they take up the sacred scriptures and philosophise concerning them, investigating the allegories of their national philosophy, since they look upon their literal expressions as symbols of some secret meaning of nature, intended to be conveyed in those figurative expressions.

They have also writings of ancient men, who having been the founders of one sect or another have left behind them many memorials of the allegorical system of writing and explanation, whom they take as a kind of model, and imitate the general fashion of their sect ; so that they do not occupy themselves solely in contemplation, but they likewise compose psalms and hymns to God in every kind of metre and melody imaginable, which they of necessity arrange in more dignified rhythm. Therefore, during six days, each of these individuals, retiring into solitude by himself, philosophises by himself in one of the places called monasteries, never going outside the threshold of the outer court, and indeed never even looking out.

But on the seventh day they all come together as if to meet in a sacred assembly, and they sit down in order according to their ages with all becoming gravity, keeping their hands inside their garments, having their right hand between their chest and their dress, and the left hand down by their side, close to their flank ; and then the eldest of them who has the most profound learning in their doctrines comes forward and speaks with steadfast look and with steadfast voice, with great powers of reasoning, and great prudence, not making an exhibition of his oratorical powers like the rhetoricians of old, or the sophists of the present day, but investigating with great pains, and explaining with minute accuracy the precise meaning of the laws, which sits, not indeed at the tips of their ears, but penetrates through their hearing into the soul, and remains there lastingly; and all the rest listen in silence to the praises which he bestows upon the law, showing their assent only by nods of the head, or the eager look of the eyes.

And this common holy place to which they all come together on the seventh day is a twofold circuit, being separated partly into the apartment of the men, and partly into a chamber for the women, for women also, in accordance with the usual fashion there, form a part of the audience, having the same feelings of admiration as the men, and having adopted the same sect with equal deliberation and decision; and the wall which is between the houses rises from the ground three or four cubits upwards, like a battlement, and the upper portion rises upwards to the roof without any opening, on two accounts; first of all, in order that the modesty which is so becoming to the female sex may be preserved, and secondly, that the women may be easily able to comprehend what is said being seated within earshot, since there is then nothing which can possibly intercept the voice of him who is speaking.

IV. And these expounders of the law, having first of all laid down temperance as a sort of foundation for the soul to rest upon, proceed to build up other virtues on this foundation, and no one of them may take any meat or drink before the setting of the sun, since they judge that the work of philosophising is one which is worthy of the light, but that the care for the necessities of the body is suitable only to darkness, on which account they appropriate the day to the one occupation, and a brief portion of the night to the other; and some men, in whom there is implanted a more fervent desire of knowledge, can endure to cherish a recollection of their food for three days without even tasting it, and some men are so delighted, and enjoy themselves so exceedingly when regaled by wisdom which supplies them with her doctrines in all possible wealth and abundance, that they can even hold out twice as great a length of time, and will scarcely at the end of six days taste even necessary food, being accustomed, as they say that grasshoppers are, to feed on air, their song, as I imagine, making their scarcity tolerable to them.

And they, looking upon the seventh day as one of perfect holiness and a most complete festival, have thought it worthy of a most especial honour, and on it, after taking due care of their soul, they tend their bodies also, giving them, just as they do to their cattle, a complete rest from their continual labours ; and they eat nothing of a costly character, but plain bread and a seasoning of salt, which the more luxurious of them do further season with hyssop ; and their drink is water from the spring ; for they oppose those feelings which nature has made mistresses of the human race, namely, hunger and thirst, giving them nothing to flatter or humour them, but only such useful things as it is not possible to exist without. On this account they eat only so far as not to be hungry, and they drink just enough to escape from thirst, avoiding all satiety, as an enemy of and a plotter against both soul and body.

And there are two kinds of covering, one raiment and the other a house : we have already spoken of their houses, that they are not decorated with any ornaments, but run up in a hurry, being only made to answer such purposes as are absolutely necessary ; and in like manner their raiment is of the most ordinary description, just stout enough to ward off cold and heat, being a cloak of some shaggy hide for winter, and a thin mantle or linen shawl in the summer ; for in short they practise entire simplicity, looking upon falsehood as the foundation of pride, but truth as the origin of simplicity, and upon truth and falsehood as standing in the light of fountains, for from falsehood proceeds every variety of evil and wickedness, and from truth there flows every imaginable abundance of good things both human and divine.

V. I wish also to speak of their common assemblies, and their very cheerful meetings at convivial parties, setting them in opposition and contrast to the banquets of others, for others, when they drink strong wine, as if they had been drinking not wine but some agitating and maddening kind of liquor, or even the most formidable thing which can be imagined for driving a man out of his natural reason, rage about and tear things to pieces like so many ferocious dogs, and rise up and attack one another, biting and gnawing each other's noses, and

ears, and fingers, and other parts of their body, so as to give
an accurate representation of the story related about the
Cyclops and the companions of Ulysses, who ate, as the poet
says, fragments of human flesh,* and that more savagely than
even he himself ; for he was only avenging himself on those
whom he conceived to be his enemies, but they were ill-treating
their companions and friends, and sometimes even their actual
relations, while having the salt and dinner-table before them,
at a time of peace perpetrating actions inconsistent with
peace, like those which are done by men in gymnastic contests, debasing the proper exercises of the body as coiners
debase good money, and instead of athletes (ἀθληταῖ) becoming
miserable men (ἄθλιοι), for that is the name which properly
belongs to them.

For that which those men who gain victories in the Olympic
games, when perfectly sober in the arena, and having all the
Greeks for spectators do by day, exerting all their skill for the
purpose of gaining victory and the crown, these men with base
designs do at convivial entertainments, getting drunk by night,
in the hour of darkness, when soaked in wine, acting without
either knowledge, or art, or skill, to the insult, and injury,
and great disgrace of those who are subjected to their violence.

And if no one were to come like an umpire into the middle
of them, and part the combatants, and reconcile them, they
would continue the contest with unlimited licence, striving to
kill and murder one another, and being killed and murdered
on the spot; for they do not suffer less than they inflict,
though out of the delirious state into which they have worked
themselves they do not feel what is done to them, since they
have filled themselves with wine, not, as the comic poet says,
to the injury of their neighbour, but to their own. Therefore
those persons who a little while before came safe and sound to
the banquet, and in friendship for one another, do presently
afterwards depart in hostility and mutilated in their bodies.

And some of these men stand in need of advocates and
judges, and others require surgeons and physicians, and the
help which may be received from them. Others again who
seem to be a more moderate kind of feasters when they have
drunk unmixed wine as if it were mandragora, boil over as it
were, and lean on their left elbow, and turn their heads on

* Odyssey ix. 355.

one side with their breath redolent of their wine, till at last they sink into profound slumber, neither seeing nor hearing anything, as if they had but one single sense, and that the most slavish of all, namely, taste. And I know some persons who, when they are completely filled with wine, before they are wholly overpowered by it, begin to prepare a drinking party for the next day by a kind of subscription and picnic contribution, conceiving a great part of their present delight to consist in the hope of future drunkenness; and in this manner they exist to the very end of their lives, without a house and without a home, the enemies of their parents, and of their wives, and of their children, and the enemies of their country, and the worst enemies of all to themselves. For a debauched and profligate life is apt to lay snares for every one.

VI. And perhaps some people may be inclined to approve of the arrangement of such entertainments which at present prevails everywhere, from an admiration of, and a desire of imitating, the luxury and extravagance of the Italians which both Greeks and barbarians emulate, making all their preparations with a view to show rather than to real enjoyment, for they use couches called triclinia, and sofas all round the table made of tortoiseshell, and ivory, and other costly materials, most of which are inlaid with precious stones; and coverlets of purple embroidered with gold and silver thread; and others brocaded in flowers of every kind of hue and colour imaginable to allure the sight, and a vast array of drinking cups arrayed according to each separate description; for there are bowls, and vases, and beakers, and goblets, and all kinds of other vessels wrought with the most exquisite skill, their clean cups and others finished with the most elaborate refinement of skilful and ingenious men; and well shaped slaves of the most exquisite beauty, ministering, as if they had come not more for the purpose of serving the guests than of delighting the eyes of the spectators by their mere appearance.

Of these slaves, some, being still boys, pour out the wine; and others more fully grown pour water, being carefully washed and rubbed down, with their faces anointed and pencilled, and the hair of their heads admirably plaited and curled and wreathed in delicate knots; for they have very long hair, being either completely unshorn, or else having only the hair on their foreheads cut at the end so as to make them of an equal

length all round, being accurately sloped away so as to represent a circular line, and being clothed in tunics of the most
delicate texture, and of the purest white, reaching in front
down to the lower part of the knee, and behind to a little
below the calf of the leg, and drawing up each side with a
gentle doubling of the fringe at the joinings of the tunics,
raising undulations of the garment as it were at the sides, and
widening them at the hollow part of the side.

Others, again, are young men just beginning to show a
beard on their youthful chins, having been, for a short time, the
sport of the profligate debauchees, and being prepared with
exceeding care and diligence for more painful services; being
a kind of exhibition of the excessive opulence of the giver of
the feast, or rather, to say the truth, of their thorough
ignorance of all propriety, as those who are acquainted with
them well know.

Besides all these things, there is an infinite variety of sweet-
meats, and delicacies, and confections, about which bakers and
cooks and confectioners labour, considering not the taste, which
is the point of real importance, so as to make the food palatable
to that, but also the sight, so as to allure that by the delicacy
of the look of their viands. Accordingly, seven tables, and
often more, are brought in, full of every kind of delicacy which
earth, and sea, and rivers, and air produce, all procured with
great pains, and in high condition, composed of terrestrial, and
acquatic, and flying creatures, every one of which is different
both in its mode of dressing and in its seasoning.

And that no description of thing existing in nature may be
omitted, at the last dishes are brought in full of fruits, besides
those which are kept back for the more luxurious portion of
the entertainment, and for what is called the dessert; and
afterwards some of the dishes are carried away empty from the
insatiable greediness of those at table, who, gorging themselves
like cormorants, devour all the delicacies so completely that
they gnaw even the bones, which some left half devoured after
all that they contained has been torn to pieces and spoiled.
And when they are completely tired with eating, having their
bellies filled up to their very throats, but their desires still
unsatisfied, being fatigued with eating they turn their heads
round in every direction, scanning everything with their eyes
and with their nostrils, examining the richness and the number

of the dishes with the first, and the steam which is sent up by them with the second.

Then, when they are thoroughly sated both with the sight and with the scent, these senses again prompt their owners to eat, praising in no moderate terms both the entertainment itself and the giver of it, for its costliness and magnificence. However, why need I dwell with prolixity on these matters, which are already condemned by the generality of more moderate men as inflaming the passions, the diminution of which is desirable? For any one in his senses would pray for the most unfortunate of all states, hunger and thirst, rather than for a most unlimited abundance of meat and drink at such banquets as these.

VII. Now of the banquets among the Greeks the two most celebrated and most remarkable are those at which Socrates also was present, the one in the house of Callias, when, after Autolycus had gained the crown of victory, he gave a feast in honour of the event, and the other in the house of Agathon, which was thought worthy of being commemorated by men who were imbued with the true spirit of philosophy both in their dispositions and in their discourses, Plato and Xenophon, for they recorded them as events worthy to be had in perpetual recollection, looking upon it that future generations would take them as models for a well managed arrangement of future banquets; but nevertheless even these, if compared with the banquets of the men of our time who have embraced the contemplative system of life, will appear ridiculous. Each description, indeed, has its own pleasures, but that recorded by Xenophon is the one the delights of which are most in accordance with human nature, for female harp-players, and dancers, and conjurors, and jugglers, and men who do ridiculous things, who pride themselves much on their powers of jesting and of amusing others, and many other species of more cheerful relaxation, are brought forward at it. But the entertainment recorded by Plato is almost entirely connected with love; not that of men madly desirous or fond of women, or of women furiously in love with men, for these desires are accomplished in accordance with a law of nature, but with that love which is felt by men for one another, differing only in respect of age; for if there is anything in the account of that banquet elegantly said in praise of genuine love and heavenly Venus, it is

introduced merely for the sake of making a neat speech; for
the greater part of the book is occupied by common, vulgar,
promiscuous love, which takes away from the soul courage,
that which is the most serviceable of all virtues both in war
and in peace, and which engenders in it instead the female
disease, and renders men men-women, though they ought
rather to be carefully trained in all the practices likely to give
men valour.

And having corrupted the age of boys, and having metamor-
phosed them and removed them into the classification and
character of women, it has injured their lovers also in the most
important particulars, their bodies, their souls, and their
properties; for it follows of necessity that the mind of a lover
of boys must be kept on the stretch towards the objects of his
affection, and must have no acuteness of vision for any other
object, but must be blinded by its desire as to all other
objects private or common, and must so be wasted away, more
especially if it fails in its objects. Moreover, the man's
property must be diminished on two accounts, both from the
owner's neglect and from his expenses for the beloved object.

There is also another greater evil which affects the whole
people, and which grows up alongside of the other, for men
who give into such passions produce solitude in cities, and a
scarcity of the best kind of men, and barrenness, and unproductiveness, inasmuch as they are imitating those farmers who
are unskilful in agriculture, and who, instead of the deep-soiled
champaign country, sow briny marshes, or stony and rugged
districts, which are not calculated to produce crops of any kind,
and which only destroy the seed which is put into them. I
pass over in silence the different fabulous fictions, and the
stories of persons with two bodies, who having originally been
stuck to one another by amatory influences, are subsequently
separated like portions which have been brought together and
are disjoined again, the harmony having been dissolved by
which they were held together; for all these things are very
attractive, being able by the novelty of their imagination to
allure the ears, but they are despised by the disciples of
Moses, who in the abundance of their wisdom have learnt
from their earliest infancy to love truth, and also continue to
the end of their lives impossible to be deceived.

VIII. But since the entertainments of the greatest celebrity are full of such trifling and folly, bearing conviction in themselves, if any one should think fit not to regard vague opinion and the character which has been commonly handed down concerning them as feasts which have gone off with the most eminent success, I will oppose to them the entertainments of those persons who have devoted their whole life and themselves to the knowledge and contemplation of the affairs of nature in accordance with the most sacred admonitions and precepts of the prophet Moses.

In the first place, these men assemble at the end of seven weeks, venerating not only the simple week of seven days, but also its multiplied power, for they know it to be pure and always virgin; and it, is a prelude and a kind of forefeast of the greatest feast, which is assigned to the number fifty, the most holy and natural of numbers, being compounded of the power of the right-angled triangle, which is the principle of the origination and condition of the whole.

Therefore when they come together clothed in white garments, and joyful with the most exceeding gravity, when some one of the ephemereutæ (for that is the appellation which they are accustomed to give to those who are employed in such ministrations), before they sit down to meat standing in order in a row, and raising their eyes and their hands to heaven, the one because they have learnt to fix their attention on what is worth looking at, and the other because they are free from the reproach of all impure gain, being never polluted under any pretence whatever by any description of criminality which can arise from any means taken to procure advantage, they pray to God that the entertainment may be acceptable, and welcome, and pleasing; and after having offered up these prayers the elders sit down to meat, still observing the order in which they were previously arranged, for they do not look on those as elders who are advanced in years and very ancient, but in some cases they esteem those as very young men, if they have attached themselves to this sect only lately, but those whom they call elders are those who from their earliest infancy have grown up and arrived at maturity in the speculative portion of philosophy, which is the most beautiful and most divine part of it.

And the women also share in this feast, the greater part of whom, though old, are virgins in respect of their purity (not indeed through necessity, as some of the priestesses among the Greeks are, who have been compelled to preserve their chastity more than they would have done of their own accord), but out of an admiration for and love of wisdom, with which they are desirous to pass their lives, on account of which they are indifferent to the pleasures of the body, desiring not a mortal but an immortal offspring, which the soul that is attached to God is alone able to produce by itself and from itself, the Father having sown in it rays of light appreciable only by the intellect, by means of which it will be able to perceive the doctrines of wisdom.

IX. And the order in which they sit down to meat is a divided one, the men sitting on the right hand and the women apart from them on the left; and in case any one by chance suspects that cushions, if not very costly ones, still at all events of a tolerably soft substance, are prepared for men who are well born and well bred, and contemplators of philosophy, he must know that they have nothing but rugs of the coarsest materials, cheap mats of the most ordinary kind of the papyrus of the land, piled up on the ground and projecting a little near the elbow, so that the feasters may lean upon them, for they relax in a slight degree the Lacedæmonian rigour of life, and at all times and in all places they practise a liberal, gentlemanlike kind of frugality, hating the allurements of pleasure with all their might.

And they do not use the ministrations of slaves, looking upon the possession of servants or slaves to be a thing absolutely and wholly contrary to nature, for nature has created all men free, but the injustice and covetousness of some men who prefer inequality, that cause of all evil, having subdued some, has given to the more powerful authority over those who are weaker.

Accordingly in this sacred entertainment there is, as I have said, no slave, but free men minister to the guests, performing the offices of servants, not under compulsion, nor in obedience to any imperious commands, but of their own voluntary free will, with all eagerness and promptitude anticipating all orders, for they are not any chance free men who are appointed to perform these duties, but young men who are selected from their order with all possible care on account of their excellence, acting as virtuous and well-born youths ought to act who are eager to attain to the perfection of virtue, and who, like legitimate sons, with affectionate rivalry minister to their fathers and mothers, thinking their common parents more closely connected with them than those who are related by blood, since in truth to men of right principles there is nothing more nearly akin than virtue; and they come in to perform their service ungirdled, and with their tunics let down, in order that nothing which bears any resemblance to a slavish appearance may be introduced into this festival.

I know well that some persons will laugh when they hear this, but they who laugh will be those who do things worthy of weeping and lamentation. And in those days wine is not introduced, but only the clearest water; cold water for the generality, and hot water for those old men who are accustomed to a luxurious life. And the table, too, bears nothing which has blood, but there is placed upon it bread for food and salt for seasoning, to which also hyssop is sometimes added as an extra sauce for the sake of those who are delicate in their eating, for just as right reason commands the priest to offer up sober sacrifices, so also these men are commanded to live sober lives, for wine is the medicine of folly, and costly seasonings and sauces excite desire, which is the most insatiable of all beasts.

X. These, then, are the first circumstances of the feast; but after the guests have sat down to the table in the order which I have been describing, and when those who minister to them are all standing around in order, ready to wait upon them, and when there is nothing to drink, some one will say . . .   but even more so than before, so that no one ventures to mutter, or even to breathe at all hard, and then some one looks out some passage in the sacred scriptures, or explains some difficulty which is proposed by some one else, without any thoughts of display on his own part, for he is not aiming at reputation for cleverness and eloquence, but is only desirous to see some points more accurately, and is content when he has thus seen them himself not to bear ill will to others, who, even if they did not perceive the truth with equal acuteness, have at all events an equal desire of learning. And he, indeed, follows a slower method of instruction, dwelling on and lingering over his explanations with repetitions, in order to imprint his conceptions deep in the minds of his hearers, for as the understanding of his hearers is not able to keep up with the interpretation of one who goes on fluently, without stopping to take breath, it gets behind-hand, and fails to comprehend what is said; but the hearers, fixing their eyes and attention upon the speaker, remain in one and the same position listening attentively, indicating their attention and comprehension by their nods and looks, and the praise which they are inclined to bestow on the speaker by the cheerfulness and gentle manner in which they follow him with their eyes and with the fore-finger of the right hand.

And the young men who are standing around attend to this explanation no less than the guests themselves who are sitting at meat. And these explanations of the sacred scriptures are delivered by mystic expressions in allegories, for the whole of the law appears to these men to resemble a living animal, and its express commandments seem to be the body, and the invisible meaning concealed under and lying beneath the plain words resembles the soul, in which the rational soul begins most excellently to contemplate what belongs to itself, as in a mirror, beholding in these very words the exceeding beauty of the sentiments, and unfolding and explaining the symbols, and bringing the secret meaning naked to the light to all who are able by the light of a slight intimation to perceive what is unseen by what is visible.

When, therefore, the president appears to have spoken at sufficient length, and to have carried out his intentions adequately, so that his explanation has gone on felicitously and fluently through his own acuteness, and the hearing of the others has been profitable, applause arises from them all as of men rejoicing together at what they have seen and heard; and then some one rising up sings a hymn which has been made in honour of God, either such as he has composed himself, or some ancient one of some old poet, for they have left behind them many poems and songs in trimetre iambics, and in psalms of thanksgiving and in hymns, and songs at the time of libation, and at the altar, and in regular order, and in choruses, admirably measured out in various and well diversified strophes.

And after him then others also arise in their ranks, in becoming order, while every one else listens in decent silence, except when it is proper for them to take up the burden of the song, and to join in at the end; for then they all, both men and women, join in the hymn. And when each individual has finished his psalm, then the young men bring in the table which was mentioned a little while ago, on which was placed that most holy food, the leavened bread, with a seasoning of salt, with which hyssop is mingled, out of reverence for the sacred table, which lies thus in the holy outer temple; for on this table are placed loaves and salt without seasoning, and the bread is unleavened, and the salt unmixed with anything else, for it was becoming that the simplest and purest things should be allotted to the most excellent portion of the priests, as a reward for their ministrations, and that the others should admire similar things, but should abstain from the loaves, in order that those who are the more excellent persons may have the precedence.

XI. And after the feast they celebrate the sacred festival during the whole night; and this nocturnal festival is celebrated in the following manner: they all stand up together, and in the middle of the entertainment two choruses are formed at first, the one of men and the other of women, and for each chorus there is a leader and chief selected, who is the most honourable and most excellent of the band. Then they sing hymns which have been composed in honour of God in many metres and tunes, at one time all singing together, and at another moving their hands and dancing in corresponding harmony, and uttering in an inspired manner songs of thanksgiving, and at another time regular odes, and performing all necessary strophes and antistrophes.

Then, when each chorus of the men and each chorus of the women has feasted separately by itself, like persons in the bacchanalian revels, drinking the pure wine of the love of God, they join together, and the two become one chorus, an imitation of that one which, in old time, was established by the Red Sea, on account of the wondrous works which were displayed there; for, by the commandment of God, the sea became to one party the cause of safety, and to the other that of utter destruction; for it being burst asunder, and dragged back by a violent reflux, and being built up on each side as if there were a solid wall, the space in the midst was widened, and cut into a level and dry road, along which the people passed over to the opposite land, being conducted onwards to higher ground; then, when the sea returned and ran back to its former channel, and was poured out from both sides, on what had just before been dry ground, those of the enemy who pursued were overwhelmed and perished.

When the Israelites saw and experienced this great miracle, which was an event beyond all description, beyond all imagination, and beyond all hope, both men and women together, under the influence of divine inspiration, becoming all one chorus, sang hymns of thanksgiving to God the Saviour, Moses the prophet leading the men, and Miriam the prophetess leading the women.

Now the chorus of male and female worshippers being formed, as far as possible on this model, makes a most humorous concert, and a truly musical symphony, the shrill voices of the women mingling with the deep-toned voices of the men. The ideas were beautiful, the expressions beautiful, and the chorus-singers were beautiful; and the end of ideas, and expressions, and chorus-singers, was piety; therefore, being intoxicated all night till the morning with this beautiful intoxication, without feeling their heads heavy or closing their eyes for sleep, but being even more awake than when they came to the feast, as to their eyes and their whole bodies, and standing there till morning, when they saw the sun rising they raised their hands to heaven, imploring tranquillity and truth, and acuteness of understanding.

And after their prayers they each retired to their own separate abodes, with the intention of again practising the usual philosophy to which they had been wont to devote themselves.

This then is what I have to say of those who are called therapeutæ, who have devoted themselves to the contemplation of nature, and who have lived in it and in the soul alone, being citizens of heaven and of the world, and very acceptable to the Father and Creator of the universe because of their virtue, which has procured them his love as their most appropriate reward, which far surpasses all the gifts of fortune, and conducts them to the very summit and perfection of happiness.

A TREATISE

TO

PROVE THAT EVERY MAN WHO IS VIRTUOUS
IS ALSO FREE.

XII. Moreover Palestine and Syria too are not barren of exemplary wisdom and virtue, which countries no slight portion of that most populous nation of the Jews inhabits. There is a portion of those people called Essenes, in number something more than four thousand in my opinion, who derive their name from their piety, though not according to any accurate form of the Grecian dialect, because they are above all men devoted to the service of God, not sacrificing living animals, but studying rather to preserve their own minds in a state of holiness and purity. These men, in the first place, live in villages, avoiding all cities on account of the habitual lawlessness of those who inhabit them, well knowing that such a moral disease is contracted from associations with wicked men, just as a real disease might be from an impure atmosphere, and that this would stamp an incurable evil on their souls. Of these men, some cultivating the earth, and others devoting themselves to those arts which are the result of peace, benefit both themselves and all those who come in contact with them, not storing up treasures of silver and of gold, nor acquiring vast sections of the earth out of a desire for ample revenues, but providing all things which are requisite for the natural purposes of life; for they alone of almost all men having been originally poor and destitute, and that too rather from their own habits and ways of life than from any real deficiency of good fortune, are nevertheless accounted very rich, judging contentment and frugality to be great abundance, as in truth they are.

Among those men you will find no makers of arrows, or javelins, or swords, or helmets, or breastplates, or shields; no makers of arms or of military engines; no one, in short, attending to any employment whatever connected with war, or even to any of those occupations even in peace which are easily perverted to wicked purposes; for they are utterly ignorant of all traffic, and of all commercial dealings, and of all navigation, but they repudiate and keep aloof from everything which can possibly afford any inducement to covetousness; and there is not a single slave among them, but they are all free, aiding one another with a reciprocal interchange of good offices; and they condemn masters, not only as unjust, inasmuch as they corrupt the very principle of equality, but likewise as impious, because they destroy the ordinances of nature, which generated them all equally, and brought them up like a mother, as if they were all legitimate brethren, not in name only, but in reality and truth.

But in their view this natural relationship of all men to one another has been thrown into disorder by designing covetousness, continually wishing to surpass others in good fortune, and which has therefore engendered alienation instead of affection, and hatred instead of friendship; and leaving the logical part of philosophy, as in no respect necessary for the acquisition of virtue, to the word-catchers, and the natural part, as being too sublime for human nature to master, to those who love to converse about high objects (except indeed so far as such a study takes in the contemplation of the existence of God and of the creation of the universe), they devote all their attention to the moral part of philosophy, using as instructors the laws of their country which it would have been impossible for the human mind to devise without divine inspiration.

Now these laws they are taught at other times, indeed, but most especially on the seventh day, for the seventh day is accounted sacred, on which they abstain from all other employments, and frequent the sacred places which are called synagogues, and there they sit according to their age in classes, the younger sitting under the elder, and listening with eager attention in becoming order. Then one, indeed, takes up the holy volume and reads it, and another of the men of the greatest experience comes forward and explains what is not very intelligible, for a great many precepts are delivered in enigmatical modes of expression, and allegorically, as the old fashion was; and thus the people are taught piety, and holiness, and justice, and economy, and the science of regulating the state, and the knowledge of such things as are naturally good, or bad, or indifferent, and to choose what is right and to avoid what is wrong, using a threefold variety of definitions, and rules, and criteria, namely, the love of God, and the love of virtue, and the love of mankind.

Accordingly, the sacred volumes present an infinite number of instances of the disposition devoted to the love of God, and

of a continued and uninterrupted purity throughout the whole
of life, of a careful avoidance of oaths and of falsehood, and of
a strict adherence to the principle of looking on the Deity as
the cause of everything which is good and of nothing which is
evil.   They also furnish us with many proofs of a. love of
virtue, such as abstinence from all covetousness of money,
from ambition, from indulgence in pleasures, temperance,
endurance, and also moderation, simplicity, good temper, the
absence of pride, obedience to the laws, steadiness, and everything of that kind ; and, lastly, they bring forward as proofs of
the love of mankind, goodwill, equality beyond all power of
description, and fellowship, about which it is not unreasonable
to say. a few words.

In the first place, then, there is no one who has a house so
absolutely his own private property, that it does not in some
sense also belong to every one : for besides that they all dwell
together in companies, the house is open to all those of the
same notions, who come to them from other quarters ; then
there is one magazine among them all ; their expenses are all
in common ; their garments belong to them all in common ;
their food is common, since they all eat in messes ; for there is
no other people among which you can find a common use of the
same house, a common adoption of one mode of living, and a
common use of the same table more thoroughly established in
fact than among this tribe : and is not this very natural ?
For whatever they, after having been working during the day,
receive for their wages, that they do not retain as their own,
but bring it into the common stock, and give any advantage
that is to be derived from it to all who desire to avail themselves of it ; and those who are sick are not neglected because
they are unable to contribute to the common stock, inasmuch
as the tribe have in their public stock a means of supplying
their necessities and aiding their weakness, so that from their
ample means they support them liberally and abundantly ; and
they cherish respect for their elders, and honour them and
care for them, just as parents are honoured and cared for by
their lawful children : being supported by them in all abundance both by their personal exertions, and by innumerable
contrivances.

XIII. Such diligent practisers of virtue does philosophy,
unconnected with any superfluous care of examining into
Greek names render men, proposing to them as necessary

exercises to train them towards its attainment, all praiseworthy actions by which a freedom, which can never be enslaved, is firmly established.

And a proof of this is that, though at different times a great number of chiefs of every variety of disposition and character, have occupied their country, some of whom have endeavoured to surpass even ferocious wild beasts in cruelty, leaving no sort of inhumanity unpractised, and have never ceased to murder their subjects in whole troops, and have even torn them to pieces while living, like cooks cutting them limb from limb, till they themselves, being overtaken by the vengeance of divine justice, have at last experienced the same miseries in their turn: others again having converted their barbarous frenzy into another kind of wickedness, practising an ineffable degree of savageness, talking with the people quietly, but through the hypocrisy of a more gentle voice, betraying the ferocity of their real disposition, fawning upon their victims like treacherous dogs, and becoming the causes of irremediable miseries to them, have left in all their cities monuments of their impiety, and hatred of all mankind, in the never to be forgotten miseries endured by those whom they oppressed: and yet no one, not even of those immoderately cruel tyrants, nor of the more treacherous and hypocritical oppressors was ever able to bring any real accusation against the multitude of those called Essenes or Holy. But everyone being subdued by the virtue of these men, looked up to them as free by nature, and not subject to the frown of any human being, and have celebrated their manner of messing together, and their fellowship with one another beyond all description in respect of its mutual good faith, which is an ample proof of a perfect and very happy life.

NOTES

1,18   the world: i.e., the cosmos; to be a citizen of the universe and to live in harmony with nature are Stoic ideals which Philo finds confirmed by the biblical account of Creation ,and of the position of the first man; see also chapters XLIX and L.

2,12   some men: mainly Aristotle, who believed in the eternity of the universe.

2,31f.   transformed into . . . this world: the transformation of inanimate matter by an active cause is a Stoic and Pythagorean view; the classical Jewish view posits a "creation out of nothing" (*creatio ex nihilo*).

3,32   the first perfect one: a Pythgorean tenet; Pythagorean, too, is the view that odd numbers are masculine, the even ones feminine. "Equal to its parts": 1 x 2 x 3; "made complete by them": 1 + 2 + 3.

4,8   first day: the biblical text (and the Septuagint) concludes the account of the first day of Creation by ". . . one day" (not "the first day"). In Pythagorean thinking, "one" is a sacred number.

4,23   incorporeal model: Philo follows Plato's view of our visible world having been formed after the model of an ideal world. According to Philo, this ideal world is the creation of the first day.

5,12f.   conceived its form in his mind: cf. Genesis Rabbah I, 2: "The Torah speaks: I was the tool of God (in the Creation). . . . God looked upon the Torah (as the blueprint) and created the world."

5,30   one of the ancients: Plato *Timaeus* 29e. Cf. Wisdom of Solomon xi. 24: "For thou lovest all things that are . . . never wouldst thou have formed anything if thou didst hate it" (tr. S. Holmes, in R. H. Charles, *Apocrypha and Pseudepigrapha of the Old Testament*).

6,24f.   the image a part of the image: man was created in the image of the *logos* which in turn was created in the image of God. Cf. the midrashic view: "Adam was created in the image of the angels" (Exodus Rabbah XXX, 12).

6,32   In the beginning: Genesis i. 1.

6,41   time: Plato thought that time came into being with Creation. Pre-Platonic Greek thinkers considered time as preceding the world.

7,11   visible Gods: the heavenly bodies which were thought of by the Greeks as rational, divine beings.

7,36   beautiful: Genesis i. 4.

8,15   darkness: *ibid.,* i. 2.

12,29   all-perfect decade: the Pythagoreans considered ten to be the symbol of perfection.

14,39   harmonious dances: a Pythagorean view.

16,20f.   signs and . . . seasons: Genesis i. 14.

18,4   cattle and beasts: *ibid.,* i. 24.

19,30   in the image: *ibid.,* i. 26.

20,1   the great Governor: cf. the talmudic sentence: "As God fills the entire universe, so does the soul fill the whole body" (Berakhot 10a).

20,21   Corybantian festivals; part of the ecstatic worship of the Phrygian goddess Cybele.

20,38   "Let *us* make man": Genesis i. 26.

21,36   assistants: responsible for the creation of evil; the Philonic God must remain outside of the realm of evil. The biblical "Let *us* make man" supported Philo in his exegesis. Plato (*Timaeus*), too, has God create "young gods" to do the dirty work.

22,4   male and female: to Philo the first, ideal, man was an androgynous being. Plato (*Symposium*) mentions such a myth. Cf. Genesis Rabbah VIII, 1: "When God created the first man, he created him as an androgynous being, as it is said: 'Male and female created he them.'"

24,27   short-lived heaven: or, a miniature heaven, or, a miniature world; man as microcosmos is also an Aristotelian, Stoic, and Pythagorean notion.

24,40   admire and worship: cf. Pirke Rabbi Eliezer XI: "All animals came, and bowed to him as to their master."

25,6   verbal appointment: Genesis i. 26.

26,25f. calling it holy: *ibid.*, ii. 3.

26,36   Here follows a discourse on the number seven (to end of chap. XLIII). For a brief account of this discourse, cf. "On the Allegories of the Sacred Laws," IV–V.

26,38   "This is the book . . .": Genesis ii. 4 f.; Philo reads these two verses as a renewed reference to the world of ideas after which the objects of our real world were patterned.

27,19   "And a fountain went up . . .": Genesis ii. 6.

28,19   Plato *Menexenus* 238a.

28,28   "God made man . . .": Genesis ii. 7.

29,4f. divine spirit: the Stoics viewed the soul as a warm, divine breath permeating the human body (Diogenes Laertius *De Vittiis* 7. 157).

32,27   same materials: here Philo follows a Pythagorean doctrine. Cf. also the talmudic view: "The dust out of which the first man was created was collected from all the parts of the world" (Sanhedrin 38a).

33,25   names: Genesis ii. 19.

35,35   good and evil: *ibid.*, iii. 5 f.

38,1   serpent fighter: Leviticus xi. 22.

40,25f. world . . . is one: this tenet is held also by Plato (*Timaeus* 31a, 32c) and the Stoa (Diogenes Laertius *De Vitiis* 7. 143). The opposite view, that of the plurality of the worlds, was maintained by the Epicureans.

40,37   providence: denied by the Epicureans.

After the Work of the Six Days of Creation (The First Book on the Allegories of the Sacred Laws)

42,3   mind and sense: "heaven and earth" of the Creation story.

42,16   the sixth day: this is the reading of the Septuagint; the Hebrew text has "the seventh day."

42,19   time: cf. "On the Creation of the World," VII.

43,8   six: cf. *ibid.*, III.

43,27   never ceases from making: cf. "On the Cherubim," XXVI.

44,5   which is said: in the no-longer-extant "Chrysippos," a drama by Euripides (Fragment 839).

44,9   seven: a longer discourse on the number seven is given in "On the Creation of the World," XXX–XLIII, omitted in this volume.

46,7   "God blessed": Genesis ii. 3.

46,13   great vow: the vow of a Nazirate; Numbers vi.

46,32   perfect reason: book-word-reason, all implied in *logos*. Cf. "On the Creation of the World," XLIV.

47,9   "On which day": Genesis ii. 4 f.

48,25   natural philosophy: or, laws of being.

49,13   "But a fountain . . .": Genesis ii. 6.

49,19   mind waters the sensations: an Aristotelian notion of the relationship of the mind (*nous*) and the senses (*aisthesis*).

49,39f.   imagination and appetite: or, power of receiving impressions (*phantasia*) and the impulse toward the object producing them (*horme*); a Stoic concept.

50,5   "And God created . . .": Genesis ii. 7.

50,8   heavenly man . . . earthly man: based on Genesis i. 27 *versus* ii. 7. Cf. "On the Creation of the World," XXIV.

50,25   devoted to the body: to Philo (and the Stoa) "earthly man" represents evil man.

51,35f.   soul . . . perceived God: of "On Abraham," XVII; the view is shared by Posidonius.

53,3   many names: according to the Stoics, too, *logos* has many names.

53,20   one and the universe: or, One and the Whole, *eis kai to pan*, designation of God also in Heraclitus and the Stoa.

54,2   husband: or, gardener.

54,7   ". . . not plant a grove": the Hebrew text refers to cultic plants.

54,35f.   "gods of silver": Exodus xx. 20.

54,40   injures himself and not God: a Stoic notion.

55,20   factitious man: or formed, moulded man.

56,3   "And God caused . . .": Genesis ii. 9.

56,19   three of its parts: a Stoic notion.

57,8   one who is uninitiated: "Philo apparently means that Moses refrained from mentioning where the Tree of Knowledge of good and evil was situated, lest its locality should become an object of awe and wonder to the ignorant" (F. H. Colson).

58,14   virtues: a Platonic and Stoic tenet.

58,33   pre-eminence: or, sovereignty; the Greek *arche* means both beginning and sovereignty.

58,40   "The name . . . Pheison": Genesis ii. 11 f.

59,7   gentle: *hileos,* which root Philo reads in the name Evilat.

59,22   "And the name . . . Gihon": Genesis ii. 13; Philo connects Gihon with *gahon,* chest (actually, belly), or with *nagah,* to butt.

59,36   "And the third river . . .": *ibid.,* ii. 14.

60,8f.   three parts: cf. Plato *Phaedrus* 246 ff.

60,38   "And the fourth river . . .": Genesis ii. 14.

60,39   Euphrates: Hebrew, *Perat,* in which Philo detects the root *parah,* to be fertile.

61,2   parts of the soul in harmony: a Platonic view (*Phaedrus* 253d), later adopted by Posidonius.

61,20   change of the mouth: probably *pi shoneh,* as an interpretation of Pishon (Pheison).

61,21   bringing forth: Havilah (Evilat) understood as based on the root *hul,* in travail (or, bringing forth).

62,1   Aaron: to Philo, symbol of the sacred, prophetic word.

62,10   gold: Genesis ii. 11.

62,26   carbuncle: *ibid.*

63,4   confession: the name Judah is derived from a Hebrew root meaning to thank, to confess. Judah's mother Leah "ceased from child-bearing," since "confession" is the acme of virtue (I. Heinemann).

63,5   Issachar: a name derived from *sakhar,* reward.

63,13   garment: worn by the high priest.

63,22   red stone: Genesis ii. 12.

63,27   laughter of Isaac: cf. "On Abraham," XXXVI.

64,22   manners: better, character.

65,1   according to merit: a Stoic notion.

65,8   "And the Lord . . .": Genesis ii. 15.

65,26   "And the Lord . . .": *ibid.,* ii. 16 f.

65,32   the first time: according to the Septuagint.

65,40   given names: Genesis ii. 20.

66,9   simple: simpletons.

66,13   the soul of the universe . . . God: a Stoic expression.

66,23   command, prohibition, and recommendation: Philo's discussion is based on a Stoic concept.

67,7   Lord God: on the two names of God cf. "On Abraham," XXIV.

67,30	wrestler: or, athlete.
68,13	assignment: appreciation.
68,15	"But of the tree of knowledge . . .": Genesis ii. 17.
68,20f.	as I have said before: chap. XVIII.
69,8f.	to alienate itself from the body: cf. Plato *Phaedo* 65a.
69,23	"In the day . . .": Genesis ii. 17.
69,30	separation of his soul from his body: cf. *Phaedo* 64c.
70,8	Heraclitus: a similar notion: Plato *Gorgias* 493a.

On the Cherubim

71,6	"He sent out": Genesis iii. 23.
72,2	Agar: Hagar.
72,2f.	middle kind of instruction: instruction preparatory to philosophy; Hagar symbolizes this lower form of education, while Sarah stands for "predominant virtue."
72,22	my authority: or, my sovereignty—meaning of Sarai, Sarah's original name; Sarai represents particular and specific virtues, while Sarah symbolizes generic and, as such, imperishable virtue.
73,1	great father of sounds: the name Abraham is interpreted as *av bar ham* (or, *hamon*). Cf. "On Abraham," XVIII.
73,8	Isaac: the name refers to laughter, i.e., to pure, passionless happiness.
73,13	Ishmael as sophist, cf. "On the Posterity of Cain," XXXVIII.
73,17	to cast out: Genesis xxi. 10.
74,9	Eden means delight: Eden as symbol of divine wisdom, cf. "On the Allegories of the Sacred Laws," Book I, chap. XIX.
75,14	notorious: known.
75,20	"all secret things . . .": Deuteronomy xxix. 28.
75,40	"he came near . . .": Genesis xviii. 23.
76,25	the spheres in heaven: here Philo follows Plato's notion of the heavenly movements (*Timaeus* 36).
76,39	Lucifer . . . Stilbon: morning star . . . Mercury.
77,30	mercy-seat: Exodus xxv. 19 f.
77,30	two hemispheres: cf. also "On the Life of Moses," Book II, chap. XX.

77,35   Vesta: or Hestia, representing the earth, firmly fixed in the center of the universe.

78,16   cherubim . . . symbols: cf. "On the Life of Moses," Book II, chap. XX.

78,18   impetuous: or, fiery; the Stoa spoke of the fiery nature of reason and *logos*.

80,8   behold reason armed . . . : better, Behold the armed angel, the reason of God, standing in the way against you (cf. Numbers xxii. 31).

On Abraham

84,13   Chaldaeans: in Philo's usage synonymous with Hebrews.

84,21   "he hoped, etc.": Philo follows the Septuagint rendition of Genesis iv. 26; the Hebrew text has, "Then began men to call upon the name of the Lord."

85,8   the fourth: Adam, Cain, Seth, Enos (Enosh); or, Adam, Abel, Seth, Enos.

85,40   "Enoch pleased God": Philo follows the Septuagint rendition of Genesis v. 24; the Hebrew text has, "And Enoch walked with God, and he was not; for God took him."

88,14   powers: Philo speaks here of seven powers; in "On the Creation of the World," XL, he follows the Stoic tenet of eight powers.

94,9   seeing God: Philo interprets the name Israel as *ish roeh el*, man who sees God (L. Cohn).

97,34   Charran: or Haran; on its allegorical meaning see "On the Migration of Abraham," XXXIV.

99,16   alpha, being doubled: In the Greek rendition, Abraham—Abraam.

99,19f. "elect father of sound": cf. "On the Cherubim," II.

102,21 natural philosophy: nature reveals higher, divine, truth.

107,16f. creative power . . . royal power: Philo interprets *theos* (*elohim*) as the creative and benevolent aspect of God, and *kurios* (*Yahve*) as His royal and judging quality.

110,7f. "The greatest cause, etc.": Menander.

114,29 good: Genesis i. 4.

119,16 Gymnosophists: Hindu ascetics devoted to contemplative life.

132,27   number ten : the four passions and five senses, all perishable and mortal, are counteracted by reason, represented by ten, the perfect number.

On the Migration of Abraham

139,19   dissolved : Heraclitus and the Stoa.
140,4   speech : *logos,* speech, reason.
141,33   wise man : Abraham.
141,39   sacred interpreter : Moses.
142,1   Exodus : *Exagoge,* leading out.
142,31   to be preserved : Genesis 1. 26.
142,35   capable of seeing : Israel, the name interpreted by Philo as *ish roeh el,* man who sees God; cf. "On Abraham," XII.
143,6f.   "Let us lie down" : wife of Potiphar to Joseph.
143,17   such a man : Joseph.
144,9   lawgiver : or, lawgiving Word (*logos*) ; in Philo, Moses is the representative of the *logos.*
145,6   to men : to Jacob, prior to his leaving Laban.
145,26   surnamed Isaac : refers to "a race" (line 22). In contradistinction to Abraham who symbolizes Wisdom acquired by teaching, Isaac represents Wisdom acquired by nature; he is "self-taught."
146,13   I am not ashamed : note the intimate autobiographical reference in this paragraph.
147,8   tree of life : Genesis ii. 9.
148,21   the soul : Abraham's.
148,28   Abraham believed : Genesis xv. 6.
149,9   speculation : better, contemplation ; *bios theoretikos* is a Stoic ideal.
149,14   people saw the voice : cf. Mekhilta, *ad loc.:* "Rabbi Akiba says : 'They saw and heard that which was visible. They saw the fiery word coming out from the mouth of the Almighty as it was struck upon the tablets.' "
150,16   tested in this manner : the thought seems to be that, while none of our sensations are visible, those of taste, smell, and touch are produced by visible objects (F. H. Colson).

151,40 wise citizen of the world: see the first note to "On the Creation of the World."

153,15 "goes upon its belly": on reptiles as symbolizing gluttonous persons, see "On the Special Laws," XXI.

153,23 serpent: symbol of the man of passions.

155,6 encyclical instruction: *enkuklios paideia,* the seven arts of Hellenic education.

155,8 sophists: Philo often criticizes sophists.

155,22 mourns over mortal things: or, to whom mortal things are a grief. Philo connects the name Abel with the Hebrew *avel,* mourning.

156,18 uttered speech: or, *logos* in utterance.

157,6 "And he shall speak": Exodus iv. 15 ff.

159,6 neglectful indifference: note Philo's emphasis on the practical aspects of religion.

159,21f. that the creature is entitled to rest from his labours: or, the non-action of created beings; the Sabbath teaches that human work is ineffectual compared with the eternal activity of God (F. H. Colson). "Among existing things which rest, is one thing only, God. By rest . . . I mean an energy completely free from labour . . . and with the most perfect ease. . . . So that rest is the appropriate attribute of God alone" ("On the Cherubim," XXVI).

160,12f. born of concubines: Genesis xxv. 6.

160,14f. natural . . . human enactment: Philo follows the Stoic division between unwritten, divine, natural laws and the man-made laws of the state.

160,34f. "the woven works": Exodus xxxv. 25 f.

161,16 miserable mind: or, the misery of the wretched mind.

161,17f. additional fire: the fire kindled by the senses is an addition to the troubles of the mind. Philo (and the Septuagint) had a text that was at variance with the masoretic reading.

162,1f. high priest . . . reason; or, the *logos* as manifested in the high priest. "The high priest is not a man, but is the word of God . . . God being his father, who is also the father of all things, and wisdom being his mother, by means of whom the universe arrived at creation . . ." ("On Fugitives," XX).

162,3   sacred garments: see "On the Life of Moses," Book III, chap. XII.

162,13   an idea of ideas: or, the original principle behind all principles; the inscription points to the *logos* as the pattern of the world's creation.

162,19   "The voice": Exodus xxviii. 35.

162,32   "its necessaries . . .": the verse refers to the duties of the master toward his maidservant.

163,1   in order that the objects, etc.: or, so that in the world of sense we may come to find the likeness of the invisible world of mind (F. H. Colson).

163,5   fact of existence: or, pure being, as opposed to seeming.

164,11   Balaam: see also "On the Life of Moses," Book I, chap. XLVIII.

165,20   "In thee": Genesis xii. 3.

165,38   prop: or, foundation. Cf. "The righteous is an everlasting foundation" (or, "is the foundation of the world"). This notion is also Stoic.

167,9f.   the measures of time: or, the threefold divisions of time; the patriarchs are symbols of virtue in the past, present, and future.

168,6   end: *telos,* aim and object; the term is used by Plato and Aristotle.

168,36   end of all knowledge: the Socratic notion.

169,14   to know yourselves: Heraclitus.

169,38f.   passed the differences in time: the three days represent the portions of time that Abraham transcended, arriving at a timeless existence.

170,15   bodily vigour: Exodus i. 19.

170,21   midwife: cf. *ibid.;* the mature soul requires no "midwife."

171,22   middle road: cf. Numbers xx. 17.

171,28   means: middle roads; cf. "On the Unchangeableness of God," XXXIV.

172,6   lover of wisdom: Abraham.

172,15   ancient disease: Lot's residing in Sodom (Genesis xiii. 12); "having been taken prisoner" refers to his capture by the four kings (xiv. 12), symbolizing the four passions; "the other" refers to Abraham.

173,11f.   smooth . . . hairy: Genesis xxvii. 11.

173,28   "mixed multitude": considered also by the Midrash as causing trouble for Israel.

174,15   "Thou shalt give me to eat . . .": masoretic text: "Thou hast fed them . . ." Philo's version of the text (future tense!) made his interpretation possible.

175,5   second chariot: Genesis xli. 43.

175,16   "not by the health of Pharaoh": *ibid.*, xlii. 15, according to Philo's Greek Bible.

175,28   worthy of honour: the meaning of this sentence is not clear.

175,36   Eschol, Annan: or, Eshcol, Aner.

175,40   fire: Philo sees a connection between Eshcol and the Hebrew *esh,* fire.

176,3   "the eyes": Philo interprets Annan (Septuagint for Aner) as related to the Hebrew *ayin,* eye.

176,7   seeing: to Philo, apparently, Mamre is related to the Hebrew *mareh,* sight.

176,24f.   arts . . . have become natures: i.e., Abraham has reached the rung of Isaac.

176,38   prophet of Moses: see chap. XV.

176,40   "voluntary": Hebrew, *nedavah,* which Philo sees in the name Nadab.

177,2   "my father": Abihu = *abi hu,* he is my father.

178,17f.   seventy-five years: Genesis xii. 4.

179,26   "God is . . .": Deuteronomy iv. 39.

181,5   "a hole": Philo derives Charran (Haran) from the Hebrew *hor,* hole.

182,22   genealogical science: i.e., astrology.

183,22   confines: i.e., the borderland.

183,32   seventy and five: according to the Septuagint. Our text has seventy.

184,13   seventy heifers: Numbers xxix. 13–36.

184,26   Joseph: to Philo, Joseph represents the earthly, sensual.

184,30   five . . . garments: Genesis xlv. 22.

184,35   fifth part: *ibid.,* xlvii. 24.

185,5   Salpaad: or, Zelophehad; Numbers xxvii. 1–5.

185,9   forgetfulness: Manasseh, which name Philo derives from the Hebrew *nashah,* to forget.

185,13   "bearing fruit": Ephraim, which name Philo derives from the Hebrew *parah,* to bear fruit.

185,16   "Our father": this refers to Manasseh.
185,27   outrun him: this refers to Joseph.
185,35   the man: i.e., Jacob; even the perfected man is, at times, when passions are high, bidden to return "to Charran," the realm of "external senses," until the passions have subsided.
187,31–188,8: The effort exerted to acquire material profit should rather be exerted to gain wisdom.
189,2   "husbandman": according to the Septuagint.
189,22   Sichem: read Simon.
189,25   attempted to pollute: Genesis xxxiv. 2.
189,33   hoped to escape notice: "Philo takes great liberties with the story, ignoring the actual seduction of Dinah and the circumcision of Hamor and Sichem. He gives, however, a sort of apology for this (in the last paragraph) by suggesting that in the spiritual sphere the defilement of the truly virtuous soul, and the 'circumcision' of the truly wicked, are only illusory" (F. H. Colson).

On the Life of Moses: Book I

198,26f.: This may be an allusion to Philo's experience in his own family; his nephew, Tiberius Alexander, abandoned his "natural hereditary customs," became Roman procurator of Judaea, later governor of Egypt (L. Cohn).
202,24: A Stoic tenet.
212,19: The rest of chapter XVII to end of chapter XXVI, here omitted, is a detailed presentation of the ten plagues.
212,22   six hundred thousand: Exodus xii. 37.
213,39   blind thing: cf. "On Abraham," IV.
214,27   property of friends: cf. "On Abraham," XL.
214,28   friend of God: Exodus xxxiii. 11.
215,4   entered into the darkness: *ibid.*, xx. 18.
216,1–220,3: cf. *ibid.*, xiii. 17–xv. 21.
220,4–221,14: cf. *ibid.*, xv. 22–26.
221,15–222,7: cf. *ibid.*, xv. 27.
222,8–226,7: cf. *ibid.*, xvi; Numbers xi. 8.
226,13   smote the . . . rock: cf. Exodus xvii. 6.
227,14–228,30: cf. *ibid.*, xvii. 8–16. By "Phoenicians" Philo refers to Canaanites.

228,28   refuge of God: Philo follows the Septuagint rendition of
          Exodus xvii. 15; the Hebrew text has, "The Lord is my
          banner."

228,30:   Chapters XL–LX, here omitted, continue to present the
          story of Israel in the wilderness on the basis of the
          biblical account in Numbers xiii–xiv, xx–xxv, xxxi–
          xxxii. Dealing in his first book on Moses with the hero's
          leadership (kingship) only, Philo omits the story of the
          revelation at Sinai and the sections on the laws; he treats
          the Sinai event in "Concerning the Ten Commandments."
          In his retelling the Balaam story (chapters XLVIII–
          LIV), Philo tones down the element of the miraculous
          in the biblical account.

          On the Life of Moses: Book II

230,8–9: Plato *Republic* V, 473d.
231,13:   A Socratic and Stoic tenet. Diogenes Laertius *De Vitiis*
          7. 125.
234,16   the yearly fast: the Day of Atonement.
234,30:   Chapters V-VII deal with the origin of the Septuagint
          translation of the Pentateuch; cf. "The Letter of Aris-
          teas" and Josephus *Antiquities* 12. 2.
234,34   Chaldaean: To Philo this is identical wth Hebrew. Cf.
          "On Abraham," II.
239,13–14: A Stoic tenet.
239,24   laws: e.g., Plato's *Laws* and *Republic*. Cf. Josephus
          Against Apion 2. 31.
242,1   four stories: The biblical account speaks of three stories
          (Genesis vi. 16).

          On the Life of Moses: Book III

244, title: Some scholars believe that the material included in
          Book III is a continuation of Book II; in his treatise
          "On the Virtues," IX, Philo mentions having presented
          the life of Moses in two books. However, it is assumed
          that Book II, chapter XII, was followed by sections no
          longer extant. These sections may have included a dis-
          course on the revelation at Sinai (L. Cohn).

247,19   fifty: $3^2 + 4^2 + 5^2$.

248,19   twenty-eight: $1 + 2 + 4 + 7 + 14$.

248,20   forty: assumed to be the period of pregnancy.

249,19   tabernacle: cf. Exodus xxvii. 9–19.

250,26   ark: cf. *ibid.*, xxv. 10–12.

251,4–5   vast knowledge and science: this Philonic interpretation of "cherubim" reappears in Clement's *epignosis polle,* Jerome's *multitudo scientiae,* and Augustine's *plenitudo scientiae* (F. H. Colson).

251,27   altar of incense: cf. Exodus xxx. 1.

251,32   candlestick: cf. *ibid.*, xxv. 31–40.

252,7   table: cf. *ibid.*, xxv. 23–30.

252,38–254,2   high priest's dress: cf. *ibid.*, xxviii.

253,18   logeum: *hoshen mishpat* (*ibid.*, xxviii. 15: "breast-plate of judgment").

253,20   manifestation and truth: Philo follows the Septuagint translation of the Hebrew *Urim ve-Tummim.*

253,23   four names: the four letters of the divine name (YHVH). According to Exodus xxviii. 36 the inscription read: "Holy to the Lord." Josephus (*Jewish War* 5. 5. 7) follows Philo in considering the inscription to have been the tetragrammaton (F. H. Colson).

258,2   paraclete: spokesman.

258,2   his son: the world, symbolically represented in the high priest's dress.

259,34–262,9:   cf. Exodus xxix; Leviticus viii.

262,10–263,17:   cf. Leviticus ix.

263,31–266,22:   cf. Exodus xxxii.

263,37   golden calf: Philo ignores Aaron's part in the making of the golden calf.

266,23–267,end: cf. Numbers xvi–xvii.

269,1   prudence, temperance, courage, justice: the four virtues of Greek ethics.

269,22   Chapters XXIII–XXXVIII, here omitted, paraphrase biblical examples of Moses as prophet.

269,23–270,21:   cf. Deuteronomy xxxiii–xxxiv.

On the Ten Festivals

272,4   every day a festival: technically, Philo's biblical reference may well be Numbers xxviii–xxix, where the series of sacrifices for the festivals starts with the daily offering. More important is Philo's intention to give liturgic expression to his (Stoically inspired) tenet that only the wise man can truly observe a festival and indeed does so every day.

275,1   virtuous mind: Sarah; Genesis xviii. 10–15. "Its (her) passions were tranquil" is Philo's understanding of verse 11.

276,13   birthday of the world: cf. "On the Creation of the World," XXX.

276,30   philosophy: study of Torah. Cf. the talmudic sentence: "The Sabbaths and the festivals were given for the pursuit of the study of Torah" (Yer. Shabbath 15a).

277,21   kindle a fire: Exodus xxxv. 3.

278,17   no man is by nature a slave: the Stoics taught that only the wise is free and only the fool a slave. Philo expanded this principle in declaring that (ideally at least) all men are free.

279,17   strangers as kindred: i.e., though the biblical law makes a ("natural") distinction between citizens and foreigners, the ideal world-state (the *megalopolis*) is ruled by a statute where only "virtue" counts.

282,36f.   athletes . . . fat and corpulent: one of several polemical references to professional athletes who are not the "true" athletes; such polemics are found already in Plato.

286,7   the fiftieth year: Leviticus xxv.

286,28   possession of God: *ibid.*, xxv. 23.

288,37   slaves: *ibid.*, xxv. 44; well-educated Greeks, too, distinguished between Hellenic and non-Hellenic ("barbarian") slaves.

289,24–25   myriads of people: cf. Exodus xii. 37: 600,000 grown men.

290,16   festival: the biblical text distinguishes between *pesah* (Passover) and *hag ha-matzot* (festival of unleavened bread). Cf. Leviticus xxiii. 5 f.

290,27 called the first: Exodus xii. 2.

290,30 world was created: cf. the rabbinic view according to which the world was created in the Fall (month of Tishre); Rosh ha-Shanah 10b.

291,10 The Philo edition of L. Cohn and P. Wendland has the following addition: "Perhaps too he wished to harmonize the feast with a past which adjoins the first day and a future which adjoins the last. These two, the first and the last, have each the other's properties in addition to their own. The first is the beginning of the feast and the end of the preceding past, the seventh is the end of the feast and the beginning of the coming future. Thus, as I have said before, the whole life of the man of worth may be regarded as equivalent to a feast held by one who has expelled grief and fear and desire and the other passions and distempers of the soul." (Tr. F. H. Colson, *Philo,* Loeb Classical Library, VII, 403.)

291,33 The Philo edition of L. Cohn and P. Wendland has the following addition: "and to employ the leisure of a festal assembly to confer admiration and honor on the old-time life of frugality and economy, and as far as possible to assimilate our present-day life to that of the distant past. These statements are especially guaranteed by the exposure of the twelve loaves corresponding in number to the tribes, on the holy table (cf. Leviticus xxiv. 5 ff.). They are all unleavened, the clearest possible example of a food free from admixture, in the preparation of which art for the sake of pleasure has no place, but only nature, providing nothing save what is indispensable for its use. So much for this." (*Op. cit.,* VII, 405.)

291,35 named the sheaf: Leviticus xxiii. 10 ff.; "on the morrow after the Sabbath" (verse 11) was interpreted by the Septuagint, Philo, and the Pharisees as referring to the second day of Passover; the Sadducees interpreted it literally: on the day after the Sabbath.

291,38 the whole land: the whole earth.

292,32 pentecost: Leviticus xxiii. 15 f.; Deuteronomy xvi. 9 f.

293,1 sacred moon: Philo does not seem to know of the New Year's festival (Rosh ha-Shanah); his "eighth festival" is the commencement of the sacred month (Tishre). For "feast of trumpets" cf. Leviticus xxiii. 24.

293,35   solemnity of the fast: cf. "On the Special Laws," Book
I, chap. XXXV: ". . . the fast which is carefully observed not only by the zealous for piety and holiness but
also by those who never act religiously in the rest of
their life. For all stand in awe, overcome by the sanctity
of the day." (Tr. F. H. Colson, *op. cit.*, VII, 207.)
293,37   sabbath of sabbaths: Leviticus xvi. 31.
294,1   week of weeks: or, a seven of sevens.
295,32   tents: Leviticus xxiii. 40–43.

On Rewards and Punishments

297,1   oracles: writings; the Pentateuch.
299,20   Triptolemus: the corn-goddess Ceres (Demeter) sent her
dragons-driven car to Triptolemus in Athens, who then
brought the gift of corn seeds to humanity.
299,39f.   learning is . . . recollection: a Platonic tenet.
300,29   worthy of being accepted: for this and the following, cf.
"On Abraham," II.
300,37   Enos: or Enosh, man; Genesis iv. 26. The Septuagint
translates this passage: "He called his name Enos, he
hoped to call on the name of the Lord God."
301,18   "He was not found . . .": the reference is to Enoch,
symbol of repentance; cf. "On Abraham," III.
302,35   Deucalion: Prometheus' son, the Greek Noah; he builds
an ark on Prometheus' advice.
303,27   Abraham: cf. "On Abraham," XI.
303,35–36   sight of God: cf. "On Abraham," XII.
304,34   Isaac: cf. "On the Cherubim," II.
305,27–28   practiser of virtue: Jacob.
307,14   spontaneously: better, automatically.
307,17   law of nature: Stoic defense of providence; cf. "On the
Creation of the World," II.
308,10f.   unit . . . two: the Pythagoreans spoke of the unity
of the Godhead and the duality of matter.
308,18   "the torpor of breadth": this refers to Jacob's wrestling
with the angel who "touched the hollow of his [Jacob's]
thigh" (Genesis xxxii. 26).
309,34   four prizes: cf. "On the Life of Moses," Book II, chap.
I.

310,27 :   The rest of the treatise (chapters X–XXIX), here
            omitted, speaks of the rewards granted to "houses," of
            punishment of offenders, and of the restoration of the
            penitent and the renewal of Israel.

            On a Contemplative Life (on the Therapeutae)

311,1   mentioned the Essenes: in a no longer extant treatise in
            which they were presented as following "the practical
            [or, active] course of life."
311,6   speculative: or, contemplative.
313,14   iris: read ibis (a wading bird related to the heron). Cf.
            "Concerning the Ten Commandments," XVI: "Besides
            falling down to statues and images, they have also intro-
            duced irrational animals, to the honours due to the
            gods. . . ."
313,41   corybantian mysteries: part of the ecstatic worship of the
            Phrygian goddess Cybele. Cf. also "On the Creation of
            the World," XXIII.
314,13 :   Anaxagoras (ca. 500–ca. 428 B.C.) and Democritus (ca.
            460–ca. 370 B.C.), Greek philosophers.
315,2 :   Hippocrates: a contemporary of Socrates; in the original
            saying, "art" refers to medicine.
315,40   country of the barbarians: the non-Greek lands.
316,32   monastery: in the text, *monasterion,* i.e., closet, or inner
            chamber.
318,41   grasshoppers: cf. also "On the Virtuous Being also
            Free," II. The notion of the fasting grasshoppers goes
            back to Hesiod and Plato.
322,11   sport of the . . . debauchees: pets of the pederasts.
323,28   Xenophon: *Symposium* 2. 1 ff. The work narrates the
            feast in the house of Callias.
323,38f.   love . . . by men for one another: cf. "On Abraham,"
            XXVI.
323,41   genuine love: Plato *Symposium* 180d ff. Philo fails to
            do justice to the Platonic presentation.
324,5–6   female disease: disease of effeminacy.
324,37   allure the ears: Plato *Symposium* 189d ff.
325,14   fifty: on the meaning of fifty, cf. "On the Special Laws,"
            Book II, chap. XXII.

325,20 ephemereutae: men who perform their services in rotation.

326,22 Lacedaemonian rigour of life: Spartan austerity.

19,18 entertainment: refectory.

19,33 Red Sea: Exodus xiv. 8 ff.

On the Virtuous Being also Free (on the Essenes)

331,1 Moreover: in the first part of the treatise (chapters I–XI, here omitted), Philo sets forth the Stoic doctrine that only the wise man is free, and teaches that "the man alone is free who has God for his leader." He points to such men in Greece, Persia, and India, before describing the Essenes.

331,1 Palestine and Syria: better, Palestinian Syria.

331,7 Grecian dialect: Philo takes the term Essenes to be a variation of *hesiotes,* holiness.

333,19 magazine: treasury.

333,41f. examining into Greek names: pedantry of Greek terms.

334,28 messing together: observance of communal meals.

334,31 happy life: in the remainder of the treatise (chapters XIV–XXII), Philo adduces further examples of the wise: the Indian Calanus, Euripides, Anaxagoras (Anaxarchus), Zeno of Elea, and others.

SELECT BIBLIOGRAPHY

Agus, Jacob. "Hellenistic Judaism." In *The Evolution of Jewish Thought,* chap. III. London and New York, 1959; 4th rev. ed., New York, 1970.

Altmann, Alexander. "Judaism and World Philosophy." In *The Jews,* ed. L. Finkelstein, chap. XIV. New York, 1949.

Andrews, Mary E. "Paul, Philo and the Intellectuals," *Journal of Biblical Literature,* LIII (1934).

Baer, Richard A. *Philo's Use of the Categories of Male and Female.* Leiden, 1970.

Baron, Salo W. "Expansion of Judaism." In *A Social and Religious History of the Jews,* rev. ed., I, chap. VI. New York and Philadelphia, 1952.

Belkin, Samuel. *The Alexandrian Halakah in Apologetic Literature of the First Century C.E.* Philadelphia, 1936.

―――. *Philo and Oral Law.* Harvard Semitic Series, Vol. XI. Cambridge, Mass., 1940.

Bentwich, Norman. *Philo Judaeus of Alexandria.* Philadelphia, 1910.

Bevan, Edwyn R. "Hellenistic Judaism." In *The Legacy of Israel,* ed. E. R. Bevan and Charles Singer. Oxford, 1927.

Bigg, Charles. *The Christian Platonists of Alexandria.* Oxford, 1913.

Box, Herbert, ed. *Philonis Alexandrini in Flaccum.* London and New York, 1939.

Bréhier, É. *Les idées philosophiques et religieuses de Philon d'Alexandrie,* 2d ed. Paris, 1925.

―――. *Philon: Commentaire allégorique des saintes lois.* Paris, 1909.

Caird, E. "The Philosophy and Theology of Philo." In *The Evolution of Theology in Greek Philosophers,* Vol. II. Glasgow, 1904.

Christiansen, Irmgard. *Die Technik der allegorischen Auslegungswissenschaft bei Philon von Alexandrien*. Tübingen, 1969.

Cohn, Leopold, and Reimer, Georg. *Philonis opera quae supersunt*. 7 vols. Berlin, 1896–1930.

Colson, F. H., Whitaker, G. H., and Earp, J. W., trans. *Philo*. Loeb Classical Library, 10 vols. Cambridge, Mass., and London, 1929–62.

Conybear, F. C., ed. *On the Contemplative Life*. Oxford, 1895.

Daniélou, Jean. *Philon d'Alexandrie*. Paris, 1958.

Drummond, J. *Philo Judaeus; or, the Jewish-Alexandrian Philosophy in its Development and Completion*. 2 vols. London, 1888.

Finkelstein, Louis. "Is Philo Mentioned in Rabbinic Literature?" *Journal of Biblical Literature*, LIII (1934).

Ginzberg, Louis. "Allegorical Interpretation," *The Jewish Encyclopedia*, Vol. I. New York, 1901.

Goodenough, Erwin R. *An Introduction to Philo Judaeus*, 2d ed. Oxford, 1962.

———. *By Light, Light: The Mystic Gospel of Hellenistic Judaism*. New Haven, Conn., 1935.

———. "Philo's Exposition of the Law and His *De Vita Mosis*," *Harvard Theological Review*, XXVI (1933).

———, and Goodhart, H. L. *The Politics of Philo Judaeus, Practice and Theory, with a General Bibliography of Philo*. New Haven, 1938.

Guyot, H. *Les Reminiscences de Philo le Juif chez Plotin*. Paris, 1906.

Hadidian, Yervant H. "Philonism and the Fourth Gospel." In *The Macdonald Presentation Volume*. Princeton, 1933.

Hart, J. H. A. "Philo and the Catholic Judaism of the First Century," *The Journal of Theological Studies*, XI (1909–10).

———. "Philo of Alexandria," *The Jewish Quarterly Review*, XVII (1904–5), XVIII (1905–6), XX (1907–8).

Heinemann, Isaak. *Philons griechische und jüdische Bildung*. Breslau, 1932.

Katz, Peter. *Philo's Bible*. Cambridge, 1950.

Lagrange, M.-J. "Le Logos de Philon," *Revue biblique*, XXXII (1923).

Leisegang, Ioannes. *Indices ad Philonis Alexandrini Opera*. 2 vols. Berlin, 1926–39.

Lewy, Hans. *Sobria Ebrietas. Zcitschrift fur die alttestamentliche Wissenschaft,* Beiheft IX. Giessen, 1929.

——, ed. *Philo Selections.* Oxford, 1946.

Marcus, Ralph. "Divine Names and Attributes in Hellenistic Jewish Literature," *Proceedings of the American Academy for Jewish Research,* 1931–32.

——. "Hellenistic Jewish Literature." In *The Jews,* ed. L. Finkelstein, chap. XVII. New York, 1949; 4th rev. ed., New York, 1970.

——, trans. *Questions in Genesis and Exodus.* 2 vols, supplementary to the Loeb edition of *Philo.* Cambridge, Mass., and London, 1953.

Marmorstein, Arthur. "Philo and the Names of God," *Jewish Quarterly Review,* XXII (1931–32).

Martin, Jules. *Philon.* Paris, 1907.

Montefiore, Claude G. "Florilegium Philonis," *Jewish Quarterly Review,* VII (1894–95).

Otte, Klaus. *Das Sprachverstandnis bei Philo von Alexandrien.* Tubingen, 1968.

Ryle, H. E. *Philo and Holy Scripture.* London and New York, 1895.

Sandmel, Samuel. *Philo's Place in Judaism; a Study of Conceptions of Abraham in Jewish Literature.* Cincinnati, 1956.

Siegfried, Carl. "Philo Judaeus," *The Jewish Encyclopedia,* Vol. X. New York, 1905.

——. *Philo von Alexandria als Ausleger des Alten Testaments.* Jena, 1875.

Smallwood, E. Mary, ed. *Legatio ad Gaium.* Leiden, 1961.

Sowers, Sidney G. *The Hermeneutics of Philo and Hebrews.* Richmond, Va., 1965.

Stein, E. *Philo und der Midrasch. Zeitschrift fur die alttestamentliche Wissenschaft,* Beiheft LVII. Giessen, 1931.

Stein, Edmund. *Philon ha-Alexandroni.* (In Hebrew.) Warsaw, 1937.

Treitel, Leopold. *Gesamte Theologie und Philosophie Philo's von Alexandria.* Berlin, 1923.

Voelker, Walter. *Fortschritt und Vollendung bei Philo von Alexandrien.* Leipzig, 1938.

Wolfson, Harry Austryn. *Philo: Foundations of Religious Philosophy in Judaism, Christianity, and Islam.* 2 vols. Cambridge, Mass., 1947.

———. "Philo on Free Will," *Harvard Theological Review*, XXXV (1942).

———. "The Philonic God of Revelation and his Latter-Day Deniers," *Harvard Theological Review*, LIII (1960).

———. *Religious Philosophy: A Group of Essays*. New York, 1965.